The
Psychoanalytic
Study
of the Child

VOLUME SIXTY-ONE

Kindly submit seven copies of new manuscripts by post
or as an email attachment in MS Word to

Robert A. King, M.D.
Yale Child Study Center
230 South Frontage Road
P.O. Box 207900
New Haven, CT 06520-7900
Phone: (203) 785-5880
E-mail: robert.king@yale.edu

The Psychoanalytic Study of the Child

VOLUME SIXTY-ONE

Yale University Press
New Haven and London
2006

Designed by Sally Harris
and set in Baskerville type.
Printed in the United States of America by
Vail-Ballou Press, Inc., Binghamton, N.Y.

Library of Congress catalog card number: 45-11304
ISBN-13: 978-0-300-11996-1
ISBN-10: 0-300-11996-8

A catalogue record for this book is available from the British Library.

The paper in this book meets the guidelines for
permanence and durability of the Committee on
Production Guidelines for Book Longevity of the
Council on Library Resources.
10 9 8 7 6 5 4 3 2 1

Contents

v

vi   *Contents*

CLINICAL CONTRIBUTIONS

The Vicissitudes of Aggression in a Toddler

A Clinical Contribution

RUTH K. KARUSH, M.D.

Clinical material from the analyses of young children may be particularly useful in understanding the vicissitudes of the aggressive drive. In this paper, the psychoanalytic work with Teddy, a boy with aggressive and angry behavior, is presented to illustrate several important, intertwining and determining factors involved in the expression of his aggressive drive. These include traumatic events, his relationship with his parents and his dread of the strength of his instincts. When the child's experience includes the lack of external control of his impulses, he may be more predisposed to violent behavior. The importance of the stage of ego development at the time of trauma is also emphasized.

TEDDY, AN ANGELIC-LOOKING CHILD, WAS FIRST BROUGHT TO MY OFfice at the age of 2 years and 7 months because of his "angry, abusive behavior toward friends and adults." The director of his nursery school had suggested the consultation because she was alarmed by his "aggressive fantasies." He would tell his teacher that he was going to kill her, and he would threaten to throw his classmates out the window. According to his mother, he didn't like being told what to do and would counter demands with such retorts as, "You're stupid. I don't like you." Teddy was a slight, fragile-looking, blond, blue-eyed

Associate Dean of Education for Child Analysis; Training Analyst; Adult, Child and Adolescent Supervising Analyst at the New York Psychoanalytic Institute.

The Psychoanalytic Study of the Child 61, ed. Robert A. King, Peter B. Neubauer, Samuel Abrams, and A. Scott Dowling (Yale University Press, copyright © 2006 by Robert A. King, Peter B. Neubauer, Samuel Abrams, and A. Scott Dowling).

boy. His articulation was poor, and although he had a huge and sophisticated vocabulary for his age, I had some trouble completely understanding him at first. It was difficult to imagine this little boy as
the terror that both his mother and his nursery school teachers described. I will use clinical examples from Teddy's psychoanalytic
treatment to demonstrate the choices of defense available to a child
in relation to his ego development and his family environment. Such
choices constitute the shaping of the aggressive drive.

Theoretically, most psychoanalysts seem perplexed by the apparent nature of aggression in the young child compared to that observed in the rageful, melancholic, or masochistic adult. Aggression
is more frequently and more directly expressed in very young children. In the first four or five years of life, it is generally more pleasurable and constructive than hostile and destructive. Indeed, from
the child analyst's perspective, as Anna Freud observed, "aggression
looms larger than sex in child analysis. [It] dominates the child
patient's acting out and transference behavior" (A. Freud, 1972,
p. 168). Yet, a developmental theory of aggression exists only in bits
and pieces. In 1972, at the conclusion of the 27th International Congress, Anna Freud also observed that discussions up to that point had
failed to remove "uncertainties concerning the status of aggression
in the theory of drives," or had failed to clarify "some urgent problems, such as the part played by aggression in normal infantile development; its involvement with the various agencies in the psychic
structure; its role for character formation" (1972, p. 163). She went
on to outline the reasons why aggression was so problematic to analysts despite its centrality in everyday life and its inescapable presence
in the lives of young children.

She noted that aggression entered analytic theory late. Long after
the erotic, libidinal drive had been securely fixed in mental functioning, Freud (1920) introduced the dualism of life and death to instinctual life. Just as all the characteristics and achievements of a younger
sibling are compared with those of the older sibling, the aggressive
drive was shaped to match the libidinal one. Standing parallel to the
libidinal drive, aggression had to meet the criteria of stage development with specific body zones and to have a source, aim, and object.
This has been difficult to do. Seeking to fit the clinical observations
of aggression into the framework of libido instinct theory did not
serve to validate aggression as a parallel, but independent drive (A.
Freud, 1972; Solnit, 1972). The presumed symmetry of the drives was
misleading and inaccurate. It led to a dilemma in understanding aggression in children in whom destructive and hostile intent was not

primary. The possible constructive, positive functions of aggression in early psychic life were obscured by the negative connotation of the term when applied to adult behavior.

Freud chose not to accept the aggressive drive in and of itself as constructively essential for normal psychic development. However, those analysts who work directly with very young children and who are familiar with infant observation know that aggression is present in the lives of young infants and consider it central to the infant's differentiating sense of self (Klein, 1957). Aggressive feelings are rooted in the most basic biologically determined patterns of behavior that are used to protect the child and bring others to him in times of need. The infant's cry is almost always perceived by adults as unpleasant and aversive yet indicative of needs. It generally arouses in the parent a sense of urgency to respond. Early motor activities are manifestations of nondestructive aspects of aggression that are part of the process of experiencing the self as autonomous (Greenacre, 1971). An example would be a toddler's struggling or running away while being dressed. Winnicott (1950) showed how a young child's vigorous muscular activity is met by opposition during physical care and that this contributes to self-definition and individuation. These body-based modes of protecting oneself and expressing one's own effectiveness become readily available schemas for how the child experiences and responds to feelings of internal or external danger, whether real or imagined.

According to Mayes and Cohen (1993, p. 152) the child's experiences with others further shape the transformation of the aggressive drive. The infant will experience himself as more or less aggressive in relation to his mother's experience of his behavior. When the 4-month-old infant vigorously sucking at the breast abruptly bites, the degree to which the mother reacts to the pain as an aggressive attack rather than a surprising but notable measure of her child's assertiveness and mastery will influence how the infant experiences similar moments in the future. When the 18-month-old about to run off and explore looks back for his mother's reaction, his excitement will be reinforced by his mother's encouragement or dampened by her look of fear or anger. "Thus, from the very beginning of infancy, any aggressive act or fantasy is embedded in a social matrix" (Mayes and Cohen, 1993). What an individual child interprets as aggressive as well as his later patterns of assertiveness, self-protectiveness, and hostility toward others stems from his earliest interactions with others. The aggressive drive may become adaptive or non-adaptive, but it is defined and refined in the context of the child's earliest experiences.

CLINICAL ILLUSTRATION

Teddy, aged 31 months, the middle child of three, entered analysis because of his angry, hostile, and abusive behavior to both children and adults. His parents, who had been married for 6 years, were both "temperamental," and their relationship was explosive, filled with fights that remained verbal for the most part, but sometimes escalated to the physical. They totally disagreed about their son Teddy. Father believed that Teddy was a "totally normal 2-and-½-year-old" and that perhaps it was the parents who needed help in dealing with his opposition to having limits set. Mother, on the other hand, felt that their son had problems. She pointed out that he tended to dwell on dark and morbid subjects. All of his play dates were problematic. They would usually end with Teddy being physically and verbally abusive to the other child. The teachers at the parent child center felt that Teddy was in "emotional distress," and they noted that he would not enter the playroom if a man was there.

Teddy was born when his older brother was 20 months old. Then when Teddy was 20 months old, another brother was born. He was breast-fed for the better part of a year and, although his mother worked, she was a "micromanager" of his care. The salient history includes the following: at the age of 5 months, he became ill with Respiratory Syncytial Virus, and was admitted to the pediatric ICU because of impaired breathing. The illness coincided with the first time he rolled over. After that, Teddy developed asthma. A diagnosis of congenital benign hypotonia had also been made. The mother said that despite this problem he was a vibrant child. He had oral motor problems and was seeing a speech therapist once a week. Father felt strongly that too much energy was being focused on Teddy's health and that this attention would "stigmatize him."

The parents remarked that Teddy and his older brother were "like twins." They baited each other and fought constantly, but the parents believed they were very close and loved each other. A very interesting and important piece of history was variably reported to have occurred when Teddy was 6 months or a year old. His brother crawled into the crib and started to attack him. He bit Teddy on the face. Mother told me that her older son had been very aggressive toward Teddy and that the turning point came when Teddy started to walk. Then things went from "bad to worse." The two boys shared a bedroom, and the bedtime routine was "torturous."

When Teddy's parents came for their initial appointment, it was extremely difficult for me to get the history of their son's life. There was an uncomfortable tension during the meeting. Mother, while not the least bit retiring, seemed to choose her words very carefully with an obvious desire not to upset her husband. He, a tall and well-built man, wanted to convey his view of the situation, but barely kept his anger under control. It appeared that he had come to my office under duress. I was reluctant to begin the consultation before trying to get a better understanding of the parents. Also, it was unclear whether the father would support a treatment if that were what I would ultimately recommend. I decided to have a series of separate appointments with each parent before seeing Teddy. Ultimately, things did not work out as I had planned because I had great difficulty getting the father to come in to see me.

In my meetings with Teddy's mother, I learned that she was in her late thirties and the youngest of three children. She was highly educated and ran a successful business. She described her husband as being extremely difficult. He was, she thought, somewhat "paranoid and a loner." He was unable to work for or with anyone. Recently, he had started his own business. She worked hard on her marriage, insisting that her husband attend counseling with her. She felt that this treatment had been beneficial in reducing the fighting between them. It was also helpful in educating the husband about expectations and appropriate discipline for small children. She believed that their son Teddy needed treatment and resolved to do everything she could to convince her husband to agree to it. I began to see Teddy in consultation once I had gotten his father to agree to an appointment time for himself.

From our very first meeting, Teddy liked to come to see me. Although he was underweight and had trouble keeping his pants up, he seemed vigorous and not sickly. He had an interest both in talking and playing imaginative games. When he first came to see me he was enthralled with the Star Wars characters, and this continued for most of his treatment. Although not even 3 years old, he had an enormous fund of knowledge, which included detailed information about the various Star Wars episodes, which he was happy to impart to me once he realized that I did not share his expertise in this area.

In a meeting with the mother, I discussed how she might prepare Teddy for coming to see me and what she might expect regarding his ability to come into my office on his own. In Teddy's first session, his mother, despite my preparation, came right into the office with him although he hadn't requested or indicated any need that she stay with him. While Teddy and I were getting acquainted and he was exploring the toy cabinets looking for Luke Skywalker, his mother lay down on my couch. The next time I glanced her way, I noticed that she was asleep. Teddy asked, "What's mommy doing? Is she sleeping?" After asking what he thought, I agreed with him that she certainly did seem to be sleeping. Uncannily, mother woke up just before the end of the session. She continued to nap on my couch for almost 6 months of the treatment and then intermittently thereafter, but she didn't always wake up on her own. Sometimes Teddy would have to wake her either by giving her a kiss or jumping on her. Of course, having the mother in the room, albeit asleep, was somewhat unnerving and inhibiting for me. While his mommy slept, however, Teddy and I proceeded to do our work together.

Once the parents had agreed to a four times a week treatment for Teddy, I tried to meet with the mother on a weekly basis. Although expressing her desire for these meetings, she demonstrated her ambivalence about them by having great difficulty finding the time to see me. It became clear that she *had* to be the person who brought Teddy to his treatment and that she *had* to know exactly what was going on in his appointments with me. Also, she believed in the importance of "enrichment" for her children. Thus, in addition to her work, she was shuttling her children to chess, French, and karate among other activities. During her meetings with me, Teddy's mother frequently commented on the effect my couch had on her: "I don't know why. It just puts me to sleep." As we discussed her worry that Teddy would become closer to me than to her, she was gradually able to leave the room and remain in the waiting room. However, Teddy's mother continued to make her presence known, by talking too loudly on the cell phone. So I also raised with her the issue of her own envy of Teddy's four times a week treatment. Her intrusive behavior did not really improve. In my sessions with Teddy's mother, I gingerly tried to point out to her that, while she was present in body, she was not always available emotionally for Teddy and that could be infuriating to him. I also thought that she avoided his intense feelings by giving him information that was too sophisticated for his age, but I never found the opportunity to discuss that with her.

Before the analysis began, I did have the opportunity to meet with the father. It was a moving session in which he told me about his problems while growing up. He had been very different from his two brothers and always felt he was the scapegoat of both his brothers and his father. He was very worried that Teddy was going to be a "wimp" and dwelled on the importance of "making a man" of him. The father revealed that he had had few friends growing up and almost no friends now. He had no relationship with his family. I was able to show the father that Teddy had a great deal of anxiety, which he was handling in a way that would ultimately be problematic for him. The father had empathy for his son who resembled him as a child. I was heartened by the father's expression of understanding and love for Teddy. He also seemed to understand Teddy's need for intensive treatment. I realized, however, that I would have to maintain a connection with the father if the analysis were to proceed. This turned out to be extremely difficult with the father agreeing to see me only on rare occasions.

Teddy's toilet training became the first major issue of the analysis because his parents were demanding that he be trained. They felt he was being very stubborn and contrary. He quickly gained control over urination and very proudly told me that he peed standing up like his brother. However, he always demanded that he have a diaper on in order to have a bowel movement. His parents continued to pressure him and he began to withhold stool. I received an irate telephone call from his pediatrician who believed that it was *I* who was demanding he use the toilet. At this early stage of his treatment, Teddy spent many of his analytic hours engaged in imaginative play in which he was Luke Skywalker, and he used his light saber to demolish his enemy—usually Darth Vader. Occasionally, Luke would get injured in the battle and lose a body part, principally his hand. Teddy's anxiety would mount, and he would want to go to the bathroom to urinate. Amazingly, he would not wake his mother to help him, and he didn't request my assistance either. If, however, he needed to have a bowel movement, he would become frantic and furious. At these times he would go on the attack and become both verbally and physically abusive. If his mother decided that he could have a diaper and did not have to use the toilet, he would usually calm down.

In the play, I began to comment on how scared Luke felt during the battle and how worried he must be about possibly losing a part of himself. Teddy agreed, but he reminded me that Luke's hand had been "fixed" for him. Then followed a period of time when Teddy tried to decide whether Luke's fixed hand was as good as the original. I told Teddy that I thought that he was really worried about losing a part of his own body and that he thought that the lost piece could never be really fixed. Teddy pondered this issue for weeks. Over and over again, Luke lost his hand in a battle with Darth Vader or another character from the Dark Side, and over and over again he had it repaired. Finally, I told Teddy that when he made a "poopee" he thought he was losing a piece of himself. His mother somehow awoke from the couch and jumped in to give Teddy a very scientific explanation of how the food that his body does not need is turned into waste products. She did, however, add that this happens over and over again. Now, Teddy considered the idea that he could always make more poopees. This was very important to him because he believed that Luke's reconstructed hand was not as good as his original one, but he finally thought that "one poopee is as good as another." After the next weekend break, Teddy ran into my office exclaiming: "Dr. K I made a poopee in the toilet!" During the session, Teddy said, "You know what? It's not a poopee anymore. It's a big shit."

At the point when Teddy's toilet training had been accomplished, his mother was able to allow him to have more privacy in his treatment. With support from me, she had the nanny bring him for some of his appointments. She felt encouraged by the improvement in his behavior in nursery school. This improvement, however, led the father to feel that Teddy could come less often or not at all. It was difficult to persuade the father that we had only begun our work together. It was only Teddy's aggressive behavior toward his brother that convinced the father that further work had to be done.

As Teddy's treatment continued, his fantasy play became more aggressive. There were huge battles between Star Wars characters, between army men, and between knights in armor. Lines were drawn and barricades built. I always had the puny army, and I was always badly defeated. During this period, he told me in a very agitated state that "Mommy fired Nanny." At first I thought he was telling me that he was upset about his nanny's leaving. However, as he played with the army and fired the guns, it dawned on me that Teddy had believed that his mother had shot and killed his nanny. He was relieved by the clarification of the word "fire," which he told me could also be a fire. Out came the fire engines and he graphically demonstrated how you could get killed in a fire as well. As the play continued, I noted that he was continually telling me that *I* could be killed either in a battle or in a fire. I interpreted his worry that he might lose me as he had lost his nanny. Teddy agreed with that, but he let me know that his worry had a basis in reality because his parents had been fighting about whether he should still see me. Then I pointed out how hard that must be for him. I said, "This is confusing. You must feel like you are in the middle." Teddy wondered whether he should stop coming to stop the fighting. In a session with the mother I pointed out Teddy's dilemma. She understood immediately and could see why he might have been expressing some reluctance about coming to his sessions. Since I was unable to get the father to meet with me again, I thought that he would continue to press for ending Teddy's treatment.

During his elaborate battle scenes, Teddy would often tell me about his brother's amazing feats. He described his older brother's daredevil behavior with both admiration and awe. I commented that he wished he could do what his brother did and that it was hard for him to be the younger and smaller one. Teddy's very mean and aggressive behavior toward his older brother escalated, and now his hostility was directed toward his younger sibling as well. His father found Teddy's behavior especially toward the younger brother very hard to tolerate.

In his analysis Teddy adamantly denied that he was angry at his older brother who would take his toys or exclude him from games. He steadfastly claimed that he loved his brother even though he would describe how his brother would abuse him. Thinking about his mother asleep on the couch made me realize that Teddy didn't have much help in countering his own inner instincts. I explained to Teddy that he must be very frightened of his angry feelings and, at a later point, that he must worry that he wouldn't be able to control what he might do if he felt really angry. Confirmation that Teddy felt a lack of assistance in countering his inner forces came in the following exchange. At the end of the session his mother suggested that they go and check on the construction in their new apartment. Teddy said, "We can see if they have put in window guards." Only after I interpreted, in numerous ways, his dread of his own instincts was Teddy able to begin to talk about his ambivalent feelings toward his older brother and later toward the younger one as well. This led to improvement in his behavior both at home and at school.

One day in the second year of his treatment, Teddy said, "I feel so happy I could cry." I said, "That's funny. Although you might cry if you were really very happy, usually you cry if you are sad." Teddy then listed various people he knew who had died including one of his grandmothers. We agreed that he was feeling sad. He said that he was "really sad because Daddy has secrets." The secrets turned out to be his father's explosive temper. Teddy said, "He blows up and you don't know when." He then described how, the previous night, his father had gotten so angry at him that he had totally destroyed the wooden toy chest. Teddy had been very frightened. Teddy then described many other times when his father had become enraged at him or at his brothers and had lost control. I thought that there was a "secret daddy" inside his regular daddy who might come out at any time and really scare him. Teddy agreed with this idea, but he pointed out that he had Foofy-Boofy (his imaginary companion) to protect him.

Following this session, there were many weeks of Star Wars play. The main theme was Luke Skywalker battling the evil Darth Vader. On occasion, Luke would be severely wounded, but usually Darth would be annihilated. Then the play would be disrupted, and Teddy would get agitated and physically aggressive. I commented that Teddy seemed to get very upset whenever Darth got killed. Teddy said, "Do you know that Darth is really Luke's father?" We discussed how Luke must have felt when he learned that Darth Vader was his father. Teddy thought that Luke would be "scared and sad." I added that maybe he was also "disturbed because no one wants their father to be a bad man." This comment had a big effect on Teddy. He said that Darth Vader was secretly Luke's father, but *his* father was "Darth Vader in secret." We could then understand why Teddy would get so frightened if Darth Vader got killed during the play. Teddy told me that Luke never *really* kills Darth Vader and Darth doesn't kill Luke. I said, "What a relief! No one wants to really kill their father." Teddy chimed in, "And no one wants their father to kill them." It was easy for Teddy to see that when his father got very angry, he worried that his father might really hurt him. He then felt he needed to protect himself and the only way to do that was to fight.

After the second summer break, Teddy was to attend a new school. He came to his session directly after having met his new teachers at the school. He burst into the office exclaiming that "Foofy-Boofy has real guns." I was amazed that his imaginary companion was back in the picture and that there was a need for real weapons. Teddy asked to take off his shirt and his mother very clearly told him that he could not do that. Being extremely defiant toward his mother, Teddy removed his shirt and paraded around bare-chested. He adamantly refused when she told him to put his shirt back on and struck many threatening poses as if he were a boxer or martial arts expert. I recalled that when he was frightened, "Teddy got tough." I thought that it must have been scary for him to meet his new teachers at a new school. He heard me and said, "You never know who someone is in disguise." I told him that while his new teachers seemed very nice, he had to be prepared for who they might really be beneath the surface. He said, "I'm really tough!" I commented that he was showing me how really tough he is and that no one was going to hurt him. I couldn't resist adding that he was probably also mad at me because I hadn't seen him in a long time. I also began to show Teddy that sometimes he acted very much the way he saw his father act. He said, "No one pushes him around. We're the same." I said that being the same kept him close to his father. Over the next couple of weeks Teddy made an adjustment at his new school and believed that the teachers were indeed nice—both on the surface and underneath. He was able to drop his exterior armor and relax.

At this point, however, Teddy's father wanted to discontinue the treatment. He reiterated that he had never really believed that his son had any problems and he thought that Teddy was being "stigmatized." He would not agree to a termination period and wanted the treatment stopped immediately. Because Teddy's behavior had improved dramatically and because he was doing well at school, Teddy's mother felt there were no real symptoms with which to convince her husband to continue. She thought she might be able to do it secretly, but I quickly discouraged this plan. We arranged for just a couple of sessions for Teddy and me to say goodbye. Unfortunately, Teddy understood that it was his father who was keeping him from seeing me. He was angry and felt he needed to "be tough" because you never knew when someone might want to hurt you. He did, however, voice his desire to please his father and expressed some feeling that his attachment to me might be causing his father's disapproval. I commented on how painful it was to be in the middle. "Of course," I said, "you love your father and you want to please him." It was particularly poignant to see Teddy struggle with his mixed feelings about leaving treatment and getting his father's approval. I felt sad to have the treatment end in this way, but I also realized that I did not want to make the situation even more difficult for Teddy.

A little more than a year later, I had a call from Teddy's mother saying that she wanted Teddy to return to treatment. In a meeting with her, she reported that Teddy had had a "fantastic year and a great summer." But now, several months into the next school year, he seemed to be having difficulties. She reported that he was constantly saying that he didn't feel well or that he was dying. She stated that he had a fixation with morbid and life-threatening things. He reported quite graphic and scary fantasies. He was, she said, "incredibly anxious" and scared about dying. Teddy's mother also reported that he "said incredibly insensitive things" such as calling his brother "useless." This, by the way, was something I recognized that the father had done. She commented that Teddy always spoke about me and now was asking to come to see me. As a side note she also reported that Teddy had a very limited diet and she claimed that he was "allergic" to many foods. Teddy was also enuretic at night. This was something the mother had never told me before probably, she said, because she herself had wet the bed until age 13. Teddy's father persisted in calling Teddy "a bed wetter." She said that her husband was "tortured" by Teddy. Father and son both spoke in hurtful and incendiary ways. Also, Teddy was having difficulty controlling himself physically and had gotten so enraged that he punched his younger brother.

In the time that I had not seen Teddy several important things had happened in the family. Another child had been born, and Teddy now had an infant sister. Mother said, "Teddy loves her. He is very sweet with her." Also, the father had become very religious. Before beginning a second round of treatment, I was determined to meet with the father to try to ascertain whether he would be supportive of analysis for Teddy at this point. With the idea that he might be convinced by outside data, I suggested to the father that we get Teddy tested. He was very much in favor of the idea. The psychological evaluation revealed "an extraordinarily intelligent boy who is concerned with some issues which absorb considerable psychological energy and adversely affect interpersonal interactions and promote anxiety." Teddy's chief concern seemed to be maintaining a balance between his strong identification with his father and his equally strong attachment to his mother. He perceived them as working counter to one another, and he seemed at odds with both parents. The psychologist highly recommended that he be in psychoanalysis. The father was convinced that Teddy needed help, but he was not in favor of intensive treatment. I believed that I would be unable to help Teddy unless he was in analysis. I was also wary of putting Teddy in yet another situation where he would have divided loyalties. The parents ultimately sent him for counseling in connection with the father's new-found interest in religion.

Discussion

Self-preservation was the overriding preoccupation in Teddy's life. Just as Luke Skywalker's world was threatened by forces from the Dark Side, Teddy also felt threatened by forces. These evil forces came from both outside and inside of himself. In the account of his treatment, I have limited my description to those aspects that unambiguously pertain to the molding of his aggressive drive. It is clear that Teddy became more violent when he felt threatened by castration or by attack from without. It is also clear that he felt a distinct dread of his own instincts.

Anna Freud, in *The Ego and the Mechanisms of Defense* (1936, pp. 58–

60), discusses instinctual anxiety or the dread of the strength of the instincts. She points out that when the ego has evolved from the pleasure principle to the reality principle, it is no longer very friendly to the instincts. It has become "alien territory" to the instincts. Usually the warfare waged against the demands of the impulses comes from the superego and the outside world. "However, if the ego feels itself abandoned by these protective powers or if the demands of the instinctual impulses become excessive, its mute hostility to instinct is intensified to the point of anxiety." Sigmund Freud wrote (1923, p. 57) that what the ego fears from the libidinal danger "cannot be specified; we know that the fear is of being overwhelmed or annihilated, but it cannot be grasped analytically." The vantage point is from the ego, which perceives its weakness relative to the strength of the id.

John Hitchcock (1996) comments that the focus in the past several decades has been on separation anxiety, emphasizing the fear of the loss of the object and of the object's love. This view has obscured another equally powerful experience of childhood, namely the loss of the object's assistance in countering those inner forces of the child, which results in the dread of the strength of the instincts. This is an affective state, which "renders an individual more vulnerable to committing an act of violence" (Hitchcock, p. 102). The word "dread" is used because it conveys awe and aversion as well as anxiety. Dread helps describe the experience of children of their powerful instincts, which they must defend against by externalization and displacement. I believe Teddy felt that he did not always have his mother's assistance in battling his own powerful impulses. This was brought home to me by seeing his mother asleep on my couch.

Dread of the strength of the instincts arises from the belief that one could really commit a violent act. It arises when an external threat is perceived. This external threat may be linked to earlier experiences in which the child felt overwhelmed. In the first year of his life, Teddy underwent several medical interventions during which he must surely have felt overwhelmed. His early experiences also included at least one "shock" trauma (Kris, 1956)—his brother attacked him in his crib, biting his face. Although it is not clear when this event occurred or even if it was an isolated occurrence, it seems to me that both his medical experiences and the attack by his brother must have made Teddy feel unprotected. And, if he was unprotected by his mother from external threats, then certainly he was not protected from the internal ones. Dread of the strength of his instincts was only partially interpreted to Teddy. A glaring omission was my failure to confront directly the feeling of dread and to analyze its origins. This oversight, I believe, still leaves Teddy vulnerable to committing or to the fear of committing a violent act.

Although the behavior of Teddy's mother during his sessions demonstrated to me her inability to be his protector, I was keenly aware of the fact that his father was also not helpful in this regard. Teddy's world was one of unpredictable violence in which there was no one to protect him. Teddy experienced his father's explosive temper as terrifying, but he also understood that his father wanted him to be "tough." He was trying to please his father and also was identifying with the aggressor. The connection that Teddy made between his father and Darth Vader is extremely interesting. I believe it was an attempt by Teddy to see his father as both threatening and loving. But it was problematic. Ultimately, there is good in Darth Vader because he kills the evil Emperor to save his son's life. Darth Vader, however, dies in the process as Luke tells him, "You saved me, Father." In other words, Darth Vader gives up his life for his son. Unfortunately, Teddy's treatment ended before his parricidal fantasies could be approached. Teddy identified with the gallant, but violent, son, Luke Skywalker, who battled against all odds and even stood up to his own threatening and murderous father.

The terror that Teddy felt when Luke Skywalker was injured in battle and lost a body part suggests, of course, castration anxiety referable to early oedipal competition with his father as Darth Vader. But, perhaps more fundamental was the underlying developmental impact of the battles that took place between Teddy and his mother around toilet training. Teddy was terrified on a preoedipal level of being defeated, demolished, crushed, broken in his spirit, and flushed away. He had to fight to preserve his pride and his self-esteem. His mother's intrusion into his analytic sessions, sleeping on the analytic couch like a dormant volcano, until she somehow awoke and sprang into action to comment on Teddy's fear of losing his poopee, reflects her propensity for interfering in the developmental process rather than facilitating it.

One difficult theoretical question to answer is whether the need to be active derives from the aggressive drive or whether aggression is a derivative of motoric impulses. It is well-known, however, that behavior which is labeled as aggressive is often enlisted when other avenues for activity are blocked. In other words, aggression is used as a defense against passivity. Teddy's brief life history is replete with traumatic episodes in which he was in a position of helplessness. It is difficult to distinguish between the effects of the different kinds of traumatic situations. Is there a difference between the effect of a single situation when reality suddenly impinges on a child's life, as when Teddy's brother bit him, and the effect of repetitive situations which are traumatic because of the accumulation of frustrating tension? I think that in Teddy's case we were dealing with an extended period in which there were real events or traumas that contributed to a premature and concretized organization of affect, particularly hate. Also, the real events began to coincide with the development of certain universal fantasies that originate during the oedipal phase. Hopefully, Teddy's treatment allowed for further development of the ego's ability to handle affects and that he now has the capacity to recognize that aggression does not always originate from without. Furst (1998) points out that the internalization of aggression is "a necessary precursor to the taming of the raw drive." When there is a failure of internalization the individual "must depend on external objects for the control of instinctual expression."

The analyses of children provide some assistance in answering the question of whether aggression is essentially destructive or constructive. In Teddy's treatment we see the adaptational value of aggression and its use in the service of mastery. There was some truth to his father's feeling that Teddy's behavior was appropriate to the situation in which he found himself. The way in which aggression is experienced and the way it is expressed is related to the particular stage of the ego's development at the time of the conflict. Teddy was reacting to intense dangers at a time when his ego was just forming, when it was unable to organize and handle the experience. His intrapsychic defense mechanisms were no match for the dangers that could be heard, seen, and felt. The external forces that threatened Teddy gave an unarguable reality to the internal ones and called for real defenses in the form of violent behaviors.

As I pointed out earlier, Teddy was beginning to identify with his aggressive father. Another aspect of this situation is that Teddy was probably acting out some of the aggressive impulses and fantasies of his father. In my meetings with the father I was always aware of a certain pride that he had in Teddy's "tough" behavior and a desire that his son not be a "wimp."

Observational studies indicate that aggressive behaviors change markedly in the preschool years, or in the terminology of psychoanalytic observation, direct discharge of aggressive drive derivatives is muted and shaped by the child's relationship with his parents or with those who most actively care for him (Mayes and Cohen, 1993). Children who are habitual witnesses of violence experience a greater sense of danger when confronted with their own aggressive feelings or wishes. Or they may experience their own aggressivity and fantasies as compatible with that which commonly occurs around them and permissible by those whom they have experienced as equally violent and destructive.

CONCLUSION

The psychoanalytic theory of aggression is not as well worked out as is the theory of libido. Questions regarding the constructive versus the destructive uses of aggression remain. Direct clinical material is the data which psychoanalysts use to develop their theories. The clinical material from work with young children may be particularly useful in elucidating the vicissitudes of the aggressive drive because a child's sense of what is internal and what is external is just evolving. Aggression undergoes developmental change and experiential factors have a determining influence on the child's subsequent ability to control aggression.

This paper offers clinical observations, which demonstrate a few of the factors involved in the vicissitudes of aggression. The data support Anna Freud's recognition of the importance of the dread of the strength of the instincts. The analytic work with Teddy, a young boy with angry and aggressive behavior, is particularly illustrative of this affective state of instinctual anxiety. It also demonstrates how the aggressive drive is molded by events that are experienced as traumatic and by the child's relationship to his parents. When the child's experience includes the lack of external control of his impulses, he may be more predisposed to violent behavior. The importance of the stage of ego development at the time of trauma is also emphasized. Unfortunately, Teddy's treatment ended prematurely and we know very well that his return for further analytic work could be invaluable to him.

BIBLIOGRAPHY

FREUD, A. (1936). *The Ego and the Mechanisms of Defense.* Revised Edition (1966). New York: Int. Univ. Press.
——— (1972). Comments on Aggression. *Int. J. Psychoanal.,* 53:163–171.
FREUD, S. (1923). The Ego and the Id. *S.E., 19:*13–63.
FURST, S. (1998). A Psychoanalytic Study of Aggression. *Psychoanal. Study Child,* 53:159–178.

GREENACRE, P. (1971). Notes on the Influence and Contribution of Ego Psychology to the Practice of Psychoanalysis. In *Separation-Individuation,* ed. J. B. McDevitt & C. F. Settlage. New York: Int. Univ. Press, pp. 171–200.

HITCHCOCK, J. (1996). Dread of the Strength of the Instincts. *Psychoanal. Study Child,* 53:102–116.

KLEIN, M. (1957). Envy and Gratitude. In *Envy and Gratitude and Other Works.* London: Hogarth Press, 1975, pp. 176–235.

KRIS, E. (1956). The Recovery of Childhood Memories in Psychoanalysis. *Psychoanal. Study Child,* 11:54–88.

MAYES, L., & COHEN, D. (1993). The Social Matrix of Aggression. *Psychoanal. Study Child,* 48:145–169.

SOLNIT, A. (1972). Aggression. *J. Amer. Psychoanal. Assn.,* 20:435–450.

WINNICOTT, D. W. (1950). Aggression in Relation to Emotional Development. *Collected Papers.* New York: Basic Books, 1975, pp. 204–218.

The Analytic Pair in Action

Finding the Missing Mental Life:
An Intersubjective Approach

JILL C. HERBERT, Ph.D.

The case of a musician/performer whose disposition and identity involved action as a privileged modality and whose initial presentation included the absence of a palpable mental life is used to show how the analyst's urge to disclose/to fill in what was unknown was midwife to the development of a symbolizing capacity and an articulated mental life. The patient at first could only tell her story by showing and doing and so the analyst's participation in the actualization of the narrative was vital to its discovery. Relationships between the patient's

Training and Supervising Analyst, New York Freudian Society; Faculty and Supervisor, Metropolitan Institute for Psychoanalytic Psychotherapy (Child/Adolescent Training Program) New York; Independent Practice in Psychoanalysis and Psychoanalytic Psychotherapy, New York.

I am grateful to Ted and Dan Jacobs whose invitation to present a clinical anecdote in their co-led discussion group on interaction and intersubjectivity at the Mid-Winter meetings, December 1997, of the American Psychoanalytic Association, held at the Waldorf-Astoria, New York, provided me with a reason and opportunity to begin work on this paper.

I wish to thank Graciela Abelin, Christa Balzert, Michael Beldoch, Zoe Grusky, and Ted Jacobs for their comments on earlier versions. I especially wish to thank Carola Chase for her editorial help.

Above all, I am enormously grateful to Sallie for permitting me to write my version of what was "true" about her/us, and with minimal disguise. In respect of Sallie's privacy, I have omitted certain information, fantasies, and symptoms—intimacies that felt too revealing and intrusive. Because of my patient's public life and because the treatment is ongoing, I am unable to report on details of her developmental or familial life and will refrain from describing personal resonances with mine.

The Psychoanalytic Study of the Child 61, ed. Robert A. King, Peter B. Neubauer, Samuel Abrams, and A. Scott Dowling (Yale University Press, copyright © 2006 by Robert A. King, Peter B. Neubauer, Samuel Abrams, and A. Scott Dowling).

*unusual mental structure, including her proclivity for action, the use
of projective mechanisms, and an ease with the concretization of fantasy are discussed with reference to her endowment as a gifted musical
composer, and her identity as an "artist." Technical strategies and difficulties in arriving at a 'best' technique are discussed as the analyst
struggled to locate the patient developmentally, and to contain and
permit difficult transference/countertransference enactments to unfold. Reflections on parallels to child/adolescent developmental necessities enabled the evolution of a viable technique.*

> "I am an assortment of dazzling, cosmic, and spectac-
> ular meteor showers in outer space. Sometimes,
> though, I feel like the painting I stare at." (Sallie)

> "Je suis ce que je suis, un clown par destin, un fabri-
> quant de masques avec la tête d'un chat, la queue
> d'une poule. Je me moque et je ris. Je suis le fils de la
> nuit, le magicien des masques. Ils pleurent; ils rient
> par ma volonte. Je suis l'enchanteur de la chauve-
> souris, l'ami du crabe et du scorpion, mon ventre
> l'aquarium où la langouste se promène avec son
> compagnon, des roses poussent de ma bouche, des
> epines surgissent de mon oreille." (caption on dry-
> point, Mordecai Moreh, *Procession*, 18/5/1966)

AN INTERSUBJECTIVE VIEW OF THE ANALYTIC PROCESS MAINTAINS
that each of the partners makes a psychological contribution to that
which emerges or is constructed as the unique narrative of a particular psychoanalysis. Albeit with varying emphases on the nature of the
analyst's contribution—as "reader" of the patient's "objective" reality, as co-constructor, facilitator, designer, or impediment—different
schools of psychoanalytic practice (see Altman and Davies, 2003)
agree that there are *two* interacting subjectivities (see for instance, Jacobs 1997) and Renik (1993) in the analytic collaboration, each affecting the intrapsychic life of the other in important and reciprocal
ways. Levine and Friedman (2000) argue for an appreciation of intersubjectivity as a necessary perspective rather than as a "school-spe-
cific" paradigm requiring modifications in technique and Green
(2000) suggests that "intersubjectivity . . . (is) the mediation necessary for gaining awareness of the intrapsychic" (p. 21).

The place and meaning of self-disclosure has been part of these
conversations about intersubjectivity. In our traditional model which
specifies that the analyst's neutrality, abstinence, and anonymity are
integral to the elaboration and exploration of the patient's transfer-

ence possibilities, analyst disclosures are problematic and the inevitable leaking of information is viewed/graded as a function of severity and degree of deviation from the "ideal of anonymity" (Renik, 1995). Seemingly good effects (such as the re-ignition of a stalled analysis) whether brought about through the happy accident of an unintended disclosure (Cooper, 1998) or through skillful planning and titration are then weighed against the transference limitations imposed by the analyst's disclosed subjectivity. Viewed through an intersubjectivist lens, however, the same disclosures would not necessarily be regarded as either deviation or contaminant.

Whether viewed as error, technical modification, well-chosen parameter, or as an inherent and unavoidable aspect of human contact, disclosures have been difficult to publicly address in a value-free way (see Jacobs, 1997, 1999), since disclosures are always revelatory actions made by the analyst and, as such, trench on those issues in psychoanalysis with which we are most passionately engaged; they are also *apparently* personal (that is, about the analyst!). If, however, we consider that *the intrapsychic field of the analyst is an arena in which the patient's story may unfold,* it is possible to regard the analyst's disclosures non-pejoratively and to treat them like any other countertransference[1] response, which is (in part) engendered by or sensitive to the transferences of the patient.

Despite having been trained to be (or inclined to be) leery of disclosure as a potential contaminant to the analytic process, I became interested in how the analyst's disclosures could be viewed as a vital and essential product of the interactive analytic process. In the case I will be discussing I was bedeviled in the first year or so by a disturbing sense of having disclosed—or wishing to disclose—too much. I came to appreciate that these experiences, albeit painful to me, were essential aspects of the treatment. *I discovered that what presented as a missing mental life in my patient at the outset was refound in and by the analyst via complex transference/countertransference enactments* which included these experiences. (see Mahoney, 1999, and Smith, 2003). As the enactments were analytically understood *and* the patient actively disabused from their manifestation (this will be discussed at some length), they subsided, and a mental life evolved. (I note at the outset that when Sallie and I had begun, I had by then been an analyst, classically trained, in practice for about 25 years, prior to which I had

1. Following Jacobs (1991) I will "use the term *countertransference* . . . to refer to influences on the analyst's understanding and technique that stem both from his transferences and from his emotional responses to the patient's transferences." (p. 140).

spent some years teaching, evaluating, and doing therapy with both "normal" and disturbed children of all ages. Some of my kids were battered and unspeakably abused; others "merely" mentally defective and with organic disturbances of various kinds. But in none of my experiences had I ever come across a person such as Sallie; no other musician I had analyzed had presented in the same way either. Her unique mélange of highly sophisticated emotional and cognitive capacities in her musical and professional life with lacunae in all other areas of the intrapsychic and interpersonal life presented me with the difficulty and demand to find a coherence (or to create one) in her mental life—and to find an appropriate technique for working with/analyzing this unique and specifically damaged extraordinary woman. In what follows I hope to provide the reader with a sense of what it was like to be in the room with this person and what the unique demands were as made on the analyst during the first two years of treatment.

I will present a few powerful and remarkable "moments," which punctuated in stunning fashion the first year and a quarter of this psychoanalysis. The events were unusually dramatic and specific to the case and to the unique analytic pair. I hope that these events will demonstrate how the intersection of self-disclosure (on the analyst's part) with acting out (on the patient's part), realized in action, that is, "actualized" (Ogden, 1986) an urgent and mysterious communication of Sallie's, "If only you could see me in action, then you would understand." My response, "Understand what?" and Sallie's rejoinder, "I don't know," was (too often) emblematic of our analytic dilemma. (See Katz's 1998 discussion of the "enacted dimension.") What neither of us knew and what was as yet unarticulated in the couple found its way into action and into the analyst's inability to see or imagine. Moreover, the analyst's wish/impulse to disclose—the content of which remained mysterious—was found to be far more important than merely a response to the pressure of the patient's demands for information and her insatiable curiosity about the analyst's life; the communication was an aspect of the patient's "presymbolic or pre-representational mental registers, . . . a baggage of experience the patient carries around. . . . outside of symbolizing or even of 'remembering.' . . . They are not unconscious contents (and) what occurs in the context of treatment does not have the characteristic of a sharing of experience, but of a much more specific function exercised by the therapist—to pre-represent in his own mind the content transmitted through the PI [Projective Identification]" (Cimino and Correale, 2005, pp. 55–56).

Both patient and analyst became entangled in action scenarios, which appeared as excitements in the evolving transference/countertransference interface and involved boundary violations (albeit of differing sorts) by both participants. They were unusually intense and demanding of the analyst in a number of ways: My patient *did* things. I presume I did things, too, in response or provocation—and that the action that was privileged by the patient's psychic structure came to roost within my countertransference in some subtle and complex ways. I needed to keep a more than usual vigil on my urges toward action and reaction, lest they be "too much." I was concerned that I not disclose too much since any revelation would change my patient's landscape; she was starving for an emotional response to shore up her narrative of deprivation and disengagement, and I was afraid that I would foreclose understanding by providing emotional sustenance to what often appeared to be a terrified little girl in desperate need of maternal warmth and sensitivity and stimulation. Internally I was split between my countertransference wish to warm and feed her spirit and my analytic ego, which insisted that I wait and analyze. This made for paralysis at times and at other times unnecessary silence as I struggled for control and understanding. I struggled for a long time too, with my experience of Sallie as a child and my awareness of her as a woman in trouble, in the sense that I could not get clear how to actually treat her. I longed to be playful and spontaneous and improvisational—literally—as I would be with a child, rather than how I am naturally with adolescents and adults in manner and demeanor; of course I was constrained then and became quite a pill at times. (See Grusky, 2002; also Ringstrom, 2001 for illustrations of the virtue and value of the creative and improvisational spirit with adult patients.)

CLINICAL BEGINNINGS: BECOMING A COUPLE

Some months after being referred by a terminating patient who had alerted me (while chuckling) that someone "unusual" would be calling, a woman called and in a tiny, breathy voice identified herself and nervously asked if I would please see her—even though so much time had passed. I reassured her that it was fine (first error?) and soon met Sallie in what would be her usual attire and stance. A small, sturdy woman of about 40 years old, dressed in jeans, boots, a form-fitting sweater, and without makeup or jewelry, Sallie greeted me shyly, averting her eyes and saying her name in a whisper. I sensed she was averse to physical contact and so, rather than offer my hand I

indicated the way to my office. She told me she was in a state of terrible hurt and disorientation, and wondered if she was "bad." When I
asked why she thought this, Sallie apologized for not calling me first.[2]
She told me she'd been seeing a couples therapist with her husband
but, "This couples person traumatized us. We were both frightened."
When I wondered aloud why she (or they) continued to see this therapist, she claimed, "I was desperate. I didn't know what to do. I
thought maybe it was supposed to be like that. But then my husband
wouldn't go anymore. So I called you." She was unable to tell me
more of her experience or reasons, looking toward me for their elaboration: "What do you think?" I wondered again aloud what I was
supposed to be thinking about or knowing. "Believe me," she said, "I
have no clue."

Sallie told me what little she could, and this was very little. She
could not describe the problems she and her husband were having.
She did not talk about any other aspect of her life; no conflicts were
accessible to her. This came later. An accompaniment to the patient's
discoveries that she had conflicts or problems in other areas rather
than a worry about a (perhaps) unfaithful husband with whom she
was symbiotically bonded—was profound shame and self-denigra-
tion. Her narcissistic vulnerabilities were enormous and entwined
with such terrible self-judgments (often projected) that it was almost
impossible for her to access and talk about having a problem. When
asked questions at this early time in treatment my patient was propelled into a panicky state and stopped making sense—at all. I
sensed that despite holding advanced degrees, being an accomplished performer, stably married, with friends and an apparently ordinary social life she was frightened—as if still a child, cast by bad
magic into the world of grownups. She was confused and made anxious by ordinary social interaction, bewildered and disoriented by inner emotional turmoil and the emotional lives of others. She had no
emotional vocabulary, and so, was at the mercy of her emotional life.
She ordered her inner world with musical composition, professional
responsibilities, and a narrative which accounted for her deprivations, even though it left her bereft of a loving family. For instance, a

2. This kind of response—at an angle to my question/way of thinking—constantly
disoriented/jarred me. When I would tell Sallie about this asynchrony, she would spi-
ral through an intensifying masochistic loop of feelings of badness, and "confess" that
she wasn't really listening to my words, but rather to her pre-thought thoughts. Eventually we were able to address Sallie's humiliation and terror at my discovery that
something was the matter with her mind. With this established we moved on to important discussions about not being able to have a dialogue with an actual other.

significantly charged conviction was held and insisted upon—that
her mother did not talk to her. I finally realized that the "not-talking
mother" was a concretization of Sallie's felt experience of not hearing what she longed to hear. It was a metaphor that was experienced
as real; that is, if the words spoken were not the words Sallie longed
for she didn't register them as words. She felt them as nothings and
did not know that the experience was in the realm of the mental. I
took these kinds of structural deficits—the mélange of absences, serious deficits in representation of content and affect, and concretizations—as evidence that there had been very early (preverbal) trauma
of the sort that leaves "vestiges" (Bion, 1962) or what Tutté (2004)
calls the "archaic" and cites de Pantazoglu (1991) as describing as
"broken threads that do not compose a weave."

At the time, Sallie's marriage was in a shambles, her husband increasingly absent physically and emotionally. She was frantic about
the potential loss of her mate and yet was unable to account for their
problems. She had not known anything was the matter—not having
taken in, or given weight to her partner's statements of dissatisfaction
with their "cocooned" life, and oblivious to any meaning for his absences other than the demands of his work. She still could only
barely entertain the possibility that he might have an extra-marital interest and that it might be romantic. For the first time, Sallie realized
that it was odd that in their many years of marriage they had never
had one conversation about having a child, sex, or their relationship.
This was mind-boggling to me—that she could *not* know so much. It
was hard for me to imagine the quality of their lives together, and almost impossible for me to imagine what her mind was like.

Sallie turned to me as an authority and pleaded with me for strategies to help her keep her husband. She related to me in an idealizing
fashion, and presented as devoid of comprehension or complexity.
She began to act. She gave me a CD (of hers) after some weeks and
then another and then another. At first, I thought that, like a child,
she was letting me know in action that which she couldn't tell me.
Then (as they kept coming) I wondered to myself why she had to
bring her successful self to me in *only* this form. I was disturbed by
the physicality of the communication. I asked her if she knew why she
couldn't use words and tell me about herself, and she said merely,
"no." Except for my first statement of acceptance, "thank you," and
then, "you are letting me know other parts of you too," I said nothing
of any substance that I recall, no intervention reflecting meaning, because I didn't know what was going on—other than that I was uncomfortable. In fact, throughout the initial consultation period—of

several months—I was confronted with a perplexing constellation of absences in my patient—an affective blanking of her history, a scantiness of accessible "facts," no apparent symptoms, and a difficulty in communicating what, if anything, might be in her mind.[3] Because of this peculiar and unusual experience for me—not knowing what/who I was confronted with—I suggested that we work face-to-face for several months (this phase of introductory work lasted three months) at a frequency of three times a week. I expected that this would give me a chance to make a beginning developmental diagnosis, and to assess the advisability of doing analytic work. Also, I felt that because Sallie was afraid and in crisis, beginning our work in this modality would be both compassionate and productive.

As for the work with her, I found myself doing a kind of crisis intervention/counseling—in an effort to help her hold the frame of the marriage until something about their dynamic acceded to some understanding on my part. The work was increasingly difficult for me as I continued to find myself confronted with blankness where there should have been a mental life. I could not make mental pictures out of what she said. My patient would, for instance, tell me a sentence or two of what was going on, fall silent, look at me expectantly or ask for advice or wisdom. I felt as blank inside as the face she turned toward me. Unable to glean what was vital within or about her, I turned inward, eventually focusing on my abortive attempts to analyze what she aroused in me. I presume I was made anxious by the impenetrability I confronted, especially as it evoked in me a corresponding sense of flatness and inaccessibility, but I was at first aware only of a thwarted curiosity. That my affective signals got derailed would prove to be an important countertransference in this analysis and a clue not only to a content of my patient's mental life (she rarely knows when she is afraid even though her voice may be shaking and her mind closed down) but to the ubiquity of the projective identificatory processes which she employed in order to communicate and/or pressure me to respond in some way (see Feldman, 1997, and Joseph, 1983, 1987). Finally, I felt compelled to tell Sallie of my inner experience. Having attempted to locate her within me and failing, I resorted to (verbal) action. I told my patient something of how I work,

3. Only recently, having already written the body of this piece, I came upon a spectacular paper by Joyce McDougall (1978) in which she almost uncannily describes and then creates a cogent theoretical narrative to account for these mysteries. She references issues of primitive communication and the meaning and function of words and actions for patients who have been traumatized even before the "acquisition of language."

about my mind and about a difficulty I was having in understanding her. I thought I was reflecting aloud on a dilemma, a variation of a usual technical device, a kind of interpretation with which I am comfortable. However, my disclosure registered in me as a *countertransference disclosure* for a number of reasons, not the least of which was that I felt I had been more personal than I was comfortable with and that I was working in an unfamiliar way. These affects were part of the induced countertransferential experience—since I was neither being very personal nor was I working so differently than usual. To borrow Cooper's (1998) felicitous phrase, my disclosure was "in the context of a *mutually held resistance*" (italics mine), a jointly manufactured transference/countertransference impasse—which I did not recognize as such.

Although my rather ordinary disclosures (educational disclosures of internal processes, spontaneous comments of pleasure at some achievement, a revelation—through word and attitude—of my musical taste) struck me as relatively minor infractions of my standard analytic posture, they were nonetheless experienced by me as other than usual and/or neutral and in fact had a particular flavor of disclothing, of *showing too much,* and in this way drew my attention to the disclosures as indicators and containers of important information. Having said to her that while I could usually feel my way into, or imagine (and usually in a dynamic, visual way) some approximation of the inner world of my patients, I told her that she was a mystery to me and that I could not see, nor feel my way, into her interior. I said this in a respectful and collegial way, I believe, trying to engage her curiosity and hoping to enlist her collaboration. She was intrigued. She immediately "got it" and was delighted at what she called my internal theater—charmed that it was just like the "virtual reality" of science fiction.

I was disconcerted by this description of hers, but I could not think about it. I was more concerned with how very uncomfortable I was with what I had said, although I had thought it through, as best I could, before the session. I had felt that I was taking a big risk in using metaphors that were potentially contaminating and seductive (a boundary violation, perhaps), since my references to getting inside her, or she in me, would have to be sexual in their elaborations. Also, I didn't know why I was telling her how I usually worked with others.

In an unsettling speedy way, my patient reversed her style of being with me; she "unzipped." We first understood this as her having gained permission to have a mental life, and I tendered an intervention—that I had been having her experience of her mother, and she was *being* her mother—that is, I was she, bewildered by an absence in my mother, and she was her mother, closed off, affectively mute. Soon, my patient began to refer to the couch and to the possibility of an analysis. At this point I still did not grasp the meanings or functions of Sallie's mental disarray and did not yet have a diagnostic sense—other than a "feel" that she had been traumatized in some way and was dissociated or numbed in her capacities to think and process information. Thus, I had a sense of unease about this desire and found myself reluctant to agree. Her reasons were as legitimate as anyone's, her felt experiences not unusual in form or expression—but something seemed "off." I felt commandeered into it, forced to accede to her request, although she was in no way pushy; she was nervous, excited, curious, and so on. I put off the formal agreement to begin the analysis, but after some weeks, I realized that I had become a participant in another transference/countertransference duet—which was worse! I felt as if I were refusing her something she was entitled to, arbitrarily and sadistically, so that she was compelled to either plead with me in a supplicant fashion or withdraw her desire. I retreated, thinking that my patient's entry into psychoanalysis should not be marked by a battle, especially one I was inveigled into by her/my unconscious and which I did not yet grasp. (The enactment continued onto the couch then, with my neither commenting on the barely disguised urgency of her demand for the couch nor bringing the "battle" to her attention. The analysis then "officially" began three months after treatment began. She moved from the chairs to the couch and from three times to four times a week.)

Instead, I think she dreamed it: "I am on an air field, running around picking things up like it's my job. Maybe it's a war! Jets are so loud I can't hear people shouting. A fire has started on the flight deck. Lots of smoke and it's hard to see what's happening. Everyone is running to put something on it—to stamp out embers. It makes it worse. I think, 'it has to run its course.' But as soon as I spoke I gave the position away and a big fire erupted. This was a nightmare and I woke terrified." I was struck by the helplessness of the people. No one seemed to be able to fix things. I commented on the dangers of speaking and how she could get "discovered" and hurt if I heard her. I told her that she was also afraid of not speaking and afraid that I could not help her or rescue her from overwhelming and out-of-control fires inside her. She tried to convince me that I was wrong—that she wanted to speak, that she loved to see me and to tell me things. But she did know that she was afraid. "Okay, okay, you're right!" (as if we were in an anal power battle). I said that her dream was telling us that she was afraid, in danger, and that she could not trust me; in fact, I thought her dream was a way of talking to me about these things.[4]

PSYCHOANALYSIS BEGINS

After a dream about marines breaching a beachhead, from which she woke saying, "I made it! I broke the surface!" she thought, "This is a dream about psychoanalysis. I was afraid psychoanalysis would be like the marines—assaulting the unconscious. I don't think I want to get assaulted." I only said, "Just analyzed?" (As I did not analyze the dream!) "Yup." Thus began the analysis, which of course, was destined to become an assault—for both of us!

My patient is currently a performance artist, although she was originally trained in classical opera, and had been an "almost star" for a decade. She described herself as a "player"—a person of action, one who makes music and makes things happen. I was thought of as a "shaman"—a magician with words. Her dreams, which are legion, are replete with visual complexity, verbal legerdemain, and puns. They partake of her multimodal sensory endowment and many times are constructed as cinematic products, complete with the perspective of the camera's eye, and reported with the detail of the camera angle, shot, etc., which creates and insists upon a perspective—the one that I am intended to incorporate. (I am herded into the corral of her vision by the detail of her implicit cinematic direction. Were I to be seduced by this I would see only that which she is allowed to see, and which she attempts to impose on me—rather than that which is available.) I loom large in the dream world. In the countertransference, I feel myself dazzled by the dreamscapes, the multidimensional repertoire she displays for my analytic pleasures and by the centrality that I am accorded in this stranger's mental life. I am everything! I am the air![5]

---

4. Some years later I appreciate an entirely different meaning of the dream—perhaps *the* meaning of the dream. My patient, who requires air for her singing, had also constructed a world—an object world—out of this air; that is, she has *created* a universe of people and meanings which was heroically about to be put under the scrutiny of the analysis. She must have known that this airfield would be blown to bits.

5. Greenacre (1957) says that the "experience of awe in childhood, the forerunner of the mystical experience" is connected to the glorification of the parents and in particular to the idealized image of the godlike father with whom there is identification. Sallie experiences me as awesome, and she wishes to benefit from my special

From the beginning there was an incipient "disagreement" brewing. She wanted to show me her feelings in actions. ("I am a doer, Doctor Herbert!"); I preferred words. She claimed that words were not her métier, only mine, and it appeared this way, at first. And yet, her lyrics and poems were superb, evocative. It was not entirely so that she was a stranger to language and its rather sophisticated use, despite the paucity of an emotional vocabulary! (I am confused for a long time by this discrepancy—that Sallie can use words beautifully and poetically and yet cannot use words to communicate meaning to me.) She was persistent in disavowing that which did not "fit" with her idea of herself: "Oh, I never could have known that" when I suggest that "Jack" in her dreams is "Jill" and despite my comment: "But *you* dreamt it." "No, it's *you* who can do these fancy word things. You discovered it. So it's yours!" she insisted.

Sallie disavowed, as well, aspects of me she didn't quite like—the hurtful person I sometimes am, however well intentioned. I show up in a dream as "Jaws," a terrifying and dangerous shark she is compelled to watch. As the petrified viewer, she is paralyzed by fear, unable to act. However, as soon as she becomes aware that I am the shark, she is entertained by her mind and amused to think of me that way. Also, to retain me as omniscient and all good, Sallie consistently resorted to an obliteration of my "not-knowings" and recast them as engineered or intended. She turned her disagreements with me into artful compliance. For example, if I were to suggest that she was envious and she disagreed, she might produce a dream with green in it— to which she would delightedly associate—as envy; she would naively come upon this sign and attribute super-powers to me, for being so intuitive, so insightful. This was a constant problem for us—that her compliance did not allow either of us to know what was "true."

Sallie consistently bemoaned the loss of visual contact with me, and longed for opportunities to fix me in mind, or feast her eyes on me. She felt "forced" to rely on whatever sounds she could glean from behind the couch—tonalities in my voice, shufflings, etc., because of the analytic "rules" proscribing her from viewing me. But sensory details of the office and me showed up in her dreamscapes— and delighted her. Her pleasure in these discoveries reminded me of the peek-a-boo game. Each time she refound me was a pleasure. She

---

qualities and not take them for her own. The sharing of the godlike and mystical with me, in this protected way, allows her the ecstasies of the illusion of our communion (on many libidinal levels) without the impingement of the rival and without the pain associated with differentiation.

almost cooed! I am intrigued by her experience of my absence and her discovery of me each night when she sleeps. Am I not seen or known by day in order to be refound at night? Am I being constructed? And why do we need to feel each other as absent or impenetrable?

Sallie continued with her compulsive gift giving. I felt trapped and experienced her as insidious in her intrusiveness and manipulative, an emotional blackmailer (not usual ways of feeling/thinking/construing for me). I feel as naive and helpless as Sallie who shyly hands me a present, something she made for me. She buys me something lovely, clever, too small to complain about!—something which reflects a moment between us; she creates something for my office, which reflects some cherished aspect of me. How cruel I would be to reject the offering (of this child). Sallie has found her way into my spaces—with things that she feels *are* her. She stakes claim to being inside me and vice versa and acts as if our "interpenetrating mix-up" is mutually desired and that to which she is entitled. I am inundated with CDs, photographs, songs she's written, books she loves—about me, for me. I try to allow the unfolding of these transferences although *they insure that I repeat something with her;* that is, I feel caught in the enactments—whether I refuse the gifts or whether I accept the gifts—either with no substantive comment or while commenting upon or attempting to interpret their particular meaning or function or "the more general, compulsive quality of her giving"—the actuality remains: she has done something which I participate in, and I don't know what the "something" is.[6]

(POWER) STRUGGLES IN THE ACTION MATRIX

Early on in the analysis, my patient was going to be singing at a prestigious venue in our city. She had indicated months before that she hoped I would come to hear her. As the week came closer, she was more forthcoming about her desire that I be there—and connected

---

6. Sharpe (1935) enriches and complicates my understanding of Sallie as artist *and* traumatized "doer" who uses me to "do to" and to impress on me and into my mind the unknowable story she contains: "Now the artist deals with his instinctual problems and psychical phantasies allied with them in terms of his body. He uses a knowledge that is diffused in his body, a body intelligence and bodily experience in dealing with emotional states. He knows *how to do things,* not by consciously thinking them out and applying his knowledge but by perfecting powers inherent in the body based upon physical rhythms. It is a method of knowing the universe, the macrocosm via the microcosm, in terms of ordering emotion" (p. 197).

her need for me to be there with her mother's alleged refusals and absences. I explain my decision not to come despite the danger that my explanation would serve as a kind of reparation; that is, both discussion of and/or coming to see her will be experienced as corrective for the wounds Sallie felt she sustained by her mother's apparent indifference.[7] (One of the interesting technical dilemmas in this treatment is that my talk is in itself reparative and experienced as the gratification of her longing for her mother's words; sometimes she listens for the "music of my sounds" and never hears a word! Not talking because of how she uses my words is not an option and so far, interpreting/describing this dilemma is merely interesting to her.) I told her that I felt that our analytic relationship needed to be protected and that I could best do that by remaining in my "seat." I also said that since we knew something of the transferential meanings of her desire for my presence, I would be foreclosing an opportunity to further our exploration. I was clear internally, and I believe with her. While I anticipated that there would be repercussions to my "no," I could not have imagined their form.

Briefly, within a month of my "no" (about one month into the analysis proper), my patient engineered a remarkable event—one which I felt as extraordinary and diabolical and which violated my/our boundaries in a spectacular way—such that I was, not for the last time, speechless. My office is on a corner where there had recently been ongoing and disturbing events. Two or three movies have been made within a few feet of my windows, including one in which Woody Allen stood outside the window giving directions while I attempted to conduct an analytic session. We had just survived a season-long project during which an enormous pit had been dug in the sidewalk under my window, and into which (after months of digging and drilling and tunneling) an enormous generator was jockeyed into the earth by impossibly noisy machines. The disruptions to my practice had been dreadful for all of us but were finally over.

Toward the end of a session, one evening shortly after the street repair work was completed, I heard and then saw some scraggly looking

---

7. I had spent some very difficult hours with myself, almost agonizing about whether to attend her show, but bewildered with myself for such concern. I considered going but remaining hidden from view—so that I could be there, accommodate her need, see her without being seen. Should I go alone? Or with whom? Finally, it dawned on me that I had never gone to nor considered going to any other performing patient's show. This was freeing of course, and I was able to analyze what it was about for me as well as to acknowledge the power of what had been lodged in me by her.

men with musical instruments and some oddly dressed women in what looked like monk's robes arranging themselves under my window. They began to play and then sing exceedingly delicate and harmonious music, and I wondered what a church choir or choral group was doing on my corner. I thought then that some friends of my patient were here—for her. I wondered if it was her birthday, or if some friends were joking with her—perhaps about her analysis, or the "magical corner" she thought of as mine.

I was finally told that this was a group of renowned madrigal singers, who had been directed by my patient to "serenade" me. I was shocked and furious. Shocked at the mind which designed and implemented this exquisite vengeance ("I told you I don't like to be said 'no' to." "Gotcha!"). Confused because I enjoyed the violation before I knew that I was being "had!" Furious on behalf of my next patient who had just come in, having seen this group arrayed outside the window, as she rushed to get here on time; now she would be delayed because I needed some time to collect myself.

The next event of similar magnitude, which also involved a boundary violation of some kind—on both sides—took place some months later during a brutally hot period in the summer. My patient wore shorts, tee shirts, or sleeveless shirts, all appropriate to the weather and her style, but I had noted that she continued to wear her socks, adorable socks with charming images on them, now with sandals, despite the intense heat. I had made the mistake—another disclosure—of commenting on them spontaneously, months before. I wondered if she continued wearing them because I liked them. Something troubled me. Why was she wearing socks, if unnecessary, in 100-degree weather? But I was determined not to comment. On one of those scorching days, though, I blurted out, without deliberation: "Do you always wear socks?" I felt strongly that I had made an inappropriate and intrusive comment, despite its mildness. Sallie responded thoughtfully, "No. I don't usually, but I do when I'm coming here. I'll think about it."

The next day she came in and sat on the edge of the couch and as she was about to lie down, she looked at me seriously and said, "There's something you don't know about me—well I guess I should just do it." She took off her socks and lay down, and I saw all over her feet up to the ankles what looked like tattoos; some cartoons, some ugly faces, a monster. I was horrified! I thought to myself, "Oh my god—she did this when she was younger and now she can't get them removed, poor thing, or maybe she's trying to tell me she has a foot fetish or this is an introduction to some perversion I don't yet know about." I was shocked. After a few minutes of my silence, she said, "I guess you don't think it's funny. Oh well. I guess you don't like my joke. That fell flat."

"Joke?" said I. Only then did I "get" that the tattoos were fake! I was dumbfounded at the lack of empathy, the violence in the joke and again, at the mind that could plan and execute such an event, although I did not agree with Sallie that the action was primarily about hurting me. I thought she was repeating something and/or undoing a separation by penetrating me visually.

CHANGE OF STRATEGY

The crescendo of present-giving had left me feeling like the victim of assaults of generosity. The gifts included precious recordings of her voice when at its peak. I brought them to a senior colleague (Michael Beldoch) who was to help me with my negative countertransference, and left them there "by mistake." Contrary to his advice that I continue to allow the transferences to unfold (and if this involved a pile of gifts, so be it!), I could not bear to receive another gift! I began to be more confrontational about the object-related implications of her gift-giving and her surprising actions. I asked, for instance, what she imagined I would do with her gifts, how she imagined I felt—receiving so much. I referred back to the socks fiasco, now with the intent of addressing her failure of empathy. I asked what she thought I was feeling or thinking when she showed me her tattooed feet. She became interested in how much she did not think about or consider, and wondered why her empathy was so attenuated. She contained more of her impulses to act, and she became more affectively conversant with herself. We were collaborating well, I thought.

About six months later on a New Year's Eve (we are now 10 months into the analysis), we were having a session, which I was experiencing as an excellent hour. I was at ease, working well, with a sense of relaxation and spontaneity. We'd had a few months of intense and good work about which I was pleased, even self-congratulatory. I was meditating on a most recent series of dreams—containing sexual imagery—to which she had associated with interpretations upward, as she talked about their metaphorical meanings. I was pleased with myself for not intruding on the evolving picture.

Sallie then told me a dream of the previous night: "I am in a bed. A woman is next to me. She has on a white sequined dress. We are not touching. We are not making love. I have a knife in my hand. It was twisting. I was horrified! I don't see her face or her feet . . . Were we wrestling? How did her body get there? What was I doing with a knife anyway, with a knife sticking up? Do you think it was you? Why would I do such a thing? I hurt someone. I didn't mean to do it." Sallie's associations were contextualized in this being our last session before the holiday: Missing me. Wanting to be ill and cared for. Angry at the separation. Wanting to get inside me somehow.

Then my patient remembered a play she had just seen, "A love story; it was silly. I'm embarrassed." Some thoughts of me, while watching the play: "I identified with a character who was always trying to use her mind to keep away from her love feelings." I said something about "being in love feels very dangerous, like a knife twisting inside you." We ended the session, I thought, having agreed that she was very frightened of this new feeling for me, and that she felt almost criminal because of its intensity. Then, at the last minute Sallie asked me, "Am I your last patient today?" I said, "Yes," without thinking and then immediately thought, "Damn! She got me!" Still lying on the couch, she threw her hand up toward me and let fly with a fistful of sequins. They were white, black, and silver musical notes and stars, tiny plastic shapes that adhered to my hair and my clothes, fell through the air to the couch, the chair, and the rug. When she sat up, I think I just stared at her. After a moment, she said quietly, while looking sheepish, "I can't control myself."

As astonishing as the act of throwing sequins on me was, the absence of the sequins in the subsequent week's session was, if possible, more stunning. Sallie began the next session with references to her worry that I would be mad about what she had told me, what she admitted to feeling for me; and for several sessions this was her topic—her love, her fear, missing me, etc.—no sequins. As the week wore on the intensifying strain between us was dreadful. My patient talked a lot, as if freely, but her words were bloodless, intellectualized, and I had become the one who would not talk, who would disclose nothing. Now I had the secret, and Sallie was behaving as if she could not figure out what was going on inside of me. "What did I say to make you not talk?" I found myself in disbelief that my patient did not know what—or even that—she had done something to me; but I was frozen and could not find words to express this.

When I was able to think I wondered aloud about Sallie's vulnerability to a kind of alternating consciousness—which disabled her capacity to make and keep in mind connections between things which she knows about, but only as isolated events, like notes which never resolve into a chord, "like when you have a dream about sequins and a pocket full of sequins but don't know they go together as a textured whole." My patient protested that even though it looked *as if* she had lied—she was always here with me, always present and always told me what she was thinking. I pointed out that she lay on the couch for an entire session with sequins in her pocket and with a sequined dress in her dream, even associating to the sequins, without talking about the sequins she was holding. She insisted, "When I was lying down here it wasn't in my mind. It's like it wasn't so. I really don't know where it was."

In the next meeting, she told me: "*I had a dream, which gives it away. In the dream, there was a devious man!* He was a master of disguise. I know it's me, that I told myself not to remember. So, maybe in the interest of doing the secret, I forgot. Maybe some guilt is part of what showed on my face. Like in the bank-robbing dream."[8] I suggested that her sense of identity, and her memory, might be compromised by this splitting up of herself.

"*But I remember everything* . . . The final step was when I was sitting in the audience and this character in a magical moment throws gold stars up; they catch in the light. As they come down, they fan out . . . [she shows me]. *I locked that moment in and then put the idea of it completely out of my mind*. Then the day before New Year's, before coming here, I put them into a pocket. Talk about planning? I take a few to see if it'll work a few days before. But, during the session, the idea is not really present; it's side by side, somewhere else. It was completely out of my mind. *I had so compartmentalized it, it was completely erased!* It was a secret—even from me."

A linked constellation to Sallie's secret keeping was what she called her practical jokes (e.g., the tattoos). When I derailed her "innocent fun" by putting words and attaching motive to the actions, I sometimes experienced myself as breaking an unspoken pact that I would pretend to enjoy her joke while being a shocked and muted audience and/or recipient, much like the mother of a little child who pretends delight or fear or shock when being performed for and used as an object in the child's play. When ensnared in what *felt* like a dilemma— in a scenario which both insisted on the analyst's silence and the

---

8. Several months into the analysis, my patient had a dream that bank robbers were tunneling into a bank's vault under the pretense of doing needed construction. The aboveground construction supervisor had no knowledge of the underground activity. This dream delighted and relaxed me. I blurted out, "Oh, that's what's going on around here! What a wonderful dream!" Sallie insisted that I was mad, despite my expressions of delight and my interpretations, which were appreciative of her clever strategies for getting the riches. Sallie did not want me to know what this dream meant, and she was furious that her secret was out.

analyst's loss of containment—my capacity to comment neutrally on
the acting out was aborted as was my capacity to take part in the play
and/or to describe it as it occurred.

Over time, what had become clearer to me was that *not* commenting on the patient's acts or their consequences communicated that
the experiences were shocking and disabling, and that my not attempting to stop these behaviors was itself an enactment. I had a
sense of having permitted my child to engage in a dangerous kind of
play and felt guilty that my maternal functions of providing safety
and boundaries had been compromised.

Certain of Sallie's actions (such as the socks incident) impacted on
me in powerful and specific ways, with each iteration provoking a
particular response constellation of shock, amazement, wordlessness,
and confusion. I felt like a character in the movie *Groundhog Day,*
compelled to repeat a nefarious traumatic experience which nonetheless felt induced and 'not me'; given the intensity of my response
along with its peculiar alien cast, I hypothesized that *an aspect of the
patient's mental life had taken up residence within me.* At these junctures I
became bedeviled by a paranoid-like indecisiveness about what was
real, and was disabled in some essential ways, such that I could not
adequately function as the container and interpreter of Sallie's experience. I could not adequately protect Sallie's mind, since I could not
ensure that I could adequately represent reality to her. As a consequence of having become so bewildered by myriad versions of events,
mental splits and dissociations, secrets, lies and contradictory reports
I (inadvertently) mistreated her, and I felt sorrowful (see O'Shaughnessy, 1990; also Steiner, 2000). I speculated that I might be coming
to know Sallie's mother from *inside me,* as I felt distressed, confused,
and abusive in my failure to be attuned to her. By extrapolating (however tentatively) from these affective experiences with 'my' little girl
to the mother's experience, I was finally able to affectively imagine
the mother who retreated, kept a respectful distance, was merely polite, perhaps who stayed away—in bewilderment—at her incomprehensible child.[9]

9. One of Sallie's cherished proofs of her mother's ineptitude is a report by one of
her brothers that their mother said, "you boys were easier to understand. Sallie's
harder 'and/or' I just don't get Sallie." I am in sympathy with this sentiment, and can
imagine a range of affective accompaniments, on the mother's part—including
pain, sadness, bewilderment, humor, which allow me to identify with her in fantasy.
Sallie regards the reported story as absolute and veridical; the brother's motives for
telling her are as unexamined as Sallie's motives for encoding it and retaining it as
concrete evidence of maternal incompetence and insensitivity. Alternative interpreta-

When I firmly said "no" to a proffered musical gift, my patient became petulant and then withdrawn. She accused me, jokingly, of "pa-
tient-abuse" and associated to her mother who left her alone "too
soon" at the piano bench. She reiterated her very anguished plaint
that neither I nor the mother would talk about her music with her.
To her chagrin, she discovered that she was sharply irritated with me
when later in the session, I used the word "synthesized" and also said
something about the "harp strings" she plucked with such deliberate-
ness, referring to a wish to control the emotional experience of a
friend and me. After a bit, my patient told me she was "mad" because
these words (synthesizer, harp) were from her domain; music was
hers alone. She was horrified to discover that after all these months
of bitterly complaining that I would not talk about music with her, it
was she who "wanted to be the only one who could."

A lost world resurfaced. We learned that she had carved out a musical identity for herself at the cost of banishing her mother's contributions to her musical underpinnings, and losing the mother who
had deliberately and lovingly introduced her to music, the piano,
and singing. There had been a time of intense connection and musical communion between them during her very early years, only now
remembered. She wondered for the first time—who was envious of
whom? Maybe it was she who kicked her mother off the piano bench
because she couldn't bear the mother's competence and not, as she
had always imagined, that the mother vacated her companionable
position out of profound envy at her daughter's superior talent. This
idea of hers, however fleeting, was confirmed by me in a countertransference wish—to disclose to the patient that I couldn't tell a
piece of synthesized music from the real thing and that I have a life-
long incapacity to distinguish one instrument from another unless I
am looking at the player. I felt that I was, in the countertransference,
the mother, wishing to deflect my little girl's envy/rivalry/anger—
and to allow her the impossible pleasures of a non-conflictual field.
In this non-disclosed countertransference event, I felt for the first
time, as did my patient, a live, substantial mother—in the room and
in me.

Memories of a happy childhood spilled out. We discovered that the
actual mother had spent hours with her little girl, cooking and gar-
dening and sharing activities and conversation. Sallie remembered
especially loving the weekends when her dad traveled, because there

---

tions for the mother's alleged statement had never occurred to Sallie, and she re-
sisted reflecting on any piece of the narrative: "*It is carved in stone,* Doctor Herbert!"

was so much playful "together time" with mother, tumbling in the bed, shopping together, hanging out. The youngest of four children, the three brothers older by three, five, and eight years, Sallie could now enjoy re-experiencing her status as the youngest, the most talented, and the only and very much desired girl, the "queen bee" during the family's happy summers—admired, indulged, and enjoyed by all.

While not presuming that this newer version of Sallie's life (amended in her mid-forties several years into a long treatment) is veridical, we are certainly left with an extraordinary contradiction between the narrative Sallie had constructed and lived from early childhood on and the narrative we, in the intersubjective sphere, were co-constructing. What accounts for the development of the barely cogent and painful narrative that is reproduced in the analysis, her marriage, and to some extent, in her relationships? How to conceptualize a mind that can say, "Words don't matter to me. I don't really care about them. I don't particularly care about making sense. Reality? It doesn't matter."

Of course, given the intensity of the treatment relationship and the disturbing experiences we incurred during our analytic life, both my patient and I were on the lookout for repressed and/or non-symbolized childhood experiences of terrible abuse or deprivation. We found nothing. What we have reconstructed of her "actual" environment is what I think of as an "ordinary" familial experience (I omit facts for purposes of privacy). Even Sallie's complaints of maternal neglect have been found to be erroneous and appear, rather, to be a function of her lifelong yearning for the imagined bliss of the early infantile relationship which she conceptualizes as a perfect union based on utter identity, but which was disturbed by age 3 (her dating) when she became aware of and then denied the generational and anatomical differences. Sallie described a "moment" of distress, rage, and decision making at around age 3, one which I take as apocryphal/condensed and located chronologically sometime around 3 to 5 years of age. She described being present for a party her parents were having with their friends. Sallie did not understand why she had not been invited, had become furious, inserted herself into the party, declaring to herself, "I am just the same as my mother. There is no difference between us. She is only bigger. Her friends are my friends." From that time forward and until I had figured out that Sallie's friends from childhood—who were actually of a different generation and often her mother's friends—Sallie never questioned her childish pronouncements. She, Sallie, also determined that there were no important differences between boys and girls, men and women, other than the privileges accorded to the male sex, which she railed against her entire personal and professional life—again, until sometime into the analysis. I have come to believe that Sallie's development ceased in profoundly important ways and that she became locked down into what should have been a moment of pre-oedipal/oedipal transition.

DISCUSSION[10] AND REFLECTIONS

The sequins incident now almost (almost!) fondly recalled by us was the last of this series of disturbing and disorienting enactments. More traditional analytic process has held sway now for about six years; the analytic work has allowed us to visit and revisit the action series as we continue to plumb them for the complex of meanings they contain and communicate.

As Sallie builds a mental life and we chip away at the structural damage, we have been able to raise new questions: Was the mother silent about her own history and/or did mother talk about her own childhood with a negative cast? Did Sallie identify with an unconscious demand of her mother that she in turn repeat this view? Did Sallie take this on to stay unified with mother? What of the mother's unconscious is being lived out by Sallie? And are my silences and wishes to disclose related to some unmetabolized aspect of Sallie's identifications?

The unusually powerful intersubjective forces that were omnipresent in this analysis—and which complicated my efforts to achieve an appropriate technique and to arrive at an understanding of my patient's unique disposition—showed up most observably in the relationship between the analyst's disclosures and the patient's various absences, and in the compelling nature of their mutual acting out. Certainly I was with a traumatized patient, but what was the nature of the trauma?

I became intrigued by these relationships and speculated that their dyadic nature was primarily a function of my patient's structural/dynamic properties, albeit in the context of my receptivity and vulnerability to certain kinds of inserted experience. I wondered with what

10. I am aware that there are many aspects of this case that would be productive to explore—especially, perhaps, an investigation into the dualities of Sallie's thinking, as reflected in her divergent capacities to use language when discussing music (any aspect of which she can discuss and analyze with a sophisticated, affect-laden, and intellectually rich vocabulary) and her "ordinary" conversational speech which retains the qualities of being unreliable, chimerical, conflict-ridden, and driven.

kinds of patients these intrapsychic (and actualized) tandem processes were more likely to occur. I wondered about the junctures at which I made what felt like disclosures and what could be learned from the impulse (or action) to do so—about the patient. I became preoccupied with conceptualizing the various meanings and functions of action for my patient, given her idiosyncratic ego structure and her constitutional proclivities as a musician/performer, and began to speculate on how these strands in the analysis impacted on me and on my technique.

I think that with many patients, the material (and what it invokes in us) feels sufficient as a primary source of analytic data, in contrast to those patients, for whom the analyst's mind—as container, or mirror, or inscription device—serves this function (Joseph, 1983; Steiner, 1993). But, when does the analyst have to regard his or her mind as an exteriorized sensory/communication organ of the patient's? I am intrigued by when this feels necessary and perhaps is a necessary and "real" component of analytic work in the intersubjective field (Herbert, 1997) and/or whether it is an artifact of the primitive interaction, or an induced countertransferential "idea" related to some fantasy of the patient with which the analyst agrees.

Abelin-Sas (1997) describes a process of "making sense" of the patient's story as arising from the systemic fit of elements *provided by the patient,* and then organized by the analyst as a hypothesis with elaborative meaning. The data is "out there"; i.e., objective elements, which, when the analyst's organization enables her to understand them, can be offered as "conjectures based on logical connections that will be validated by their consistent, repetitive reappearance *in the text the patient provides*" (p. 100) (italics mine). I am struck by differences between Abelin's patient and my own—and *where* Abelin and I experienced the meaning as emerging from. She talked about the patient's communication of vital information (a symptom, fears, memories, dreams, an historical narrative, affective experience), which although misapprehended by the patient, described to the analyst a powerful, effective, coherent and unconscious structure which ruled the patient's life. To the analyst the information array was compelling and told a story which appeared to constitute itself as a rich display of interlocking meanings. The analyst was able to see into the material, which came from *the patient's side of the couch,* and it was experienced as such. My patient provided information of a different sort, negative information (a space, a lacunae), and was experienced by me as opaque. I felt compelled to develop hypotheses about information derived from *the analyst's side of the couch,* from within.

I suspect that when patients are able to contain their story, own it (despite its unconsciousness), it is told in a different way and thus, lands in a different place in the analyst—and is experienced as a story being told to the analyst. I don't think my patient has been able to contain her story—and so, is not able to tell it to me, only to show it to me, or do it to me. Its telling and retelling thus invoked other capacities or regions of the analyst, and was experienced as told from the analyst's, and only later, from the patient's mind.[11] My disclosures and my relation to them led to the discovery that I had disclosed, or unearthed, in some convoluted and derivative way Sallie's own narrative, which had embedded itself in my unconscious. My disclosures then provided an affective language for the emotional life she had never articulated. Like McDougall's (1978) patient, Sallie was not able to consistently communicate "ideas, moods, and free associations" but seemed "to aim at making the analyst *feel* something, or stimulating him to *do* something; this 'something' (was) incapable of being named and the patient himself is totally unaware of this aim" (pp.177–178). My countertransference disclosures served as the vehicle by which the "something" could be put into words and come to be known. The patient acted out that which she could not know or remember by behaving in the transference-countertransference, and *I did her remembering for her,* through the circuitous route of taking part in various enactments and only afterward, becoming able to articulate their structures, and speculate on their meanings. Tutté (2004) discussing trauma talks of the unusual experience of the analyst when "the patient is unable to narrate, either by allusion or by any type of symbolization, what is an operational item, a procedural memory of his way of relating, which in analysis cannot be recovered as a declarative memory or by decoding the narration, but only through being acted out in the analytic relationship" (p. 916).

The architecture of Sallie's more elaborate and dramatic performances[12] (those which inveigled me into some enacted response)

11. Dupont (1984) referencing Freud's 1922 paper on telepathic communication, describes a special kind of primitive communication which sometimes occurs between analytic partners and is reflected in uncanny clinical moments. These moments between analyst and patient are reminiscent of Winnicott's "primary maternal preoccupation" (1958) and Bion's "maternal reverie" (1962) and are not necessarily diagnostic, but bespeak a deep level of unconscious communication that remains to be understood.

12. Fenichel (1945) also describes a kind of acting out which he finds "similar to the characteristic 'repetitions' of the traumatic neurotic." Often the actions which are repeated have a *very impressive and dramatic character; we may speak of "traumatophilic"*

had something of the quality of the "concretizations" of Blos's (1971) delinquent adolescents who acted out important and forbidden pieces of their history, constellations of profoundly important "facts," truths that they had not been allowed to know in words or in consciousness. An important difference between Blos's adolescents whose concretizations, once recognized as such, became knowable aspects of their identity, and Sallie's concretizations lies in their different functions. For Blos's (1971) young people the concretizations functioned as vehicles and containers for vital information about the self and object world, and as such were destined to become central to the resumption of identity development. For Sallie, the concretizations appeared to be condensations of and defenses against her inner kaleidoscopic experience, and they functioned, in part, as stabilizing acts of creation—which were essential to her identity sense. Her actions were intended to be bewildering and revisionary as well as shocking and exciting to the analyst. Her identity as creator and creative was defined by the elaborate preparations and performances in which the analyst was designated both audience and actor. The mysteries qua mystery also had self-enhancing functions (See Blos, 1963). Sallie's unknowability was delicious to her, as well as protective; she was not as interested in the deciphering of her performance pieces as she was in their various effects.

McDougall (1978) suggested that with someone like Sallie we are in the presence of early psychic trauma of which we become aware only through the effects of the "unconscious pressure it exerts upon the analyst's way of being and speaking (which) may only be accessible if captured through our countertransference reactions" (p. 175). For a long time, Sallie's language usage and its effect on the analyst served the functions of an "action symptom"; her words were not used to communicate symbolically or to inform in the ordinary way; nonetheless they were intended to reach or connect with me, the other. Sallie's speech was idiosyncratic (in much the same way as McDougall's patient's was); it was neither in the primary process nor firmly in the secondary process (see also Rizzuto, 2002).

The complexity of my patient's structural idiosyncrasies included

---

persons (italics mine). The repetition symptoms . . . serve the purpose of achieving belated mastery of experiences which brought too great an amount of excitement" (p. 300). The skilled and planful performance aspects of Sallie's dramas, however, complicated (or obfuscated) my analysis of them as traumatic re-enactments since the exhibitionistic and artistic needs of this patient whose internal requirements included the need for an audience or fellow actor were related also to her constitution as composer and performer.

an ego, which was distressed by its splits and imprisoned in its dis-
avowals (see Freud, 1927, 1940) and which relied on sensory/body
knowledge and various projective/introjective processes for its information gathering; the ego's deformation had been further enforced
by processes of "enactive remembering" in which secondary processes (had been) substituted by "processes of timelessness and lack
of differentiation" (Loewald, 1980, p. 165). Thus, Sallie was often in
trouble in social interactions as well as in the analysis since her belea-
guered ego was exhausted by the verbal/logical expectations of others; she would fade or withdraw, too anxious when under the siege of
required relatedness and coherence (see Gaddini, 1982). The analyst, on her part, felt threatened as she entered a world of fused and
part identities and was called upon to tolerate not only fusions but
also incursions of primitive and sometimes chaotic material, as well
as involvement in actions. Greenacre's (1963) description of "acting
out in attack form (which is) mainly provocative and (designed) to
seduce the analyst into some sort of reality involvement with him" is
what I came to experience as "action attacks," and what she characterized as a "tantrum form (of attack) but of a special kind in which
there is a relentless demand for reciprocation and discharge through
or with the other, the analyst" (pp. 702–03). (I find it useful to think
of this enacted intrapsychic dynamic as a complex set of projective
identifications, which included the press to action; my participation
enabled me to both experience and subsequently reflect upon what
were echoes of Sallie's unarticulated experience [see Tuckett, 1997,
and Smith, 2000]).

At other times I experienced Sallie's actions like the "playacting" of
Ekstein and Friedman's (1957) adolescents—which functioned for
them as a primitive state of reality testing in which solutions to conflict were entertained in action (a kind of trial thought) rather than
thought. When Sallie's actions served this function, I felt, not attacked, but like a detective-partner in serious important play. This
countertransference experience was reminiscent of how one works
with child patients, and enabled me to locate Sallie developmentally
as well as to access a different, more playful model of doing analytic
work, such that even my tone of voice and intonations shifted. I came
to see Sallie as a latency age child who had been thrust into this phase,
profoundly hampered by a harsh and terrifying superego, straining
to use ego functions appropriate to her age but at enormous cost—
she felt the need to hide what she didn't know or understand, her
self-esteem was shaky except in the area of her musical expertise, and
she felt like a fraud or crazy. Sallie was not relieved by latency; she

didn't have the tools for its tasks. She was incompletely differentiated from the mother of symbiosis, alienated by the mother of separation, and beset by projections of the "bad" mother which disabled her from knowing her "real" mother and from knowing her own impulses, which continued to frighten her; as she, of course, remained identified with her unwelcome and non-comprehended impulses she was constricted in her relationships and in her creativity, and frightened of the object world. She was at her wits' end and desperately in need of help from a seemingly whimsical and terrifying other whom she had to engage, but repel at the same time. I, all too often, experienced as violent and traumatic violations (the "attack form" of Greenacre) Sallie's internal hodgepodge of excited, sometimes sadistically engineered secrets of seeing and showing, telling too little or too much, aggression masquerading as love and vice versa, and shocking and mind-numbing actions. When I "forgot" that Sallie was not necessarily being aggressive with these insertions but that she was desperately attempting to find a way in,[13] I would, via a countertransference action, shut her down with a critical/judgmental edge to my voice. Nonetheless, Sallie (with stubbornness as her ally) persistently searched for ways to make contact with and feel loved by me/mother. She struggled to keep up with my reasoning and to find words that *appeared* communicative, despite the suffering induced by my countertransferential refusals to bear her painful experience and her self-inflicted insistence on remaining vigilant about "hiding the holes in my mind you will find and then tell me about in a shocking way." Sallie, in these ways, submitted to what she intuited were my demands for coherence while retaining an inner sense of incoherence and maintaining her familiar mélange of despair and excitement. So, again, Sallie did things and continued to suffer. When I made "interpretations" about these states, often merely playing back in words what had just occurred (a kind of verbal rewind) I had eerie sensations, and would be momentarily disoriented, not knowing what was true or real. I often felt as if I was disclosing something secret about my insides, my mind, but I came to trust that I was telling a story about Sallie from inside of me, rather than making a more "ordinary" interpretation that grew out of a different kind of observation of her, as external.

My patient could not tell me her story—other than as a perverse scenario and as a performance (see Chasseguet-Smirgel, 1984; Mc-Dougall, 1986; and Etchegoyen, 1991, for further discussion of per-

---

13. I have Graciela Abelin-Sas to thank for this immensely helpful hypothesis.

version as performance in the transference) which could not bear interpretation or for which ordinary interpretations of meaning were profoundly beside the point, and *also* because she needed to disavow the analyst as different, separate, and therefore dangerous to her organization (Bass, 2000). Her inner world remained correspondent to a psychic reality long ago concretized and encoded as *so* and not as a "perhaps" alternative among a range of what was possible (see also Ekstein, 1966, and Caper, 1996). Hence, reality could not be tested because it was conceived of as exactly what she imagined, not as something to "test."

All that could be contained was what had already been thought. As Sallie herself told me, change is categorized as "inconsistency," and consistency must be insisted upon even though that means understanding herself "exactly as I did as a child." When asked to think more deeply about this, Sallie was confused by my request, as if I had requested her to exercise a "mentalizing function" (Fonagy and Target, 1996) she had yet to possess: "Think about what?" and "I can't. *If I'm inconsistent who will I be?*" Since the dangers in changing were so extreme for her (identity fragmentation!) a version of annihilation anxiety overwhelmed her intention and paralyzed her even as she heroically labored to change via analysis; that is, while Sallie understands intellectually that the danger she dreads is not real, and that she is imprisoned by defenses which seem to ensure her survival but which actually keep her both fragmented and afraid of fragmenting, she cannot yet tolerate their abatement.

Caper (1998) focused on those pathological solutions which radically interfere with the patients' capacity to learn: "the persistence of states of narcissistic identification when supported by omnipotent projections and introjections sets in motion an inability to learn from experience (in that unconscious 'delusions' remain inaccessible)" (p. 342). If we construe my patient's refusal/inability to learn from experience (I include here the analyst's interpretative ministrations and presentations of reality via secondary process communication), the analytic enterprise must expand to include unusual and non-verbal strategies (typical strategies in working with children!) such that the analyst's imagination of the patient's mind and its attendant damage will enable her to enter it on a most primitive and sensorial level.

The analyst was also often struggling to keep straight what/who/ what parts of whom were being projected, introjected, and identified with—on both sides of the couch. I found that asking deceptively simple questions like, "What do you mean?" "Who said that?" "Does that sound like something I would have said?" "To what are you referring?" often brought the barely disguised non object-related sentences to consciousness, and it allowed us to intervene quickly enough so that the perverted version was not crystallized as so, and discarded in some way that rendered it no longer available to consciousness. However, a countertransference enactment of a sadomasochistic relationship was always nibbling at the edges of these interchanges. The patient acted scared of the analyst's questions, even before they were posed, and the analyst often was caught up in a kind of counterphobic defense against colluding with the patient's "reversal of perspective" (Bion, 1963). That is, it was not the patient who had perverted reality but the analyst who was perverting the relationship by suggesting that the patient had engaged in a destructive act—the destroying of their collaborative meanings. My collusion with this perspective and my worry about colluding with the patient's fantasy of the harm I would do her by pointing out some inconsistency, some symptom of perverse thought processes, led to some tactless, poorly timed, chilly-sounding questioning, which I imagined as re-traumatizing (see Chassequet-Smirgel, 1990; Sanchez-Medina, 2002).

Undoubtedly Sallie was traumatized; that is, she was so frightened by an internal uncontained morass of non-symbolized experience that she could not think or feel in a secondary process, and was frozen in her mind; her strengths, though, were twofold: she could—with some action or acting out—express, however inchoately, the affects associated with impulses/fears, and she could make beautiful sense of her emotional life via musical composition and performance. Her trauma seems to be of the sort Freud (1925) considered to be an essentially economic condition that derived from the psychic helplessness of the infant rather than the kind of traumatic situation which (actively) involved an object, who in some sense misused the child. I think, with Sallie, that the mother may have missed cues which would have enabled her to protect and imagine the mind of her baby in a way that would have allowed Sallie to internalize the ego function of mentalization, but she was not traumatogenic in a severe, pathological way (see Hartke 2005 for historical/clinical discussion of the concept of psychic trauma). La Farge (2004) and others would focus perhaps on the mother's inability to imagine the mind of her child giving rise to an *incapacity* in the child to think about her own mind, or to appreciate the psychic realities of others or to differentiate psychic and external reality, and so, as a consequence, foster a narcissistic organization with specific ego deficits. Certainly one way of thinking about Sallie's overall transference is that it *was* a kind of narcissistic transference which permitted Sallie to repair, via her use of me, certain of her damages. Happily, Sallie's defect in the area of imagining/mentalizing has been profoundly modified by the analysis in which she has, through ordinary analytic means, been increasingly able to internalize the analyst's ego functioning, to cease acting as a way around grappling with affects associated with impulses, to think and to think about thinking.

I continued to struggle, though, for a number of years to find a proper and effective technique. By treating Sallie's propensity to action as a problem for the analysis (rather than for the analyst!) and insisting on the verbal analysis of the powerful currents between us, I had at times precipitated a frightening, shameful, and exciting disruption of her organization. Without action as her ally, Sallie had (too often) been propelled into a state akin to terror that I would uncover the holes in her narrative and expose the fraudulence of her communications of coherence. I also prematurely forced Sallie into an effortful attempt to talk to me "like a grownup" (her phrase) and deprived her of her primary and most advanced modality for communication—her music and its elaborations in various non-verbal transformations. (See Charles, 2001, and Knoblach, 2000 for therapeutic strategies which address the musical and sensory dimensions.) My apparent disregard for this most precious source of self-valuing precipitated a narcissistic crisis, one which replicated, in another key, her childhood experience of being ejected from the maternal orbit. Sallie, whose omnipotent fantasies flourished in the light of the profound admiration and attention she received because of her musical gifts, was left unusually unprepared for what she experienced as an abrupt dethroning and traumatic separation engineered by her mother when she was treated as ordinary, "even normal." When her grandiose fantasies were debunked, however momentarily, my patient suffered such profound mortification that she rushed to re-erect her position, unfortunately through various deformations of her ego structure, and she became something of an imposter (see Greenacre, 1958).

Perhaps mother was not able, once early (and fantastic) language appeared, to provide or sustain an effective reliable verbal frame which would enable and support the development of reality testing and so, because of these limitations, was not able to be made use of as an object, who would become internalized as an aspect and guardian of the integrity of the mental structure (Winnicott, 1969). Sallie was too able to present a "false face" and to surround it with proper sounding words (they may not have been the correct words!). This unfortunate capacity may have led her mother astray, and I think mother became somewhat bewildered and ineffectual with this prodigy of hers. Sallie took refuge in the illusionary delights of their oneness. I breached this illusion of oneness by asking questions which insisted, albeit gently, that she locate her referents, that she grapple with inconsistencies, that she use a mutually understood lingo, that she/we had to find words that will make sense of things and enable us to secure a realistic connection. This may well be a reflection of the longed-for words (from mother) which would have served as a scaffolding for the ego's reality building.[14] Nonetheless I may have, because of my distress at being impinged upon by "inappropriate actions," reproduced with countertransference impatience but in the guise of analytic frame and technique—a version of what did in fact happen to her; that is, I expected that she was like me, and therefore should privilege the use of language over action. I did not, at first, appreciate what her constitution was bringing to the table. My point here is that the transference/countertransference interface included a kind of collusion with the unattuned maternal object such that I *also* fostered the presentation of a false face/self and was "impostergenic" (my word) instead of empathic with the plight of Sallie, the artist.

Greenacre's (1957) seminal work on the childhood of the artist, and Nass's (1984) contributions to the psychology of the composer suggest, too, that I did err in not finding ways to integrate an appreciation of the unique contribution of Sallie's psychology as an artist into my formulations of the meaning of our actions; that is, I had given short shrift to what "doing" meant for her, qua artist, and my technique for interpreting the action modality and for coping with the impact of these actions on me, and the limitations on her ego that the action propensity imposed on her reasoning, was misguided. I wonder if for Sallie, *the artist,* fantasy and reality remained an admixture, not because the parents were pathologically deficient but because Sallie's precocious musical ability and her exquisite sensory sensitivities as artist, countermanded the "good enough" attunement of (especially) her mother to imagine the inner world of her child and provide a language for it. As a consequence, the primal fantasies, which were motors for and contained within Sallie's compositions,

---

14. The press for re-enactment in the analytic relationship may have been in part a wordless plea for a mother to provide the proper nutriment for the resumption of ego and psychic development.

may have been felt to be real, and Sallie's inner reality, not articulated in a modality in which it could be reframed by the parent, was taken as *so!* It is possible that the imaginative inner world of the little girl she was, in this way became exceedingly dangerous and so, required massive defenses against even its existence. Except in its musical form, it could not and would not be accessed; hence, one source of the absence (the walled-off inner life) the analyst is introduced to in the beginning, and that Sallie expresses as, "It was a secret—even from me."

Sallie remains with a sense that something is "terribly wrong, even crazy" because she cannot count on internal, automatic cogency—*except* when she is making music or in its presence. It is important to reiterate that Sallie, internally fulfilled by her musical universe and capable of representing her emotional experience to herself in musical language, did not (and often does not) say out loud what she was/is thinking, and/or did not put her affective experiences into words. When still a very little girl, she surmised that she could not use words as other people did, and she imagined a universe in which "true talk" would not be welcomed. (I presume this to be a projection.) In a session in which neither of us could find words to express a particularly painful inner state, Sallie had given up and was instead using language to hide her confusion and shame at the wordless cacophony she couldn't communicate. When she does this, she stops making sense to me, and as I have indicated, gets increasingly frightened about her loss of me, and her sense of craziness. I stopped her and asked if she could tell me what was going on "in music." She laughed nervously and said, "I can't tell it but I could do it with a musical phrase." And she did! She composed on the spot! It was a fully communicative phrase. It was structured, directional, the key chosen reflective of the affect, the dissonances contained and framed by her tone, the timbre of her voice, the shifts in rhythm. We both marveled that what was almost frantic gibberish when she felt compelled to use words was absolutely intelligible and as sophisticated a communication as one could wish for—when the modality shifted.

We agreed to try to remember to do this when we find ourselves in that awful place of mutual frustration and misery; that is, to find the musical language when words are not available for communicating. As interesting and extraordinary as this particular interaction was, I think that what it provided for us was a glimpse into a creative analytic space in which we could make use of the many communicative tracks which are available to us for furthering the analytic enterprise. While I remain the one most interested in the communication of and elaboration of meanings and Sallie remains the one most interested in the music of our encounter, we have achieved a relationship in which our determination to communicate with and find one another "in the real" has overcome the seductions of the fantastic; words, actions, music, and others are used in the service of a dialogue that is intended to be meaningful and elaborative.

BIBLIOGRAPHY

ABELIN-SAS, G. (1997) The First Interview: From Psychopathology to Existential Diagnosis. *Journal of Clinical Psychoanalysis,* 6:95–106.

ALTMAN, N., AND J. M. DAVIES. (2003) A Plea for Constructive Dialogue. *Journal of the American Psychoanalytic Association,* 51/Supplement: 145–161.

BASS, A. (2000) *Difference and Disavowal, the Trauma of Eros.* California: Stanford University Press.

BION, W. (1962) *Learning from Experience.* London: Heinemann.

——- (1963) *Elements of Psychoanalysis.* London: Karnac.

BLOS, P. (1963) The Concept of Acting Out in Relation to the Adolescent Process. *Journal of the American Academy of Child Psychiatry,* 2:18–136.

—— (1971) Adolescent Concretization. In (Ed.) I. M. Marcus. *Currents in Psychoanalysis* (pp. 66–88). New York: International Universities Press.

CAPER, R. (1996) Play, Creativity, and Experimentation. *International Journal of Psychoanalysis,* 77:859–869.

—— (1998) Psychopathology and Primitive Mental States. *International Journal of Psychoanalysis,* 79:539–552.

CHARLES, M. (2001) Nonphysical Touch: Modes of Containment and Communication Within the Analytic Process. *Psychoanalytic Quarterly,* 70:387–416.

CHASSEGUET-SMIRGEL, J. (1984) *Creativity and Perversion.* New York: Norton.

—— (1990) On Acting Out. *International Journal of Psychoanalysis,* 71:77–86.

CIMINO, C., & A. CORREALE. (2005) Projective Identification and Consciousness Alteration: A Bridge Between Psychoanalysis and Neuroscience? *International Journal of Psychoanalysis,* 86:51–60.

COOPER, S. H. (1998) Analyst Subjectivity, Analyst Disclosure, and the Aims of Psychoanalysis. *Psychoanalytic Quarterly,* 67:379–406.

DE PANTAZOGLU, URIARTE C. (1991) Traumatismos Precoces; Cicatrices Y Lagunas Dentro De lo Psíquico (Precocious Trauma; Scars and Lagoons within the Psychic). *Rev Urug Psicoanal* 74:147–160 (cited in Tutté).

DUPONT, M. (1984) On Primary Communication. *International Review of Psychoanalysis,* 11:303–311.

EKSTEIN, R. (1966) *Children of Time and Space, Action and Impulse: Clinical Studies on the Psychoanalytic Treatment of Severely Disturbed Children.* New York: Appleton-Century Crofts.

EKSTEIN, R., & S. FRIEDMAN. (1957) The Function of Acting Out, Play Action and Play Acting in the Psychotherapeutic Process. *Journal of the American Psychoanalytic Association,* 5:581–629.

ETCHEGOYEN, H. (1991) *The Fundamentals of Psychoanalytic Technique.* London: Karnac.

FELDMAN, M. (1997) Projective Identification: The Analyst's Involvement. *International Journal of Psychoanalysis,* 78:227–241.

FENICHEL, O. (1945) Neurotic Acting Out. In *The Collected Papers of Otto Fenichel, Second Series.* New York: W. W. Norton, Inc. [1954].

FONAGY, P., & M. TARGET. (1996) Playing with Reality: I. Theory of Mind and the Normal Development of Psychic Reality. *International Journal of Psychoanalysis,* 77:217–233.

FREUD, S. (1914) Remembering, Repeating and Working Through. *Standard Edition* 12:145–156.

——— (1925) Inhibitions, Symptoms, and Anxiety. *Standard Edition* 20:87–172.

——— (1927) Fetishism. *Standard Edition* 2:49–157.

——— (1940) The Splitting of the Ego in the Process of Defense. *Standard Edition* 23:271–278.

GADDINI, E. (1982) Acting Out in the Psychoanalytic Session. *International Journal of Psycho-Analysis,* 63:57–64.

GREEN, A. (2000) The Intrapsychic and Intersubjective in Psychoanalysis. *Psychoanalytic Quarterly,* 69:1–39.

GREENACRE, P. (1957) The Childhood of the Artist: Libidinal Phase Development and Giftedness. *The Psychoanalytic Study of the Child,* 12:47–72.

——— (1958) The Relation of the Impostor to the Artist. *The Psychoanalytic Study of the Child,* 13:521–540.

——— (1963) Problems of Acting Out in the Transference Relationship. In *Emotional Growth, Psychoanalytic Studies of the Gifted and a Great Variety of Other Individuals* (Vol. 2, pp. 695–712). New York: International Universities Press.

GRUSKY, Z. (2002) Conviction and Interpretation: Hiding and Seeking with Words. *Psychoanalytic Quarterly,* 71:81–112.

HARTKE, R. (2005) The Basic Traumatic Situation in the Analytical Relationship. *International Journal of Psychoanalysis,* 86:266–290.

HERBERT, J. C. (1997) The Haunted Analysis: Countertransference Enactments and the Dead. *Journal of Clinical Psychoanalysis,* 6:189–221.

JACOBS, T. J. (1991) *The Use of the Self: Countertransference and Communication in the Analytic Situation.* Madison, Conn.: International Universities Press.

——— (1997) Some Reflections on the Question of Self-Disclosure Symposium: Aspects of Self-Revelation and Disclosure: Analyst to Patient. *Journal of Clinical Psychoanalysis,* 6:161–173.

——— (1997) In Search of the Mind of the Analyst: A Progress Report. *Journal of the American Psychoanalytic Association,* 45:1035–1060.

——— (1999) On the Question of Self-Disclosure by the Analyst: Error or Advance. *Psychoanalytic Quarterly,* 68:159–183.

JOSEPH, B. (1983) On Understanding and Not Understanding: Some Technical Issues. *International Journal of Psychoanalysis, 64:*291–98.

———— (1987) Projective Identification: Some Clinical Aspects. In J. Sandler (Ed). *Projection, Identification, Projective Identification.* Madison, Conn.: International Universities Press.

KATZ, G. (1998) Where the Action Is: The Enacted Dimension of Analytic Process. *Journal of the American Psychoanalytic Association, 46:*1129–1168.

KNOBLACH, S. H. (2000) *The Musical Edge of Therapeutic Dialogue.* Hillsdale, N.J.: Analytic Press.

LA FARGE, L. (2004) The Imaginer and the Imagined. *Psychoanalytic Quarterly,* 73:591–625.

LEVINE, H. B., & R. J. FRIEDMAN. (2000) Intersubjectivity and Interaction in the Analytic Relationship: A Mainstream View. *Psychoanalytic Quarterly, 69:*63–92.

LOEWALD, H. (1980) *Papers on Psychoanalysis.* New Haven: Yale University Press.

MAHONEY, P. (1999) Forepain and Forepleasure in an Enunciatory Perversion: A Countertransference Ordeal. *Journal of Clinical Psychoanalysis, 8:*93–123.

McDOUGALL, J. (1978) Primitive Communication and the Use of Countertransference—Reflections on Early Psychic Trauma and Its Transference Effects. *Contemporary Psychoanalysis, 14:*173–209.

———— (1986) *Theatres of the Mind.* London: Free Association Books.

NASS, M. (1984) The Development of Creative Imagination in Composers. *International Review of Psycho-Analysis, 11:*481–491

OGDEN, T. H. (1986) *The Matrix of the Mind: Object Relations and the Psychoanalytic Dialogue.* Northvale, N.J.: Jason Aronson, Inc.

O'SHAUGHNESSY, E. (1990) Can a *Liar* Be Psychoanalyzed? *International Journal of Psychoanalysis,* 71:187–195.

RENIK, O. (1993) Analytic Interaction: Conceptualizing Technique in Light of the Analyst's Irreducible Subjectivity. *Psychoanalytic Quarterly, 62:*553–571.

———— (1995) The Ideal of the Anonymous Analyst and the Problem of Self-Disclosure. *Psychoanalytic Quarterly,* 64:466–495.

RINGSTROM, P. (2001) Cultivating the Improvisational in Psychoanalytic Treatment. *Psychoanalytic Dialogues,* 11:727–754.

RIZZUTO, A. M. (2002) Speech Events, Language Development and the Clinical Situation. *International Journal of Psychoanalysis,* 83:1325–1343.

SANCHEZ-MEDINA, A. (2002) Perverse Thought. *International Journal of Psychoanalysis,* 83:1345–1360.

SHARPE, E. F. (1935) Similar and Divergent Determinants Underlying the Sublimations of Pure Art and Pure Science. *International Journal of Psycho-Analysis,* 16:186–202.

SMITH, H. F. (2000) Countertransference, Conflictual Listening, and the Analytic Object Relationship. *Journal of the American Psychoanalytic Association, 48:*95–128.

———— (2003) Analysis of Transference: A North American Perspective. *International Journal of Psychoanalysis*, 84:1017–1041.

STEINER, J. (1993) The Recovery of Parts of the Self Lost Through Projective Identification. *In Psychic Retreats: Pathological Organizations in Psychotic, Neurotic and Borderline Patients* (pp. 54–63). London: Routledge.

———— (2000) Containment, Enactment and Communication. *International Journal of Psychoanalysis, 81*:245–255.

TUCKETT, D. (1997) Mutual Enactment in the Psychoanalytic Situation. In (Eds.) J. Ahumada, J. Olagaray, A. K. Richards, and A. D. Richards, *The Perverse Transference and Other Matters* (pp.203–216). New Jersey: Jason Aronson, Inc.

TUTTÉ, J. C. (2004) The Concept of Psychical Trauma: A Bridge in Interdisciplinary Space. *International Journal of Psychoanalysis.* 85:897–921.

WINNICOTT, D. W. (1958) The Capacity to Be Alone. *International Journal of Psychoanalysis, 39*:416–420.

———— (1969) The Use of an Object. *International Journal of Psychoanalysis, 50*:711–716.

Children's Turn-Arounds
in Psychotherapy

The Doctor's Gesture

LENORE C. TERR, M.D.,
JOSEPH H. BEITCHMAN, M.D.,
KENNETH BRASLOW, M.D., GERI FOX, M.D.,
AUBREY METCALF, M.D.,
MARIA PEASE, M.D., LYNN PONTON, M.D.,
WILLIAM SACK, M.D.,
and SAUL WASSERMAN, M.D.

Over the past year, a number of us have been examining the organizing principles behind dramatic turning points in the psychotherapies of children. We wondered whether any particular techniques or occurrences in therapy promoted childhood change. Method: One of us (L.T.) asked the health care professionals on the UCSF child psychiatry grand rounds email list and 50 colleagues across the United States and Canada to select key "moments," or turning points, in their treatments of young people. No organizing principles were suggested in the request letters. Over 3 months, 21 vignettes telling of major changes in children and adolescents arrived in San Francisco. Some of them came from psychotherapies—others, from consultations or very brief thera-

Drs. Terr, Braslow, Metcalf, Pease, and Ponton are at the University of California, San Francisco; Dr. Beitchman is at the University of Toronto; Dr. Fox is at the University of Illinois; Dr. Sack is at Oregon Health & Sciences University; and Dr. Wasserman is at Stanford University.

The Psychoanalytic Study of the Child 61, ed. Robert A. King, Peter B. Neubauer, Samuel Abrams, and A. Scott Dowling (Yale University Press, copyright © 2006 by Robert A. King, Peter B. Neubauer, Samuel Abrams, and A. Scott Dowling).

pies. *Eleven are included in this paper. Results: Gestures from the psychotherapist were shown to effect dramatic turn-arounds in some young people. These shifts in the doctor's emphasis or behavior included: (1) making an entirely unexpected statement; (2) advocating strongly for the youngster; (3) confessing personal flaws and/or frustrations to the patient; (4) feeding or rewarding the young patient; and (5) inquiring deeply into something personal with the child. A gesture never given—in this instance, an undelivered inquiry into incest—is shown to have left an adolescent patient unchanged. The young people described in this report suffered from anxiety, trauma, neglect, cancer, anorexia, bulimia, and personality disorders. Two were institutionalized at the time of their dramatic changes. One had been previously hospitalized 4 times. Another small child had suffered a double amputation. These children came with a far broader spectrum of problems than the relatively mild disorders for which child-psychodynamic psychotherapy was originally tailored. Although we were not primarily concerned with the "ground" on which the doctor's gesture fell, in 5 of our cases there had been little to no therapeutic relationship prior to the gesture; in 4, the relationship had been primarily positive; and, in 2, it had been negative. Conclusions: Doctors' gestures are usually given on impulse and unexpectedly during psychotherapy. To the child, these gestures appear counter-intuitive and surprising. From the therapist's perspective, they first generate a brief sense of confusion in the patient, and then a strong sense of connection between the young person and the adult. In the cases we report, the physicians' gestures created a new alliance. The tone of the therapy switched, leading to a noticeable psychic shift in the child. Summary: A doctor's gesture may elicit a dramatic turn-around in a young patient. This therapeutic climax is implicitly understood between the two parties and then may be converted to consciousness and worked with explicitly. Therapeutic "moments" occur in a broad range of disorders, that in many cases are also being treated simultaneously with medications, and with family or institutional counseling.*

Keywords: Psychotherapy, psychodynamics, turning points, moments, gestures, advocacy

INTRODUCTION

RAYMOND WAGGONER, M.D., CHAIRMAN OF PSYCHIATRY AT THE UNIversity of Michigan from 1937 to 1970, once treated an adult woman whose problem was so interesting that he took session-by-session

notes. What Dr. Waggoner did not know, he told his resident staff,
was that the patient herself had made detailed jottings about the very
same sessions. Then she died. In her will, she left all her notes to Dr.
Waggoner. He sat down and compared each hour—his impressions,
her impressions. They did not coincide. Each participant thought
something important had happened at the various junctures of treatment. But each experienced a different reason for the woman's
change. One "moment," however, stood out in the patient's mind.
Dr. Waggoner had helped her on with her coat! She saw this moment
as an instant of change. Dr. Waggoner did not take any note of it. But
clearly, the doctor had made a "gesture."

In this group effort at capturing key "moments" in children's and
adolescents' psychoanalytically derived psychotherapies (and brief
interventions, or even consultations), we will demonstrate that the
doctor's gesture sometimes leads to an important turning point in
the child. Of course, unlike Dr. Waggoner, the doctor must have
been conscious of the gesture in order to record it for our purposes.
And equally obvious, too, we can only offer these vignettes from the
psychiatrist's point of view—unless our patients "will" us their notes,
or write us, or tell us about it.

In the spring of 2004, the lead author of this article (L.T.) collected 7 vignettes describing "moments" in child psychotherapy from
friends of Saul Harrison, M.D., who had recently passed away (Terr,
2005). That project turned out interesting enough to impel the lead
author to ask both the health care professionals on the UCSF child
psychiatry grand rounds email list and a group of 50 colleagues in
child/adolescent psychiatry for 500-word vignettes telling of a crucial "moment" in their young patients' psychotherapies (including
the meaning of the "moment" and one reference). No therapeutic
principles were suggested in the request letters. No preplanned principles existed in the lead author's mind. Twenty-one new vignettes
promptly arrived. This paper will include 11 of these "moments" in the
treatment of 7 adolescents, 3 latency-age children, and one toddler.
Each "moment" had to do with a gesture the psychiatrist made (or
didn't make). Each had the potential to prompt a dramatic change.

In our two past writings in this series on turn-arounds in children,
we have demonstrated that attending to the realities of the doctor-patient relationship (Terr et al., 2005) and purposely taking a playful
approach (Terr et al., 2006) lead—at times—to important therapeutic shifts. Most likely, there are other important principles also operating in achieving dramatic childhood readjustments. This article
will show that a psychiatrist's gesture, such as: (1) making an unex-

pected statement; (2) advocating for the youngster; (3) confessing a personal flaw or frustration; (4) feeding or rewarding; and (5) inquiring deeply with the child, may contribute to a notable turnaround in the young patient. The article will end on a sad note, however. It will tell of a lost opportunity—a doctor's gesture, missed.

MAKING AN UNEXPECTED STATEMENT

A young patient may do a double-take when his psychotherapist does not speak the way he had assumed. With a catch of the breath, shake of the head, and a probable rise in blood pressure, the mind (and brain) marks the "moment" as particularly important. In the first case we present here, the psychotherapist surprised an adolescent patient he had only recently met by insisting on returning to an old treatment plan that this boy had felt was useless and "no fun." Yet once their "moment" came and went, the young man's treatment was well on its way toward achieving success. In the second case, the doctor caught a latency-age child, who had been relishing her symptom during a relatively positive psychotherapeutic relationship, completely off guard with a verbal confrontation. Luckily (and knowingly on the doctor's part), the girl's relationship with the doctor was strong enough to withstand the power of his well-timed, confrontative gesture. Finally, in the case of a 2-year-old double amputee, the doctor was willing—from the very first day she met the child—to bring up and/or discuss such "unspeakable" topics as body-part disposal, how long "time" really takes, and how one can learn to use plastic limbs. This repeated, but entirely unexpected gesture broke through the child's logjam of grief-stricken and terrified emotion, giving her a jump-start toward recovery.

BEGINNING IN MIDSTREAM

Timothy is a big, strong, 14-year-old eighth grader, adopted at 3 months of age by two gay men. He had been abandoned by his young, single mother shortly after his birth. Timothy began his therapy in our clinic with another psychiatric resident, a half-year prior to his new start with me. His diagnoses included ADHD and severe parent-child relationship problems. It was noted that he acted extremely oppositional with both "Papa" and "Daddy," and frequently "got in their face." The patient had been originally referred to UCSF by a private family therapist who did not think her family work had been successful with the trio. She suggested individual psychodynamic therapy, which had been carried out for 6 months by a male resident, while another resident on our staff managed Timothy's medications.

When Timothy was transferred to me, I was his fourth therapist in one year. He had not made much progress. He repeatedly challenged Daddy physically, and he verbally sassed Papa. When we first met, Timothy was taken aback that I asked him anything at all about his family—he said he had talked about "mostly girls" to his first UCSF therapist and had enjoyed it tremendously. He wanted us to go on in exactly the same vein so that he could begin dating. In a separate session, his fathers told me that, even though they had done all the "homework" that their private family therapist had given them, Timothy was far too hostile to accept their efforts. They wished to bow out of the boy's treatment altogether. His aggressiveness was his own problem.

Since everyone's complaints were about the family and nobody wanted to talk about it, it appeared that family therapy was indicated once again. Perhaps this time we could make a success of it. I surprised Timothy by requesting to see the three males together. "Do I *have* to?" he protested. Arriving in my office, they argued on and on against the idea of resuming family work. I noticed that each time the fathers failed to validate Timothy's concerns, the boy, step by step, escalated his belligerence. When I pointed out this process, each suddenly appeared to appreciate the value of having me there in the room. Our therapeutic "moment" came, however, the next time we met. I had again confronted them with their usual pattern of behavior, when Papa announced, as if he considered this a fresh idea of his own, "Maybe we should consider family therapy." Everybody joined in with gusto. Timothy's change had finally begun.

Meaning of the Moment

Making a decision about whether to pursue individual or family therapy, especially when an adolescent is the identified patient, can be one of the most challenging considerations in the treatment process (Whitaker, 1975). This boy's gay adoption, too, could have been considered challenging in and of itself. Most of all, however, it was challenging for a resident to inherit somebody else's treatment plan. In my therapeutic "moment" with Timothy and his fathers, not only did I surprise the three of them with my approach to their treatment, but the appropriate modality for this particular boy was finally chosen. Over the next few months, as we worked together, Papa and Daddy became able to yield more freedom to their son. In return, they received far more friendliness, maturity, and constructive behavior from young Timothy.

Kenneth Braslow, M.D.

BETTY AND THE OLD LADY'S GHOST

Betty was 10 when she began her individual psychotherapy. She was afraid to sleep alone, fearful that she might become possessed. She imagined herself turning into a mean, devil-like figure. By the time her treatment started, she'd been sharing her parents' bed with her father, while her mother slept by herself in Betty's room.

We were beginning to make progress with the sleeping arrangements when Betty suffered a setback. She and a friend, named "Lynn," went to visit Lynn's grandmother and discovered the poor woman dead. Betty believed that the ghost of Lynn's grandma would haunt her. She returned to the parental bed, forcing, of course, Mother to abandon it once again. By fixing all her anxieties on the ghost of Lynn's dead grandmother, Betty seemed unable to explore the more intimate meaning and source of her worries.

After many weeks of therapy, as Betty chatted on animatedly about the ghost and all the individuals who were trying to convince her that Lynn's grandmother's spirit would not be harmful, I deliberately took the little girl aback, by saying, "It must be fun to have a ghost around. After all, it gives you lots of attention, considering all those people who like to talk about it." Betty sat bolt upright. She looked shocked. Then I added that because of the ghost, Betty got to sleep with her father and maybe even liked that, too. Maybe she even preferred sleeping with Dad, compared to Mom.

Following her initial surprise, Betty became furious at me. I was telling her lies, she declared. In her next session, she stayed completely silent, with her body and face deliberately turned away. During the following appointment, however, Betty confessed to having a crush on her dad and feeling that her mom was upset about it. Soon after this, she decided she would be able to sleep in her own bed. Miraculously, the ghost of Lynn's grandmother evaporated without a trace.

Meaning of the Moment

As long as Betty "was afraid" to sleep on her own, she could share her parents' bed and satisfy her oedipal wishes guilt-free. After all, she was "sick" and could not help herself. As soon as the secondary gain afforded by her symptoms emerged in my surprising delivery of a confrontative statement, a window opened to Betty's conscience. She realized she had to conform to more mature expectations.

Betty's and my "moment" involved my stating aloud an action, wish, habit of hers, which previously had been ignored, avoided, or entirely unconscious. This amounted to a "confrontation." It was a very strong and surprising gesture from me, and could be considered from two angles. From Betty's perspective, it was my sudden, unexpected attempt to get her to face something she was avoiding. From my perspective, it was a move that produced a strong emotional reaction and started her thinking. The confrontation led to significant changes in Betty's behavior and attitudes. It worked because we already had a positive therapeutic alliance. It also worked because I wasn't expressing negative countertransference with my gesture. I had taken care to proceed with tact. I had timed my gesture, as well, to occur after a number of Betty's admissions of secondary gain had been made aloud.

I have found that skillfully employed and strategically timed confrontations are extremely helpful in treating children (Beitchman, 1978). One has to be careful, but it works.

Joseph H. Beitchman, M.D.

MEET BILL DENBY!

A shell-shocked-looking, 24-month-old girl, named Marcella, lay in bandages on my office carpet (Terr, 1990). She had been discharged from the hospital one week earlier—she suffered from a rare condition, in which her feet had turned gangrenous following an operation to release bilateral, congenital contractures. She had just been through a double amputation. The child lay virtually motionless, while her unhappy parents—sitting on my couch—whispered to me. They believed that no one, in or out of the hospital, had told Marcella what was done to her. This apparently was my assignment.

The toddler looked up. My plan was to offer her "good news" right along with the "bad." I said, "Do you know what was done to you at the hospital?" Not a flicker of movement. "The doctors took your feet off. Right?" She nodded solemnly. Her parents looked shocked. "They did it to stop all the pain you were having. And your feet had turned black. That meant they *had* to come off." Again she nodded. She was bright. She already knew. "There is something wonderful you need to hear about, though—artificial feet," I went on after just a short pause. "And there's a man you must watch on TV—Bill Denby. He has them."

I told Marcella's parents to ask DuPont Chemical Company to send them their commercial featuring an athlete, Bill Denby, who had lost both legs in Vietnam. The commercial showed Bill playing basketball on artificial limbs. I explained artificial feet to the toddler and asked her to watch the tape that her parents would show her. She must understand what could be done to correct her condition before she would be able to mourn the loss of her feet.

By the time the family returned the following month, Marcella's parents said she had already watched "her" tape at least a hundred times. The little girl, still lying on my floor, looked far more animated. She smilingly told me about Bill Denby's feet. Her mother and father, however, seemed confounded about some questions Marcella had recently been asking. "What is *soon?*" for instance, "Why is *soon* not *now?*" I explained that Marcella's questions concerned her new hopes for the future—the artificial feet. She needed adults to help her understand "time" in that context. We all went on to talk about "time" and how long "time" sometimes takes.

During Marcella's third visit, her parents were terribly concerned about how much she had been mentioning the word "garbage" at home. When I asked the child, "Did you think the doctors threw your feet into the garbage?" her parents looked mortified, but Marcella said adamantly, "Yes." As her mother and dad continued to cringe at our conversation, most likely sure that *no one* should ever speak to children of such terrible things, I explained to Marcella the idea of hospital bottles filled with formaldehyde, pathology slides for looking into microscopes, and little feet that no longer would grow. Her feet might help doctors understand how to work with other children's painful feet some day. I asked her parents for one more visit. With extreme reluctance, they agreed.

Meaning of the Moment

I had shocked and upset a set of good, but fastidious, parents by delivering the unexpected to their little girl in a series of talks about amputation, artificial limbs, "time," and the disposal and preservation of body parts. These commentaries were meant, not to shock, but to provide a very young, traumatized patient with the chance to *abreact* (express her emotion), fully understand the *context* of her trauma, and find *corrections* for it (Terr, 2003). The last time I saw her, Marcella came to my office to demonstrate her new "made by

DuPont" feet. (In a phone call beforehand, her parents had said they objected to the red shoes she wanted—they wished for something unobtrusive like brown or buff—but I had insisted she exert her only vote in the entire process). That morning, as she showed me that she could walk, the beaming little girl in the ruby slippers lit up my room (and my life).

Lenore C. Terr, M.D.

ADVOCATING FOR THE YOUNG PATIENT

Within a family, there are numbers of conflicting as well as complementary interests. Although the elders of the family—or the guardians representing the state and/or community agencies—hire the child/adolescent psychiatrist, at times the psychiatrist must be the one to advocate solely for the child. This advocacy must be sincere. (Children almost instinctively smell out phony attempts to join their legions.) Also, the advocacy may come into direct conflict with parents' or guardians' wishes. Representing a child, when needed, must be done as tactfully as possible. But a statement of advocacy also needs to be delivered as strongly and as persistently as required. In cases of suspected child abuse, of course, it requires a report to the law enforcement and/or child protection authorities. This kind of state-mandated advocacy often backfires, as many of us sadly realize. The unavoidable loss of the patient and family to psychotherapy will hopefully lead to a cessation of whatever abuse is occurring, and later, the resumption of some form of effective psychiatric treatment for the young victim. But it doesn't always work that way.

In the first case reported here, the psychiatrist barely had a moment to contemplate how best to advocate for her patient when, within the blink of an eye, she had to jump up and made her support for her adolescent patient absolutely clear. Not only was the psychiatrist taken aback by her own dramatic gesture, but the patient and her family, new to this particular therapist, were taken aback as well. This led to an immediate and welcome change in the dynamics of the entire group. In the second case, the psychiatrist, who already had a positive relationship with her patient, suggested to the bright, energetic adolescent a new and surprising piece of dialogue. "Wouldn't it be easier just to say . . . ?" The doctor's words suggested that the teenager advocate her own interests, not necessarily everyone else's. This moment of agreed-upon advocacy symbolized therapeutic permission for behaviors that this particular girl could not previously have allowed in herself. She went off and running with it.

STAND UP

Sixteen-year-old Nathalie, who had struggled in vain for 2 years with treatment-resistant anorexia nervosa—4 hospitalizations, 7 therapists, and a current weight of 80 pounds—was sitting with her mother, brother, and me in my office, waiting for her father to arrive. He was 20 minutes late. This was Nathalie's and my third evaluative session together, and I had requested that the entire family attend. On this day, the usual entrance to my office was obstructed by a large mud-filled construction ditch. Nathalie was complaining that her father was never on time, when his head suddenly became visible through the glass door at the rear of the office, opening onto a muddy pit. I opened the door and her father, who had failed to notice the large signs in the front of the building, indicating the alternative entrance, hoisted himself in, muddy shoes and all. We were at a loss for words. Then, Nathalie laughed and began poking fun at her father. He hadn't seen the signs. Right? What a joke!

His face turned red, his mouth twisted, and he walked in Nathalie's direction, raising a hand to hit her. I was still reeling from his unexpected and extremely dirty entry into my office. But I swiftly stood up. I faced him and declared, "Not in *my* office, you don't!"

He slumped over and sat down. Nathalie shouted a profanity at him and ran out. Her father began to talk, holding back sobs about how hopeless he believed his daughter's situation to be. He then apologized for getting ready to strike. When I questioned them further, Nathalie's parents told me he had hit her a couple of times years ago. As they said this, I looked over and spotted Nathalie's younger bother smashing his hand into a chair. Then minutes later, a crying Nathalie knocked at my other door. All 5 of us spent the last minutes of the session discussing the very obvious problems that the family was struggling with.

Meaning of the Moment

In the next session, Nathalie thanked me for "standing up" for her and speaking out when her father got ready to strike. I responded that I would work with her family to try to make sure it would not happen again. I had already referred her father to an anger management class. She and I talked about the fact that her father had missed all the signs, indicating an alternative entrance, just as he had missed all the early signs of her anorexia. But I also noted that he had expended considerable energy to climb through the mud pit and hoist himself into my office. Recalling the moment, she giggled, "I guess he stood up, too."

Nathalie, her family, and I continued to work together for almost 3 years, during which time she graduated from high school, started college, and slowly recovered. Many times, she and her family referred verbally back to our "moment," calling it, "The Day of the Mud." It became part of family mythology about how they all had changed. From their perspective as well as mine, it had been a pivotal instant.

Lynn Ponton, M.D.

"Thanks, but No Thanks"

At the age of 17, Emily felt sad and confused about her direction in life. She had recently developed bulimia. A school counselor suggested psychotherapy. The girl had been a spectacular, Olympic-bound swimmer until she turned 14, when she developed an osteosarcoma, requiring total replacement of her left femur. During her subsequent chemotherapy, she could not hold down food and became almost skeletal. She then developed into another "star" of sorts. She became an inspirational public speaker for childhood cancer. Gradually, she began gaining weight to the point of mild obesity.

Emily started her self-induced vomiting a few months before she met me. Taking this new "fork in the road" (Schulman et al., 1977) seemed to create in Emily a sense of shame and alarm. She hated herself. But her vomiting persisted, even after her weight returned to normal.

I learned that Emily's family constantly "focused on food." Her brother was a chef. Her mother loved to cook. Her father emphasized the importance of not wasting food, and he routinely finished the leftovers on others' plates. Emily was frequently in conflict with her dad over eating (and other topics in which he attempted to control her behavior).

One morning in her psychotherapy session, Emily spoke about a bulimic episode from the day before. She had been at a luncheon she did not want to attend, at a time when she was not hungry, with food she did not enjoy, coupled with an anticipated visit to her relatives' home that evening, where she would have to eat once again, and be polite to boot.

I said, "Sounds as if your body knows what you want and don't want. Wouldn't it be easier just to say, 'No thanks'?"

Meaning of the Moment

Emily had taken a "good girl" approach to much of her life, wanting to please others, especially her father and coaches. She now struggled to define herself as a separate human being. She had finally entered the normal, but delayed, developmental phase of adolescence. I believed that Emily was painfully trying to forge a new identity (Erikson, 1968) other than "athlete" or "cancer survivor." She needed to tune in to her own internal signals and affirm them. My question had said so. I was advocating for Emily herself, no matter what her family, coaches, charity groups, and peers might say. In order to listen to her own voice, Emily first needed a positive relationship with me. Then she needed my strong approval. My "gesture" gave her permission to say "no" to anyone. In the long run, Emily would have to realize it was completely okay to become her own person and make her own decisions. Eventually, she would have to become her *own* advocate.

By our next session a week later, Emily told me she had completely stopped vomiting. She came in wearing an attractive, comfortable-looking outfit she had purchased by herself. She reported holding her own in a disagreement with her dad. There was a hiking club she had decided to join. She went on to mention some career options she was considering. No longer a symbolic "hero," Emily was enjoying the sensation of becoming an ordinary, not-to-be-duplicated young woman. The turn-around was one of the quickest and most dramatic I have ever seen. She simply needed permission to say no to others and yes to herself.

Geri Fox, M.D.

DIRECTLY CONFESSING PERSONAL FLAWS OR FRUSTRATIONS

In our first paper on "moments" (Terr et al., 2005), we found that being real with a child—despite traditional admonitions to preserve psychiatric anonymity in order to prompt transference—is often an excellent way to promote youthful change. The three cases we presented along these lines in that 2005 paper, however, did not require that the psychiatrist say something negative about himself or herself. The two cases which follow demonstrate that when the psychiatrist willingly admits to flaws or frustrations, the child may suddenly abandon his "good guy-bad guy" approach to treatment. Interestingly, both of these expressions of psychiatric fallibility were virtually blurted out. This demonstrated that instantaneous gestures—when made by well-trained, experienced professionals—often lead the treatment in a helpful direction.

EATING HUMBLE PIE

When one works with adolescents one must be prepared for silence, refusal to admit even pressing needs, contradiction, and outright verbal abuse. Such behaviors are so wearing, they eventually may provoke a response from the psychiatrist that ends the treatment. This outcome was nearly the case with John, the 14-year-old, sullen, only child of an elderly pathologist and his attractive second wife. John had been forced to see me because of the upset he was causing at home and at school. He was a master of all exercises in negativity. His grades were poor while his intelligence was high. His insults flowed to friend and foe alike. He seemed to function from a mountain top, looking down at his fellow humans as mere peons. This clinical picture suggested to me several types of serious disorders, including antisocial personality, while I remained completely in the dark about the reasons John behaved this way.

The boy's persistence in derogatory and disdainful exchanges inside his psychotherapy came close to provoking me, in my exasperation, to counter with something I knew would be fatal to our work together. He maintained his characteristic bravado for weeks, while I exhausted all my techniques of engagement and doggedly restrained my retaliatory impulses. Finally he asked me a straight question that called for a straight response, "Why do I have to come here?" He listened and then contemptuously said, "You think you know all the answers, don't you?" I swallowed yet another devastating riposte. Thinking back to my own personal analysis, I spontaneously blurted out, "No, I don't have all the answers. But I do know something about my own deficiencies." Unexpectedly, a torrent of feeling was released in John. He said, "Well, I know *mine!* I'm just a lump of shit."

Meaning of the Moment

My uncalculated but self-reflective response to John's question suddenly pried his low estimation of himself out from under his defiant defenses. He instantaneously saw that his negativity was brittle and only partially effective. John merely *seemed* to have a personality disorder. Inside, he hated himself—and he knew it, now that he could hear himself say it aloud. I came to learn much later the origin of John's conflict. His father doted on this child of his late-middle age and, in fact, unconsciously identified with his braggadocio. Dad had unwittingly encouraged John's behavior (Johnson, 1949). John's mother had been extremely, but unconsciously, critical of her husband's weaknesses, inadvertently punishing him by refusing to help him deal with the boy. These parents, though loving, had not been able to act authoritatively because of their own unconscious conflicts.

From what he said to me during our dramatic "moment," I could see that, far from being amoral, John was actually hyper-moral. The boy's recognition of his internal situation changed the entire course of his treatment. We began working together.

Aubrey W. Metcalf, M.D.

A Moment of Despair

Brett was an almost 11-year-old boy who was quick to feel humiliated and rejected. He was far too aggressive. He attended a private school that was on the verge of expelling him. Still sucking his thumb in public, he recently had been found lying in a fetal position in a school closet. He twice ran away from class, and his school attendance was spotty. When angry, Brett had begun to say he was suicidal. Therapy had been recommended the year prior, but the boy refused. His mother experienced great difficulty setting limits; his father relied on shaming him and physical punishment.

During his first session, Brett bolted as he approached my office door. The next time, we met in the waiting room for only a few minutes. Once inside my office, he kicked at my dollhouse. "Get me out of here," he pleaded with his mother, who had stayed with him in my room. "You are stupid!" he screamed at me. I respected Brett's unwillingness to engage with me, but I needed to assess his suicidality. I discussed this dilemma directly with him, and he gave me a few necessary, but short answers. Over the next several months Brett was mainly silent, punctuated by bursts of his fury. Once he pitched his heavy, wheeled backpack down my long stairwell. More than once, he ran out. He kicked at me on the sidewalk when I found him.

Our turning point came after Brett announced at school, "Guns don't kill people. I do!" This potentially serious threat necessitated an emergency session. He was dragged in by his parents and kicked a hole in a wall along the way. He crawled under my office couch and began kicking and pushing it upward with all his might. I was afraid I was losing any opportunity to build an alliance with this wildly angry boy. Kneeling on the floor, my face inches from his, I said, with desperation in my voice, "Maybe we should try medication. Maybe what we are doing here isn't enough to help." "No," he screamed. "No medicine!" While still under the couch he looked directly into my eyes for the first time and said, "I'll talk to you. I will give you five questions," he said with the ghost of a smile. And with that he engaged me in a game of wits; in subsequent sessions he began playing with me constructively.

Meaning of the Moment

As I thought aloud about medicating him, Brett experienced this idea and my accompanying affect as a crucial moment between us. Did he see my gesture as a threat? I have wondered about it since, but I don't think so. At the time, I felt as if I was giving up on being able to treat Brett with psychotherapy—yet I didn't really want to give up.

I was painfully ambivalent about what to do next. I still wanted to help Brett, but his behaviors and statements had made me feel help-less. I believe it was my desperation that ultimately moved him. From that moment on, he chose to have a genuine relationship with me. He could get hurt in the process of healing, but he was now willing to take the chance. Two years after he began to work with me in earnest, Brett was elected the student body vice president of his school.

Maria Pease, M.D.

GIVING FOOD AND REWARDS

A direct "gift" from the psychiatrist may prompt a climactic turn-around in the child. The gift must be meaningful, not like a lollipop after a shot at the pediatrician's office or a toothbrush at the den-tist's. In this section, we will consider two particularly meaningful gifts, the first of them a true feeding, and the second, a group of more intangible, but always positive rewards—like congratulations, trophies, and gold stars. Both examples occurred in institutional set-tings where the psychiatrist—as part of a premeditated program-matic decision (case 1) or an individualized preference (case 2)—consciously set himself up always to act positive. In many instances, this behavior seems counter-intuitive. Yet the idea eventually worked even better than could have been predicted. The doctors' positive gestures, because they were genuinely felt by both the psychiatrist and the patient, were accepted and taken in as the foundations for youthful change.

SECURITY IS IN THE FREEZER

On the inpatient unit, we saw many children who had been seriously mistreated. As a policy, we decided to revise our treatment strategies toward the positive, to correct for old negative life experience. As a part of that process, we liked to serve meals family style. One day, the kitchen sent up a 5-gallon tub of ice cream for dessert. While most of the children patiently waited in line, a 10-year-old girl, named Susie, aggressively pushed her way to the front, disrupting everyone. I didn't previously know her, but I took Susie aside and we talked. I asked her if she had ice cream in her home, and she said, matter-of-factly, all they ever had in the refrigerator was beer. I took her down the hall to the unit kitchen where we had a big freezer and surprised her with the statement that she could have all the ice cream she wanted. Naturally, Susie took a giant bowl and ate every bit. We did this for several days, and I noticed that her self-served portions were getting smaller. Finally, one day while she was playing with friends, I offered to take her down to the freezer for her ice cream and she smiled and said, "That's OK, I know it's there if I want it."

Meaning of the Moment

In my view, the most basic function a parent serves for a mammalian child is feeding the child. While one might tend to generalize the term "nurturance" to include a wide variety of ways in which a parent cares for a child, for me, feeding remains at the core of maternal love. The infant rapidly learns to associate the process of being fed with the feeder. The primal relationship that soon develops becomes the prototype of all positive human relationships.

For children who have been abused and neglected, with a very damaged pattern of relationships and a world view that reflects the harsh treatment they have received, the sense of deprivation, of "not having gotten enough," can be very strong. The urgency of the needs and the anger over "not getting" can easily lead the child into problematic behavior. Part of the therapist's task is to instill within the child some hope that the child's needs can be fulfilled by adults, and that the child has enough worth for the adult to want to do this (Rosenfeld and Wasserman, 1990). This sense, that we are worthy and have a reasonable possibility of getting our needs fulfilled, is a significant part of the development of inner security. Security is not something that can be learned by talking about it. It must be experienced by the youngster in the concrete and specific way in which a child views the world. Thus, my first and last trips to the freezer with Susie became moments I clearly remember today. She did reasonably well in our program and ultimately went to live in a therapeutic foster home.

Saul Wasserman, M.D.

WAITING FOR THE WORDS TO FLOW

Tom was a 16-year-old convicted sexual offender who had been committed, the year before I met him, to the juvenile correctional institution where I work. I saw him every few weeks for medication management and behavioral assessment. Tom had failed several outpatient treatment programs before being incarcerated; and at the one-year mark, he was also seen as a treatment failure by our facility. He hated the cottage staff and avoided his peers. Periodically, he would have horrible blow-ups, blacking someone's eye or kicking somebody down. He'd then have to be sent to a secure facility to "cool-off." In our 15-minute get togethers, Tom presented as a surly, alienated young man with a huge chip on his shoulder. He would answer my inquiries with a condescending rebuff or a sneer. Around the hard edges, however, there was a loneliness to Tom that gave me hope.

I had always been taught to proactively "go for the affect" in working with a behavioral problem. One needed to know what feeling was generating the patient's unacceptable actions. But here, my instincts told me not to probe. Tom might fight me! Instead, I focused, time after time, on positive things (see Omer, 2004, for a Gandhi-like twist to this approach). In asking about his daily routines, for instance— his sleep, his medications, his visits with his family—I consistently tried to find something good for which I could give Tom institutional "points" or personal kudos (Winnicott, 1958). I was waiting for his words to flow. It took a year.

One afternoon, after he shoved an attendant aside and had to go to the secure unit, Tom came to his session with me, looking furious. I waited, tossing off a few phrases about the weather, the time of year, the flora and fauna outside. Suddenly (it seemed out of the blue), came a torrent of tears, rage, and choked-out words. Tom hated all men and couldn't trust them. "Men abuse you!" he blurted out. Then came a graphic description of how, as a young kid, he was repeatedly sexually abused by his grandfather. My inner response was one of relief. I now knew why Tom was so enraged. I also knew why he had been driven to commit a *sexual* crime. I immediately endorsed the legitimacy of Tom's anger and the importance of his sharing it with me—and my pleasure that he hadn't acted on his feelings with me, but instead, had expressed them out loud.

Tom's verbal catharsis, late as it was, brought about a significant change in his life. He began to make progress in his sexual offender treatment group, and his peer relationships turned positive. No more trips to the secure facility! As I write, Tom will be leaving our institution soon.

Meaning of the Moment

This therapeutic turning point taught me to revise the old dictum of "*going* for the affect." At times, it is better to "*wait* for the emotions to arrive." It also reminded me that therapeutic moments can happen, even if one isn't doing formal office-based psychotherapy. It reinforced the idea of heeding your own instincts. And it encouraged me to keep on accentuating the positive, even in the occasional case of a child who is pathologically violent.

William H. Sack, M.D.

INQUIRY: A GESTURE CONVEYING THE DOCTOR'S CURIOSITY

Asking a probing question about the patient sometimes represents the gesture that the entire case was waiting for. In our first example, one from family, rather than individual psychotherapy, the adolescent patient dramatically turned around because he suddenly realized—through his doctor's dissection-like inquiry—that his mother was repeating the same pattern with him that she had painfully experienced herself as an adolescent girl.

In the second example, the doctor noticed a new behavior that she thought about, but did not doggedly investigate. This turned out to be a lost opportunity, a gesture missed. As a general rule, we rarely realize what we *didn't* do that might have caused a turning point in a child's psychotherapy. Once in a while, and long after the fact, however, children—as adults—inform us of "moments" lost. If we don't ask, we won't know what we need to understand about our patients. If our curiosity arises during psychotherapy, we must inquire. Who knows how many turning points could have come about *if only we had known?*

CROSSED WIRES

Sixteen-year-old Jack was not performing up to his academic potential in a competitive high school. Because of Jack's B's and C's, his mother, Marion, was afraid she was failing as a parent. Marion was taking antidepressants and seeing her own individual therapist. Jack's father, Bernard, habitually functioned as family mediator. I decided to see the threesome together. It was one of our first sessions.

A key incident had occurred 2 years before we started. Fourteen-year-old Jack had asked for a cat. His mom countered that he would first need to demonstrate his responsibility by keeping his room neat. Jack did not measure up. When the cat never materialized, Jack verbally excoriated Marion, accusing her of purposely setting him up for failure—"You never really wanted me to have a pet!" Hurt to the core, Marion refused to speak to Jack for months. Bernard acted as go-between. After Marion and Jack finally resumed talking, the teenager developed an attitude of indifference.

I decided to inquire about Marion's life story. I requested that her husband and son listen carefully. When Marion was 14, she told us, her hardworking, distant mother divorced her easy-going alcoholic father. Marion believed the rift was entirely her own fault. Her dad's parting words—"Take good care of your mother"—didn't help. When Marion was 15, her mother attempted suicide. Again, Marion was riddled with guilt. Her mother remarried a year later, and Marion lurched prematurely into adulthood, completing high school in 3 years so that she could escape home. When her father withdrew his child support halfway through college, Marion felt utterly devalued. She stopped speaking with her father entirely.

At this juncture in Marion's story, I commented to the family that Marion's decision not to talk to her father was exactly what she had done later to Jack. Bernard noted in response that Jack was the living image of Marion's father. Jack looked intensely surprised at this. I then remarked to Marion, "Your emotional wires are crossed between Jack and your parents. You feel responsible for every single thing that happens to Jack, as you did long ago with your mom and dad. When Jack rejects your maternal efforts, it triggers the failure you felt when your mom attempted suicide, and the hurt you felt when your father stopped paying for college. Despite yourself, you also react to Jack the same way your mother and father reacted to you." Jack silently listened, still looking a bit taken aback.

Within the next few family sessions, Jack told us proudly that he had begun working on his own personal goals. His grades were improving. Bernard could now stop acting as a go-between. Marion became less rejection-sensitive. She began to reach out to Jack, telling him she loved him, "no matter what." It was what she had always yearned for, she told us, from her own mother.

Meaning of the Moment

A probing psychotherapeutic inquiry is often aimed at linking past with present. This can be a powerful technique in somewhat unusual places, such as family therapy (Ackerman, 1958). In this case, my inquiry and the interpretation that followed connected the meaning of events in the mother's past with the meaning of events in her boy's recent life. Making such an interpretation in each other's presence was an unexpected gesture that improved the life of the entire family far into the foreseeable future.

Geri Fox, M.D.

MISSED MOMENT

Sandrine was a sad, slightly overweight, virtually ignored high school sophomore. She received B's and C's at school, participated in no extracurricular activities, came home and did housework and babysitting, and walked the family dog. She had two younger sisters, one of whom I had previously treated. Marlena, the girl's mother, was born in Europe and married and conceived the children by an American soldier stationed there. They chose to maintain their American citizenship, despite the fact that the father of the family went AWOL and disappeared when Sandrine was 7. The girls' mother had always worked as a secretary and translator on army bases. She eventually moved to an air force base where she met and married her second husband, Hobie. Soon, they were deployed in Northern California.

I attributed both the oldest and youngest sisters' sadness to their sudden, inexplicable paternal loss. I also saw them as suffering from a difficult change in cultures (Erikson, 1950). Working along these lines with 10-year-old Bridget, the youngest, led to a brightening of her affect and considerably improved efforts at school. When I declared Bridget "better," Marlena decided to have me treat, instead, her oldest daughter, Sandrine. Both mother and stepfather came to see me in conjunction with Sandrine's treatment. I learned that there were some ongoing air force problems with Hobie. He'd been late for work, for instance, absent a couple of times, and suspected of pilfering (but not caught). The couple, however, seemed relatively devoted and happy. Marlena worked long hours. Hobie prided himself on coming home early to tend to his stepdaughters.

Under my care, Sandrine did not complain, nor did she respond much. She was not really suffering from father-loss or cultural adjustment, she insisted. She looked bored as we talked and often drifted into hazy, day-dreamy states. In general, however, she was pleasant and cooperative. Then one day she announced she had joined a "born-again" church. Within weeks, Sandrine, a Catholic, was attending fundamentalist Protestant church activities almost every day. She barely had the time to come to my office. She told me that religion had "saved" her. Nobody danced, drank, or swore. Skirts were long. Tops were loose. She no longer helped much at home. All her friendships revolved around church activities. Weekends were totally taken up. Although Sandrine's dismal affect and pessimistic statements did not change, she insisted that she felt better now and no longer needed me. Her parents concurred.

I received a letter from Sandrine 30 years later. "Why didn't you know?" she wrote me. "My stepfather was sexually abusing me!" Not only had Hobie repeatedly abused Sandrine, she wrote, but later—when she became a teenager—he also sexually abused Bridget. Eventually Hobie and Marlena divorced. Hobie was never prosecuted. I invited Sandrine to my office for a no-pay session. During a Christmas holiday break, she came to visit her mom and to see me. She was still sad, slightly overweight, lonely, and dreamy. Her love affair with Christian fundamentalism had lasted only a couple of years. I strongly suggested psychotherapy and told her several low-cost ways to obtain it near her home (in a distant state). I doubt she ever did.

Meaning of the Moment

Sandrine did not tell me, while I was treating her, that she was actively being sexually abused. Her symptoms—dreaminess, sadness, aloneness, pessimism, so-so grades, aloofness from peers—might have suggested incest, but I don't think I could have acted on this group of symptoms alone. Hobie's minor antisocial run-ins may have suggested incest, too, but they were not enough to lead me there. Marlena's work, work, work ethic, while ignoring the girls, suggested a family incest dynamic, as well. The church, however, should have been the clincher for me. When a child independently throws herself into 7-day-a-week rule-bound religious activity, the professional cannot accept this behavior as a given. It was too extreme and far too different from this particular child's background. Here was reactive, defensive, self-protective behavior (Terr, 1991) that I should have recognized. I could not have known exactly what was happening. But I should have asked—and not just one question, but a gentle and tactful probe.

Lenore C. Terr, M.D.

CONCLUSION AND SUMMARY

In this group investigation of the reasons for climactic change in young peoples' psychotherapies—or even in consultations or institutional care—we found that in at least 10 situations (and an eleventh, in which the opportunity was missed), the psychiatrist's verbal and/or motoric gesture toward the child patient was (or would have been) what made the crucial difference. The meaningful gesture could occur with the doctor's unexpected words; the doctor's advocacy; his or her confession of fallibility; direct feeding or rewarding; or the doctor's probing inquiry. The 10 gestures we describe in this paper were entirely conscious on the doctor's part. Although they were delivered in a "blink" in 7 cases out of 10—in other words, on impulse (see Gladwell, 2005, for an interesting discussion of this sort of immediate, unconsciously-precipitated, psychological response)— they were founded on good training and considerable experience. The old dictum, "First of all do no harm," always lay at the base of what the doctor did.

In the design of this group inquiry into dramatic changes in children and adolescents, we put most of our emphasis on the "figure" (the doctor's gesture), while we purposely put the "ground" (the pre-existing relationship) into the background. We wish to bring this "ground" into the forefront for just a moment. It is interesting to note that in 5 cases (Drs. Braslow, Fox [case 2], Ponton, Wasserman, and Terr [case 1]) there had been little to no therapeutic relationship prior to the doctor's gesture. Each of these cases had been in the early evaluative or treatment phases at the time of the dramatic "moment" of change. In 2 of our cases (Drs. Metcalf and Pease) the child's transference had been highly negative from the very beginning of the relationship, and the gesture fell upon that hostile ground. In the 4 remaining cases, including the one in which a gesture never occurred (Terr [case 2]), the therapeutic ground had been relatively positive (Fox [case 1], Beitchman, Sack). Of course, we report our own perceptions of the "ground," which obviously is only part of the whole story.

Looking once again at the gesture itself, we found that in the large majority of our cases (9 of 10) the psychiatrist did something the child and/or parents would have seen as entirely unexpected. Ranging from discussing body-part disposal to giving ice cream to the disrupter of a food line, the shift from routine to unusual must have felt strange to the child—and thus, must have earmarked the "moment" as special. Another frequent item among our 10 dramatic turn-arounds was the tendency for the psychotherapist to do something counter-intuitive. As long as the doctor's behavior was genuine and there was "method to his madness," the tactic worked. In 8 of our 10 delivered gestures, the physician did something defying common sense (standing up to a very large, angry man, for example), or going up against an old accepted psychotherapeutic dictum (in confessing personal fallibility, for example). It appears, in other words, that the suddenness, counter-intuitiveness, and common-sense defying qualities of these gestures come, largely, from the therapist's unconscious. Even so, as long as the doctor is well-trained and sensitive, the gesture seems to serve the young patient well.

Our description of these 11 cases, marked by the doctor's gestures, can be broken into smaller categories—for example, children with major physical illnesses (3 cases), personality problems (6 cases), and traumatic exposures (5 cases). In the 4 instances of trauma, which were known to the therapists treating it, it was interesting to find that during the "moment" of climax, at least one of three important principles of trauma psychotherapy (Terr, 2003)—*abreaction, context,* or *correction*—was at work. An important general point here is that effective psychotherapy is not strictly limited to latency and adolescent

neuroses or developmental disturbances, as might have been assumed in the past. In this article, we have described one preschooler,
2 institutionalized youngsters, 5 treatment-resistant adolescents, and
3 children adjusting to massive cultural, family, or physical change.
This large range of psychiatric, social, and medical conditions certainly represents a broader usefulness of psychotherapy than might
previously have been assumed. But it also demonstrates that today, in
many successful instances of psychotherapy, more than one treatment modality are simultaneously being utilized.

Many of our therapeutic turning points gave youngsters the singular chance to cognitively understand the ins and outs of their dilemmas and disorders. In each of our cases, the "moment" captured
something that could be immediately grasped unconsciously, but
then thought out in full consciousness afterward. Cognitive work
with patients ranks much higher today than it did in the days when
psychodynamic psychotherapy was first being formalized (Colby,
1951; Tarachow, 1963; Wolberg, 1977). In most of our cases, the impact of the implicit moment, experienced almost nonverbally between two people, was subsequently translated into an entirely conscious and cognitive framework with the child. (See Daniel Stern,
2004, for an interesting and somewhat similar formulation by his
Boston group, regarding key moments that occur in adult psychoanalysis.)

It seems to us that a climactic "moment" in child psychotherapy
represents a sudden irreversible switch from one set of silent assumptions between a couple of people to another set of more mutual understandings. Whereas the assumptions of the dyad before the "moment" were separate and individualized, the assumptions afterward
become conjoined and united. Gestures made by the doctor appear
to be one of many possible ways that this union comes about. The
doctor's playfulness with the young patient and the doctor's willingness to acknowledge the realities of the relationship and of the
child's life are other means to help effect dramatic change. Most
likely there are other important principles that did not emerge from
the 28 vignettes we collected. We will be eager to hear of these from
our readers.

To conclude and to summarize this group of, what turns out to be,
3 papers written by 23 authors (see also, Terr et al., 2005, and Terr et
al., 2006), we sought to examine only one aspect of child psychotherapy—climactic change in the patient. We put no restrictions into our
inquiry, suggesting no categories or causes for the massive turn-
arounds that some youngsters exhibit. What emerged were 3 trends.

The doctor's gesture—the point of this article—was vitally important to children in therapy, as were the realities of the doctor-patient (analyst-analysand or psychologist-client) relationship, and a playful, imaginative approach. What overlaid the 3 reasons behind massive childhood change was an irreversible switch from one set of silent assumptions between doctor and patient to another set of more mutual understandings. Before the "moment," doctor and patient were riding on separate tracks. At the "moment," and thereafter, they rode the same rail.

Although our study design was not set up as a prototype of evidence-based research into psychotherapy, it might be seen as one possible approach to this kind of study. Why not consider psychotherapeutic turn-arounds in various groups of children? Why not compare the effect of individual dynamic psychotherapies to what happens with similar children on waiting lists, or with similar children receiving group cognitive-behavioral treatments? As long as the children in each subgroup and the methods used for each subgroup can be determined to be strongly alike, the research might turn out useful. Also, why not compare individual cognitive-behavioral work to individual psychodynamic psychotherapy, not just immediately, but 4–5 years later? Instead of looking only at symptom lists, why not compare some additional factors, too, such as the child's developmental levels, personality traits, family relationships, peer connections, identity formation, intelligence? Befores and afters for some of these measures might eventually put individual psychotherapy on the same level—or even higher—than the other "evidence-based" treatments (see Kazdin and Weisz, 2003). It would have to take careful planning, but we think such studies would be worthwhile. It is our hope that our group of 3 papers will inspire further psychodynamic research.

Just as Raymond Waggoner, M.D., told his story of a case in psychotherapy—"he said, she said"—to his young residents so many years ago, we have reported our therapeutic examples of childhood turn-arounds in order to inspire new thinking, questioning, and scientific study. May the new crop of psychiatrists, psychoanalysts, and allied professionals find happy hunting in grounds such as these!

Each one of the vignettes sent to author L.T. was used in the set of 3 articles that we have now published. All of these psychotherapies were conducted by physicians. It remains highly important for psychiatrists-in-training to formally learn psychodynamic psychotherapy, treat children with it, be supervised in it, and utilize it throughout their training years. Psychotherapy is equally important for advanced training in psychology, social work, psychiatric nursing, counseling, and related fields. If our younger colleagues carefully learn child and adolescent psychotherapy, they, like us . . . and their patients, like ours . . . may eventually experience the miracle of the "moment."

BIBLIOGRAPHY

ACKERMAN N (1958) *The Psychodynamics of Family Life: Diagnosis and Treatment of Family Relationships.* New York: Basic Books.

BEITCHMAN J (1978) Confrontation in Psychotherapy with Children. *Psychiatric J Univ Ottawa* 3:5–11.

COLBY K M (1951) *A Primer for Psychotherapists.* New York: Ronald Press.

ERIKSON, E (1950) *Childhood & Society.* New York: Norton.

——— (1958) *Identity: Youth & Crisis.* New York: Norton.

GLADWELL M (2005) *Blink: The Power of Thinking Without Thinking.* New York: Little, Brown.

JOHNSON A (1949) Sanctions for Superego Lacunae of Adolescents. In: *Searchlights on Delinquency*, Eissler K, ed. Oxford, England: International Universities Press, pp 225–254.

KAZDIN A & WEISZ J (2003) *Evidence-based Psychotherapies for Children and Adolescents.* New York: Guilford.

OMER H (2004) *Non-violent Resistance: A New Approach to Violent and Self-Destructive Children.* S London-Sapir & H Omer, trs. UK: Cambridge.

ROSENFELD A R, WASSERMAN S (1990) *Healing the Heart, a Therapeutic Approach to Disturbed Children in Group Care*, Washington D.C.: Child Welfare League of America.

SCHULMAN J L, DELAS FUENTE M E, SURAN B G (1977) An Indication for Brief Psychotherapy: The Fork in the Road Phenomenon. *Bull Menninger Clinic*, 41:553–562.

STERN D L (2004) *The Present Moment in Psychotherapy & Everyday Life.* New York: Norton.

TARACHOW S (1963) *An Introduction to Psychotherapy.* New York: International Universities Press.

TERR L (1990) *Too Scared to Cry.* New York: Harper & Row.

——— (1991) Childhood Traumas: An Outline and Overview. *Am J Psychiatry*, 148:10–20.

——— (2003) Wild Child. *J Amer Acad Child & Adolesc Psychiatry* 41:1401–1409.

TERR L, MCDERMOTT JF, BENSON RM, BLOS JR P, DEENEY J M, ROGERS R R, ZRULL J P (2005) Moments in Psychotherapy. *J Amer Acad Child & Adolesc Psychiatry* 44:191–197.

TERR L, DEENEY J M, DRELL M, DODSON J W, GAENSBAUER T J, MASSIE H, MINDE K, STEWART G, TEAL S, WINTERS N (2006) Playful "Moments" in Psychotherapy. *J Amer Acad Child and Adolesc Psychiatry* 45:604–613.

WHITAKER C (1975) The Symptomatic Adolescent—an AWOL Family Member. In: *The Adolescent in Group and Family Therapy,* Sugar M, ed. New York: Brunner/Mazel, pp 205–215.

WINNICOTT D W (1958) Clinical Varieties of Transference. In: *Collected Papers: Through Pediatrics to Psychoanalysis.* New York: Basic.

WOLBERG L R (1977) *The Technique of Psychotherapy* (2 vols., 3rd ed.). New York: Grune & Stratton.

The Grandparent Syndrome

A Case Study

LANDRUM TUCKER, JR., M.D.

"The Grandparent Syndrome" was first defined by Rappaport in 1956 as "the development of detrimental character traits brought on by the identification with a grandparent. . . ."

This paper first reviews some of the various descriptions in the analytic and anthropologic literature of the significance of grandparents in the human psyche and in culture in general. Then, the analytic treatment of a young man with an unconscious identification with his grandmother is described. He has a particular type of identification, precipitated by melancholia in childhood, which lasted well into his adult life. In the treatment the effects of the deeply entrenched identification are brought to light and the parental and grandparental transference elements which develop are analyzed over a six-year period. The difficult analysis of the patient's negative therapeutic reaction, which was intensified by his unconscious guilt, is discussed. There is a 15- and 20-year follow-up of the analysis when the patient, an only child, returns to the analyst to do more analytic work in grieving the deaths of his parents.

MANY YEARS AGO, JONES, ABRAHAM, AND FERENZI FIRST DESCRIBED aspects of the significance of grandparents in the development of personality. (1, 2, 3)

Jones pointed out that the grandfather is naturally suited to be-

Supervising and Training Psychoanalyst, Psychoanalytic Institute of the Carolinas; Adjunct Professor, Department of Psychiatry, University of North Carolina.

The Psychoanalytic Study of the Child 61, ed. Robert A. King, Peter B. Neubauer, Samuel Abrams, and A. Scott Dowling (Yale University Press, copyright © 2006 by Robert A. King, Peter B. Neubauer, Samuel Abrams, and A. Scott Dowling).

come an ideal substitute for father in a child's "family romance." He has power over father, and he may be kinder and more indulgent to the child. Also Jones notes that there is a common childhood wish to reverse roles with the parents and become their parents.

In this manner the child can then order about those who control him and satisfy hostile, aggressive wishes toward the parents; and, also, it is an exaggeration of the incestuous wish to take father's place.

Jones goes on to describe how rivalry with grandparents can become more intense when the child realizes that a grandparent has specially favored a mother or father. For example, if mother actually loves grandfather more than father, then it is him the child has to replace.

Jones adds that parents can also identify their children with their parent and thus love the child with incestuous intensity as a replacement of the grandparent. He concludes that all members of a family or ancestry can be replacements in the original image of the trinity of Father, Mother, and Child. Jones also referred to the writing of Rank and Abraham about the oedipal significance of ancestors in myths and ancient history. In the myth of Perseus and Medusa, Rank points out that in the final part of the myth, Perseus returns to play the grandfather fulfilling a prophesy and freeing the daughter, his mother, for his father and himself.

Abraham (4) discussed the life of the Egyptian pharaoh Echnaton who destroyed the image of his father and his father's religion. Echnaton then turned to the older religious principles of early ancestors to displace father with the mother with whom he was closely attached, that is, to gain the power of the grandfather over father (4).

In 1913, Abraham (2) went on to discuss his clinical impression that a patient who emphasized grandparents had violently rejected a father or mother. He pointed out that a child may play grandparents against parents to get even with parents and that children take the word "grand" at face value, literally "grander than parents." He described brief clinical vignettes to illustrate, in one case, idealizing grandfather as more powerful than father and, in another, displacing anger from mother onto grandmother. Finally, he concluded, as Jones did, that grandparents are used to neutralize the power of the Oedipus complex by denial and debasement of the original parent figures, that is, a variation of the "family romance."

Ferenzi (3) makes some brief additional comments about identification with a powerful or feeble grandfather imago depending upon how the grandparents were treated by the family in reality. He also pointed out the use Little Hans made of grandparents in forming an oedipal compromise with his father in the wish that he could give grandmother to father to handle things justly, that is, "I sleep with my Mama, you sleep with your Mama."

Then, in 1956, Rappaport (6) first described what he called "The Grandparent Syndrome." He defined the syndrome as the development of detrimental and grotesque character traits brought about by the identification with the grandparent. He said the identification was motivated by the fantasy of reversal of generations and intensified by the situation of the grandparent being in the same household with the family. Rappaport noted, in contrast to the earlier emphasis on the grandfather, that it was *grandmother* who was usually involved in the cases he reported.

In discussing the reversal of generations as a motivating factor in such identification, Rappaport says that a child fantasizes that, as he grows older, he will become the parent to his own parent, that is, his grandparent. This fantasy is reinforced by its being, in essence, identification with the strongest member of the household or identification with the aggressor and by turning passive into active; that is, being able to do to his parents what was done to him. Rappaport illustrated how this fantasy is ingrained in human culture by pointing out similarities in diverse languages of the word for infant and grandparent. He also described rituals in which the fear of the grandparent returning in the child motivates some act to signify the parents' dominance over the child,* and themes of fairy tales, like *Little Red Riding Hood,* where birth and death motifs involve a grandmother figure. Rappaport said that such identification is amplified when the grandparent, usually the grandmother, has been a powerful force in running the household. This identification also is exaggerated if the child has had to nurse a sick grandparent or *if there has been an unresolved grief reaction after the death of a grandparent.* Many times the introjection is grotesque, grandiose, and omnipotent, and the parents are

*In English, both grandparent and grandchild are "grand." The German word for grandchild, *Enkel,* is a diminutive *of Ahn,* ancestor. Grandmother in Italian is *nonna* and in Spanish, *nino* is infant. The Russian word for grandmother is *baba,* and the English word for infant is "baby."

The Nukahiva on the Marquesas Islands believe that the soul of the grandfather is transmitted by nature into the body of the grandchildren. In West Africa, children have been put to death in certain tribes because the fetish doctor declared it to be the king's father come to life again.

In *Little Red Riding Hood,* the grandmother becomes the wolf (bad mother?) but the good grandmother is rescued from the wolf's stomach. Rappaport says this theme expresses the notion that grandmother is a powerful, frightening figure but also symbolizes grandmother being born again as the grandchild.

degraded and demeaned as relatively weak and flawed. Also, Rappaport claimed that since the sexual differences in old age fade, such identification might reinforce the already confused concept the child has of sexuality and interfere with the child's sexual identity and full psychosexual development.

In relating the identification with the grandparents to the Oedipus complex, Rappaport saw this as an attenuation of the latter or an avoidance of it. He also noted that mothers who choose to have their parents or in-laws live with them may themselves have strong infantile needs and then compete with their own children and promote a pre-oedipal situation in which the child is tied to an omnipotent mother of vague or bisexual identity.

LaBarre, Jessner, and Ussery (7) noted the frequency of grandmothers being important in children's personality development in a review of cases presenting for treatment in a child guidance clinic. In 41 cases reviewed, 26 children were either taken care of much of the time by grandmother or the grandmother lived in the same house with the child. The influence of the grandmother was seen as positive in some cases providing stability or nurturance but also led to confused identification and splitting of good and bad parent images.

Erikson (8) discussed two analytic cases. In one the patient's identification with his powerful, maternal grandfather was encouraged by a mother disappointed in her weak husband, intensifying the patient's oedipal conflict. In another, the patient's affects are stifled when her identification with her warm and loving grandfather was no longer nourished after his death.

Parker (9) discussed a case in which an adolescent girl presented with depression following the death of her grandmother. She had a childhood wish to have a baby by grandfather and take grandmother's place and was very guilty when her childhood wish was gratified by the grandmother's death. Identification was not the major issue in this case; rather oedipal wishes were conscious and amplified by the patient having taken the mother's place and grandmother's place with father and grandfather respectively. The mothering figures had been chronically ill, and the father figures had turned to the daughter for affection many times.

Marui (10) discussed a case in which *a young man became melancholic and sado-masochistic after the death of his grandmother and declared himself to be worthless.* The grandmother was remembered as strict and critical but also overly affectionate and pampering. The father was always under the thumb of the mother and grandmother. The patient initially identified with father and was himself docile and obedient. Then, when he was 25, his grandmother died of stomach cancer; subsequently, he developed stomach distress, felt like an old man, and thought he was the vilest creature on earth for his loose sexual activity with girlfriends. Marui emphasized that *since the introjection of grandmother and identification with her was unconscious, and the ego was impoverished, this was true melancholia as opposed to grieving where sadness over a death is recognized or pathologic mourning where symptoms are present but recognized as connected to feelings about someone who has died.* Marui pointed out in this case that the patient's extreme self-criticism was a result of introjection of grandmother's superego after her death; and that, when he was growing up, the grandmother's extreme doting on him had interfered with his own superego development, resulting in his poor impulse control before her death.

The following case is much like the case Marui reported in that there is an identification with the grandmother after her death. Also, the case is consistent with Rappaport's statement that the grandparents' living in the same household intensifies the identification and development of the syndrome. *What is unique about this case is the fact that the analysand felt responsible for his grandmother's death, and this interfered with mourning and further intensified the identifications with her. That a latent melancholic reaction is a particularly intense variant of the grandparent syndrome is something that Rappaport did not stress in his definition.* This case material will illustrate how such identifications were uncovered, and how melancholia was rekindled and resolved in the analysis.

CASE REPORT

Mr. B, a 23-year-old paralegal, was referred to the psychoanalytic clinic by a friend, because of anxiety around authority figures, premature ejaculation, and an inability to allow himself small pleasures in life.

In initial interviews he talked mainly about his relationship with his mother and a girlfriend. He described his mother as dominant, controlling, and overindulgent, and his father as pleasant but passive. He and the girlfriend had been seeing each other for three years, and marriage was being considered but with several reservations. There was only brief mention of the grandmother having lived with the family until she died when he was 10 years old. When Mr. B asked early on about how the analysis might affect his outside life, the analyst said that important decisions in his life would be a part of the analysis, and he would be encouraged to explore his thoughts before he took action. But when Mr. B began analysis, he immediately told his girlfriend he might have to wait until he finished treatment before he could consider marriage. Upon hearing this she broke up the relationship and later married his best friend with whom—he found out later—she, covertly, had been having intercourse all along. He was in a rage over this rejection and humiliation, but after being in analysis a few weeks, he began living with a woman 10 years older than himself. He described his new partner as a plain but nurturing woman who needed his attention because she had diabetes, which she poorly controlled. (Regarding the patient's primary presenting symptom, in the relationship with the older woman, premature ejaculation was not reported to be a problem, and has mainly recurred when Mr. B began new relationships with women his age.)

In the early analytic situation, Mr. B was talkative, extremely punctual, and polite. He stayed with superficial topics or became vague and intellectual.

The first dream of the analysis was in the 13th hour when he reported the following dream:

> I had a dream night before last. There was a large woman in it. She wasn't my grandmother, but kind of like my grandmother.

During the next week he made the first mention of his grandmother, a memory of her finding him in the basement with another male friend spanking a little girl's bare buttocks. He had no memory of what happened after he was discovered.

Within a few weeks, Mr. B complained that he had to be the mother to his girlfriend—the older woman—and revealed that she was the former girlfriend of the older male friend who had referred him for analysis. This was the first clear indication that the patient was identifying with his grandmother, that is, "mother to his mother" and repeating an observation and wish of his childhood in his relationship with the older girlfriend. At the same time, Mr. B was satisfying oedipal wishes in having intercourse with the former girlfriend of the man toward whom he felt "like a father." Also, the sick girlfriend represented the grandmother and sexual wishes for her were satisfied as well. In fact, the woman was safer than a younger woman in that she was not so "oedipal." But, at this time, Mr. B was able to see only that his relationship with the girlfriend had something to do with the past and "maybe something oedipal was going on" to use his words. The analyst interpreted the defense of intellectualization, which led to Mr. B's awareness of his fear of being criticized and rejected by the analyst, rather than a full understanding of his acting out behavior. The analyst thought this fear of rejection was related to an early unconscious transference experience of the analyst as a care taking, omnipotent parent.

With interpretive work on the more conscious transference resistance of fear of criticism by the analyst, Mr. B became more trusting, and a positive transference dream followed:

> I had a dream. This guardian angel had a talk with Mr. M in the firm, and that's how I got to keep my office. The guardian angel looked an awful lot like you. I'm embarrassed about that.

In the next several sessions, Mr. B's reactions toward the analyst and the analytic situation vividly repeated the past. For example, when the analyst noted Mr. B's excitement and interest in an associate's account of spanking prostitutes, Mr. B became very anxious and began worrying in his associations about losing his musical equipment. (Mr. B was an avid amateur musician, and the analyst saw this worry as a possible displacement of castration anxiety since "beating fantasies" might have their root in masturbatory oedipal wishes.) Then he protected himself by telling the analyst that the elderly woman who lived next door to him approved of him and his girlfriend living together. After systematic interpretation, Mr. B saw the connection between his fear of being punished by the analyst in the present and grandmother's reaction to finding him spanking the little girl in the basement.

The complicated pre-oedipal themes at this time included a wish for sadomasochistic sex with a woman and a fear of punishment by castration by the pre-oedipal mother for this wish (the "bad" grandmother imago). There was also the possibility that this was a screen memory in which Mr. B projected his own masochistic, feminine identification; that is, he was the little girl being spanked.

Other thoughts and descriptions of himself then emerged reflecting his identification with his grandmother such as Mr. B revealing that he had used his grandmother's brush and comb for his very long, shoulder-length hair ever since her death. He also remembered the need to have with him a variety of phallic objects.* For ex-

---

*Bak (11) has described the attachment to such objects in latency and referred to them as "prosthetic," saying that they reassure body integrity in the face of object loss (separation anxiety) as well as allay castration fears.

In a personal communication Freeman (12) has referred to the intense attachment to objects as an extension of the body image, such as Peller (13) describes in the play of infancy. For example, an individual really feels incomplete and anxious without the physical presence of the object such as a pen or piece of clothing, jewelry, etc. Also, he may extend himself and merge with the object such as when one is driving a dearly loved automobile or a carpenter using his special hammer.

ample, he cherished pens and little play guns during his childhood. He also described fears in the session that the analyst would think he was homosexual when he admitted weakness in needing objects for security, or passive wishes to be cared for, or preference for his father over his mother. Mr. B's understanding that his particular attachment to these objects was intensified after his grandmother's death was followed by his first primal scene memory. However, he denied his parents' sexuality, saying, for example, "they were just in bed together, looking funny."

All this was followed by the first recovery of the intense memory of grandmother dying the day he fell out of a tree and broke his arm. Mr. B broke into sobbing and tears. He felt much guilt and remorse about grandmother's death because Mr. B remembered that she was extremely upset by his accident. And he was not supposed to be climbing the tree!

Following the recovery of these memories with the affective and cognitive components now integrated, the analysand lost interest in his older girlfriend and ended the relationship. That this had been an unconscious enactment of his past desire and fantasy was strongly suggested when he was very afraid that she would die because of his rejection of her and was surprised when she didn't.

After this, the grandmother transference was no longer split, and symptomatic actions outside the analytic situation lessened. Both positive and negative feelings toward the analyst became more intense, and Mr. B feared that the analyst would die because of his anger. When he also expressed concern that the analyst liked females better than Mr. B, the analyst thought he was revealing his past jealousy toward the mother for grandmother's affection.

Then, after some months, father transference began to develop as well. Mr. B remembered his father falling off a ladder he was holding for him, breaking his leg and almost dying from an embolus. After he talked about warm feelings toward his father, he became concerned that homosexual urges in him would erupt, and this frightened him. (The thoughts would not be intentionally connected by Mr. B; first, he might talk about his father and then, via free association, other thoughts came to mind of a homosexual nature. Then the analyst would wonder about the sequence, and the patient would say more with affect.)

At this point, Mr. B became involved with a younger woman but had trouble with premature ejaculation again when attempting sex. (Tyson [14] speaks about self-constancy issues after childhood loss, and the ejaculation problem could represent vulnerability of the "sexual or gender self" as well as castration anxiety and anger/fear of mother.)

After expressing his sexual desire and frustration, he lost his car keys and couldn't find them. He talked of women having their hooks in him and feeling like a fish. But, also at about this time, Mr. B began to dress in a more masculine manner with hard-soled shoes instead of moccasins, and he had his shoulder-length hair cut shorter. In a parapraxis he confused his girlfriend with his mother when he said she called his penis "ma's little fellow," meaning to say "my little fellow." The analyst wondered if this reflected both Mr. B's concern about the female taking his penis from him as well as actually feeling that he was mother's little penis.

Though the material focused more on oedipal sexual wishes for his mother at this point in the treatment, the conflict and fear was also pre-oedipal; that is, he was more afraid of the powerful mother castrating him during intercourse rather than retaliation from father.

Then mother's birthday stimulated memories of grandmother's death, which Mr. B now remembered, had occurred in the same month, October. He followed this connection of mother's birthday with grandmother's death by reporting he takes warm baths in an old bathtub every morning before coming to sessions, just like being bathed by grandmother and also how she bathed herself. He reported that he still has with him the same bicycle she had given him on the Christmas before her death.

One day Mr. B suddenly remembered that it was in a psychiatrist's back yard where he climbed the forbidden tree and fell when grandmother died. He wondered if this coincidence intensified his ambivalent feelings toward the analyst, and was stunned at the irony of his parents never seeking any psychiatric help for him when he was so depressed afterward. He remembered no mention of his grandmother after her death, and he knew of no funeral.

Returning from a holiday interruption, Mr. B again revealed his fear that his anger at the analyst might have caused him to die while on holiday. He blamed his mother for his grandmother's death and quit the new girlfriend, perhaps acting out his anger at mother and analyst. Then he felt guilty for blaming mother so intensely. (His anger at the analyst was stirred by Mr. B's conviction that the analyst disapproved of him and made the analysis too intense to punish him.)

After this revelation of feeling, Mr. B lingered in the warm tub at home before sessions and was late because he went to sleep there.

(Typically he was scrupulously on time.) Then, during an hour, he saw a breast on the ceiling, and said he wanted to be warm. He thought he deserved to feel more pain and should be punished for grandmother's death, and then he got a traffic ticket for speeding. A dream followed:

> I was thinking of mother and father being paired up leaving me with Granny.

This brief dream reflected one particular way Mr. B handled his oedipal rivalry, a reversal of the Little Hans solution. He had his woman, grandmother, and father had the other, mother; but he wanted mother too. He called the analyst at home to change an appointment time and was frightened after he talked to the analyst's wife. (He usually called the business phone if necessary; but he had decided to try the home phone instead on the weekend.) He was afraid that she thought he was a dangerous person and that the analyst would retaliate. He expressed anger at his mother again, and he wished his mother would die before father. And he also denied interest in mother, saying he liked his father much better. Then he feared the analyst was angry because he might be trying to take the analyst away from his wife.

So, at this time Mr. B moved away from positive oedipal strivings into a negative oedipal regression in the transference; that is, he strongly claimed preference for his father over his mother. He also asserted that he had preferred grandmother over mother as well. With such underpinnings of denial, Mr. B comfortably denied sexual feelings for his mother. But then there was a dream that frightened him:

> A woman is sucking on my dick [while I'm] in a group of people.

This fellatio dream may have reflected negative oedipal wishes toward father and the analyst as well as the wish to identify with grandmother and be mother's mother—the grandmother with the big breast to be sucked on.

Then he met another young woman, and again there was trouble with sex; this time, Mr. B was not able to maintain an erection. He feared the analyst disapproved of his sexual activity just like grandmother did, and he had dreams of the analyst being a sheriff or a policeman coming after him to punish him. When he developed a venereal infection, he projected onto the analyst the elements of his "grandmother" superego, saying for example, "you think she's a dirty girl and gave me a disease."

When the extra-transference sexual involvement and projection were interpreted, Mr. B described oedipal themes, feeling extremely competitive with other professionals at work as well as with the analyst, and he feared attack by the new girlfriend's father. Again, the analyst saw that when defensive attitudes and actions were analyzed, Mr. B would reveal underlying fears of retaliation.

Then the analyst's vacation stimulated anger and fear again that the analyst might die and not return, just like grandmother. During a vacation break, there were the following dreams. One was of rejection by mother, leaving him holding his present:

> In my dream last night, I was wishing Mother "Happy Birthday" and being real nice to her. Then I had a fantasy of her giving me hell and leaving me standing with the present.

The other of a woman coming back from the dead, reflecting fear of the grandmother:

> I had a nightmare Sunday night. It was from a horror movie I saw 6–8 years ago. A woman had died, a medium, and people from the funeral home came to get her the next day. She stole this ring. The lady's eyes kept popping open. It was real dark. The medium came back from the dead, there was noise, and then someone strangled her. I woke up with the image of mother standing over me, really frightened.

Following the dreams, Mr. B recovered a vivid memory of an episode when he was four years old involving his going into the bedroom to sleep with his mother. He remembered that saying he was scared at night was only an excuse to get sexual gratification from being close to mother, and this realization was stimulated by seeing his girlfriend's little brother, age 6, coming to her bedroom with the same wish—to sleep with his big sister at night on a visit. Then, during the session, he had a visual image of a penis being cut off, and he denied any interest in his mother and claimed he liked his father much better.

With continued working through of the identification with grandmother and its defensive function, Mr. B's oedipal conflict became more cathected. There was less emergence of pre-oedipal issues and less of a grandmother transference. He had recognized sexual wishes for mother, then expected castration and quickly denied the interest. Indeed, at this point he moved to a negative oedipal position, claiming interest in the father and using projection, wondered indirectly if the analyst was homosexual, saying the analyst reminded him of a professor in college who had been homosexual.

The fear of castration for his oedipal wishes was followed by actively seeking out information from his mother, while she was visiting him, about grandmother's death. He learned that after her death, he was very depressed for a long time, and also remembered that his grandmother used to tell him "you'll be the death of me" when he was naughty. Then he felt very guilty about grandmother's death in the session and had a strong wish to be punished; he also felt guilty about the idea of his mother learning about his sexual activities with his new girlfriend. Following this, he again received a traffic ticket and felt very ashamed and humiliated and thought he was punishing himself unconsciously. Mr. B feared his mother would die if she learned about the girlfriend just like grandmother did after finding out about the little girl in the basement he had spanked. He had a dream of cutting off his belt to please father and thought father didn't want him to grow up and function sexually. This time his fear of castration and oedipal guilt merged with the fear of his omnipotence and pre-oedipal shame.

When his parents learned of his living with the girlfriend and had little reaction, Mr. B was very puzzled. Then his mother had a cyst removed from her urethra, and a Pap smear report was suggestive of pre-cancerous changes. Although Mr. B realized that the mother's problem was very treatable and there was little cause for alarm, he became quite concerned that she would die soon, and that he had caused her problem by his birth. When his exaggerated concern about mother's death was interpreted in light of his past experience with grandmother, the patient responded with less of a masochistic regression in his behavior.

SUMMARY AND THE FINAL COURSE OF THE ANALYSIS

In summary, this paper was written to show how the material in an ongoing analysis reflected aspects of the Grandparent Syndrome described by Rappaport. In the unfolding of the analysis, it was revealed that the analysand had a strong identification with his grandmother, intensified by her being a dominant force in his household as well as by the fact that he felt responsible for her death. Pre-oedipal regression was evident in the analysand's fear of powerful female figures. Oedipal wishes were split into a desire for both mother and grandmother; and the interest in the grandmother at certain times served as a defense against the more threatening oedipal wishes for mother. In the childhood situation of being the only child in a family of three adults, the analysand had developed a complicated pattern of maneuvering to try to be the favorite of each of the three adult figures (see Arlow's comments about "only children" [15]). In the transference, the analyst found himself initially being related to as the critical mother or the abandoning grandmother; only later in the treatment was he feared as the jealous, punishing father and demeaned and ridiculed because of rivalrous feelings.

The major resistances in the first two years of the analysis were the multiple identifications with grandmother and the repression of both all memory of her and the affect connected with her death. Mr. B didn't even remember what his grandmother looked like or when she died, even though she lived with him for ten years. Gradually, the identifications were clarified and analyzed; to restate them, they included the wish to be the mother to his girlfriends, brushing his shoulder-length hair with his grandmother's comb, his passive feminine demeanor, his preference to live in old houses, his excessive dieting and vitamins to protect himself from illness, his fear of a heart attack, his prolonged bathing in the morning, his prudishness, and his wrapping himself in a blanket for a coat. Along with these identifications, there was the wish to repeat the experience of being with grandmother both in and out of the transference. For example, Mr. B chose to live with a much older girlfriend sick with diabetes, and then he lived beside an elderly woman in a duplex; he expected the analyst to condemn him for his sexuality, and he enjoyed the smell of sausage in the mornings outside the analyst's office, which was just like his mornings with grandmother when she fixed him sausage.

With the analysis of the identifications and repetitions, Mr. B began to vividly recall the circumstances of grandmother's death and to experience the strong affects of guilt, remorse, grief, and anger, which he had suppressed after her death.

During the third and fourth year of analysis, Mr. B spoke less and less of his grandmother and when she did come to his thoughts, his affects were less intense. More vivid memories were gradually recovered of her face, body, style of dress and of her demands for cleanliness and prudishness. In these areas, he remembered her scolding both his mother and himself. The recovery of the memories of her scolding him and his mother came after he himself had been very critical of a colleague having sex with a co-worker.

A reaction to the analyst's decision to change offices also included a strong fear of being abandoned as he'd been with his grandmother, but Mr. B soon analyzed this and his reaction was modified.

Also, his internalized mother imago was split into "good" grandmother and "bad" mother initially with vague good qualities of grandmother being allowed into consciousness and leaving the mother as a bad, demeaned image. For example, grandmother gave him presents and fed him good food, but mother fed him only what she thought he should eat and expected him to always behave perfectly and gave him presents that she liked regardless of what he liked or wanted.

All in all, the Grandparent Syndrome in Mr. B included the repetition of the grandmother experience with the analyst and with others, identification with grandmother in Mr. B's actions and in his object relations, the repression of memories of his grandmother, the splitting of the mother imago into "good" grandmother and "bad" mother, the fear and disgust of "bad" mother and the projection onto her of all that was bad and weak in himself and his grandmother, the displacement of oedipal wishes from mother to grandmother as a defense to lessen the intensity of the oedipal wishes for mother, and the separation anxiety and guilt over his omnipotent power to kill grandmother condensed with oedipal anxiety and castration fears.

CONCLUSION

The analysis continued for a total of six years. In the last two years Mr. B was functioning at a high level in the world outside of analysis. He had a steady girlfriend with whom he was comfortable and successful sexually (and whom he later married), got along well with his colleagues, was assertive at work, and took on more leadership responsibilities.

In the analytic situation in the termination phase the patient was enraged and dismissive toward the analyst. He blamed the analyst for putting him through unnecessary suffering and for being unfair, sadistic, and selfish when he raised his fee after the patient's financial situation improved in life. He said that the analyst was cold and dismissive toward him and put forth little help to comfort him. He cried and sobbed for weeks on end as he remembered and recounted again and again the pain of his childhood, the coldness of his mother, and the feelings of aloneness and guilt after the death of his grandmother. This left the analyst feeling frustrated, helpless, and concerned that he should somehow soften Mr. B's painful sobbing and rage; gradually, the analyst felt more like an empathic silent companion to Mr. B in his grief. Mr. B was enraged at his father for his passivity and failure to protect him from his mother's dismissive and hostile attitude toward him as a child and not talking to him about the death of his grandmother or getting him professional help as a child.

The analyst interpreted Mr. B's feelings toward him as intensified by the reliving of his past in the regression of the analytic situation. The analyst was experienced intermittently as the mother, the grandmother and/or the father and, also, the patient treated the analyst as he, himself, had been treated in the past. (Kernberg [16] has described the concept of the "activation of internalized object relationships" in which the patient may interchange positions in the activation of the old relationships in the present with the analyst.)

Eventually Mr. B and the analyst felt he had worked through much of his conflict and grief in the analysis, and he was more and more able to do the analytic work himself. (Schlessinger and Robbins [17] have described the formation and internalizing of "self-soothing" and "self- analyzing" functions as primary goals in analysis.)

After he and the analyst agreed on his termination date for a day in October, Mr. B worked intensely in the treatment up to the last day, and, on the last day of treatment, he was startled to remember that this day—he thought he had chosen it mainly to overlap with the day of a concert by his favorite band the Grateful Dead—was actually the anniversary day of his grandmother's death!

In the final sessions Mr. B was tearful and joyful and expressed much appreciation to the analyst for the work they had done together.

Several years passed with no contact. Then one day Mr. B called to ask to come in again to consult with the analyst. His father was dying, and he was overcome with grief. As the only child with no extended family, he had been the only resource of help for his aging parents, who were also only children. Arlow (15) has written about the unique dynamics and concerns of only children in the past and the guilt they may harbor because of "secretly" relishing their special position. Mr. B's family members and he himself were all only children. For Mr. B it meant when everyone died he was the sole survivor and alone.

The analyst saw Mr. B for a few sessions during this time. The love and empathy he felt for his father was striking in contrast to the rage and anger that had been expressed in the past. Then he left again and a few more years passed before he returned once more to see the analyst when his mother was dying. As with his father, he was deeply grieving for his mother, and when she died, he felt a tremendous sense of love for her and loss. He was by then married, but he felt alone in terms of his past and his childhood. Talking to the analyst helped him feel more in touch with his past and with someone who knew his whole story; he felt it also helped him to grieve the past and to move forward with his life.*

After several sessions another warm goodbye was said, and Mr. B departed.

BIBLIOGRAPHY

(1) JONES, ERNEST. (1913) "The Significance of Grandfather for the Fate of the Individual," *Papers on Psychoanalysis,* 3rd edition, pp. 688–696.

(2) ABRAHAM, KARL. (1913) "Some Remarks on the Role of the Grandparents in the Psychopathology of Neurosis," *Clinical Papers and Essays on Psychoanalysis,* Vol. II. New York: Basic Books, 1955, pp. 44–47.

(3) FERENZI, SANDOR. (1913) "The Grandfather Complex," in *Further Contributions to the Theory of Psychoanalysis,* New York: Basic Books, pp. 323–324.

(4) ABRAHAM, KARL. (1912) "Amenhotep" IV: A Psychoanalytic Contribution Toward the Understanding of His Personality and the Monotheistic Cult of Aton," in *Selected Papers of Karl Abraham,* Vol. 2, 1955 Ed.

(5) FREUD, SIGMUND. (1909) "Analysis of a Phobia in a Five Year Old Boy," in *The Std Ed of the Complete Psych Works of Sigmund Freud,* ed. J. Strachey, Vol. X. 1955 Ed.

(6) RAPPAPORT, ERNEST A. (1958) "The Grandparent Syndrome," *Psychoanalytic Quarterly,* pp. 518–538.

(7) LaBARRE, MARIANNE B., JESSNER, LUCILLE, & USSERY, LOH. (1960) "The Significance of Grandmother in the Psychopathology of Children," *American Journal of Othopsychiatry,* 30:175–185.

(8) ERIKSON, ERIK. (1959) "Identity and the Life Cycle," *Psychological Issues,* 1, No. 1.

(9) PARKER, GORDON. (1956) "The Little Nell Complex—An Oedipal Variant," *Australian and New Zealand Journal of Psychiatry,* 10:275.

(10) MARUI, K. (1935) "The Process of Introjection in Melancholia," *International Journal of Psychoanalysis,* 16:49–58.

(11) BAK, ROBERT C. (1953) "Fetishism," *J.A.P.A.,* 1:285–298.

*Baker (18) says that in successful mourning objects are not so much "detached from" as positively embraced. This seems more the case with Mr. B and his parents and, maybe, even later on, with his grandmother.

Anzieu (19) says that guilty feelings and a grieving patient's wish for punishment can create more motive for the development of a negative therapeutic reaction. This may have happened to some degree the last two years of treatment, but the alliance was strong and the patient eventually worked through these feelings states. Mr. B's return to the analyst for connection while grieving for his father and mother might have reflected his seeking out the constancy of the analyst and the analytic situation, particularly in his state of being alone and being the only child with no other relatives.

(12) FREEMAN, DAVID. (1977) Personal Communication.

(13) PELLER, LILLY. (1954) "Libidinal Phases, Ego Development and Play," *Psychoanalytic Study of the Child,* 9:178–199.

(14) TYSON, ROBERT. (1983) "Some Narcissistic Consequences of Object Loss: A Developmental View," *Psychoanalytic Quarterly,* 52:205–224.

(15) ARLOW, J. (1972) "The Only Child," *Psychoanalytic Quarterly,* 41:507–536.

(16) KERNBERG, OTTO. (1988) "Object Relations Theory in Clinical Practice," *Psychoanalytic Quarterly,* 57:481.

(17) SCHLESSINGER N., & ROBBINS F. (1974) "Assessment and Follow-up in Psychoanalysis," *J.A.P.A.,* 22:542.

(18) BAKER, J. E. (2001) "Mourning and Transformation of Object Relations," *Psychoanalytic Psychology,* 18Z; 55–73.

(19) ANZIEU, D. (1987) "Alterations of the Ego Which Make Analysis Interminable," *International Journal of Psychoanalysis,* 68:9–19.

THE CHILD ANALYST
AT WORK

Anna, Leaving Home—An Adolescent Girl's Journey

Rachel G. Seidel, M.D.

The author presents an in-depth exploration of psychoanalytic process from her work with Anna, a young woman in treatment from age 15 through her 18th birthday, when she left for college. Anna came to treatment with attachment problems and bulimic symptoms embedded in her character structure, the deformation of which had impaired relationships and disrupted developmental processes. A noteworthy aspect of Anna's analysis is a treatment resistance that repeated early issues of abandonment and loss, and that allowed the analyst to experience the centrality of Anna's sadomasochistic relatedness. As this material is analyzed, an erotized transference emerges in which Anna both longs for and fears a special intimacy with her analyst. Talented at working and playing in the transference, Anna is able to use the transference to remember her early life, to learn to experience and tolerate a range of affects, and to explore old and new kinds of attachments. Psychoanalysis helps to put developmental processes back

Faculty, Boston Psychoanalytic Society and Institute, Boston, Massachusetts; Practicing Child, Adolescent and Adult Psychoanalyst, Cambridge, Massachusetts.

Shorter versions of this paper were presented first as a Plenary paper at the meeting of the Association for Child Psychoanalysis, Tampa, Florida, in March 2005, and then as part of a panel at the Conference of the International Psychoanalytical Association, Rio de Janeiro, Brazil, in July 2005. A revised version of this paper was given as The Beata Rank Lecture on May 24, 2006, at The Boston Psychoanalytic Society and Institute, Boston, Massachusetts.

The author wishes to thank Drs. Sarah Birss, Ruth Karush, and Judy Yanof for their careful readings and thoughtful comments. Dr. Steven Ablon has been an invaluable consultant.

The Psychoanalytic Study of the Child 61, ed. Robert A. King, Peter B. Neubauer, Samuel Abrams, and A. Scott Dowling (Yale University Press, copyright © 2006 by Robert A. King, Peter B. Neubauer, Samuel Abrams, and A. Scott Dowling).

Rachel G. Seidel

on track and results in significant intrapsychic and interpersonal change, allowing Anna to separate and to leave home.

INTRODUCTION

I AM GOING TO TELL YOU ABOUT ANNA, A REMARKABLE, INTELLIGENT adolescent who was in psychoanalysis with me for three years. Though Anna and I worked on many issues during the course of her treatment, my focus in this paper will be on the vicissitudes of separation as they were expressed in her life and explored in her analysis.

Most often, by late adolescence, a teenager is sad and somewhat anxious but also eager to leave home. What are the psychological developments starting in infancy and leading up to mid-adolescence which, when accomplished in a "good enough"[1] fashion, permit an adolescent to separate from home in a relatively uncomplicated way? To answer in one way, in order to separate psychologically and leave home, a teenager needs to start from a secure attachment base, then to individuate[2,3], that is, to have an established sense of self[4] and a reasonably consolidated identity[5,6]. Stated in a more phenomenological way, she needs both the capacity for good affect tolerance in order to manage the increased libidinal and aggressive drives accompanying puberty, and also the ability to sublimate those drives and neutralize conflicts related to primary objects.[7] In some instances, however, when leaving home is an issue—as it was in Anna's case— an adolescent may also need both insight-oriented and developmental help[8] in order to be able to take this basic and necessary step into young adulthood.

1. Winnicott, D. W. (1965) *The Maturational Process and the Facilitating Environment.* New York: International Universities Press.

2. Mahler, M. (1975) *The Psychological Birth of the Human Infant: Symbiosis and Individuation.* New York: Basic Books.

3. Blos, P. (1962) *On Adolescence.* New York: Free Press.

4. Kohut, H. (1971) *The Analysis of the Self.* New York: International Universities Press.

5. Erikson, E. (1959) *Identity and the Life Cycle.* New York: W. W. Norton.

6. Stern, D. (1985) *The Interpersonal World of the Infant: A View from Psychoanalysis and Developmental Psychology.* New York: Basic Books.

7. Freud, S. (1905 [1953]) "Three Essays on the Theory of Sexuality," *S.E.* 7. London: Hogarth Press.

8. Hurry, A., ed. (1999) *Psychoanalysis and Developmental Therapy* , Monograph Series of the Psychoanalytic Unit of University College, London and the Anna Freud Centre, London, No. 3. New York: International Universities Press.

Anna Freud[9] wrote that the regressive and dependent pulls of psychoanalysis run counter to the strong developmental push toward action and independence in adolescence. In my work with Anna, this push was expressed dramatically in a resistance that developed during our early analytic work and required sensitivity and technical patience to resolve. Separations and reunions—with their power to evoke early attachment issues—gave us ample opportunities to learn about the many impediments to Anna's leave-taking, and so all my clinical material is taken from sessions before or after separations. As I hope to show, in Anna's case, psychoanalysis permitted a re-working of her capacity for relatedness and seemed to facilitate the process of separation, perhaps because Anna was able to work out her issues in the transference.

ANNA

Anna's treatment began when she was 15 years 2 months old, just before the beginning of her sophomore year in high school, and ended soon after her 18th birthday, when she left for college. Initially, she was referred to me for problems with anxiety, depression, and bulimia. As we soon learned, however, for Anna, the biggest issue was that of forming new age-appropriate attachments, both social and sexual, and detaching from primary objects. In this essential developmental task of adolescence, Anna was hampered by the internalization of a complicated nexus of relationships in her family—including difficulties in her earliest attachment to her mother and complexities in the triangular situation of the oedipal period.[10]

INITIAL MEETINGS

Anna's parents were urgently concerned about their daughter's struggles around food and her dislike of her body. They described her as irritable and depressed, competitive and unable to maintain friendships, problems that had existed at least since late latency. Her perfectionism and drive to excel at school caused Anna great anxiety which she could not contain. Her parents, in turn, either felt over-

9. Freud, A. (1958) "Adolescence," *PSC,* 13: 255–278. New Haven: Yale University Press.

10. Lothane, Z. American Psychoanalytic Association Open-line (listserve) communication, August 14, 2003. "The oedipal situation is first and foremost a social reality, a nexus of relationships in the triangular situation of the child, both parents, and siblings."

whelmed by her outbursts or entered into sadomasochistic struggles with her.

Anna's parents provided little historical information about Anna or their family. Instead, they pressed me to see their child the very next day. I noticed that I felt as if they had abandoned Anna to me, and I thought this was an interesting way to begin, with important issues concerning dependency and abandonment already affectively available.

I found Anna to be a very attractive mid-adolescent girl with feminine curves and an expressive face. She was warm and friendly, engaging me robustly with her eyes as well as with her feelings and words. Sitting in the chair closest to me, Anna spoke eloquently about her life and her relationships, especially about her conflicts with her family and about her difficulties with friends. She told me of a period the previous summer of food restriction that led to significant weight loss and temporary cessation of menstruation, and I noted that this anorexia had occurred at the time of a first sexual exploration. Now Anna engaged in bingeing and purging.

FAMILY HISTORY

Anna was the second and last child—two years younger than her sister—born to older parents. Anna spoke of her parents' marriage as highly conflictual, held together by sexual activity and passionate arguments, both of which were open knowledge in the family. Anna's father was a successful professional and an avid athlete. He told of coming from a family with a father who was "lost" to him due to serious depression and a mother who was narcissistic, critical, and controlling. He saw himself as like his mother, "a bear to live with," and described his own alternating cycles of being sadistic on the one hand, and guilty, contrite, remorseful, on the other. Anna's mother, also highly educated, nevertheless had difficulty finding work and progressing in her career. In regard to her family of origin, Anna's mother told me she experienced her father as very critical of her and her mother as hostile or absent.

Though there were times when Anna felt a physical and even an emotional closeness with her mother, I learned later that Anna more often experienced her own mother as similarly hostile or absent. For example, she recounted angrily that she was left in full-time daycare from the age of two months. She also told me about wetting her bed at night into early adolescence in what I thought of as a bid for maternal attention and care[11] that was only partly successful; as Anna remembered it, her mother responded to her enuresis by putting a towel over the wet area, or simply by leaving Anna to change the bed linens alone.

While an anxious primary attachment to her mother and sexual overstimulation were issues for Anna, an additional complication was the fact that her father had become her primary nurturer as well as her oedipal love object. He took Anna to medical appointments and to shop for clothes; the latter included showing Anna catalogues with photos of models wearing lingerie. He also shopped for food and prepared most meals, intruding into Anna's eating habits and problems in a sadistic manner, for example, by humiliating Anna with empty food cartons taken from the trash as evidence of her eating binges. Anna was initially unaware of the ways in which she also invited her father to engage with her in this passionate and hurtful way.

PSYCHOANALYTIC PSYCHOTHERAPY

While everyone in this family appeared to be relationally hungry, it seemed to me that Anna was starving. This word *starving*—as it came to be used by Anna and me—proved to be a helpful metaphor in the early stages of our work, allowing Anna to move from blaming her parents and socio-cultural pressures (external) to exploring her mental life (internal), from focusing solely on her concretized issues with food and weight to examining the complex realm of her emotions and attachments, a play space[12,13,14], which gave us much more room and food for thought.

Though I felt psychotherapy was beginning to prove helpful to her, Anna let me know that she continued to have difficulties at school and at home. In sessions, I observed that Anna had trouble tolerating anxiety. Such was the case, for example, when—after beginning to talk about sexual feelings and her first sexual experiences of the previous summer—she came late or missed sessions entirely. At the

11. Winnicott, D. W. (1956) "The Antisocial Tendency," *Through Pediatrics to Psychoanalysis*. New York: Basic Books, 1975: 306–321.

12. Freud, S. (1914), "Remembering, Repeating and Working Through," *S.E.* 12.

13. Meares, R. (1992) "Transference and the Play Space—Toward a New Basic Metaphor," *Contemp. Psychoanal.*, 28: 32–49.

14. Gill, M. (1985) "The Interactional Aspect of Transference," in *The Transference in Psychoanalysis: Clinical Management*, ed. E. A. Schwaber, New York: International Universities Press.

same time, however, after a few months of working together twice weekly, Anna let me know that she wanted to see me more often, and I found that I welcomed this wish. I felt she needed intensive treatment in order to prepare for psychological separation from her parents and to be able to leave for college, to create and maintain intimate relationships, and to build toward a fulfilling career.

Anna explored her feelings about starting psychoanalysis with me and decided to discuss it with her parents. She brought her parents to a meeting with me, and when her father and mother expressed concern about the cost of an analysis, she offered to contribute the majority of what she had earned the previous summer. Though I thought that this unusual willingness to participate in the financing of her psychoanalysis was another example of Anna's premature self-care and internalization of her early deprivation which would also need to be analyzed, I was nevertheless impressed by the depth of Anna's desire, her new-found capacity to speak up for herself, and her success at getting her parents on board. Anna's parents readily accepted her offer to give them a lump sum payment that would be used toward payment of my analytic fees. This arrangement continued over the three years of treatment and derivatives appeared repeatedly in our analytic work.

Anna's Psychoanalysis — The Beginning

By this time, understanding something about how Anna's presenting symptoms were a way of expressing feelings related to deeper and earlier issues, we began Anna's four times weekly psychoanalysis. At this point, Anna was 15 and ½ years old, and in the middle of her sophomore year of high school.

We explored whatever Anna brought to sessions, which at first focused mostly on the feelings and meanings of her symptoms, including her relationship with food. We began to learn more about her problems with her parents, and how the same difficulties she encountered with them were repeated in her friendships. For instance, she often seemed self-sufficient to her peers, while actually feeling lonely, needy, and unlikeable. Fearing rejection and abandonment on the one hand, and coercion on the other, Anna repeated familiar sadomasochistic/dependent patterns of relating with friends and family alike.

One healthy development—though it may also have been an expression of her ambivalence about getting closer to me—was finding her way into a first intimate and sexual relationship with Bob, a kind and sensitive male classmate. While Anna welcomed discussions about birth control and relished sharing with me delight in her sexual explorations, she also felt stimulated and ashamed when it came to talking with me about the details of her sexual experiences and fantasies.

During the summer, as her sister prepared to leave for college, Anna felt abandoned and angry. Mobilized perhaps by counter-dependent defenses, she expressed some independence by obtaining a driver learner's permit and also by beginning to resist her growing dependency on me. Anna asked for schedule changes and then missed sessions when I disappointed her. In a way that was reminiscent of her relationship with her mother, she was demanding more of me and felt angry when I couldn't give it. I understood that there were early contributions to this defense against longings for someone reliable in her life, which we needed to analyze. However, developmentally, her conflicted wish to depend on someone like me also interplayed with her appropriate and growing need to separate, individuate, and become more autonomous in preparation for leaving home, a development which I felt I also needed to support.

As so often happens in adolescent treatments with so much put into action[15], Anna managed these feelings and anxieties by arriving late and missing sessions more frequently. I noticed feeling frustrated that we had so little time to work on this resistance before my vacation, confused by all the projections coming my way, hurt and angry that Anna threatened to abandon me this way. In fact, I was aware of wishing to force her to stay. Anna likened our encounters at this time to "mother-daughter fights." While I understood that this type of engagement—a repetition in the treatment of the sadomasochistic interactions Anna also invited outside the consulting room—was part of the transference/countertransference mix, I believe Anna was sensitive to the anger I was working, with difficulty, to metabolize. My very attempts to help her analyze her actions were felt as coercive, as you will see in the analytic hour that follows, which took place after a cancellation and just before our first summer break.

The session began with Anna referring to a phone message she had left for me in which she had requested a schedule change. Anna said, "You got my message yesterday? I was really hoping you could change the time—it doesn't seem fair of me. I felt disappointed but quickly tried to psyche myself into thinking it would be OK." Anna's

15. Chused, J. (1990) "Neutrality in the Analysis of Action-Prone Adolescents," *J. Amer. Psychoanal. Assn.*, 38: 679–704.

Rachel G. Seidel

self-reflection, "It doesn't seem fair of me," evoked my empathy and I stayed with her affect, hoping to help her deepen it. I said, "You were disappointed." A bit later she complained, "Everybody's always asking me to change my schedule for them."

I believe I was hoping to expand our space for reflection when I replied, "I notice that there are a lot of strong feelings between us. I wonder if it has anything to do with my going away soon." Anna said, "Maybe it is because you're going away again. Again I do feel like I don't want to come so often—it's really not worth it—I have to bend over backwards for something I don't feel so good about." This phrase sounded promising to me, so body-based and evoking sado-masochistic trends. I repeated, "Mm, bend over backwards," after which Anna associated, "What comes to mind is going to grandma's when I don't want to, because she needs it." Then she expressed her feelings toward me directly: "I'm coming here for you, not me, to prove something to you. I am again thinking how much is it worth it? I feel kind of powerless—you're the authority, you surprise me by how much you understand, but there's part of my life I don't think you understand. If you could grasp the full scope of my life then you wouldn't feel I have to come as often. Looking ahead is really, really nerve-wracking. I could come twice per week and then I wouldn't have this relationship with you where we go deeper."

I felt relieved to glimpse the anxiety underlying her anger, and to have an opportunity to expand our understanding. I said, "Oh, I see, this relationship with me where we go deeper—perhaps that's what these feelings are about. Getting closer brings up a deep anxiety and you want to get away from it, see me less often."

Anna then went on to relate the following dream: "I went to my pediatrician and my blood pressure was skyrocketing. They did some tests and found I had 'Stress Syndrome,' and she called you up and said I couldn't come here anymore."

Anna associated to her anorexia of the previous summer and then to the stress of having me go away. She blamed me and psychoanalysis for her illness, "Stress Syndrome." My attempt to speak to her anger at me and how that frightened her felt to Anna like an attempt to make her stay. I told Anna that I thought she felt I didn't care about her. She replied, "Or only in an experimental way. I might pay the price of 'Stress Syndrome,' but that seems secondary to you." I played with this projection of me as sadistic analyst and wondered aloud why I might want that. Anna thought of a famous therapist who traumatized orphans in order to make them stutter so that he could study them. She declared angrily, "You've adopted psychoanalysis as your religion! It's unbelievable to you that I could value other things above that. This analysis is what has become a center of my life!"

I thought that Anna's anger served partly as a defense against feeling sad and abandoned in anticipation of my approaching August break and I said, "I'm going away. It feels like I don't make you the center of my life, but I insist you make your psychoanalysis and me the center of your life." For a while, she continued expressing—and I continued clarifying—her anger and disappointment. Then she softened and said more plaintively, "You're going away; I'm feeling neglected. You're almost like this god and I've built my whole life around you, and you go away, and I realize how alone I am."

I felt moved by her sadness and saw that we had been able to penetrate her anger and to approach the deeper feelings of loss she had been defending against. Anna agreed that my going away left her feeling starved, uncared for, like an orphan. Through her dream and her associations, she had begun to tell me how difficult our relationship—with all that it evoked about her confusing relationships with her parents—had become for her.

Her need to extricate herself from the pressures of the transference relationship with me was reminiscent of her conflicted wishes for care from her mother and for independence from her father, both of whom she also loved passionately. In a way, this need was expressed during the time we were apart when Anna broke up with her boyfriend, Bob, who had gone on vacation without her. Bob had abandoned her, her sister had abandoned her by leaving for college, her father by going abroad and, of course, I had been away. We had all left her. Anna's response to the abandonment included her retaliatory rejection and abandonment of Bob. I realized that she was also engaged in enacting[16,17] something like this with me.

This resistance, which evolved after the summer break into a demand to cut back her sessions to one per week, took some time to be worked through. At first, Anna couldn't or wouldn't work with any interpretations or clarifications, was too immersed in her adolescence and her need for autonomy, too frightened by her anger at my having left her. Since she couldn't yet analyze the resistance, I understood that I needed to protect the alliance even if she had to cut back for now: It was better for me not to struggle with her over it, but to let

16. Jacobs, T. (1986) "On Countertransference Enactments," *J. Amer. Psychoanal. Assn.,* 34: 289–307.
17. Chused, J. (1991) "The Evocative Power of Enactments," *J. Amer. Psychoanal. Assn.,* 39: 615–639.

it unfold.[18] I knew that she was attached to me, and I believed we might eventually be able to analyze the resistance together.

Over time, I heard that she had been terribly hurt, had deep feelings about my being away: that I didn't care about her, that she was better off on her own—perhaps a repetition of feelings from the first years of life, feelings of worthlessness and of being incapable of holding her object's interest and love.[19] These few months seemed iconic for so many experiences with her passive mother and sadistic father. She wished I could've been—could still be—her mom. It seemed progressive for her that I neither left her in day care (so to speak), nor passively accepted that she came to sessions less often, but that I treasured and appreciated her, tolerated her anger at me, and continued to work with her to understand her withdrawal from her analysis and from me.

Perhaps because of my interpretations or perhaps because I had let her know she was important to me, Anna was able to express positive feelings for me. She also let me know about her progress and growing independence. Still saddened that she wasn't doing well with friends, however, Anna began to think about returning to her analysis four times per week. Gradually, the resistance was worked through, attended by a strengthened alliance. After two months of once weekly analytic work, Anna returned to four times weekly psychoanalysis.

ANNA'S PSYCHOANALYSIS — THE MIDDLE

Anna's second year in analysis was notable for a deepening capacity to remember her early life and a growing ability to work to understand it and how it continued to affect her. This, her junior year in high school, was also marked by a general decrease in symptoms and an increase in autonomous activity. She spent less time at home and engaged in fewer battles with her parents. She reached out to different groups at school and was deeply involved in its intellectual and social life.

Anna pursued several younger, sexually aggressive male athletes at school and became sexually involved with some of them. Often these relationships repeated the sadomasochistic dynamics related to oedi-

18. Sandler, J. (1976) "Countertransference and Role-Responsiveness," *Int. R. Psycho-Anal.*, 3: 43–47.
19. Barros, I. (2005) from the Discussion of the shorter version of this paper, given in Brazil.

pal aspects of her relationship with her athletic father. As with her father, not infrequently, she wound up feeling disappointed, narcissistically injured, rejected, and enraged. During this time, Anna also retrieved an early memory of having intruded on her parents during intercourse, which she now envisioned as her father raping her mother. Anna and I came to understand something about how her interest in the young men was multi-determined: In engaging with them sexually, Anna was both enacting something to do with her transgressive longings for her father while also playing out a masochistic identification with her mother. In time, some of these issues about boundaries and differences also arose in the transference, as I shall soon describe.

Having worked well in advance of this summer vacation to understand all that my pending absence evoked, Anna decided that she would come to see me for June and July, thereby both depending on me and tolerating my leaving in August. For her last sessions before the summer break, Anna was able to say directly that she felt angry and abandoned "in my time of need, not having figured everything out, eating too much when I'm at home and making myself throw-up [a return of symptoms after a period without bulimia]. It'll feel like our relationship will be gone, a friend or a family member, whichever you are at the moment; thinking I'll feel depressed without you to talk to."

At home, the bathroom was located next door to her parents' bedroom, and Anna reported that she thought of "doing it" with her parents in the next room. On the surface, by "doing it," she intended throwing up, but I heard these words, "doing it," also as sexualized, reminding me of Anna's overstimulating awareness of her parents' intercourse. I wondered whether the reappearance of her (in/out) bulimia at this point was not only an ambivalent request for care, but also a symptom[20] representing anxiety about primal scene fantasies.[21,22,23] I thought this anxiety was related to sexual feelings toward me in the transference.

Anna wondered if her parents would stop her or confront her afterward. I wondered if, by showing up late, Anna was both reproaching me for being about to leave her and showing me she wanted something more from me. Now able to work with early memories

20. Freud, S. (1926) "Inhibitions, Symptoms and Anxiety," *S.E.* 20.
21. Freud, S. (1905) "The Three Essays on Sexuality," *S.E.* 7.
22. Esman, H. (1973) "The Primal Scene," *PSC*, 28: 49–81, New Haven: Yale University Press.
23. Blum, H. & Isay, R. (1978) "The Pathogenicity of the Primal Scene," *J. Amer. Psychoan. Assn.*, 26: 131–142.

and to play with them in the transference, Anna said, "maybe I want you to say, 'I'm not gonna go on this vacation; I'll come with you so I can know that you're OK,' set up one of those baby monitors so you could listen to me all the time." I responded, "I think you want to know if I care about you and, if I do, why would I go away from you?" This seemed to give her permission to explore further, "Yeah, and you get paid to see me! It's disgusting, but I think of prostitutes who do it for the money." There was that expression "do it" again: Prostitutes "do it" for money. Do I only "do it" with her for the money? I thought that this association was connected to giving her father the gift of a coin collection and whatever that might mean on a fantasy level about unconscious wishes for exchange or intercourse between them, but it was certainly also connected to her fantasies about the meaning of the contribution from her earnings toward payment of my fee.

In tandem with the incestuously based yearnings for me, Anna expected that I would find her "disgusting" and eminently rejectable. She gave examples of ways in which she found herself annoying or uninteresting and thought that I might, too. I thought about the defensive aspect of this line of thinking, and saw it as a way of warding off a longed for but intolerable, perhaps sexual, closeness with me.

Anna had developed a new capacity to express and discuss the complexities of her feelings, and she spoke to her issues concerning intimacy even before I could: "I get awkward and shy, not wanting to face up to the caring feelings; if we are just doctor and patient, there's only so far our relationship can go. It really is hard when someone shows they care about me. I have a dream of being close, but don't want to do it when the opportunity comes. I kinda like it when people can do just as well without me—it's kind of a predicament." As Anna was aware, it was almost time to end this last meeting before our summer break. She continued, "I come back to thinking about good-bye. I stopped and just saw you there—this is about us. I don't want to get into anything; I'm afraid I'd just be left hanging." The feelings of longing and sadness, fear of rejection and loss hung heavy for a few moments. It was very rich, full of her early wishes for her parents and her increasingly complex feelings for me.

ANNA'S ANALYSIS — THE FINAL YEAR, TERMINATION

While issues relating to separation were woven throughout Anna's analysis, they became particularly prominent and affectively alive in the transference during our final year of working together, her senior year of high school.

This was an eventful and stressful time in Anna's life. While, to some degree, all adolescents count on body integrity and utilize fantasies of invulnerability in order to face a frightening world, Anna's adolescent defenses were severely challenged when she was diagnosed with a serious chronic medical illness initially expressed in the form of musculo-skeletal pain and fatigue. While Anna responsibly pursued a full and lengthy medical work-up, we continued to work analytically with the associations evoked by her body's vulnerability and with her efforts to find or make meaning of this sudden impingement on her health and psychological development: She wondered, for example, if her illness was a result of her bulimia or of her sexual activities.

In addition, Anna's physical weakness and pain redoubled the regressive, dependent longings for care which had preceded this condition, and which also now accompanied it. In the past, Anna had often enacted these wishes, for instance, by delaying getting her driver's license so that she continued to need her parents to bring her to school and to appointments. By this time, however, Anna took greater responsibility for herself—including obtaining her driver's license—and used her analysis as a place to explore her regressive fantasies, such as imagining herself in a wheelchair, helpless and totally dependent upon her parents who would now be forced to be her caretakers. The sadomasochistic elements of this fantasy were salient: Though Anna masochistically and passively suffered her illness, her need for care was understood as a sadistic demand on her parents, a retaliation for their failures.

In the arena of her family life, although Anna had been aware of problems in her parents' marriage from an early age, during this last year of high school, the discovery of an infidelity resulted in a parental separation, and Anna's mother moved to a town some distance away. I thought that it was not insignificant that Anna's parents' marriage dissolved and Anna's mother became more distant just as Anna was preparing to separate and leave home. Old and partly unresolved yearnings for a special relationship with her father were revived alongside the old longings for nurturance. Moreover, living with her father and seeing him become involved in new relationships once again evoked rage toward him, and jealousy of the women as well as some attempts at identifying with them.

Although a revival of any of these symptoms, feelings, and wishes might have been expectable during the termination year of Anna's analysis, the impact of Anna's illness and of her parents' separation cannot be denied. It is to Anna's credit that, even in this rocky sea with its regressive currents, Anna worked hard to understand herself and was able to hold her developmental course.

Perhaps partly as a result of the regressive pulls created by Anna's illness and by her parents' marital separation, but also because Anna was committed to the work we were doing, Anna considered several times the idea of staying at home and continuing to see me after graduation. Although I felt that we might still have more to do by the end of the year, and I would have liked her to stay in town so we could continue, I also thought that it would be developmentally progressive for her to try to be on her own. Ultimately, it was Anna's decision to make, and Anna decided that she really wanted, and felt ready, to go.

I felt sad that Anna planned to go away for college, but my growing attunement and knowledge of Anna's inner world made this final year of our work go more smoothly. Worrying less about abandonment and, therefore, needing less to do battle, Anna accepted her wish to be close to me and tolerated the complementary sadness of leaving. We worked together to attend to Anna's multiple and simultaneous losses, and to mourn the pending loss of our analytic relationship. This work was rich in affect, associations, and insight, and very moving for both of us, as I hope to show you in the clinical material that follows from the middle of our final year, just after a two-week break.

Anna, now 17 and ½ years old, began a session by reviewing the various relationships she'd be leaving soon. She worried about what would happen to our relationship. She let herself imagine it: "We wouldn't see each other or remember each other, or when we did, it would be so long since the last time. Partly it's resentment, hard things to deal with, it's inevitable. When two people are apart—with you, even a week makes a difference. You're still my analyst, unless we become friends, but I don't know if that would be helpful. Maybe I'd want to see you during school breaks; being friends might ruin that. There'd be lengths of time that would go by that would feel like only 'mine,' but when I see you often it feels like 'our' time. You were away for two weeks; that feels like an 'unknown' time."

I felt that she was talking about all that she had missed as a young child, and I said feelingly, "It felt like a time when I didn't know you." Anna exclaimed with anger: "There were fifteen years you didn't know me! Those two weeks you were away, you didn't see me; it's just me re-telling to you." I heard this as a reproach for not having been present earlier in her life, but also as a worry about the reliability of her evocative memory, and I said, "you worry that, being apart from me, I won't know you and maybe you won't know me." I felt very moved when Anna responded, "I'm realizing how important seeing you is in my life—it's huge."

Anna started to think about the progress she'd made and what had not yet been done. Now good at self-reflection and freer in her associations, Anna began another session on a familiar note: "I didn't feel like coming to analysis today," but then Anna reflected, "I'm wondering why. I thought: only a few more months before I go away to college. Wouldn't it be good to come as much as possible? Yeah, I thought about the importance of seeing you. I guess I enjoy seeing you every day, well four times each week. But I really think I'm quite good at being my own therapist now. Wondering what you think about where I am now. I have been a bit depressed. I hate to ask you what you think. Maybe I shouldn't come so often. I don't want to be offensive, but this is your business. I hate thinking that—it's like my dad in my head. This is your livelihood. I notice I have my jacket on. [Takes it off] I guess I feel vulnerable. I also question my own not wanting to come, because I'll feel very vulnerable without that other half of me, which is you; such an important part of my life. But maybe I don't want to see you so many times a day."

I had been following the ebb and flow of her conflicts with interest, but without comment. When I heard Anna's parapraxis, I felt it was time to interpret. I said, "I hear your slip: You said you don't want to see me so many times a day. Maybe partly you'd like to see me 24/7— it's the other side of wanting to slow down, see me less. I understand that you feel vulnerable with and without your other half, me, and you might want to dilute all the different feelings you have towards me, so you wouldn't miss that other half so much when you leave, so it wouldn't be so painful."

Anna was able to work with this interpretation. "I'm conflicted," she said. "I'm thinking about the process of leaving. This relationship is like a fantasy, a lie; it's not like I have a friend in you. You're an adult and I'm not. We don't share things like me and my friends do, and we don't see each other outside this room. But I feel closer to you than I do to my parents! When I talk with them or with friends, you're always in the back of my mind. Maybe it would be an easier way to leave if I could taper the dose of you! What am I gonna do when I don't have you?"

After a long pause, Anna gave voice to a wish, "I would like to hear from you, if you think it's OK to tell me. I think you do have my best interests in mind." Although I did not know precisely what Anna wanted to hear, I understood that it had been hard for her to express this wish. I felt I wanted to give her something of myself in return and thought, in the context of termination, it was appropriate to do so. I spoke about the strong feelings in the room, hers and mine, about our relationship and about her getting ready to leave, thinking about what we've done together and what still remained to be done. I knew that I would miss her. Feelings of sadness and loss emerged and my eyes welled up. Anna teared up, too. It was a very tender, shared "now moment."[24] After a while of sitting with these feelings, I handed her the box of tissues and used a tissue myself.[25] I commented that maybe Anna had needed to see that I had feelings for her, too. Anna agreed, "I think you're right. Seeing emotion from you shows me it is more than fantasy, too."[26]

During this final year of her analysis, Anna elaborated a rich fantasy life about me and showed a growing capacity for a relationship with me. At the same time as developing greater detachment from her parents and increased independence of action and thought, Anna had a fantasy of fusion with me: that I was her other half, her soul-mate, and she expressed poignantly that separation meant a loss of "we-ness." Saying good-bye was very hard; she was angry that I was letting her go. She tried to ward off feelings of loss by imagining a different kind of relationship with me, but realized that she still needed me as her analyst, because—though she had done a lot—she did not feel finished.

A session from before my summer vacation, only a few sessions before our last meeting, began:

> *A:* I didn't feel as much as usual that I wanted to come in today. I'm definitely angry—wish you could stay. I know that time is limited. How do I usually act it out? Partly by spending as much time with you as possible. I don't want to leave with a bad feeling with a person—or maybe I don't want to leave with a good feeling about them, because then I'll be sad. So, I don't want to leave with bad or good feelings!
>
> *Dr:* Maybe not wanting to come in today is about not wanting to have any feelings, good or bad, with me.
>
> *A:* That would be easiest. Maybe I ration out the feelings: don't want to come on too strong, though I do.

24. Stern, D. et al. (1998) "Non-Interpretive Mechanisms in Psychoanalytic Therapy: The 'Something More' Than Interpretation." *Int. J. Psychoanal.*, 79: 903–921.
25. Sandler, J. *op. cit.*
26. Fonagy, P. (2004) "*Initiating Change Through Change in Psychoanalytic Technique.*" Paper presented on November 5, 2004, at the Scientific Colloquium at the Anna Freud Centre, London.

Dr: You worry about coming on too strong with me.

A: Maybe I don't want someone to have that kind of control over me.

And later that session:

> *A:* I will feel lost. I'm going away in a month. I don't want to start any-thing. I feel attractive and people notice. I don't feel too bad. Really enjoying my life. Maybe it's a way of telling you, "I don't need you, Dr. Seidel," and trying to convince myself that's true. I'll miss you. There's nothing more to explain. [Her cell phone rang] Wonder who phoned me? I know it's not Dr. Seidel calling!
>
> *Dr:* I suppose that's a fantasy.
>
> *A:* [Anna playfully mimicked her end of a superficial phone conversa-tion with me, then said:] I don't want to go through that fake conver-sation! On the phone, you're not you and I'm not me. And what about on-line? IM'ing could be a scary place to go: "Do you want to enlarge your penis size?" like pop-up ads. On the phone, maybe I feel the connection is so fragile. I don't know what people are thinking. Conspiracy theory: They're on the speakerphone at the "I Hate Anna" rally!
>
> *Dr:* You have a fantasy of continuing to talk with me by phone after you go to college, but then you worry what I might be thinking, or that I might hate you and you wouldn't know it. [The reality of Anna's pending departure emerged out of our playfulness and I said with feeling:] Your going is only a few weeks away.
>
> *A:* Oh, God! I got teary when you said that. It's surreal. At times I feel like gripping it—it's not quite real but it's close. The last day, should I wear black for mourning, or dress up? It's not like graduating from high school and getting a diploma, or finishing elementary school and having juice and cupcakes. My temptation is to give you some-thing, a gift or a card. The kid comes back next year to see if the teacher still has it.
>
> *Dr:* You'd want to see if I remember you.

Anna had learned to tolerate her feelings and to put them in per-spective, using humor. She was better able to balance love and hate, and her aggression toward me softened, lost its sadistic edge. I saw my work, at this time, as staying with her affects, especially sad and angry feelings related to loss. She had come to explore the inner workings of her mind, taking on with curiosity and pleasure, the ana-lytic functions of self-observation and reflection. She was more able to sublimate sexual impulses and looked forward to the intellectual pursuits of college. She liked herself better, had established a "good enough" sense of self, and had started to consolidate an identity and to imagine a future that featured interesting work and satisfying rela-tionships, including roles as wife and mother.

POST-ANALYTIC CONTACT

Though Anna had become more ready and able to leave home, I was aware that she was still struggling with oedipal issues which lingered. In addition, to some degree, her earliest feelings of deprivation remained a vulnerability. I had concerns about whether Anna would run into trouble at college and need to return to her analysis. She had similar worries, but felt that she would be able to come home and continue her work with me if necessary.

We thought about what, if any, further treatment Anna might want after leaving for college and considered a referral to a colleague near her college, but Anna was eager to see how she would do on her own. Anna Freud wrote that no one would terminate with a child of her own free will because of the maternal transference.[27] Anna was a very compelling person and her need for care was great; my maternal responsiveness was also great. As a result, we decided that it made sense for us to maintain some sort of contact after termination.

Anna left for college in the fall and came to see me a few times in the months that followed. She let me know that she was doing well, and—with me in mind—doing self-analytic work by "taking time to think" or writing in a journal when she felt unhappy. She told me about two close friendships with young women, and expressed gratitude that her analysis had helped her to make these ties, something she had not been able to accomplish with peers during high school. Though Anna was dating and having sexual experiences with a few men at her college, she was saddened when she saw that old sadomasochistic dynamics re-emerged. As yet unable to create a sexually intimate relationship that was also mutually caring and enduring, she recognized that she still had some issues to work out in this regard, and she thought about whether she'd like to see me intensively again the following summer to work on them.

DISCUSSION

Early in our work together, it became clear that—due to conflicts about autonomy and sexuality—Anna was having considerable trouble loosening the constraining bonds to her parents, developing age-appropriate friendships, exploring sexual relationships, and becoming more independent in preparation for leaving home. We came to

---

27. Freud, A. (1970[1957]) "Termination of Child Analysis," *The Writings of Anna Freud*, VII. New York: International Universities Press, 3–21.

believe that, in these developmental tasks of adolescence, Anna had been derailed by the complications of her early relationships with her parents: Issues with her mother had led to feelings of deprivation and longing as well as to fears of abandonment; in turn, these early impingements upon oedipal longings for her father were further complicated by his additional role as primary nurturer and by pervasive sadomasochistic trends in the family.

A noteworthy, though by no means unique, aspect of Anna's analysis was the prominence of action. I thought of the resistance expressed in the first year by Anna's briefly cutting down to once weekly meetings after my summer vacation surely as an expression of anger at me, but also as an enactment involving anger at her mother for felt abandonments and at her father for what Anna experienced as his sadistic and controlling ways with her. This formulation was important in helping me to tolerate Anna's anger and also mostly to resist countertransference pressures such as my wishing to force her to stay.

Anna developed a talent at working and playing with diverse transferences: maternal, paternal, sibling, grandmaternal, teacher, buddy or best friend,[28] and even Spiderman! Since much of the real work of Anna's analysis was done in the transference, it became possible not only to recognize but also to experience the intensity and centrality of her sadomasochistic relatedness.[29] Anna, who had felt abandoned first by her mother and then by me, threatened to abandon me. Needing to extricate herself from the control of her father who did not want to let her go and, in the transference, from me and the intolerable closeness that analysis brings, Anna wished to cut back the frequency of our meetings so our relationship would not go "deeper." Attempts at clarification and interpretation were felt as persecutory, intrusive, or seductive. As a result, I believe it was helpful technically that I was flexible with Anna and let her cut back so that we were able to maintain an alliance and to analyze these issues over time.

We had begun to understand some of the complexities of Anna's identifications with both her mother and her father, though—at the end—we felt that there was still more to learn. I was aware, for exam-

28. Yanof, J. (2005) Personal Communication. Yanof refers to a transference in which the patient relates to the analyst as she would to a "best friend." The "best friend" is often useful during normal development in helping the early adolescent girl separate psychologically from her mother.

29. Brenner, I. (1996) "On Trauma, Perversion, and 'Multiple Personality,'" *J. Amer. Psychoanal. Assn.*, 44: 785–814.

ple, that Anna had not developed a full-fledged oedipal transference with sustained competitive strivings in relation to me.[30] Though I would have liked us to go further in our work, I understood that—by dint of a developmental thrust[31] that was palpable—Anna had a sense of what she needed, and she wanted to go; she had to experience leaving me as well as her parents. Although there were probably opportunities to talk more about what Anna was avoiding or resisting by leaving, I believe I didn't press because I felt it was progressive and important for this young woman to try to make a go of it on her own.

While, in a way, Anna's entire analysis dealt with the need to grieve early disappointments and losses, in the final year of the analysis, our work together focused on loss and mourning. Anna and I recognized that sexuality was still an issue for her. She had played with a fantasy of phone contact with me, but it had seemed overstimulating, as we saw when Anna thought of ads such as, "Do you want to enlarge your penis size?" In the end, it was Anna's decision that we touch base from time to time in the office that had become an important space for her.

Perhaps because Anna was so able to work out her issues in the transference, psychoanalysis—despite its regressive pulls—seemed to facilitate the process of separation. Working in the transference—the containing play space in which Anna and I could experience a range of affects and explore old and new kinds of attachments—put developmental processes back on track and released the force of life,[32] resulting in significant intrapsychic and interpersonal change.

30. Yanof, J. (2005) Personal Communication.
31. Winnicott, D. W. (1971) "Therapeutic Consultations in Child Psychiatry," *International Psycho-Analytical Library*, 87: 1–398.
32. Winnicott, D. W. (1971), *op. cit.*

COMMENTARIES ON
RACHEL G. SEIDEL'S "ANNA,
LEAVING HOME — AN ADOLESCENT
GIRL'S JOURNEY"

Discussion of Anna

CHARLES E. PARKS, Ph.D.

Adolescence is generally defined as the psychological response to the physiological process of puberty. Surging hormones, and the accompanying rise in instinctual tension, push the young adolescent toward a thorough-going reworking of her relationship to her body, parents, peers, and, of course, toward her sense of who she is. The young adolescent is confronted with an entirely new set of experiences and accompanying intense affect states that, in the beginning, are difficult, if not impossible, to understand and control, much less articulate. The maturing adolescent is becoming capable of performing sexual activity that could only be fantasized about before. Many aspects of the child's sexual life, experience, and fantasy had been driven underground and/or relatively contained during the latency years preceding adolescence. Now, as adolescence proper approaches, old, partially buried impulses are reawakened and push for gratification. This heightened intensity of the drives is, of course, partially terrifying to the adolescent, who feels eerily out of control of her own body and has a variety of conflicts and fears associated with ideas of instinctual gratification.

Partially in response to the upsurge in tension and anxiety, there is a regression, literally, a moving backward to earlier, less mature forms of psychological functioning. We are all only too aware of the dramatic emotional volatility and rapid mood swings; of the impulsiveness, erratic behavior, and poor judgment; of the messiness, irresponsibility, and difficulty concentrating; and of the exquisite, narcissistic

Child and Adolescent Supervising Psychoanalyst, Baltimore Washington Institute for Psychoanalysis. Adjunct Instructor in Clinical Psychology, The George Washington University.
The Psychoanalytic Study of the Child 61, ed. Robert A. King, Peter B. Neubauer, Samuel Abrams, and A. Scott Dowling (Yale University Press, copyright © 2006 by Robert A. King, Peter B. Neubauer, Samuel Abrams, and A. Scott Dowling).

preoccupations and vulnerabilities seen in varying degrees in most adolescents. While these regressive moves and experiences make life difficult for adolescents, their parents, and their analysts, these experiences of reliving less mature ways of functioning also provide opportunities to revisit and rework earlier problematic experiences. As adolescence proceeds, so does cognitive maturation. Gradually, newly acquired cognitive strengths, including the ability for more rational judgment, planning, anticipation, introspection, organization, and synthesis can be brought to bear on old problems which are becoming alive again in the present. Difficult though they may be, the regressive processes in adolescence are necessary for the kind of movement forward that leads to the development of a healthy, vital adult. To be more precise, one might describe the adolescent process as containing both progressive and regressive potentials. In no other stage of life do the movements between regression and progression oscillate and reverberate with each other so dramatically and rapidly as in adolescence.

Peter Blos (1976) has stated that four developmental tasks must be accomplished for the adolescent to move into young adulthood: (1) The second separation-individuation phase of adolescence; (2) Establishment of a stable ego identity; (3) Integration and detoxification of residual trauma; and (4) Development of a comfortable sexual identity. Because she had not completed her adolescence by the end of her treatment, Anna had not fully negotiated any of these four developmental challenges at that time. Nevertheless, an examination of how her analysis fostered important work in each of these four areas and thereby facilitated movement into late adolescence provides one useful way of approaching Dr. Seidel's paper. After briefly outlining the central tasks of each of these areas, I will provide clinical summaries illustrating how Anna's analysis addressed each of these core developmental issues. Needless to say, progress in each of these four areas does not proceed in isolation. Movement in each is intimately tied to, reverberates with, stimulates, and is stimulated by movement in the other areas.

SECOND SEPARATION-INDIVIDUATION PHASE OF ADOLESCENCE

Predictably, the adolescent, confronted with a variety of novel and disturbing challenges, turns to earlier ways of coping, specifically turning to the mother and secondarily to the father for support and protection. However, this increased dependency, though strongly desired, is also unacceptable to the adolescent for two reasons. First, the dependency seriously threatens the sense of autonomy and independence for which the adolescent is striving. Second, with the resurgence of sexual feelings, these wishes for love and care from the parent tend to take on sexual meanings. To avoid this possibility, emotional investment has to be withdrawn from the parents and redirected toward substitutes in the world outside the family. This process of detachment from internal representations of the parents involves a very real and deeply felt loss of a sense of safety, well-being, and gratification. This loss is mourned by the adolescent who now has to confront intense loneliness. Frantic searches for substitute persons, causes, or activities to which she can passionately attach herself ensue. Much of the need for frenetic action, for the experience of vivid affects and excitement and even defiant rebellious behavior, characteristic of many adolescents, derives from the need to ward off underlying sadness, emptiness, and neediness. At other times, the adolescent may reinvest the emotional energy in herself, leading to the states of utter self-absorption and grandiose fantasies that we are all familiar with.

Noting that adolescents are so fully involved in states of mourning, falling in love with parental substitutes, or denying connectedness with and distancing themselves from parents and parental figures, Anna Freud (1958) raised questions about whether they had enough emotional energy left over to become productively involved in a treatment relationship. Today, we would be more appreciative of the ways in which these involvements with substitutes are in and of themselves transferences, that is, expressions of old themes and conflicts in the present that can be worked with in their own right. It is, in fact, these displacements onto others that enable the adolescent to become meaningfully and passionately involved with peers, causes, and interests outside the family. In Anna's case, we see how, with an intensive enough treatment, the adolescent's core conflicts can also be experienced directly in the transference to the analyst. Often enough, this relationship becomes the primary focus of the analysis, providing maximum opportunity for the clear emergence and working through of unconscious conflict.

From the beginning, Anna seemed to experience Dr. Seidel as a new object, as someone whose clear warmth and emotional connectedness made her different from Anna's mother, whom she had experienced as hostile and abandoning. While one might view these initial, positive feelings as manifestations of defenses against an underlying negative transference, it is important to also understand that Dr. Seidel's sensitivity to her patient's state of emotional starvation and her "welcoming" her patient to treatment were new experiences for the patient. Anna seemed to recognize in her analyst a potential developmental object who could help her rework old difficulties in the context of a relationship with a new, more fully responsive, person. Her subsequent asking her analyst for more time together had both its mature and regressive aspects. As the analysis began, and then deepened, Anna began to receive very real help from her treatment, among other things, beginning to modify her sado-masochistic/dependent pattern of relating to boys. The help she was getting could be expected to fuel Anna's regressive, dependent longings toward her analyst. Because these longings were, at the same time, unacceptable to her, negativity and denial of the importance of the regressive pulls toward her analyst became the order of the day.

As the first summer break approached, Anna increasingly arrived for sessions late or missed them entirely. After the break, she demanded that she attend sessions only once a week. Her feelings were further complicated by an emerging transference in which Dr. Seidel was experienced as sadistically coercive, yet abandoning, interested in relating to her patient only in terms of her own, that is, Dr. Seidel's, needs, not Anna's. The therapist "traumatized orphans in order to make them stutter so that he could study them," or exploit them for his own ends. In fantasy, this transference lent powerful content to the fear of the dependent pull. To become dependent, to care, and to "build your whole life around the analyst," risked not only despair and abandonment, but vulnerability to submission to an array of cruel, hurtful exploitations. One could hardly underestimate the challenges posed by thinking through how to respond to behavior that represented a complex blend of need, wish, and resistance to accompanying longings for closeness; hurt, anger, and fear; and transference and defense.

Dr. Seidel's narrative portrays the intensity of the affect felt by both patient and analyst during this time in the treatment. Anna felt enraged, abandoned, deeply hurt, and coerced. Dr. Seidel also felt angry as well as coercive, guilty, and hurt. Despite intense pressure, Dr. Seidel maintained an atmosphere in which feelings could be expressed, tolerated, and increasingly understood. Importantly, she maintained an analytic stance without becoming defensive or affectively withdrawing from her patient. For example, at one point she told Anna that there were "a lot of strong feelings between us," acknowledging her own emotional involvement in the treatment. Dr. Seidel states that "perhaps because of my interpretations or perhaps because I had let her know she was important to me . . . the alliance seemed stronger." Anna then resumed four times per week psycho-analysis. In my mind, the resumption of intensive treatment, as well as some therapeutic gain, was contributed to by the regressive revival and, then reworking, of earlier affects and conflicts in a personality with considerably more cognitive capacity to process them than Anna had when she was much younger. Now, as an adolescent in the treatment situation with vastly more mature cognitive capacities, Anna had more resources available to understand and modulate her experiences and place them in an understandable context.

At any rate, we learn that, from this point on, "Anna spent less time at home and engaged in fewer battles with her parents. She reached out to different groups at school, was deeply involved in its intellectual and social life, and became interested in Latino culture and issues of race." These behaviors—the increased affective involvement with other persons, groups, and causes outside the family, accompanied by diminished affective enmeshment with parents and siblings—are the external markers of the inner process by which infantile attachments to representations of the parents are beginning to be replaced by attachments outside the immediate family. The process of object removal (Katan, 1951; Blos, 1967) seems to have been facilitated by an intermediate phase in which the infantile object ties were re-experienced and reworked within the psychoanalytic relationship resulting in a more affectively-modulated, less sado-masochistically tinged turn to the outside world. What is being described is not a process by which all emotional attachment to the parents is relinquished, but the infantile quality of that attachment. Such relinquishment does not result in the loss of the parent, but instead provides the space for the development of a more mature, less instinctively-infused, relationship. At issue is the transformation of a relationship, not its removal (Novick and Novick, 2005).

ESTABLISHMENT OF EGO IDENTITY

The adolescent process involves establishing a sense of one's self as an autonomous individual with an identity that is unique and specifically her own. This identity should be one that provides a stable, coherent sense of who one is, how one's personality fits together and into the larger social context, and a sense of continuity between who one was in the past, is in the present, and intends to be in the future. Until this occurs, however, the question, "Who am I?" looms urgently in the adolescent's mind.

Anna's treatment initiated a process in which a progressively clearer understanding of her current conflicts and how these conflicts had grown out of and represented transformations of earlier experiences developed. The consequent sense that central, ongoing concerns, often over sexuality and aggression, had had a complicated, but at least a partially understandable evolution, helped to lessen the guilt, shame, and anxiety associated with them. Part of the change involved movement away from externalization of conflict, an expression of conflict through action, toward an ability to verbalize and tolerate her conflicts and to accept responsibility for them as part of her self. The subsequent development and freeing up of Anna's capacity for introspection allowed her to see herself as being conflicted about having a loving and sexually satisfying relationship with a male rather than only engaging in unreflective forays into sado-masochistic encounters with boys.

The process of emotional disengagement from representations of the parents described above allowed Anna to more fully engage outside her family, providing experiences with a richer, more varied, surround. Dr. Seidel worked patiently to help Anna better understand herself, her feelings, and her fears as they emerged. Significant shifts in ego identity occurred as defensively required views of herself as disgusting, eminently rejectable, annoying, and uninteresting began to be relinquished. As these defenses became less necessary, Anna was able to develop a much more emotionally complex relationship with her analyst and others. To take but one example, Anna was able to permit fuller access to her wishes for closeness with others. These new relationship experiences, in turn, provided an array of core, affective experiences of herself and herself with another, which could begin to be consolidated into a richer, more complex sense of herself as a person.

THE DETOXIFICATION AND INTEGRATION OF RESIDUAL TRAUMA

We all have emotional bumps and bruises in life. To varying degrees, these experiences can be traumatic and have a major organizing effect on the experience of the remainder of one's life. These effects can never be eliminated. However, adolescence does allow one final chance for a more mature, resourceful personality to experience and reintegrate, in a more adaptive way, the effects of earlier troubling experience. Such a reintegration can mean the difference between being stuck in a pattern of misery and self-destructiveness on the one hand or finding a solution that enhances one's feeling of mastery and even enables a certain passion or depth of meaning to a particular pursuit or set of pursuits in one's life.

Dr. Seidel's paper focuses on Anna's reworking of current versions of traumatic loss, disappointment, hurt and anger at her experience of her mother as unavailable to her and her traumatic, sadomasochistic relationship with her father. Anna feared both closeness and dependency and identified with the aggressor, torturing her analyst with threats to abandon her. Anna's progressive ability to articulate, rather than simply enact, feelings related to experienced loss and abandonment represented the first step toward detoxification. In the latter part of the analysis, we hear more about developing an interest in setting aside time for herself to think and writing in her journal while away from her analyst. Anna also began to consider her wishes to become a wife and mother. One is justified in asking whether these wishes and interests were fueled, in part at least, by their roots in earlier traumatic experiences, representing increasingly adaptive attempts to master earlier experiences of painful aloneness. In other words, to what extent do these more adaptive identifications with her mother and analyst represent attempts to repair earlier hurts and disappointments by providing the kind of nurture and care for others that she felt deprived of in her own life? The following section will demonstrate how closely, in Anna's case, movement toward development of a comfortable sexual identify interdigitated with other attempts at mastery and reintegration of trauma.

DEVELOPMENT OF A COMFORTABLE SEXUAL IDENTITY

Sexual identity refers not to gender identity, that is, whether one experiences oneself as a male or female, but to one's choice of sexual partners, sexual preferences, and so on. Such choices should permit the individual to feel good about her sexuality and to experience the freedom to pursue sexual pleasure in the context of a caring, intimate relationship. For this to take place, at least three things have to happen. First, there has to be a softening of the relentless, strict, rule-bound superego so that sexual pleasure becomes permissible and inhibition minimal. Second, childhood fantasies and theories about sexuality that lead to undue anxiety about sexual functioning need to be revisited so that the anxiety can be modulated. Third, some of the adolescent's need to admire and be admired and loved by her parents as well as her idealizations of her parents need to be displaced onto and invested in goals, values, and causes with which the adolescent can feel passionately involved. This involvement and devotion to ideal others and gradually becoming like them by adopting their goals and standards compensates for some of the lost love and admiration from the parents and can make the pursuit of certain aims in life deeply meaningful to the individual. At times, though, before such compensatory values and accomplishments can be established the decathexis, and concomitant deidealization, of the parents can significantly contribute to the lonely emptiness and narcissistic vulnerability of the adolescent who suddenly feels she has no one's admiring gaze to bolster her and her self-esteem.

Anna had begun to restrict her food intake and lose a significant amount of weight immediately after her first sexual experimentation with a boy when she was fourteen years old. Her deep rage at her mother, whom she felt had abandoned her at an early age, as well as her identification with her mother's masochism, precluded more healthy feminine identifications. Earlier experience with an erratic, sadistic, sexually over-stimulating father compromised her development of a capacity for caring, trusting, and giving in a sexual relationship. With regard to the superego, Anna's pattern of repeating sexual relationships with boys, a pattern in which she ended up feeling hurt, rejected, and enraged, was partially determined by intense guilt over incestuous feelings for her father. As the analysis progressed and Anna began to work on her transference to her analyst as a coercive, seductive, sadistic, and rejecting object she also began to become involved in a series of hurtful, potentially dangerous, relationships with a series of younger, sexually aggressive male athletes. As Dr. Seidel states, Anna, through this involvement, worked on the "sado-masochist dynamics related to the oedipal aspects of her relationship with her athletic father." As with her father, not infrequently, she wound up feeling disappointed, narcissistically injured, rejected, and enraged. Her identification with her mother's masochism was also addressed and reworked in this context.

Anna's involvement with the athletes was then related to (1) earlier memories of having intruded on her parents during intercourse, an activity she experienced as her father raping her mother; (2) possible sexual meanings to her bulimic symptoms; and (3) an eroticized, sado-masochistic transference in which Anna felt exploited and potentially abused. As Anna's awareness of the sado-masochistic nature of her sexual conflicts deepened, her need to enact them was attenuated. The gradual analysis of her need to ward off intimacy and feelings of love for her analyst lessened the presence of the defensively motivated retreat into a sado-masochistic stance. Although clearly freer to love and feel loved by the end of her analysis, Anna, after she had left the analysis, was saddened by her continued propensity for sado-masochistic involvement with men.

We are left with the question of whether Anna's development can continue in this area or whether additional treatment will be necessary to achieve a more comfortable, satisfying sexual identity. In this regard, Dr. Seidel notes that, in her analysis, Anna did not develop a "full-fledged oedipal transference with sustained competitive strivings." Particularly given her mother's failures as a professional and a mother and Anna's deep emotional involvement with a father who provided much of her nurture, one would expect this to be a highly charged area for her. A fuller experience of these oedipal strivings in her relationship to her analyst might have both lessened the pressure for regressive sado-masochistic solutions to sexual conflicts and enhanced the possibility for more satisfying, adaptive feminine identifications. In fact, our tendency to focus on experiences of separation and loss as the adolescent leaves analysis and home to attend college may lead us to vastly underestimate, or entirely overlook, the contribution of oedipal and competitive conflicts to such leave taking. Such conflicts often include guilt-laden fantasies that academic and then professional success will be damaging to or invite retaliation or punishment from a parent. In a certain sense, we have now come full circle since conflicts over success, succession, fantasies of parricide, loss, and mourning all reverberate with each other in complex ways (Loewald, 1979; Marrill and Siegel, 2004).

Turning to the process material from the session prior to Dr. Seidel's vacation may illustrate this point. Anna, after expressing a wish that Dr. Seidel had changed the time of one of her appointments, stated that wanting the change didn't "seem fair of me." Dr. Seidel did not address this statement as Anna's way of defending against her wish to ask, demand, insist on, etc., more from her analyst. Instead, she spoke to the patient's feelings of disappointment about Dr. Seidel's leaving and not being more available to her patient. From that point on, the trend in the session is in the direction of Anna experiencing herself more and more as a victim, on the receiving end of her analyst's sadism, as opposed to her initial experience of herself as *conflicted* about derivatives of her own wishes to control and dominate her analyst. Anna does, as the session progresses, become more openly angry but her anger is about what she feels is being done to her. This is very different from the earlier internal struggle over whether or not Anna will actively (and without feeling she is being unfair) be able to push her analyst to do something that she (i.e.,

Anna) feels is to her advantage. Throughout her narrative Dr. Seidel's emphasis in discussing Anna's anger is on the defensive function of warding off fears of loss and attachment. Being able to move
beyond these defensive uses *of* anger was indeed an important aspect
of the treatment. However, one is left wondering whether more attention to Anna's discomfort with and need to defend against her aggressive, assertive, at times sadistic feelings, would have over time allowed for the clearer emergence of competitive oedipal themes,
including guilt and fears that competitive success would lead to further loss, abandonment, and/or punishment.

Similarly, there are hints in the material that Dr. Seidel presents of
Anna's underlying fantasies that her leaving would be painful or destructive to Dr. Seidel ("I have a dream of being close, but don't want
to do it when the opportunity comes. I kind of like it when people
can do just as well without me.") and of conflicts over asserting her
autonomous wishes and fantasies ("But I really think I'm quite good
at being my own therapist now. Wondering what you think about
where I am. I have been a bit depressed . . . I don't want to be offensive."). In both of these cases, Dr. Seidel chooses to address Anna's
concerns over her feelings of attachment to her analyst rather than
her transference fantasies about the effects of her fledgling independence on the analyst. Dr. Seidel's interventions were clearly helpful
and led to the emergence of affect around the impending separation. However, it is important to note that other technical choices, including exploring Anna's fantasies about someone not being able to
get along without her or asking about her need to ask her analyst's
opinion and the associated depression and concern about being offensive right after she asserted her ability to be her own therapist,
were available. Would taking one of these alternative tacks have more
potential in terms of helping access more competitive feelings toward the analyst?

These clinical choice points raise a number of interesting and
complex questions for our on-going consideration. For example,
what is the relationship between the developmental assistance an
adolescent receives in a treatment and the nature of the emerging
transference? In what ways does the real help a child or adolescent
receives from her analyst facilitate the emergence of certain aspects
of the transference and in what ways does it impede them? When
dealing with regressive wishes in the treatment of an adolescent, how
does one maintain a balanced view of the complexity of these wishes
that express both longings for attachment, which one wants to help

the adolescent tolerate, but also passive defenses against more active, assertive, competitive experiences of oneself?

In the end, Dr. Seidel was faced with the question frequently faced by the adolescent analyst at work: Was it really in Anna's best interest to leave her hometown and her analysis to attend college in another locale? Dr. Seidel, correctly, attempted to remain neutral, helping her patient explore both sides of her conflict. She recognized that, as would be expected at this stage of development, all of the inner conditions necessary for the closure of adolescence had not been fully attained. While she believed more could be accomplished if the analysis were to continue, Dr. Seidel also believed that the external action of leaving for college had the potential to facilitate continued internal development. One wonders whether Dr. Seidel also considered the possibility that such an external move away from home and her analyst might actually disrupt the process of developing an inner sense of separation and independence that was occurring with the aid of Anna's analysis. External leavings, especially abrupt ones, can foreclose the gradual, internal individuation processes that ultimately lead to true autonomy. There are times when the internal task of leaving home might be facilitated by externally remaining at home or at least in one's hometown and continuing one's treatment. Analysts at work in this country may feel constrained from seriously considering with their adolescent patients the possible advantages of staying around for more analytic work, as opposed to taking what, in North American culture, is viewed as the developmentally normal step of leaving home for college.

Peter Blos (1962, 1976) has spoken of the process of adolescent development as one in which regressive processes allow earlier conflicts to be re-experienced and reworked in the new context of more mature cognitive and emotional functioning. Psychoanalytic treatment in adolescence facilitates this development. Old problems resurface with an aliveness and affective vividness that may never again occur in one's life. This process allows the opportunity to address crucial, unfinished business head on at a time when the personality is still in flux and the potential for change in the patient is great. It is the aliveness, the emotional intensity and the urgency of the adolescent's wish to grow and develop, as well as the privilege of participating in this great second chance, to prepare for a satisfying, productive adulthood that makes work with an adolescent so exhilarating and so personally moving when it goes well. Dr. Seidel is to be congratulated for presenting a narrative of a treatment that so clearly portrays the intensity, aliveness, and deep emotional involvement, in both members of the analytic dyad, regularly encountered by the adolescent analysis at work.

BIBLIOGRAPHY

BLOS, P. (1962). *On Adolescence: A Psychoanalytic Inquiry.* London: The Free Press.
—————— (1967). The second individuation process of adolescence. *The Psychoanalytic Study of the Child,* 22:162–186.
—————— (1976). Where and how does adolescence end: Structural criteria for adolescent closure. *Adolescent Psychiatry,* 5:3–17.
FREUD, A. (1958). Adolescence. *The Psychoanalytic Study of the Child,* 13:255–278.
KATAN, A. (1951). The role of displacement in agoraphobia. *The International Journal of Psychoanalysis,* 32:41–50.
LOEWALD, H. W. (1979). The waning of the Oedipus complex. *The Psychoanalytic Study of the Child,* 27:751–775.
MARRILL, I. H., & SIEGEL, E. R. (2004). Success and succession. *Journal of the American Psychoanalytic Association,* 52:673–688.
NOVICK, K. K. & NOVICK, J. (2005). *Working with Parents Makes Therapy Work.* Northvale, New Jersey and London: Jason Aronson Inc.

Navigating the Cross-Currents of the Treatment Relationship

A Discussion of Dr. Seidel's Case Presentation

SAMUEL ABRAMS, M.D.

THE TREATMENT RELATIONSHIP IS THE CONCEPTUAL CENTER OF THE theories that inform clinical psychoanalysis. Consequently, it is useful to differentiate its many components. Regrettably, the word "transference" tends to obscure rather than illuminate what transpires within that remarkable exchange, so I prefer the more descriptive term "treatment relationship" or "therapeutic interaction." There are aspects of the relationship that arise from past conflicts and earlier mental organizations; there are aspects of the relationship that reflect the realistic features of the participants as they encounter one another; there are aspects of the relationship that express externalized and projective features of each of the players. Distinguishing these *old*, *real*, and *externalized* features is always a formidable task, a task that is further burdened when the distinctions are ignored and all are huddled together under the global Babel-term, transference.

When dealing with children and adolescents another feature surfaces. The path to maturity is guided by an unfolding biological program. The potential of that program is actualized by structured stimuli provided by at least a "good enough" environment. Separation-individuation requires persons to titrate the anxiety of loss and

Clinical Professor, The Psychoanalytic Institute Department of Psychiatry at N.Y.U. Medical Center; Editor, *The Psychoanalytic Study of the Child*.

The Psychoanalytic Study of the Child 61, ed. Robert A. King, Peter B. Neubauer, Samuel Abrams, and A. Scott Dowling (Yale University Press, copyright © 2006 by Robert A. King, Peter B. Neubauer, Samuel Abrams, and A. Scott Dowling).

make available the pleasures derived from engaging in a "love affair with the world." Oedipal consolidation is promoted when parental caring is measured and balanced with appropriate regulations. Latency can move along in the presence of capable auxiliary authorities and the opportunities for expanding friendships. During these stages, the people in the surround provide the stimuli to actualize the newly emerging organizations inspired by the inherent biological program. Consequently, when addressing children and adolescents, the treatment relationship contains the seeking out of something *new,* as well as old, real, and externalized; the analyst can be one of those providers. That is why the analytic treatment of younger persons is far more complex than the treatment of adults.

Anna, Dr. Seidel's patient, is caught in the cross-currents of these dynamic features which Dr. Seidel houses in the term "transference." There is a developmental pull (Dr. Seidel says "push," but I find "pull" more metaphorically appropriate) toward the new, along with a powerful "regressive and dependent" pull back to the old. Quite early, Dr. Seidel stakes her position in respect to these conflicting pulls. She writes that the pull forward toward a new organization is to be conceptualized as a "resistance" to the earlier (and deeper) conflicts and impaired relationships. My own inclination in treating adolescents is to see that issue the other way around. The principal goal in child analysis is to make certain that development pursues its expected course. The pull forward reflects the expected course; consequently, I view the pull backward as a major resistance however useful it may be for examining earlier conflicts. Naturally, I also recognize that there is a set of inevitable minor obstacles to engaging those conflicts.

Adolescents seek adults in their environment to assist in "removing" them from the intense intra-psychic attachments to their primary objects so that they may be introduced into the opportunities of personal freedom, individuality, and the establishment of their own world view. The process of removing often involves idealizing, which is why college students become so enamored with social movements and have crushes on professors. Such idealizing readily finds its way into treatment settings as well. When analysts insist on cultivating only the past conflicts and old relationships, they interfere with the possibility of patients finding that necessary new figure to abet primary object removal within (as well as without) the therapeutic interaction. For example, in the midst of an excessively idealized view of the analyst, I have heard therapists actively account for such idealization as defenses against the latent aggressiveness being deployed within the treatment relationship. They worry that the idealization, a frequent defense, is a resistance to the past. Actually, sometimes careful observation may demonstrate that it is a corollary of object-removal, especially if a judgment has been made to attentively engage contemporary conflicts evoked by the inevitable discontinuities. Pulling the patient backward by way of a historical intervention may unnecessarily stall the advance and simply cultivate a resistance to the treatment goal. When adolescents attack us it is always tempting to explain the attack as deriving from past feelings and old conflicts. Sometimes I find it better to say, "In the midst of what you're going through these days I suppose you're reminded about how angry you used to get about similar matters when you were younger." This approach addresses the anger within the setting without drawing the patient away from what is going on in the present.

Of course, it is perfectly understandable that there are times when analysts must cultivate and confront the old. That approach is honored by tradition and validated by successes in practice. There is a historical reason for this. The examination of the continuities in disorders is far more useful when treating adults than is the examination of the discontinuities which is more the purview of the child analysts. Treating adults was well established in our discipline long before the systematic approach to treating children analytically came into being. Activating the past in children can be successful as long as those old "neurotic" entanglements are recognized as resistances to the new opportunities rather than the clinical core of the treatment. The past needs to be engaged for conflict-resolution, of course, but only in order to make the prospect for discontinuities more readily available. The technical dilemmas of navigating such cross-currents become intense, however, when the therapeutic dwelling in the past inadvertently serves to intensify the drag backward and thereby interferes with the pull forward. There are moments in the reading of Dr. Seidel's case material when that danger seems perilously near.

Perhaps that impression is an artifact of the aim of this case write-up. Dr. Seidel wishes to emphasize the problems of separation and the adhesiveness to the past relationships that have led Anna's lure backward to be more intense than ordinary. Naturally, under those circumstances, it is necessary that such issues be engaged and Dr. Seidel does that with competence. The course of the treatment suggests that Anna's pull forward remained sufficiently strong so that she could overcome any kind of treatment ambiguity, that is, she was one of those kinds of children who assertively reach out for what they need in spite of all sorts of impediments. Indeed, the analyst's draw toward genetic explorations aside, in my opinion Anna faced far more serious obstacles to autonomous growth than the emphasis upon old conflicts. She became seriously ill—the nature of the illness is not described but its disabling potential casts a dark cloud. Furthermore, there is what appears to be a sudden and dramatic split between her parents; her mother goes off and her father seeks out other women. A disabling illness, a fragmenting family life, and a treatment that implicitly invites the regressive pull—any one of these could be enough to derail the path toward maturity. Yet, even bunched together, they don't seem to throw Anna off.

I suspect that Anna's inherent pull forward (a dispositional feature) was more than adequate to overcome all of these impediments. I also believe that she found in Dr. Seidel the caring, affectively attuned person that differentiated her from the internalized parents. Dr. Seidel may have further buttressed the differences by way of her interpretations of Anna's misperceptions that were informed by the past. From a technical point of view, I believe that many adolescents like Anna are sometimes helped to find the necessary new object within the therapeutic interaction when an analyst addresses the past in ways that facilitates differentiation—even if those interpretations are primarily motivated by the wish to resolve infantile conflicts. When we say, "You are behaving toward me as if I'm one of your parents," that not only facilitates old conflict-resolution but implies "I'm not like them, I'm someone different." Being "someone different" allows the treatment relationship to become a vehicle for whatever is necessary for growth, even as it also promotes a valuable authentic real exchange.

Although Dr. Seidel and I have slightly different views as to where therapeutic action was joined, I am as pleased with the outcome of the case as she must be.

Discussion of Anna

JUDITH A. YANOF, M.D.

RACHEL SEIDEL FRAMES HER CLINICAL PAPER AROUND THE SUBJECT OF separation in adolescence. She points out that "being able to separate from home in a rather uncomplicated way" is a normal developmental task of adolescence. She states that her patient, Anna, was stuck at this developmental crossroad. The paper discusses separation from the analyst at three different times during the treatment. This organization enables the reader to appreciate the changes that evolved during the analytic work as well as the different levels of developmental conflict that were revived and reworked in the treatment. Seidel poignantly conveys Anna's intense affective engagement in the analytic process, while noting her simultaneous ability to step back from her feelings to self-reflect and think analytically, using humor and metaphor. This sophisticated and nuanced analytic work led to a termination of the analysis after three years and a successful move away from home to college.

Seidel implicitly conceptualizes the therapeutic action of this psychoanalysis as involving Anna's use of her analyst as an important attachment figure during a crucial developmental time. The analyst provided stability and availability during a period when the patient was struggling to get needed emotional distance from an enmeshed, sadomasochistic relationship with her parents. Once she loosened her dependent ties to her parents by attaching herself to the analyst, Anna used her psychoanalysis to work on conflicted feelings about dependency and autonomy that came alive in the analytic relationship. In my experience this is a rather common role that the analyst

Training and Supervising Analyst and Child Supervising Analyst at the Boston Psychoanalytic Society and Institute; Instructor in the Department of Psychiatry, Harvard Medical School.

The Psychoanalytic Study of the Child 61, ed. Robert A. King, Peter B. Neubauer, Samuel Abrams, and A. Scott Dowling (Yale University Press, copyright © 2006 by Robert A. King, Peter B. Neubauer, Samuel Abrams, and A. Scott Dowling).

serves in adolescent analyses, whether it is conceptualized explicitly by the analyst or not.[1] This phenomenon also mirrors something that arises in normal adolescent development. It is not uncommon for adolescents to make strong attachments to adults outside the family, like teachers, coaches, or friends' parents. Often these chosen adults become the repository for idealized feelings that once belonged to the parents, providing the adolescent with some needed perspective on the parental relationship. When the analysis was over Anna continued to use her analyst as an attachment figure by checking in periodically when she was home from college.

The analyst also functioned simultaneously as a transference figure, and through this experience Seidel learned a great deal about Anna's earlier relationships. As soon as Anna began a more intensive treatment, a regressive transference was mobilized. The analyst became tinged with conflicted and threatening aspects of the primary objects. Anna longed for closeness, but feared that her powerful dependent needs would easily consume her, endanger her autonomy, and lead only to disappointment. She brought her deeply ambivalent wish for closeness into the treatment in enactments with her analyst. She distanced herself by coming late and missing appointments. She simultaneously demanded "too much" by asking Seidel to continually change scheduled appointments, so that her needs might be met no matter what inconvenience was caused to the analyst. Anna let the analyst know firsthand how difficult it was for her to feel reciprocity in a close relationship. In the transference/countertransference paradigm each partner was experienced alternately as abandoned or abandoning; frustrated or frustrating. In these ways Anna engaged in a transference repetition, "proving" that this new relationship, like those in the past, would become predictably disappointing. At times the transference also became erotically tinged. The immediacy of the counter-transference allowed Seidel to use her own feelings to understand how Anna had experienced her early relationships and how she now, defensively, turned the tables and withdrew from others when her fears of closeness and disappointment were stirred up. Through the use of the analyst as both transference figure and developmental object, Anna gradually learned to tolerate more affect, increasingly became more aware of her behavior, and eventually risked new ways of relating.

Yet, a case such as Anna's raises some interesting questions about

1. I have used the term *attachment figure,* but the terms *developmental object* or *object removal* have similar meanings.

the role of parent work. One of the striking things about this case is that while Anna made major internal and external changes through her analytic work—disengaging from the sadomasochistic struggles with her parents, successfully relating to peers, and recognizing herself to be more capable of making her own decisions—the family disintegrated. An infidelity was discovered, the parents separated, mother abandoned the home and her daughter, and father became sexually active with multiple partners in a way that seemed like a return to his own adolescence. Anna was not entirely unscathed either; she was diagnosed with a chronic medical illness. As Seidel observed, the timing of all of this was coincident with preparing for Anna's imminent physical departure from the home, her senior year of high school.

In retrospect, it is easy to see that Anna's hovering on the brink of a major developmental step (the internal changes that enabled her to leave home as well as the actual event of leaving) put Anna's parents into crisis. Why this did not happen with their first child and how that sibling relationship functioned for Anna and her family we do not know. However, a major coping style in this family appears to have been to retreat and withdraw rather than risk being left or feeling disappointed, and this reaction became most apparent as Anna was poised to leave.

Seidel noticed this pattern at the very beginning of the treatment. Anna's parents felt overwhelmed by their daughter's eating disorder, depressed mood, and provocative behavior toward them. Perhaps, like many parents, they also felt overwhelmed by her adolescence— her transformed body, her burgeoning sexuality, and her forays into more autonomous functioning, which are often accompanied by de-idealization, or in some cases devaluation, of the parents. When they consulted Dr. Seidel, Anna's parents did not want to talk about their daughter's developmental history or think about themselves or learn how they could help Anna. They wanted Dr. Seidel to see their daughter *the very next day* and fix the problem. Seidel felt as if they had *"abandoned Anna to me."* In a way they had. Feeling incompetent as parents, they wanted to get rid of the shameful, helpless affects that left them feeling so out of control, much as Anna did.

It seems that the same issues emerged again when Anna discussed with her parents her wish to intensify her treatment and to begin psychoanalysis. Her parents were concerned about money. However, the cost of analysis is never simply financial. I suspect that Anna's parents were also concerned about the consequences of Anna's increased connection to her analyst (as most parents are), and perhaps in particular, the potential loss to them if Anna moved closer to someone else. Anna's willingness to contribute her own money to pay for her analysis was over-determined, as Seidel suggests. It was a new move in terms of her ability to give voice to her own wishes more loudly and clearly than she ever had before, but it was an old move in terms of her attempt to relieve her parents of their parental duties, to provide for herself, and by reversing the roles, to take care of them. Seidel rightly felt that Anna's issues about who was paying and why could be analyzed later in the treatment. However, Anna's successful negotiation of this hurdle left her parents' concerns unspoken and unaddressed. Some parents might have inserted themselves into the process at this point, perhaps even disrupting the treatment. Anna's parents, however, seemed instead to withdraw further, their familiar way of coping.

Psychoanalytic theory has consistently emphasized the goal of separation from the primary objects as a fundamental developmental task during adolescence (Freud, 1958; Blos, 1962, 1967). However, psychoanalytic theory has been less articulate about the importance of forging affiliative connections in adolescence, both the goal of deepening the capacity for intimacy with others, and the goal of redefining the relationship to parents, rather than relinquishing it (Gilligan, 1982; Hauser and Levine, 1993). The Novicks state this quite clearly, "the goal of adolescent development and hence of treatment is not *separation* [my italics], but transformation of the parent-child relationship and integration of the new self-representation" (Novick and Novick, 2005, p. 122). Certainly some would disagree with this, but whether we agree or disagree depends largely on how we define separation.

There is frequently confusion in our literature when we talk about separation in adolescence. It is often difficult to tell if we are talking about the *internal* work of giving up childhood ways of thinking about the self in relation to parents or if we are talking about an actual external separation from the parents, as in living or functioning independently. The two are related but not the same. Sometimes what seems to be independent functioning can be erected on a very tenuous foundation of self. Moreover, this confusion is exacerbated in a cultural milieu in which the definitional endpoint of adolescence is to leave home to go to college, a goal that is narrowly seen in terms of outward behavior without reference to internal state (Novick and Novick, 2005). Truly becoming one's own person in a psychological sense is a much slower, arduous, and more gradual process.

The emphasis on separation in psychoanalytic theory has often led analysts to conduct the analytic treatment of the adolescent without seeing or working with the parents in an ongoing and regular way. The rationale for this approach is to protect the adolescent's need for separation, or as in Anna's case, to encourage that separation. However, it is clear that adolescents do better in achieving their developmental goals when their parents are connected, stable, and available to them during adolescence (Offer, 1980; Kaplan, 1980), and even into young adulthood. Parents have the important task of gradually ceding to their adolescent the role of decision-making, believing in their adolescent's increasing ability to make life decisions, supporting adolescents when things do not go well, and responsibly vetoing what is frankly dangerous. Unfortunately, this is no easy task. Adolescents are forever giving their parents conflicting messages about their actual capabilities for independent functioning, and the most intuitive parents have a hard time deciding when to hold on and when to let go.

This raises the question: How do we determine when it is our task as adolescent analysts to help parents during this truly difficult stage of parenting? There most certainly would have been a great deal of resistance from Anna and her parents to interfering with the familiar dance they had developed with each other. In a family that denies the need for connection and uses controlling behavior instead of dealing with feelings of loss, it is difficult to help family members acknowledge their need for each other and their sadness. While it is difficult to second guess the analyst who has done the work and knows the situation better than anyone else, the fact that this family totally spun apart during the analysis makes one wonder if perhaps additional efforts could have been made to help the parents feel more important to their daughter, more involved in the treatment, and more effective in their role as parents.

It may be easier to tell in retrospect that more intervention with a family would have been advantageous, but how does the analyst make that decision in the beginning of a treatment? While this needs to be a decision made on a case by case basis, working with parents often means going against what has come to be the standard practice for an adolescent treatment. Such a decision, therefore, requires an extended state of open-mindedness and a willingness to encounter resistance from all parties. There is certainly a tension between the adolescent's need to feel that the treatment is his or her own and the analyst's wish to have direct contact with parents (with or without the adolescent present) to work on a better environment for growth and development. While this tension exists in child treatments, it becomes much greater in adolescent treatments, where privacy, confidentiality, and the need to feel independent are more loaded issues. Nevertheless, parents need to be involved and need to be negotiated with by their adolescent children. It is not surprising then that analysts will have to struggle with these issues in adolescent treatments, and at times will find themselves embroiled in their patients' ambivalent struggles with family around separation and connectedness.

BIBLIOGRAPHY

Blos, P. (1962). *On Adolescence: A Psychoanalytic Interpretation.* New York: Free Press of Glencoe.

———— (1967). The second individuation process of adolescence. *The Psychoanalytic Study of the Child,* 22:162–186.

Freud, A. (1958). Adolescence. *The Psychoanalytic Study of the Child,* 13:255–278.

Gilligan, C. (1982). *In a Different Voice.* Cambridge, Mass.: Harvard University Press.

Hauser, S. T., & Levine, H. A. (1993). Relatedness and autonomy: Links with ego development and family interactions. *Adolescent Psychiatry: Developmental and Clinical Studies,* 19:185–227.

Kaplan, E. H. (1980). Adolescents, age 15 to 18: A psychoanalytic developmental view. In *The Course of Life,* ed. S. I. Greenspan and G. H. Pollack, pp. 373–396.

Novick, K. K., & Novick, J. (2005). *Working with Parents Makes Therapy Work.* New York: Jason Aronson.

Offer, D. (1980). Adolescent development: A normative perspective. In *The Course of Life,* ed. S. I. Greenspan and G. H. Pollack, pp. 357–372.

Discussion of "Anna, Leaving Home" by Rachel Seidel, M.D.

E. KIRSTEN DAHL, Ph.D.

"ANNA, LEAVING HOME" IS A VIVID PORTRAIT OF HOW PSYCHOANALYSIS enabled an adolescent girl to psychologically separate sufficiently for her to leave home in a relatively uncomplicated way. Dr. Seidel argues that for an adolescent to leave home she needs to start from the base of a secure early attachment, to have a reasonably consolidated identity, and good affect tolerance. She must have begun to find avenues for sublimation and neutralization. Dr. Seidel uses the clinical process to illustrate how the re-working of early attachment issues of separation and loss can lead to the development of a solid platform from which to leave home.

Anna came into treatment, perhaps not surprisingly for a mid-adolescent girl, with an eating disorder and difficulty in making and sustaining age-appropriate sexual and social relationships with her peers. We learn that Anna's parents had a stormy and sexually charged relationship that dominated the household. Anna reported feeling abandoned by her mother from early on and that her father had been her primary, if sometimes sadistic, care giver. Anna had wet her bed until early adolescence.

Dr. Seidel gives us a picture of a girl caught in what she experiences as a simultaneously over-stimulating and depriving environment in which she feels unseen and unheard. A shared metaphor that developed between Anna and Dr. Seidel was that Anna was "starving" for nourishment in every form. Anna demonstrated a gift

Training and Supervising Analyst at The Western New England Institute for Psychoanalysis, where she is Chair of the Child Analysis Program. She is in private practice in New Haven.

The Psychoanalytic Study of the Child 61, ed. Robert A. King, Peter B. Neubauer, Samuel Abrams, and A. Scott Dowling (Yale University Press, copyright © 2006 by Robert A. King, Peter B. Neubauer, Samuel Abrams, and A. Scott Dowling).

for reflecting on her inner world, and Dr. Seidel was able to sustain
her analytic attunement to the shifts in Anna's contact and withdrawal from moment to moment as well as during enactments
around canceling appointments. Over the course of the analysis the
pair was able to understand the many intra-psychic meanings of
Anna's disturbed relationship to food and eating. This symptom condensed conflicts at all developmental levels: her early sense of abandonment, her struggles to sustain relationships sado-masochistically,
and her exciting and frightening erotic tie to her father. All of these
developmental epochs become reflected in the transference so that
Anna is "starving" for a good feed from Dr. Seidel. She becomes enraged and provocative when Dr. Seidel is unavailable, fleeing her and
at the same time wanting Dr. Seidel to "force" her to come back. She
develops an erotized transference containing both the wish and fear
that Dr. Seidel's love can be "bought" like sex with a prostitute. The
developmental progress Anna has made is demonstrated in the final
year of her analysis where she is able to weather the consequences of
being diagnosed with a chronic illness and her mother's actual abandonment of her to live in another city. Anna moves toward leaving
her analyst to go away to college. This paper gives us a window on
how earlier conflicts become re-awakened with renewed force during
adolescence. We can see how early trauma suffuses and organizes
each subsequent developmental phase.

Because of Anna's early experience of her mother as hostile and
withdrawn as well as the on-going sadomasochistic relationship between the parents and between Anna and her father, we may be
tempted to view Anna's adolescent crisis only in terms of disturbed
attachment and separation anxiety. As Dr. Seidel shows us with Anna,
by adolescence the girl's push to separate from her mother has acquired multiple and complex meanings. Employing the term separation anxiety for the internal dilemma of mid-adolescence may make
us miss the nature of the intra-psychic struggle during a girl's adolescence which is not so much about separation as it is about the processes involved in psychic structure building. Throughout her analysis we see how Anna makes use of oral imagery: she is "starving,"
she feels "disgusting," and of course she makes vivid use of her symptoms
of bingeing and throwing up. The mid-adolescent girl struggles not
with the fear that she will lose her mother's love but with the conflicts
stimulated by the wish to both identify with and obliterate the
mother as a sexual woman. If we think of identifications as linked to
unconscious fantasies of being or becoming like another individual,
they are then best viewed as complex psychic structures, along the

lines of compromise formations. As such, these fantasies weave together derivatives of the drives, wishes, fears, defenses, and object relations (Abend and Porder 1995, p. 468). Loewald (1973) argues that identification should be seen as a "way station" in the process toward internalization. Identification reflects a merging or confusion of subject and object. In contrast, internalization involves a new differentiation between subject and object; aspects of the object are no longer experienced as outside the self but have become metabolized as new psychic structure.

The development of the mind involves a reciprocal relationship between the construction of subjectivity and the construction of the object world. Both the drives and psychic structure emerge not just in the *context* of relation to the object, but the object is critical in *shaping* drives and psychic structure (Freud 1914, 1915). Inherent in the mind, then, is the subject's relation to the object. In contrast to identification in which there is a blurring between subject and object, internalization involves assimilation of the object, a breaking down of the object relationship into its basic elements and a re-organization and restructuring of these elements into new psychic structure (Loewald 1973).

The processes of identification and internalization constitute oscillating poles of mental life (Loewald 1973). Adolescence is a period especially dominated by these oscillations which involve a loosening of current ego structures in preparation for the internalization of the identifications of late adolescence. Many writers (Erikson 1963, Blos 1962, Ritvo 1971) point to the necessary psychological moratorium, or second latency, during adolescence and early adulthood, during which the process of internalization is at work creating and consolidating new inner structures. There is an elaboration and deepening of ego functions as well as a stabilization of those structures protecting psychic integrity. Adult psychological functioning comes about not as a result of disengagement from the familial objects but from a consolidation of new internalizations of these familial objects (Behrends and Blatt 1985).

The developmental push is toward identification with the mother as a sexually mature adult. For a mid-adolescent girl like Anna, the process of internalization of the mother as sexual woman is complicated immeasurably by the merging of boundaries that is at the core of identification. This blurring of boundaries is further complicated by the bodily isomorphism which reverberates with representations of the tie to the archaic mother. For Anna, this archaic mother is stamped with experiences of deprivation and hostility. As she begins treatment she is making use of her body to give representation to her ancient conflicts around her longings for maternal closeness and her fears of merging with the desired object. Anna demonstrates how the danger posed by the loosened distinctions between self and object may be avoided by recasting the dilemma in sado-masochistic terms where the unconscious dilemma is then experienced as one of either triumphant isolation or humiliating surrender. Anna wants to be "forced" to come to her sessions and then experiences herself as disgusting and hateful.

Internalization of the sexual mother is experienced as intolerably aggressive. Projected onto the mother in an effort at escaping internal conflict over her own intense aggression, the girl experiences her own aggression now in the form of a deadly mother who will destroy her daughter's sexuality. No new psychic structure can be created because the daughter fears the destructive power of internalization. The girl "has" her mother in reality but is unable to metabolize her. Stripped of the resonating representations of the sexual mother and their links to earlier more archaic imagoes, the inner world becomes impoverished. At the beginning of treatment, this is the intra-psychic territory Anna has entered. She will starve if she leaves her parents, but if she stays she fears returning regressively to the sado-masochistic tie to both. Anna has not been able to move forward into age appropriate sexual intimacy. Her deepest and most exciting relationship is with her own body; how she can control its shape and its functioning through her anorexia, bingeing, and vomiting. Anna is left, however, with feelings of abandonment and isolation, deprived of emotional sustenance.

As Anna's analysis proceeds and she becomes increasingly able to make use of her analyst as a nurturing, stable object who permits Anna to control her comings and goings, Anna begins to move forward into pleasurable relationships with her peers and her first sexual relationship with a boy. This developmental progression ushers in new symptoms, this time within the transference in which Dr. Seidel is experienced as a sadistic, depriving mother who will either "force" Anna to eat (attend her sessions) or abandon her to a false sense of self-sufficiency which is accompanied by feelings of starvation. Anna wants her analyst to be the all-giving, perfectly attuned mother she had never had but she fears the loss of psychological boundaries this implies. As analysis of her longings for and fears of the archaic mother proceeds, Anna begins to reveal the erotic aspects of her maternal transference. Dr. Seidel gives us a remarkable picture of the internal struggles that an adolescent girl encounters as she begins to internalize the mother as a sexually mature woman.

Internalization of identifications with the mother as a sexual woman, however, awakens the unconscious fantasies associated with the processes of internalization: that is, that the metabolization of the identificatory object will result in the object's destruction. We can "hear" the derivatives of Anna's struggle with the unconscious primitive fantasies associated with internalization in the metaphor of "starving," in her actions around eating, her wish that Dr. Seidel "force" her to come to her sessions, and her conscious fantasy of fusion with Dr. Seidel, of being her soul mate. Anna's internal conflict is represented in the transference by her struggles over: Who "controls" the sessions? For whom is Anna coming, herself or Dr. Seidel? Is torturing the beloved exciting or frightening? Is it dangerous to want so much power over another? As this material is analyzed, a more erotized transference emerges in which Anna longs for and fears a special intimacy with her analyst.

The aggression inherent in the process of internalization stimulates both the wish and the fear that to claim sexual agency the mother must be eliminated. This conflict takes the form of a wish for the mother's sexual potency and a fear that in claiming sexual agency the mother must be destroyed. For the daughter, given her multitudinous identifications with the mother during each developmental epoch, absolute destruction of the mother would result in internal impoverishment (Dalsimer 2001; 1994). The girl's identification with her mother as mature sexual woman leads to an inherent confusion about who has been or is being destroyed. The defensive projection onto the mother-in-reality of the aggression associated with internalization, although it results in the experience of the mother as malignant, may nevertheless be employed in the service of disavowing the process of internalization.

This is a developmental crisis unique to female adolescence. Although it may appear to echo some of the conflicts of early childhood or the oedipal period, the dilemma created by the demands placed on the psyche by the sexually mature body do not revive earlier conflicts; earlier conflicts are now fundamentally transformed by the presence of a sexually mature body. The new body, now in reality so like the mother's, intensifies identificatory processes, weakening differentiation between self and object, and loosening ego organization. Primitive and intense aggressive fantasies associated with psychic structure building are re-awakened. These in turn may resonate with fantasies of the archaic omnipotent mother which contribute to a deepening of an internal climate of overwhelming aggression experienced as originating sometimes within and sometimes outside the self. The intra-psychic dilemma for the adolescent girl is created by the need to integrate her sexually mature body as a functioning part of her inner world. To accomplish this, identifications with the mother as sexual woman must be metabolized as psychic structure. Because the body is central to the territory to be navigated, archaic strata of the mind are enlivened, now transformed, however, by present conflict. These questions press urgently for resolution: To whom does my body belong? What are the conditions for satisfaction of my bodily desires? With whom will I satisfy my desires? The achievement of sexual agency is a narrative primarily about the body and its appetites. At the center of the intra-psychic terrain of the sexually mature body stands the mother as a sexual woman. Linked as this figure is to archaic fantasies of omnipotent bodily power, for some adolescent girls, their unconscious fantasies may entail the mother as the desired object who, however, bars the way to the daughter's autonomous sexuality.

As Anna moves into the termination phase of her analysis, she is better able to tolerate the aggression inherent in her desire to take Dr. Seidel "inside." She acknowledges Dr. Seidel's "huge" presence in her life; she is in "the back of" Anna's mind all the time. She sees the "we-ness" of the two but begins to envision a time when Dr. Seidel will be a "remembered" presence, rather than an absence. Anna is more comfortable with her own sexuality. As she fantasizes about a telephone conversation with the absent Dr. Seidel, however, erotic imagery is quickly replaced by the imagery of death and mourning. What will it mean to take Dr. Seidel with her? Can Dr. Seidel survive and become a usefully remembered presence, or will Dr. Seidel be destroyed by Anna's absence? Will only one sexual woman survive this life and death struggle?

The dilemma for the adolescent girl is how to transform the earlier representations of the mother as a source of solace and comfort while simultaneously metabolizing as psychic structure the mother's sexual agency. For some young women, these multidimensional maternal representations of mother as originary source of life, bodily pleasures, comfort, morality, and sexual agency present an insurmountable obstacle on the path toward adulthood. By the conclusion of her analysis, however, Anna is able to contemplate a time when Dr. Seidel will be a consoling remembered presence. As Anna moves into her future developmentally, we can imagine her as a vibrantly alive young woman with a rich inner world. We can imagine that Anna's inner world will contain useful representations of Dr. Seidel's ability to tolerate strong aggressive and erotic affects. Dr. Seidel will become a forgotten/remembered presence who continues to help Anna consolidate her identity as an actively sexual young woman no longer at risk for sado-masochistic submission with its accompanying, defensively driven glacial isolation.

BIBLIOGRAPHY

ABEND, S., & PORDER, M. S. (1995) Identification. In: Moore, B., and Fine, B. (Ed.). *Psychoanalysis: The Major Concepts.* New Haven: Yale Univ. Press. Pp. 463–471.

BERHRENDS, R., & BLATT, S. (1985) Internalization and psychological development throughout the life cycle. In: *The Psychoanalytic Study of the Child.* 40:11–39.

BLOS, P. (1962) *On Adolescence.* New York: Free Press.

DAHL, E. K. (1995) Daughters and mothers: Aspects of the representational world during adolescence. In: *The Psychoanalytic Study of the Child.* 50:187–204.

——— (2004) "Last night I dreamed I went to Manderlay again": Vicissitudes of maternal identifications in late female adolescence. In: *Psychoanal. Inquiry,* 24:5, 657–679.

DALSIMER, K. (2001) *Virginia Woolf: Becoming a Writer.* New Haven: Yale Univ. Press.

——— (1994) The vicissitudes of mourning. In: *The Psychoanalytic Study of the Child.* 49:394–411.

ERIKSON, E. (1963) *Childhood and Society.* New York: W.W. & Norton Co.

FREUD, S. (1915) Instincts and their vicissitudes. In: *Standard Edition.* London: The Hogarth Press. 14:109–140.

——— 1914. On narcissism: an introduction. In: *Ibid:* 67–102.

LOEWALD, H. (1973) On internalization. In: Loewald, H. 2000. *The Essential Loewald: Collected Papers.* Hagerstown, MD: Univ. Publ. Group. Pp. 69–87.

RITVO, S. (1990) Mothers, daughters and eating disorders. In: Blum, H. P., Kramer, Y., Richards, A., and Richards, A. (Ed). 1990. *Fantasy, Myth and Reality: Essays in Honor of Jacob Arlow.* Madison, CT: Inter. Univ. Press. Pp. 423–434.

THEORETICAL
CONTRIBUTIONS

The Dialectic Between Self-Determination and Intersubjectivity in Creating the Experience of Self

MITCHEL BECKER, Psy.D.,
and BOAZ SHALGI, M.A.

This paper explores the concept of delineation in light of the dialectical process as currently defined in the relational or intersubjective literature. Although this concept is also based on projective identification processes, we see it as a broader concept. Using the modern dialectic model we propose two modes of delineation. One mode involves an interaction between the subjective organizing principles of the family and its members, on the one hand, and the child's own subjective organizing principles, on the other hand, in a mutual process of construction, destruction, and reconstruction of self-definition. We term this concept mutual *intersubjective delineation. The second mode of delineation is the individual experience of selfhood or "me"-ness as a monadic entity removed from all contextual interaction with other and thus termed the* self-determined *delineation. These two modes of delineation are seen as inherent, mutually defining processes of personality development. The manner in which the adolescent negotiates the dialectic tension between these two modes of delineation is seen as an essential process in the development of a dynamic, vital, and integrated self.*

The authors are clinical psychologists in private practice in Israel.

The Psychoanalytic Study of the Child 61, ed. Robert A. King, Peter B. Neubauer, Samuel Abrams, and A. Scott Dowling (Yale University Press, copyright © 2006 by Robert A. King, Peter B. Neubauer, Samuel Abrams, and A. Scott Dowling).

An Early Object Relation Perception of Delineation

ERIK ERIKSON (1950) SAW THE ADOLESCENT'S STRUGGLE WITH IDEN-
tity as being "primarily concerned with what they appear to be in the
eyes of others as compared with what they feel they are" (p. 261).
This dialectic between the interpersonal or social self and the inner
self is reflective of the innate essence of psychological experience as
expressed in the idiom of "one mind two mind psychologies." Within
the vast concept called "identity" we are interested in focusing on the
manner in which we self-define ourselves as seen through the prism
of the dialectic between intersubjective and intrapsychic being. Zinner and Shapiro (1972) coined the term delineation to represent the
"realm of parental behavior, acts and statements which communicate
to the adolescent his parents' image of him . . . and are the raw material for adolescent internalization and identification" (p. 524).

We see the term delineation as enabling the clinician to remain
"experience near" when interpreting how the family and adolescent
consciously and unconsciously create representations of the adolescent's self. The term delineation is synonymous with describing,
defining, and declaring what properties and characteristics make up
the self of the adolescent. Delineations are the "raw material" used in
the processes of creating self representation. Zinner and Shapiro describe an additional mode of parental delineation as follows: "Among
parental delineation are those which are more determined by their
service on behalf of parental defensive needs than by their capacity
to appraise or perceive the *realistic attributes* of the adolescent. Those
defensive delineations are the expression of parental defensive organizations" (ibid, p. 524, italics are ours).

Thus, Zinner and Shapiro make a clear distinction between "realistic delineation" based on a more healthy and objective perception of
the adolescent's traits and abilities and "defensive delineations,"
which are mainly an expression of parental defensive needs and are
thus seen as a distortion of reality and pathological. The defense delineation acts in accord with the interpersonal dynamic of a projective identification. Family members and the family system project
from themselves and deposit within the child, unwanted, threatening—though at the same time life giving and gratifying—parts of the
parents' selves. The parent is able to simultaneously distance himself
from the unwanted characteristic while remaining in relation to it.
This does not imply that the adolescent is a "tabula rasa." Rather, as
Ogden (1994) describes, projective identification usually seeks a suit-

able carrier, who a priori possesses the hints and traces of the traits projected on him. Family dynamics evoke and emphasize these pre-existing traits in the adolescent and delineate him as being-that. As a loyal recipient of a defensive delineation, he begins to experience the projection as an authentic aspect of self. In Zinner and Shapiro's words, the family dynamics of defensive delineation "leads to authentic and lasting structural change in the recipient of the projection" (ibid, p. 523).

The prospect of an adolescent releasing himself from a defensive delineation and consequently returning the projection to the parent evokes the same painful turmoil that originally motivated the parent to project the repudiated yet gratifying characteristic from himself. The intensity of the parent's defensive need and the degree of dependence and lack of autonomy of the child determine the level of motivation to sustain the defensive delineation. Zinner and Shapiro ponder the question, "How do we account for the extent to which adolescents may collude in this activity with the result that parental defensive delineation becomes a self-fulfilling prophecy? The motivation which may need to be most reckoned with is the adolescent's fear of *object loss* which might ensue were he not to act on behalf of the parental defensive organization" (ibid, p. 526, italics ours). In Ogden's (1982) terms, "the muscle behind the demand" of the projection is an ongoing and emotionally laden threat that disloyalty to the assigned role will cause the adolescent to be "invisible" to the projector. Not being seen by the significant other evokes the most basic existential and abandonment anxieties.

The above stated model of psychopathology implies a need for an object relations family therapy orientation. Therapy is designed to increase the awareness of the system of projections cast onto the adolescent. The family's enhanced ability to contain previously repudiated traits enables the family to gradually loosen the hold, reshape the defensive delineation, and create the psychological space essential for the growth of individuation and autonomy of the adolescent.

We (Becker and Shalgi 2002) contended that the adolescent's motivation to participate in the family's inappropriate perception of the adolescent stems not only from his desire to protect himself from object loss but also because of the adolescent's still-fluid immature state of self-representation. As his self is not yet distinct, he is dependent on the family's delineation. Negation of these projections is experienced as a perilous foray into emptiness and void. "If this is not who I am, then I do not know who I am, or if I am." Thus the adolescent plays out his role of loyal recipient of the family members' defensive delineations of him to maintain his object bonds and establish his sense of identity—even at the cost of authenticity, growth, and vitality.

In this vein, we therefore suggested a therapeutic model that therapy aims to create a reciprocal process of release from the system of defensive projections (Berkowitz et al. 1974, Shapiro 1979), together with the gradual construction of new "building blocks" of the self. New experiences of the self in his world encourage new experiences of separateness from the old definitions of self. In addition, the family's capacity for containment of their own separateness is simultaneously enhanced by their perception of their child's successful psychological growth. This is a step-by-step process of growth and release in which a defensive delineated identity is exchanged for an identity established through a genuine search for experience and sensation of self, constructed into a complementary system of self and object representations.

This conceptualization of adolescent psychopathology and the corresponding process of therapeutic change which it suggests is based upon two assumptions which characterize what we term the classic dialectic and correspondingly classic psycho-analysis. The first assumption is that change is a process formed by substituting the old with the new. In accord with this assumption, the therapeutic model is one of releasing the family members from interactions characterized by pathological projective identification and creating developmentally enhancing interactions in which the family members see and relate to the adolescent for who he is, free of projection while simultaneously allowing the construction of a transitional space in which the adolescent constructs a new sense of identity out of his own experiences and self-created building blocks. The second assumption is that there is a clear dichotomy between the real objective attributes of self and the distorted delineation of self produced by interpersonal interactions marked by pathological projective identifications. Therapy attempts to differentiate between real attributes and defensive delineations.

The ongoing influence of what we term the modern dialectic, both in philosophy and contemporary psychoanalysis, puts these two assumptions in question and thus brings new light to the process of creating identity and change. Describing the classic and modern dialectic, we offer a new perspective to adolescent delineation focusing on two ways of creating a sense of identity.

The Dialectic — Classic and Modern

The philosophical concept of the dialectic has a long developmental history in Western thought. The dialectic was born out of the recognition of man's capacity to sense, think, and pursue knowledge. It began in early Greek philosophy as a science of argument and investigative method. This dialectic method engaged in a confrontational exercise of logic in which basic assumptions were mutually explored and logical contradictions were exposed thus establishing a compelling need to search for a new mode of thinking and knowing.

Inherent in this ancient Greek dialogue was the moral stance that humans sin and do "wrong" because they think and perceive erroneously. This metaphysical vantage is a pursuit for an objective kind of knowledge and stance obtained by virtue of man's pure reason. The dialectic served to debunk erroneous subjective assumption and crowned objective knowing as the correct recognition of reality.

The modern dialectic was born out of a disillusionment in the classic dichotomy between objective reason and subjective apperception of historical actuality. This dichotomy of classic philosophers (including philosophers of the enlightenment) cast human existence as a product of creation and change, whereas knowledge and reason uniquely assumed a pure objective and eternal existence. Modern philosophers, such as Kant (1790) and, even more so, Hegel (1807), postulated an integration of conceptual process and actual history. Reason and knowledge were seen not only as creating the reasoning subject but also as being created by the very same subject. Reason is no longer an external entity standing in dualistic relation to the experiencing subject but rather a dialectical concept created, negated, and preserved by the subject(s). This dialectical process does not aim to substitute "erroneous" with "correct." It consists of negating and preserving contents, which by virtue of their co-existing tension and opposition mutually create their existence and definition (Hegel chose the term Aufhebung to describe this process). Pure reason and existence of the subject become mutual creators. The ontological world is self-explicated by the subject's experiences and recognition, which at the same time defines his own being as a subject. In this sense, the modern dialectic can be seen as an existential leap that brings together objective and subjective as mutually recognizing and defining and views the pursuit for a uni-dimensional objective reality as incomprehensible and irrelevant.

The above-described development of the dialectic concept shaped the theoretical development of conflict in psychoanalysis. Freud's (1930) initial conception of conflict is based on opposing biological drives in conflict with the demands of reality. Instinctual satisfaction versus abstinence is a uni-dimensional conflict between contradictory forces arguing their case in which the upper hand in normal development goes to the presenter of reality. The role of the analyst is to correct the logic of primitive libido and superego and thus free the patient to accept the objective though frustrating reality. In Ghent's (1995) words: "Classically . . . interpretation is aimed at helping the patient see, or perceive, things differently, that is, from a new perspective. The implicit assumption was that changed perception would result in changes in ways of being and doing in the world [we can see here the stance stated above that "people do 'wrong' because they perceive erroneously, the basic assumption of what we have termed 'classic dialectic' that is . . . *insight* will lead to change" (pp. 486–487)].

Despite Freud's continued development of new personality models culminating in the structural theory, which can be seen as a system of interpenetrating agencies of mind, psychoanalytic theory still remained, to some extent, under the influence of the "Law of conservation of energy." The analytic process was concerned with bolstering the preferred mode of function—secondary process over primary process. This was aptly expressed in Freud's (1933) credo "where id was ego shall be" (p. 80). The implication being that there exists a more objective and preferred mode of mental functioning.

In a similar vein, early object relation and self-psychology theories postulated development from fragmented object and archaic self to consolidated, integrated, and whole objects and self. In essence, their therapeutic credos were, "where paranoid-schizoid position was, there depressive position will be" and "where archaic self was, there cohesive, continuous and vital self will be." Development is a linear and temporally sequential process evolving from primitive to more mature and realistic states or stages.

Modern psychoanalytic thinking has increasingly been influenced by the Hegelian dialectic which is eloquently described by Thomas Ogden: "Dialectic is a process in which opposing elements each create, preserve, and negate the other; each stands in a dynamic, ever-changing relationship to the other. Dialectical movement tends toward integrations that are never achieved. Each potential integration creates a new form of opposition characterized by its own distinct form of dialectical tension. That which is generated dialectically is continuously in motion, perpetually in the process of being created and negated, perpetually in the process of being decentered from static self-evidence" (1994, p. 14).

Contradictory or opposing concepts and forces are no longer perceived as competing but rather "dialectical relationships are always generating mutual influence, so that each pole is not only dependent on its opposite for its meaning but is actually imbued with qualities that are more prominently defining of the opposite" (Hoffman 2001, p. 480).

The relational or intersubjective literature has investigated many issues in psychoanalysis as reconceptualized in this modern dialectic. The self-explicated meaning of change has been delved into via the prism of ritual and spontaneity (Hoffman 1999), meaning and death (Becker 1973), old and new (Greenberg 1999), and repetition and transformation (Lachmann 2001). Issues focusing on the tension between the self and object relation have been expressed in the dialectics of mutuality and autonomy (Aron 1996, Mitchell 1997), recognition and destruction (Benjamin 1992), self-expression and self-subordination and presence and absence (Peltz 1998).

All of the above stated theorists conceptualize these opposing modes of being as standing in a mutually enhancing coexistence. This "dialectic requires that the tension be sustained between both terms in such a way that neither is fully negated and a space can exist between the terms—a space in which meaning can flourish and the recognition of freedom can be embraced" (Peltz 1998, p. 391).

This dialectical model describes psychological experience as comprised of simultaneously coexisting and interrelated modes of being. We see the adolescent's existential struggle to define himself through this very same prism of dialectic. We will use the concept of delineation to illustrate this adolescent's struggle to define his sense of identity as being created both through his context and within himself. These two modes of delineation are not exclusive, but create, negate, and enhance each other.

THE MUTUAL INTERSUBJECTIVE DELINEATION

Modern dialectic thinking as described above brings into question the distinction between objective, reality oriented definition of the adolescent and distorted definitions based on erroneous subjective projections. In contrast, the relational or intersubjective perspective describes a meeting of all interpersonal interactions as a mutual meeting of the subjects' experience, perception, and need. Thus, the adolescent's development takes place in "the evolving psychological field constituted by the interplay between the differently organized subjectivities of child and caretaker" (Orange, Atwood, and Stolorow 1997, p. 4). From this vantage point, one can no longer aim at differentiating between realistic perception based on the true reality and idiosyncratic perception based on subjective psychological need.

This interaction between family and child is a continuous meeting of subjectivities in which each member creates, nurtures, influences, and shapes the other's perception of self and other. In this sense there exists a continuous mutual process of establishing and re-establishing representations of all members of the interactional system in an assimilation—accommodation manner. Each individual assimilates the interactional experience into the pre-existing representations and organizing principles and simultaneously accommodates these representations in response to the new experience, thus creating change. Each member's experience of the other serves to shape and reshape the other's experience in a circular feedback loop of mutual influence. The individual is seen as both creating and being created by his social system's organizing principles of experience, an intersystemic process. This mutual, continuous, and ever-changing exchange of interactions, perceptions, and conceptions constructs the process of delineation within the family and social system. We call this mutual dance among members of the system the *mutual intersubjective delineation.*

The child's perception of the system's delineation of himself inspires a natural, yet complex resistance to or negotiation with the system's way of experiencing him, the meanings attributed to him, and the "use" extracted from him. The adolescent experiences his struggle and confrontation with parental expectation, authority, acceptance, and rejection as the intersubjective field in which aspects of self, aspirations, characteristics, and coping style are shaped and defined. We see argumentative stands such as "You can't run my life," "You don't understand anything (i.e. me)," or "You always think you're right" represent ways in which the adolescent negotiates and even attempts to negate the content of the parents' representation or schematic perception and organization of their experience of him. This is a struggle between adolescent and family system regarding the content, manner, and process of defining the adolescent who never intends to deny or disconnect from the existence of a family definition. This struggle, therefore, remains an essential part of the intersubjective mutual definition. Thus, the representation of the adolescent is endlessly negotiated in a process in which the self is developed and constructed through the patterns of experience and apperception in the intersubjective field of adolescent and family system.

THE SELF-DETERMINED DELINEATION

The intersubjective school of thought that sees relations, mutual influence, and creation of the I-you encounter as the focal point of understanding human experience and development simultaneously seeks to account for the experience of individuality and I-ness within the matrix of co-created minds. Perhaps, Mitchell's (1993) description of the relational school best illustrates the dialectic struggle between social embeddedness and autonomous self-definition. "It feels as if our personal self is ours in some uniquely privileged way; we control access to its protective layers and its core; only we know and understand its secrets. It feels as if the self is not inevitably contextual and relational but has an existence and a life that is separate and autonomous from others. Yet the self that seems so personal and interior is, in a broader perspective, deeply embedded in relations with others" (p. 111). Similarly, in Benjamin's (1992) words, "Respect for the inner world—including the bad—leads me to prefer a theoretical perspective in which intersubjectivity rivals but does not defeat the intrapsychic. Such a theoretical approach can then explicitly try to account for the imbalance between intrapsychic and intersubjective structures" (p. 46).

In the vein of the above mentioned efforts to create a synthesis of one mind—two mind psychology, we present, in addition to the mutual intersubjective delineation heretofore described, a second mode of delineation. This second mode of being is based on those moments of complete and pure introspection into the inner depths of self-experience, which we will term the *self-determined delineation*. As will be discussed later, our postulate of dialectically opposed modes of being implies that the self-determined delineation is mutually created and influenced by the intersubjective delineation. Yet, we believe that this self-determined delineation has separate and unique experiential and ontological qualities, which should be examined and understood within themselves.

This self-determined experience of self is constructed via the individual's capacity to sense himself, feel his own feelings, think his own thoughts and reflections of self, and experience his own wants and desires as stemming only from his own inner self. This experience is not a negotiated response to others' subjective experience of himself, nor is it a negation of how the other sees him. Rather it is a momentary suspension of the possibility of being perceived by the environment. This delineation is constructed by the mental states in which the individual temporarily yet purposefully disconnects from the essence of intersubjective being and constructs an autonomous state of individuality.

A brief clinical vignette aptly illustrates the disconnection from the mutual intersubjective delineation. During a session, an adolescent describes an interaction with his father. "I don't know how he does it but Dad always gets me to tell him things that I shouldn't. So I told him how I liked this girl and how she didn't seem interested. I started to feel myself crying and my father began his usual macho speech that I have to show absolute confidence and certainty. What most hurt was when he began to poke fun at my feelings—I know he cares but what a fuckin' way of showing it." The adolescent's experience of being loved by his father intersubjectively connects him to the undesired delineation of being soft and feminine. The unstated and unconscious dynamic is that the father brought to the family system a deep and intense emotionality whose presence the father simultaneously denied within himself and vicariously experienced through others. The adolescent continues, "so I stormed away to my room and began strumming on my guitar, thinking about the times I played for some friends and how a couple of girls gave this look, like you're pretty damn cool—don't stop playing." At this point, the adolescent is still in an interactional or relational mode. He wrestles with his father's representation of himself by conjuring competing representations of himself as related by other subjects in his psychological world. The girls' "look" is an emotional intersubjective appreciation of the very same emotional life of the adolescent which father connects to and delineates as negative. This is a monumental intersubjective achievement in which building blocks of self are reconstructed by interacting with subjective perceptions of others, thus, expanding the more constricted mutual intersubjective delineation of the father.

However, in this scenario the adolescent has not as of yet touched upon the monadic individual experience, from which stems the self-determined delineation. But at this juncture the experiential mode shifts. "As I was playing, the image of the girls left my mind and I felt myself in my own music world. I was fascinated with the movement of my own fingers, the touch of the strings and the notes just seemed to touch my soul. It was *my* music for *my* pleasure and it was great." This time his eyes gleamed a genuine euphoric moment of autonomous selfhood relinquished of all environmental context. He was neither accepting nor negotiating others' perception of himself, but rather creating a sense of being that momentarily denied the presence of outside or formerly outside elements of self-definition. This is an aspect of selfhood in which the self constructs experiences of excitement, sensuality, and satisfaction that serve to self-define without any contextual meeting with another's subjectivity. The self experiences a monadic moment of being *with and only with oneself.* We term this process of self-definition the *self-determined delineation.* Monadic experiential moments such as these arise at critical crossroads of development as well as in the daily routine of life. Cooking the perfect idiosyncratically desired tastes, moments of artistic creativity, eroticism, and daydreaming can all serve as monadic moments, potentially free of all context. In our view, this monadic experience of self is an essential, unique, and imperative component in the adolescent's endeavor to create and maintain his experience of cohesivity, continuity, and positive affective coloration (Stolorow and Lachmann 1980).

A Modern Dialectical Approach to Delineation

Having described two modes of self-definition and experience, the mutual intersubjective and self-determined, we explore the relationship between the two modes of experience. The modern dialectic approach serves us well in our attempt to describe these delineations' co-existence. In this line of thought, these two modes of being can be seen as mutually creating, negating, and enhancing each other.

Each mode is comprised of elements whose essence and origin were derived from the other. An individual ensconced in a mutual intersubjective moment of experience brings to that relational moment sensations and experiences of self born out of the self-determined experience of self. Similarly, the non-contextual, non-relational self-determined monadic moment of self-experience brings with it a sense of self-representation based on previous mutual intersubjective delineations. Each newly created aspect of monadic selfhood by nature of its co-existence must ultimately influence the mutual intersubjective selfhood and vice versa. These two extremes of human existence co-exist in an interminable dialectic tension: They mutually create, destroy, negate, and nurture but never replace each other. In our opinion, the adolescent's capacity to manage and negotiate the dialectic tension between these two delineations is one of the primary determinants of psychological health. Child and system strive to create a healthy dialectical balance in which each mode of delineation is experienced as mutually enhancing each other. In this sense we see a need for a language to describe this dialectic balance. We borrow terms from movement therapy, family systems therapy, and mother-infant literature to create this language. We are interested in the rhythm, activity level, and intensity of interplay between the vectors, which construct the dialectic tension. Is the movement from one mode to another smooth or jerky, slow or quick? Is the manner in which the delineation is addressed direct or indirect, predictable or unpredictable? What is the adaptability of the dialectic-rigid or flexible, easily influenced or entrenched? To what degree can the dialectic be modulated in tune to the needs of the life stages of the family and the developmental stages of the child? This language can potentially enrich our psychoanalytic aspiration to phenomenologically describe the tension between inner self-experience and relational experience.

In this sense, we are in debt to Winnicott's perspective on the human condition as an existential paradox of simultaneously creating an inner and outer world. In Winnicott's words, "the individual is engaged in the perpetual human task of keeping inner and outer reality separate yet inter-related" (Winnicott 1951, p. 230). This is the "inherent dilemma, which belongs to the co-existence of two trends, the urgent need to communicate and the still more urgent need not to be found" (Winnicott 1963, p. 185), the urgent need to experience oneself in the relational intersubjective context and the no less urgent need to experience oneself as a non-relational, non-contextual monadic being.

Summary

In this paper, we have attempted to construct a model of psychological development of self-definition which entails an integration of the intersubjective experience of I-You (Buber 1927) with the inner meness experience of the monadic-self. The intersubjective school casts the human relational experience as consisting of not only reflection and introspection with regard to the place of the other in one's psychological world (object relations), but rather as the network of subjectivities in constant relation which mutually experience, wrestle and create each other (the meeting of subjectivities). This intersubjective conceptualization contributed to our revised definition of delineation from a potentially undesirable projective identification resulting in developmental arrest to the perspective of the mutual intersubjective delineation as an inherent, continuous, and mutual experience which serves by its basic nature to define each other's subjectivity.

The modern dialectic approach as presented in this paper is seen as a major cornerstone of relational school theory. Relational theory not only profoundly reconceptualizes the intersubjective delineation but it similarly revolutionizes how we perceive the monadic experience of self. In contrast to classic psychoanalytic theory's perception of the monadic self as an objective observable entity that undergoes an incessant process of being differentiated from distorted perceptions of self, the relational school and its allegiance to the modern dialectic approach leads us to see the monadic individual as a dynamic narrative of self-determined subjective delineations struggling to create a sense of autonomy. Furthermore, we see this monadic experience as a crucial player in the adolescent's struggle for self-definition. These two delineations, self-determined and intersubjective, stand in dialectic tension as complementary modes of experience reciprocally resisting and establishing each other in the drama of creating the adolescent self-narrative. Thus, although at polarized moments we can be swallowed in the intersubjective experience with an other, or bathe in an absolute self-autonomic singlehood, each mode of the dialectic never ceases to maintain its essence and simultaneously mutually define each other. This view enhances our appreciation of the incessant struggle to weave into the existential narrative our quest for attachment and individuation, identification and self-creativity, empathic attunement and the capacity to be alone.

BIBLIOGRAPHY

ARON, L. (1996). *A meeting of minds.* Hillsdale, N.J.: Analytic Press.
BECKER, E. (1973). *The denial of death.* New York: Free Press.
BECKER, M., & SHALGI, B. (2002). A psychoanalytical approach to integrating family and individual therapy. *Psychoanalytic study of the child,* 57. New Haven: Yale Univ. Press.
BENJAMIN, J. (1992). Recognition and destruction: An outline of intersubjectivity. In Skolnick, N. J., and Warshaw, S. C. (Eds), *Relational perspectives in psychoanalysis,* 43–60. Hillsdale, N.J.: Analytic Press.
BERKOWITZ, D., SHAPIRO, R., ZINNER, J., & SHAPIRO, E. (1974). Concurrent family treatment in narcissistic disorders in adolescence. *International journal of psychoanalytic psychotherapy.* 3:379–396.
BUBER, M. (1927). *I and thou.* Trans. W. Kaufman. New York: Scribner.

168 *Mitchel Becker & Boaz Shalgi*

ERIKSON, E. (1950). Childhood and society. Norton: New York.
FREUD, S. (1930). Civilization and its discontents. *Standard edition, 21,* New York: Norton, 1964, pp. 59–145.
—— (1933). New introductory lectures on psychoanalysis. *Standard edition, 22,* New York: Norton, 1964, pp. 3–184.
GHENT, E. (1995). Interaction in the psychoanalytic situation. *Psychoanalytic dialogue 5,* (3), 479–491.
GREENBERG, J. R. (1999). Theoretical models and the analyst's neutrality. In Mitchell, S. and Aron, L. (Eds), *Relational psychoanalysis: The emergence of a tradition,* 131–152. Hillsdale, N.J.: Analytic Press.
HEGEL, G. W. F. (1807). *Phenomenology of spirit.* Trans. A. V. Miller. London: Oxford University Press (1977).
HOFFMAN, I. Z. (1999). *Ritual and spontaneity in the psychoanalytic process: A dialectical constructivist view.* Hillsdale, N.J.: Analytic Press.
HOFFMAN, I. Z. (2001). Reply to reviews by Slavin, Stein, and Stern. *Psychoanalytic dialogue 11,* (3), 469–497.
KANT, I. (1790). *Critique of judgment.* Translated by G. H. Bernard, New York: Hafner Publishing (1951).
KLEIN, M. (1935). A contribution to the Psychogenesis of manic-depressive states. In: *Contribution to psychoanalysis.* London: Hogarth Press, 1968, pp. 282–311.
LACHMANN, F. M. (2001). Some contributions of empirical research to adult psychoanalysis. *Psychoanal. Dial.* 11 (2): 167–185.
MITCHELL, S. A. (1993). *Hope and dread in psychoanalysis.* New York: Basic Books.
—— (1997). *Influence and autonomy in psychoanalysis.* Hillsdale, N.J.: Analytic Press.
OGDEN, T. H. (1994). *Subject of analysis.* Northvale, N.J.: Aronson.
—— (1982). *Projective identification and psychotherapeutic technique.* Northvale, N.J.: Aronson.
ORANGE, D. M., ATWOOD, G. E., & STOLOROW, R. D. (1997). *Working intersubjectively. Contextualism in psychoanalytic practice.* Hillsdale, N.J.: Analytic Press.
PELTZ, R. (1998). The dialectic of presence and absence. *Psychoanal. Dial.* 8(3): 385–409.
SHAPIRO, R. L. (1979). Family dynamics and object-relations theory: An analytic, group-interpretive approach to family therapy. In: *Adolescent psychiatry: Developmental and clinical studies,* ed. S. C. Feinstein and P. L. Giovacchini. Chicago: University of Chicago Press.
STOLOROW, R. D., & ATWOOD, G. E. (1992). *Context of being.* Hillsdale, N.J.: Analytic Press.
STOLOROW, R. D. & LACHMANN, F. M. (1980). Psychoanalysis of developmental arrests. Theory and treatment. New York: International university press.
WINNICOTT, D. W. (1965). Communicating and not communicating leading

to a study of certain opposites. In: *The maturational process and the facilitating environment.* London: Karnac, 1990, pp. 179–192.

———— (1975). Transitional object and transitional phenomena. In: *Through pediatrics to psychoanalysis.* New York: Basic Books.

ZINNER, J., & SHAPIRO, R. (1972). Projective identification as a mode of perception and behavior in families of adolescents. *Int. J. of Psychoanalysis,* 53:523–530.

On an Evolving Theory of Attachment

Rapprochement—Theory of a Developing Mind

ILAN HARPAZ-ROTEM, Ph.D.,
and ANNI BERGMAN, Ph.D.

This paper adds a new dimension to the evolution of attachment and of representation formation in the toddler stage. During rapprochement, under appropriate conditions, symbolic activity begins to take prominence over sensorimotor activity to guide and regulate affective experience. We propose that as the toddler comes to increasingly reorganize early sensorimotor experiences under the influence of language, the mother plays a new and vital role in helping the toddler achieve new and higher levels of organization. The intensity of the toddler's proximity seeking-behavior, as described by Bowlby, takes on a new element in light of the toddler's need for mother as an essential interlocutor who helps him or her to verbally articulate and organize experience. The toddler's need to seek proximity with mother, particularly pro-

Ilan Harpaz-Rotem is Assistant Professor of Psychiatry, Yale University School of Medicine; Anni Bergman is Associate Professor and Supervisor, NYU Postdoctoral Program in Psychotherapy and Psychoanalysis; Training and Supervising Analyst, New York Freudian Society.

The authors would like to thank The Margaret Mahler Foundation, especially Dr. William Singletary, for providing video extracts of Mahler's original observational data. We also would like to thank Drs. Sidney J. Blatt and Robert King for their gracious help in forming the ideas that helped to shape this paper.

The Psychoanalytic Study of the Child 61, ed. Robert A. King, Peter B. Neubauer, Samuel Abrams, and A. Scott Dowling (Yale University Press, copyright © 2006 by Robert A. King, Peter B. Neubauer, Samuel Abrams, and A. Scott Dowling).

found during the rapprochement phase, serves not only to safe-guard the toddler's physical well-being but to ensure the survival of the child's developing mind. Moreover, the mother's failure to respond appropriately during this time to this emerging need for her as a verbal interpreter of experience may result in disruption of the toddler's burgeoning ability to make appropriate use of verbally mediated representations of the world, self, and others.

This paper discusses the rapprochement stage in light of this new developmental perspective.

INTRODUCTION

IN RECENT DECADES, PSYCHOANALYTICALLY INFORMED RESEARCH IN child development has blossomed, especially in the area of infant studies, and yielded important contributions to the psychoanalytic literature with implications for psychoanalytic treatment and the nature of therapeutic action (Beebe and Lachmann, 2002; Bruschweiler-Stern et al., 2002; Lachmann, 2001; Lyons-Ruth, 2000; Tronick, 1998).

The aim of this paper is to expand our understanding of early childhood relationships, specifically that of the toddler with his mother, by highlighting previously under-appreciated changes in the child's mind during the development of rapprochement. This perspective augments attachment theory (Bowlby, 1969) by proposing that during rapprochement the toddler uses the primary caregiver as a focal point in a shift from the infant's existing sensorimotor regulatory systems to new forms of regulation rooted in verbal representations. The intensity with which these new forms impel the toddler to reach for his mother are no less affectionately intense than the motivational factors of attachment that Bowlby describes. Indeed, this developmental stage requires the mother to respond to her toddler's need in new ways. We believe that during this proposed phase, the toddler has a unique opportunity to rework previously existing, maladaptive forms of early mother-child interaction. At the same time, however, deficiencies in this transition can endanger a previously secure relationship. This view of the mother-child relationship thus provides a richer understanding of the developmental processes of representation formation and affect regulation than has been previously available.

As Hofer (1996) noted, existing developmental theory lacks a clear account of how the sensory physiology of early infant social interaction becomes transmuted into the complex patterns of symbolic behavior characteristic of inner experience, often referred to as mental representations (Blatt, 1995; Fonagy and Target, 2000) or as internal working models of attachment (Bowlby, 1969). To quote Hofer: the "developmental events through which this remarkable transition takes place are not yet established" (1996, p. 177). Moreover, as the infant matures, the influence of early maternal regulators gradually wanes as the child becomes more independent and learns to take by himself. In some respects, regulation of the infant's biological systems becomes increasingly autonomous, while in others, regulation remains primarily influenced by key features of the child's environment, such as light, time of day, temperature, and interactions with caregivers or social companions (Hofer, 1996). Until recently, it has been unclear how these early regulatory processes become incorporated into mental representations or how they shift from regulation at the sensorimotor level to regulation at the cognitive-affectual level. This paper considers the developmental context within which this transition occurs.

We suggest that the transition from the sensorimotor level of regulation to the verbally mediated level of mental representation and affect regulation is a key feature of the rapprochement stage of development. In the context of the infant's growing cognitive capacities, language becomes a primary organizing agent for affective experience, and the child experiences a new and heightened need for the mother as a verbal interlocutor or interpreter of inner and outer experiences. The mother's role during this stage can be understood as helping the child to organize the self-object structure derived from sensorimotor experience into a new structure increasingly governed primarily by language. Seen in this light, the anxiety observed during the rapprochement stage of development stems not only from the child's growing apprehension of mutual separateness but also from the child's awareness of an intense need for the mother in a new way. This paper will examine this new aspect of rapprochement to explain how early representations of affect, self, other, and self in relation to other come to be organized processes accessible (or potentially accessible, if unconscious) to analysis within a two-person developmental model.

BACKGROUND

Instruments such as the Adult Attachment Interview (AAI; George, Kaplan and Main, 1985), Differentiation-Relatedness Scale (D-R; Diamond et al., 1991), Reflective Functioning Scale (RF; Fonagy et al., 1998), or Object Relation Inventory (ORI; Blatt et al., 1981) assess adult respondents' ability to reflect on current or early emotional relationships and have provided rich empirical methods for examining individuals' implicit and explicit schema of self and of self in relation to others. The knowledge gained by the use of these instruments raises such questions as: What constitutes the ability to reflect on one's emotional life? How does one come to talk about feelings? What gives one person the ability to reflect accurately (as much as one can) on self and others while another will reflect almost exclusively on fantasies of self and others? Although some models of development root these capacities in the mother-child relationship during the child's first year of life (Fonagy and Target, 2000) and focus on the context in which early forms of representations are formed, they fail to explain how the child develops verbal access to sensorimotor encoded experiences.

Researchers agree that the unique emotional relationship between mother and child appears to crystallize in the first year of a child's life (Bowlby, 1969; Cassidy, 1994; Main, 1999; Sander, 1980; Sroufe, 1979; Tronick, 2002). However, the mechanisms by which an infant represents and regulates emotional experience differ from those of the older child and adult. Therefore, a better understanding of the transition from infant to toddler forms of experiencing and understanding is necessary for the understanding of adult relationships, including the analytic dyad.

The idea that the early mother-child interaction lays the foundation for self-structure, in the form of early emotional representations of the dyad, was explicated in Stern's theory of the structure of the self (1983). Stern and others argued that early preverbal forms of interaction provided the basic structure of the self. Stern proposed that the mood, style, quality, and rhythm of the mother-child dyad allowed for the creation of RIGS (Representations of Interactions that have been Generalized), which are the foundation of the self. Lachmann and Beebe (1989) also suggested that the patterns of these early representations were the basic forms of identity. In later work, Beebe and Lachmann (1991) described the principles by which representations take form: ongoing regulations, rupture and repair of the dyadic activity, and heightened affective experience.

However, an essential component in the formation of identity is self-reflexivity—the ability to make transitions between subjective and objective perspectives of the self (Bach, 1994). The capacity for self-representation, inherent in emerging self-awareness, appears as the ability to reflect on oneself as an object. As a result, self-awareness has two main facets (Blatt and Bers, 1993): subjective self-awareness and objective self-awareness. The ability to integrate these two forms of self-awareness appears to emerge between 18 and 24 months (Auerbach and Blatt, 2004). Fonagy and Target (1996) explained that this type of consolidation normally begins in the second year of a child's life and is largely completed by the sixth year. Mayes and Cohen (1996) argued that although the child experiences his body separate from his mother's at around the second year, it is only by the fifth or sixth year that the child fully understands that his mind is distinct from his mother's.

This description of emergent self-awareness (Auerbach and Blatt, 2004; Fonagy and Target, 1996) appears to parallel the rapprochement phase of development described by Mahler, Pine, and Bergman (1975). It also coincides with the start of pretend play (Piaget, 1945) and with the use of transitional objects (Winnicott, 1971). All of this evidence points to the significance of the child's transition into the third year of life and calls for a closer look at the mother's relationship to the child at this time. We strongly believe that a healthy development of self-awareness is dependent upon the successful resolution of rapprochement. The observations of Mahler, Pine, and Bergman (1975) provide a rare opportunity to better understand this transitional period, during which the child's capacity to view his mind as separate from his mother's emerges out of a dialectical process.

Early psychological differentiation of self and other begins over sharing affective states between mother and child, a type of sharing that is preverbal and dialectical, fluctuating between mutually gratifying involvement and experienced incompatibility. This view is shared by Anna Freud (1963) who stressed the role of the dyadic exchanges between mother and child around issues of pleasure and pain as crucial experiences for cognitive growth and development. The centrality of preverbal affective processes in the formation of the self is also apparent in the writing of Bion (1962), Fairbairn (1952), Kohut (1977), and Winnicott (1956). The child's early ability to form mental representations of self and others is, then, rooted in early object relationships and is initiated in the early process of mirroring that occurs between infant and caregiver (Fonagy and Target, 1997). Fonagy and Target (1997) have suggested that infants gradually learn that they have feelings and thoughts and, in particular, feel that their caregivers respond to their internal experiences. Through this learning, primary representations of experience are organized into sec-

ondary representations of mind and body. Flawed parental responsiveness, however, leads to delayed or distorted secondary representations of affect, with serious consequences for the development of
the child's psychic reality.

Integrating various theories of intersubjectivity (Aron, 1998; Blatt
and Auerbach, 2001; Benjamin, 1995), Auerbach and Blatt (2004)
propose that children become independent subjects only when regarded as such by their parents and can only complete the process of
separation when they recognize their parents' subjectivity—that is,
when children understand that their parents have minds independent of their own. According to Auerbach and Blatt, "this basic intersubjective situation, this mutual recognition by caregiver and infant
of each other's independent subjectivity, is just as crucial as are phy-
logenetic processes to the child's development of reflexive self-awareness and of the theory of mind that enables a child to understand the
beliefs and desires of others" (p. 82). We believe that the rapprochement phase marks a crucial change in the child's representation
structures and thus requires a new level of attendant parental emotional availability, as emotional narrator, and thus provides new opportunities (and risks) for change.

It is our view that the transition between early forms of representation of affect and the newly emerging organizing forms of verbally
mediated thought occurs during rapprochement and is the product
of the dialogue between self and other, which is a crucial component
in the capacity for intersubjectivity (Auerbach and Blatt, 2001; Behrends and Blatt, 1985; Benjamin, 1985; Ogden, 1994). We believe that
these dialogues should be part of the investigation into the formation of mind. The centrality of the transition from a preverbal to a
verbal level of representation is also seen as the child's growing capacity for verbalization, increased ego control over drives and affects,
and the ability to test reality (Katan, 1961). The new understanding
of rapprochement, with its emphasis on the significant role of language, adds a new and crucial dimension to the perspective offered
by Mahler and her colleagues (1975).

VYGOTSKY AND LANGUAGE

Although development is a continuous process, there are several milestones that mark the achievement of each stage of organization (Piaget, 1954; Erikson, 1982; Freud, 1957). Each stage allows for not
only the assimilation of new information but also the reorganization
of previously integrated representations, both of which give the child

the opportunity to look back, to derive new understanding and meaning, and to create more complicated mental constructs. During rapprochement, the role of language acquisition and language use, particularly in dialogic contexts, marks a major transition period from sensorimotor to linguistic representational forms of experience.

Vygotsky (1978) offered a dialectical approach to linguistic development that provides a model for understanding the child's psychological development during rapprochement. His dialectical approach to development integrates well into the line of thinking presented here regarding the formation of higher-level representations of affect and interactions that emerge during rapprochement. The relationship between psychoanalysis and Vygotsky's developmental theory was examined by Wilson and Weinstein (1990, 1992a, 1992b, and 1996). They saw the psychoanalytic investigation of word meaning and sense as providing clues to the context and affective conditions under which word meanings were originally created, and thus opening a window into hidden emotional climates (1992a).

Vygotsky (1978) claimed that higher mental functions develop through social interaction rather than solely as a result of internally generated cognitive change. More specifically, social interaction fosters cognitive growth by providing the child with the necessary tools for higher thinking. Vygotsky (1966; 1978) observed that just as humankind has developed tools to master the environment it has also created psychological tools to master its own behavior. He called the various psychological tools that people use to aid their thinking and behavior *signs*. Vygotsky went on to argue that we cannot understand human thinking without examining the signs that cultures provide. For Vygotsky, the most important sign system was undoubtedly speech. According to Vygotsky, when humans use signs, they engage in mediated behavior. That is, they do not just respond to environmental stimuli, their behavior is also mediated by their sign system.

Speech, according to Vygotsky (1966), is more than just a communication tool which enables a child to participate in social life; it also facilitates the child's own individual thinking. As speech develops children begin to carry out with themselves the kinds of dialogues they have previously had with others. At first this is done aloud; by about six years of age they carry on such dialogues more inwardly and silently. To talk to ourselves is to think with the help of words. The general model underlying cognitive development, according to Vygotsky (1978), is one of the internalization of social interactions, and the means for such internalization is speech, at first guided by others, but ultimately becoming an intrapsychic process.

Egocentric speech, with which at first the child talks aloud to himself, was observed by Vygotsky as helping and directing the child's behavior. Slowly, as speech becomes inner speech, the child develops the ability to have a silent dialogue within himself. Vygotsky (1987) saw this as a "verbal self-regulation process." Words, for Vygotsky, have a power through which the child masters his behavior. We believe that verbal self-regulation evolves to replace sensorimotor level of representation primarily during rapprochement. Moreover, verbal self-regulation which is first guided by parents and then becomes an intrapsychic process not only serves to regulate the child's behavior but most importantly assists both the child and the parents to regulate emotional states.

WORDS AS TRANSITIONAL OBJECTS

Harris (1992) has integrated Winnicott's (1971) concept of transitional objects with Vygotsky's notion that words are tools to perform cognitive and social tasks. As interpreted by Harris (1992), Winnicott's (1971) developmental theory suggested that language could serve as a transitional object. Winnicott highlighted the importance of the mother-child relationship as the context for the child to experience symbolic thought and creativity. The mother provides the child with the environment to learn how to distinguish self and other, a function that she performs through verbal and non-verbal interactions with her child. Increasingly, as the infant grows, she uses language as a means of communication and, in the process, provides him with a tool for achieving independence and subjective autonomy.

The notion of language as a transitional phenomenon is crucial to our argument. With language as a transitional object, the child can use language successfully to transition between different modes of organizing experience and between different patterns of relating to others. As Harris (1992) noted, it is the transitional experience between early *subjective omnipotence*—where the mother's response to the child produces the illusion that the child's wish creates the object of his desire (and which later on allows for the experience of spontaneous desires and gestures as real, important, and deeply meaningful even though they must be integrated in adaptive negotiations with another person)—and *objective reality*, by which the child employs language to negotiate.

Entry into the speech system can be viewed as one of the greatest milestones in the child's developmental process. There is no doubt that verbally mediated thinking designates a new level of conscious and unconscious representation and that language use marks a significant leap in the child's capacity to organize, reorganize, and regulate his experiences. The absence of language capability in the child's first year of life limits the organizational structuring of emotional experience to a more primitive level of representation. Although these internalized representations are crucial to the child during the first year of his life, the question we seek to address is how these experiences become available and reworked by the child as he later develops the capacity to give voice to his experience, past and present.

The Mother's Role as Interlocutor and Interpreter during Rapprochement

The unique space for enacting the transition between early forms of sensorimotor representation and the child's newly emerging verbal capacities for organizing experience in the form of verbally mediated thoughts emerges vigorously during the rapprochement phase of development. It is our contention that what was originally thought to be anxiety associated with the experience of separateness and the loss of the child's object of love can, in fact, also be understood as anxiety mainly associated with the emergence of the child's new capacity for organization and new need to put previous experience into verbally mediated representational form. In this context, the child's need to return to the mother reflects a desire and need for the mother as an organizing agent for his emotional experiences and as a narrator or interpreter for both new experiences and those that were formerly structured and internalized on a sensorimotor level. During rapprochement, then, the child not only begins to separate from the mother but increasingly seeks her out so that she can put his current and earlier experiences into words. Thus dialogues are a new terrain both for anxiety which arise through misunderstandings and for pleasure through the shared experience of understanding.

Separation-individuation processes, present almost from birth (Beebe and Lachmann, 1991), play a significant role in the formation of self-other representational schema. Not only physical separation and reunion but also understanding and misunderstanding are a crucial arena in which differentiation seems to occur. These events take place through various forms of ruptures and repairs on a daily basis and evoke anxiety, as the child must find new ways to understand self and other. This anxiety propels the developmental process and, if appropriately contained, leads to a new and more accurate view of self, other, and the world.

Given that the process of separation-reunion is ongoing from birth, why does heightened anxiety accompany the rapprochement phase? It might be expected that the child's growing capacity for self-regulation would, over time, lead to a decrease in the anxiety associated with this process. Mahler and her colleagues (1975) proposed, for instance, that the child's increasing capacity for locomotion creates the occasion for physical separateness by making it possible for him to dart away from the mother. Because the child actively leaves and returns to the mother at this age, one might also expect that the child's initiated, intentional moves away from the mother would be less anxiety provoking than the mother's moves away from the child.

There is a rich body of developmental literature indicating that before rapprochement, by 16–18 months, the child achieves evocative constancy (Fraiberg, 1969; Piaget, 1954; Werner, 1957; Werner and Kaplan, 1963) defined by Fraiberg (1969) as the child's capacity to establish and sustain a representation of the caregiver, independent of her physical presence and of variations in the infant's need states. Since the child's anxiety does not seem to decrease as might be expected but is heightened as toddlers enter rapprochement, we suggest that the anxiety observed during the rapprochement phase deserves fresh examination and broader explanation.

RE-ATTACHMENT

One observation which defined rapprochement for Mahler and her colleagues was that children wanted to return to their mothers after leaving them. During the prior practicing stage, the children approached their mothers in what was described as the *"refueling"* type of bodily approach. But during rapprochement, the child's physical approach was observed to be compounded with a much higher level of symbolic engagement, characteristically governed by the use of language, play, and other forms of intercommunication, as if the child sought re-attachment to his caregiver. Consequently, coming back to the mother during rapprochement included a richer array of behaviors and emotional resonances than observed during refueling. Mahler and colleagues saw the increased separation anxiety as a new feature of the child's experience at this stage, as was the child's tendency to approach the mother more frequently when she was present, often filling her lap with objects from the environment. Sharing, both physically and linguistically, became one of the most distinctive characteristics of their interaction. Furthermore, the child *demanded* the mother's full attention to his wish to share experiences, orienting the mother into a dyadic state of emotional exchange. No matter how the mother was previously experienced by her child, separation anxiety coincided with the child's desire to reunite and share with the mother. As a result, we believe that the transition from the practicing stage to rapprochement deserves further investigation since the child's need to return to the mother seems to emerge suddenly and vigorously. Additionally, the implications of this need require attention, as the child initiates a new type of engagement with the mother during rapprochement and as the effects of the child's engagement with the mother at this time may influence adult emotional relationships.

Secondly, a change in children's reactions to their mothers' location was manifested in increased distress or sadness in response to separation together with signs of greater vulnerability, impotent rage, and helplessness. In their observation, Mahler and her colleagues did not explain why there is more distress and anxious attunement to the mother's whereabouts. We suggests that at this crucial junction, the mother becomes no longer just "home base" for the child, but rather someone with whom the child wishes to share the world. With a newly heightened wish to share experiences with her in a new way, it becomes important for the child to give the mother objects and to show her, by gestures or by words, that he needs her to be interested.

In our present view, these rapprochement phenomena support the notion that this crucial phase of development is marked by reorganization of the child's representations of self, other, and self in relation to other. This reorganization process not only replaces previous sensorimotor representation but also lays the foundation for structuring new experiences by language. During the rapprochement crisis the child must approach the mother with what must be seen as an internal need similar to the one operating in the child's first year of life when the child seeks the mother in order to reduce fear associated with internal or external stimuli (Bowlby, 1980). During rapprochement, however, the child needs the mother as an interlocutor to reorganize current and past experiences, thus allowing the child to internalize and to later retrieve a new form of representation.

This heightened need to reach for the mother as interlocutor is not solely dependent on previous experiences of her as either a good or bad responder. Rather, it seems to appear as a new, autonomous imperative whose vicissitudes unfold without respect to earlier attachment style. In other words, the toddler *must* approach the mother in this new way during rapprochement, even if she was previously experienced as a source of fear or anxiety or was not emotionally available. However, we believe that pre-existing attachment classifications manifest themselves and mediate the quality of the child's reaction to the mother in reunion and separation. The emergence during rapprochement of new levels of relatedness and new reaction patterns governed primarily by language create the opportunity for intervention, with the unique potential to correct previously consolidated maladaptive interpersonal and representational patterns. At the same time, mother's failure to respond appropriately to her child's new developmental demand during rapprochement can lead to the disruption of a previously secure relationship.

This issue is crucial because during rapprochement mothers face new unexpected demands, at times counterintuitive to their expectation that the child will function more independently. Instead, as he insistently seeks emotional narration, the toddler demands the mother's full attention and emotional availability to his sharing overtures and heightened separation anxiety. Thus, during rapprochement the mother needs to take a new step to understand her child as she most likely experiences this behavior as a regression. As rapprochement represents a new potential developmental achievement, the mother needs to understand that her toddler's primary mode of experience is changing and correspondingly to reorganize herself to understand and meet his new and emerging needs.

In some respects, our view of rapprochement is more in line with that of Horner (1985) who stated that, "rapprochement, then, is not a process of dealing with lost symbiotic bliss but a process of restoring positive equilibrium following perturbations, a process of re-attaining basic love and security when frustrations and resistance/opposition, and their correlated affects, have been effectively dealt with" (p. 21). We do not share Horner's conviction, however, that the restoration of equilibrium is prompted by the clash between the child's growing capacity for willful assertiveness and the mother's expectations of greater obedience and self-regulation.

Mahler, Pine, and Bergman (1975) observed that after several months the child's need to reach out to the mother appeared to diminish. Through the exchange of emotional experiences with the mother and the experience of her availability as an organizing agent, the child comes to an implicit conclusion at this time about how the mother satisfies, or fails to satisfy, his emotional needs.

Most likely, assuming that the mother's way of being with her child did not change during rapprochement, the same patterns of interaction present in the child's first year of life repeat themselves in this phase, leading him to maintain pre-existing cognitive-affective representations of self and others and the original attachment characteristics he had before rapprochement.

But now these affective representations are organized (or in the case of a borderline child, fail to be organized) and accessible in verbal utterances, in re-enactments during play, or later on, in adulthood, either in transference or through empirical instruments such as the Reflective Functioning Scale (Fonagy et al., 1998), Object Relations Interview (Blatt et al., 1981), and Adult Attachment Interview (George, Kaplan, and Main, 1985). This reorganization process can also be viewed as the child's "retrospective study" of early relationships, whereby the child tries to organize earlier forms of sensorimotor representation into new forms of thought guided by language.

The resolution of the rapprochement crisis marks the beginning of this representational achievement; the toddler's representational and internalization processes are not completed at this point and remain open to further modification or refinement. The rapprochement phase re-defines the extent to which the child can rely on the mother as an organizing agent for his affective experiences. If the mother fails to attend to her role appropriately, the child will be burdened by a disproportionate share of the responsibility for organizing his affective experiences, even though he is not yet sufficiently equipped to do so. Under such circumstances, fantasy will play a major role in the child's capacity to represent affect and self and others. Clearly, the mother's emotional attunement to the needs of her child during rapprochement determines the child's successful completion of this developmental phase. According to Mahler, Pine, and Bergman (1975), "one cannot emphasize too strongly the importance of the optimal emotional availability of the mother during this subphase (rapprochement). It is the mother's love of her toddler and the acceptance of his ambivalence that enables the toddler to cathect his self-representation with neutralized energy" (p. 77).

As stated earlier, the child's intense need for the mother's availability during rapprochement resembles the child's need for the mother's presence in the first year of his life when she regulates the infant's anxiety associated with the experience of an internal or external fear. During rapprochement, however, the child's anxiety, associated with the need for proximity, is triggered by his emerging need for the mother to help him put the experience of both internal and external stimuli into words, into a theory of mind. During rapprochement, therefore, the need for the mother can be understood as "mental survival," crucial to adaptive functioning. The ability of the mother to respond to the child's new developmental needs is "tested" during rapprochement. If the mother fails to respond appropriately to these newly emerging needs, the child will no longer turn to her as a reliable resource. Mahler and her colleagues (1975) recognized the consequences associated with the mother's unavailability at this phase of development. They noted, for example, that if the mother is not available "this process drains so much of the child's available developmental energy that, as a result, not enough energy, not enough libido, and not enough constructive aggression are left for the evolution of the many ascending functions of the ego" (p. 80).

A mother who is attuned to her child's newly emerging needs can be viewed as the child's emotional narrator during rapprochement. At this stage, with the help of his mother, the child begins to narrate and, therefore, represent the complexity of the relationships that were formed in the first year of his life. One of the primary tasks during rapprochement is this reorganization of his more primitive level of emotional experience, which is in need of articulation, verbal expression, and narration. During rapprochement, verbally mediated thoughts begin to become the primary level of organization. Although the importance of verbal interchanges during rapprochement was clearly observed by Mahler and her colleagues, the adult consequences of incomplete narration during rapprochement were not incorporated into their understanding of this developmental phase or its influence on pathogeneses. They observed that "verbal communication becomes more and more necessary; gestural coercion on the part of the toddler or mutual preverbal empathy between mother and child will no longer suffice to attain the goal of satisfaction—that of well being" (1975, p. 79).

The observed intensified vulnerability on the part of the child during rapprochement can be recognized in light of this fuller understanding as a broader need, a new motivation for relationship, where the mother serves as a narrator agent for the child's affective experience, allowing the child to reorganize previously internalized sensorimotor representations of self, other, and self in relation to others. This stage paves the way for symbolic activity to replace the primary sensorimotor regulatory systems. Sensorimotor representations have to be renegotiated with the mother during rapprochement, to be accounted for by her, and then to be narrated by her, to become suitable for the child's newly emerging representational structures where language becomes the primary psychological organizing mechanism. Early representations are thus re-internalized in a new form, giving rise to the child's ability to further elaborate feelings, experiences, and fantasy.

Language not only comes to be the organizing feature of representations at this stage but it also comes to have the potential for affect regulation (Vygotsky, 1978; Wilson and Weinstein, 1990, 1992a, 1992b, 1996). From rapprochement on, affect regulation previously achieved by non-verbal communication can now be also accomplished through language. For example, when the mother says to her child, "it's scary, but don't worry, I'm here right next to you," the words "don't worry" have the potential to regulate the anxious mood associated with a potentially fearful experience. This principle applies to positive emotional experiences as well; if the child approaches an attuned mother, happily sharing his experience of the world (i.e., a toy or a new discovery) with her, the words "You are so excited; it makes you so happy" mark the child's emotional experience with appropriate signs and sense. During rapprochement, therefore, it is crucial for the mother to be emotionally available to the sharing experiences the child initiates since it is the nature and the content of particular affective-sharing experiences that make each exchange linguistically unique.

The mother must not only be emotionally available to the child during rapprochement but she must also convey to the child that she has feelings associated with those the child experiences choosing to share his world with her. In other words, if a child puts a stuffed bear in his mother's lap at this phase, the child is not interested in the mother naming the object, as children can respond to objects' names as young as one year of age. He needs, instead, her emotional narration of the sharing experience and of the feeling attached to the object. In this way, the childhood developmental phase of rapprochement is comparable to aspects of the adult therapeutic process, as the therapist helps the patient consciously organize his emotional experience in a relational context.

We can think of the mother as a psychoanalyst during rapprochement, organizing and verbalizing as yet unspoken emotional experiences. In a therapeutic setting, an emotionally unavailable analyst will produce an ineffective interpretation for the analysand. Similarly, a child will be unable to internalize his mother's narration if she is emotionally removed from her child's sharing experiences during rapprochement.

CONCLUSIONS

The seminal observations of Maher and her colleagues (1975) draw our attention to the importance of maternal emotional availability during rapprochement as a crucial factor in the move from early forms of sensorimotor representation to higher order representations and regulation processes. As Mahler and her colleagues noted:

> It is, however, the mother's continued emotional availability, we have found, that is essential if the child's autonomous ego is to attain optimal functioning capacity, while his reliance on the magic omnipotence recedes. If the mother is quietly available with a ready supply of object libido, if she shares the toddling adventurer's exploits, playfully reciprocates, and thus facilitates his salutary attempts at imitation and identification, then internalization of the relationship between mother and toddler is able to progress to the point where, in time, verbal communication takes over, even though vivid gestural behavior—that is, affectomotility—still predominates (p. 79).

In this paper we have emphasized that the need for the mother during rapprochement is similar in many ways to the need experienced earlier, but with new and crucial features that the mother is redefined, and affectively rediscovered, as a source of emotional narration. At this point in the child's development, reflective functioning (Fonagy et al., 2002) is highlighted by the mother's capacity to think about her child's experience and her ability to articulate and narrate it back to him. The capacity for verbal emotional regulation and interchange slowly replaces the pure physical touch and preverbal vocalizations, which were the primary tools previously available to the mother. This process can be described as the "power of words" to cure, comfort, or reassure, where the sign's meaning and sense come to inherit the power of regulation.

In light of this expanded understanding of rapprochement, the separation-individuation process can be viewed as a linear developmental continuum (beginning with birth and stretching into adulthood), rather than as a singular achievement of the rapprochement phase. Rooted both in mundane interactions and more complex emotional interchanges, the process of separation-individuation is propelled by sequences of understandings and misunderstandings, ruptures and repairs between the child and the persons or objects with which he interacts (Beebe and Lachmann, 1991; Harris, 1992; Lachmann and Beebe, 1989; Stern, 1985; Tronick, 1989). From the child's motoric indications that he would like to disengage from dyadic activity (implying, "I don't like it") to his transition into verbal exchange (i.e., the mother feeds the toddler, saying "yummy banana," and the child utters a genuine reply, "yucky"), the child makes it known to his mother that he already thinks and operates independently of her. The more complex mirroring of affective experiences during the first year of the child's life as well as the emotional narration that takes place during rapprochement are both central to the child's ability to recognize his own emotional experiences.

The child's heightened anxiety during rapprochement should therefore be viewed and treated as triggered not solely by the separation-individuation process but also by the child's need to seek proximity to the mother to nurture and regulate his new need to understand affect, self, and others with the help of words. As a result, we strongly believe that the resolution of rapprochement carries fateful implications for the internalization of representations and affect regulation processes from childhood into adulthood, as language becomes the primary organizing mechanism of affective experience. Moreover, this new understanding of rapprochement provides broader and productive insights into the processes of relational psychoanalysis as well as the mechanisms underlying therapeutic change. Further elaboration of this model and its implications for child development and adult psychoanalytic interventions will be discussed in future papers.

BIBLIOGRAPHY

Aron, L. (1998). The clinical body and the reflexive mind. In L. Aron and F. S. Anderson (Eds.) *Relational perspectives on the body.* 3–37. Hillsdale, N.J.: Analytic Press.

Auerbach, J. S., & Blatt, S. J. (2001). Self-reflexivity, intersubjectivity and therapeutic change. *Psychoanalytic Psychology,* 18:427–450.

——— (2004). The concept of mind: A developmental analysis. In R. Lasky (Ed.) *Essay in honor of Bertram Freedman.* New York: Guilford.

Bach, S. (1994). *The language of perversion and the language of love.* Northvale, N.J.: Jason Aronson.

Beebe, B. (1988). The contribution of mother-infant mutual influence to the origins of self and object representations. *Psychoanalytic Psychology,* 5:305–337.

Beebe, B., & Lachmann, F. (1991). Representational and self-object transferences: A developmental perspective. *Progress in self psychology,* Vol. 8. Hillsdale, N.J.: Analytic Press.

——— (2002). *Infant research and adult treatment: Co-constructing interactions.* Hillsdale, N.J.: Analytic Press.

Beebe, B., Lachmann, F. M., & Jaffe, J. (1997). Mother-infant interaction structures and presymbolic self and object representations. *Psychoanalytic Dialogues*, 7:133–182.

BEHRENDS, R. S., & BLATT, S. J. (1985). Internalization and psychological development through the life cycle. *Psychoanalytic Study of the Child*. 40:11–39.

BENJAMIN, J. (1985). *Like subjects, love objects: Essays on recognition and sexual difference*. New Haven: Yale University Press.

———— (1988). *The bounds of love*. New York: Pantheon Press.

BION, W. R. (1962). *Learning from experience*. London: Heinemann.

BLATT, S. J. (1995). Representational structures in psychopathology. In D. Cicchetti and S. Toch (Eds.) *Rochester symposium on developmental psychopathology. Vol. 6. Emotion, Cognition and Representation*. Rochester: University of Rochester Press.

BLATT, S. J., & BERS, S. A. (1993). The sense of self in depression: A psychodynamic perspective. In Z. V. Segal and S. J. Blatt (Eds.), *Self representation and emotional disorders: Cognitive and psychodynamic perspective*. 171–210. New York: Guilford.

BLATT, S. J., CHEVRON, E. S., QUINLAN, D. M., & WEIN, S. (1981). *The assessment of qualitative and structural dimension of object representation*. Unpublished research manual, Department of Psychiatry, Yale University.

BOWLBY, J. (1969). *Attachment and Loss:* Vol. 1. *Attachment*. New York: Basic Books.

BRUSCHWEILER-STERN, N., HARRISON, A. M., LYONS-RUTH, K., MORGAN, A. C., NAHU, J. P., SANDER, L. W., STERN, D. N. & TRONICK, E. Z. (2002). Explicating the implicit: The local level and the microprocess of change in the analytic situation. *International Journal of Psychoanalysis*. 83, 1051–1062.

CASSIDY, J. (1994). Emotion regulation: Influences of attachment relationships. In N. A. Fox (Ed.) *The development of emotion regulation. Biological and behavioral considerations*. 228–249. Chicago: University of Chicago Press.

DIAMOND, D., BLATT, S. J., STAYNER, D., & KASLOW, N. (1991). *Self-other differentiation of object representations*. Unpublished research manual, Department of Psychiatry, Yale University.

ERIKSON, E. H. (1982). *The life cycle completed*. New York: Norton.

FAIRBAIRN, W. R. D. (1952). *Psychoanalytic studies of the personality*. London: Routledge and Kegan Paul.

FONAGY, P., & TARGET, M. (1996). Playing with reality I: Theory of mind and the normal development of psychic reality. *International Journal of Psychoanalysis*. 77, 217–233.

———— (1997). Attachment and reflective function: Their role in self-organization. *Development and Psychopathology*. 9, 679–700.

———— Playing with reality III: The persistence of dual psychic reality in borderline patients. *International Journal of Psychoanalysis*. 81, 853–873.

FONAGY, P., TARGET, M., STEELE, H., & STEELE, M. (1998). *Reflective-functioning manual, version 5, for application to AAI*. Unpublished research manual, sub-department of Clinical Health Psychology, UCL.

FONAGY, P., GERGELY, G., JURIST, E., & TARGET, M. (2002). *Affect regulation, mentalization, and the development of the self*. New York: Other Press.

FRAIBERG, S. (1969). Libidinal object constancy and mental representation. *Psychoanalytic Study of the Child.* 24, 9–47.

FREUD, A. (1963). The concept of developmental lines. *The Psychoanalytic Study of the Child, 18:* 245–265.

FREUD, S. (1957). Civilization and its discontents. *Standard Edition, 21.* London: Hogarth Press.

GEORGE, C., KAPLAN, N., & MAIN, M. (1985). *The Berkeley adult attachment interview.* Unpublished manuscript, Department of Psychology, UC Berkeley.

HARRIS, A. (1992). Dialogues as transitional space. In N. Sckolnick (Ed.) *Relational Perspectives in Psychoanalysis.* Hillsdale, N.J.: Analytic Press.

HOFER, M. (1996). On the nature and consequences of early loss. *Psychosomatic Medicine. 58:* 570–581.

JOHNSON, D. B. (1983). Self-recognition in infants. *Infant Behavior and Development, 6:* 211–222.

KATAN, A. (1961). Some thoughts about the role of verbalization in early childhood. *Psychoanalytic Study of the Child, 15:* 184–188.

KOHUT, H. (1977). *The restoration of the self.* New York: International Universities Press.

LACHMANN, F. M. (2001). Some contributions of empirical infant research to adult psychoanalysis: What have we learned? How can we apply it? *Psychoanalytic Dialogues.* 11:167–185.

LACHMANN, F., & BEEBE, B. (1989). Oneness fantasies revisited. *Psychoanalytic Psychology,* 6:137–149.

LEWIS, M., BROOKS-GUNN, J., & JASKIR, J. (1985). Individual differences in early visual self-recognition. *Developmental Psychology, 21:* 1181–1187.

LEWIS, M., SULLIVAN, M., STANGER, C., & WEISS, M. (1989). Self-development and self-conscious emotions. *Child Development, 60:* 146–156.

LYONS-RUTH, K. (2000). "I sense that you sense that I sense . . .": Sander's recognition process and the specificity of relational moves in the psychotherapeutic setting. *Infant Mental Health Journal.* 21:85–98.

MAHLER, M., PINE, F., & BERGMAN, A. (1975). *The psychological birth of the human infant.* New York: Basic Books.

MAIN, M. (1995). Recent studies in attachment: Overview, with select implications for clinical work. In S. Goldberg, R. Muir, and J. Kerr (Eds.) *Attachment theory: Social, developmental and clinical perspectives.* 407–474. Hillsdale, N.J.: Analytic Press.

MAYES, L. C., & COHEN, D. J. (1996). Children's developing theory of mind. *Journal of the American Psychoanalytic Association, 44:* 117–142.

OGDEN, T. (1994). *Subjects of analysis.* Northvale, N.J.: Jason Aronson.

PIAGET, J. (1945). *Play, dreams, and imitation in childhood.* New York: Norton.

——— (1954). *The construction of reality in the child.* New York: Basic Books.

SANDER, L. (1980). New knowledge about the infant from current research: Implication for psychoanalysis. *Journal of the American Psychoanalytic Association,* 28:181–198.

SROUFE, L. A. (1979). The coherence of individual development: Early care, attachment and subsequent developmental issues. *American Psychologist,* 34:834–842.

STERN, D. (1983). *The Primary Relationship.* Cambridge, Mass.: Harvard University Press.

TRONICK, E. Z. (1989). Emotional and emotional communication. *American Psychologist.* 44:112–119.

——— (1998). Dyadically expanded states of consciousness and the process of therapeutic change. *Infant Mental Health Journal.* 19:290–299.

——— (2002). A model of infant mood state and Sanderian affective waves. *Psychoanalytic Dialogues.* 12:73–99.

VYGOTSKY, L. S. (1966). Development of higher mental functions. In *Psychological Research in the USSR.* Moscow: Progress Publishers.

——— (1978). Tool and symbol in children's development. In A. R. Luria and M. Cole (Eds.) *L. S. Vygotsky: Mind and Society.* Cambridge, Mass.: MIT Press.

——— (1986). *Thought and Language.* Cambridge, MA: MIT Press.

——— (1987). The problem of will and its development in childhood. In R. W. Rieber and A. S. Carton (Eds.) *The collected work of L. S. Vygotsky.* New York: Plenum Press.

WERNER, H. (1957). *Comparative psychology of mental development.* New York: International Universities Press.

WERNER, H., & KAPLAN, B. (1963). *Symbol formation: An organismic-developmental approach to language and the expression of thought.* New York: Wiley.

WILSON, A. & WEINSTEIN, L. (1990). Language, thought and interiorization—A Vygotskian and psychoanalytic perspective. *Contemporary Psychoanalysis.* 26, 24–39.

——— (1992a). An investigation into some implications of Vygotskian perspective on the origins of mind: Psychoanalysis and Vygotskian psychology, part I. *Journal of the American Psychoanalytic Association,* 40:349–379.

——— (1992b). Language and the psychoanalytic process: Psychoanalysis and Vygotskian psychology, part II. *Journal of the American Psychoanalytic Association.* 40:725–759.

——— (1996). The transference and the zone of proximal development. *Journal of the American Psychoanalytic Association,* 44:167–200.

WINNICOTT, D. W. (1956). Mirror role of mother and family in child development. In D. W. Winnicott (Ed.) *Playing and reality.* 111–118. London: Tavistock.

——— (1958). *Through pediatrics to psychoanalysis.* London: Hogarth Press.

——— (1971). *Playing and reality.* London: Tavistock.

A Note on Some Microprocesses of Identification

FRED PINE, Ph.D.

Identification is examined in terms of inferred processes through which it comes about. Three such processes are described, inferred from the intimate mother-infant relationship. They are referred to as (1) the overlay of the mother's organizing characteristics, (2) magnification processes also emanating from the mother (though stimulated by the child), and (3) appeal processes emanating from the infant or child. These identification processes are then set within the broader context of a developmental line running from global, undifferentiated states, through increased differentiation, and culminating in integration of the now-differentiated parts.

THE TERM "IDENTIFICATION" IS ORDINARILY APPLIED TO AN OBSERVA-tion of a child's psychological or behavioral likeness to a significant person in his or her life. But how (aside from genetic transmission) did such a likeness come about? Calling it an "identification" labels it without describing a process. "Identification with the aggressor" (A. Freud, 1936), which we may see in an older child or adult, is a term, for example, that is more suggestive regarding an identification *process,* presumably around an inferred effort by the person to achieve safety or mastery by taking on the characteristics of a hostile other. What can we infer regarding identification processes in the infant?

Emeritus Professor, Albert Einstein College of Medicine.

This paper is a section of a larger talk prepared for and presented at a conference on Mind and Body at Delphi, Greece, sponsored by the Hellenic Psychoanalytic Society, October 2004. It was also given earlier as the Honorary Maurice Friend Lecture in Child Psychoanalysis of the Psychoanalytic Association of New York, October 2003.

The intimate relationship between mother and infant, and especially its close-up bodily aspect, creates forms of influence and interaction which bear upon the "transfer" of dynamic and structural features from mother or other caretakers to the child. These shall herein be conceptualized as microprocesses of identification—identification as seen close-up through a microscope. Freud (1915) originally developed the idea of a process of object linkage through identification in his paper on Mourning and Melancholia. His formulation there that the shadow of the object falls upon the ego is his way of saying that the internalization of the other, appearing as an identification, is a form of interconnection with the other, in that instance presumably a holding on—whether motivated by love, longing, guilt, rage, or whatever.

Some Microprocesses of Identification

I shall describe three interactive mother-infant processes that can be seen as microprocesses of identification. My choice of these (inferred) processes reflects an attempt to imagine concrete and describable events in the formation of the very young child's beginning "identifications." Other processes, perhaps more fully intrapsychic and certainly carrying with them unconscious wishes and fantasies, are not my focus here. The three to be discussed are: (1) the superimposition of the mother's forms of organizing and disorganizing, (2) the mother's "magnification" behavior, and (3) the "appeal" phenomenon in the child. Each may be powered in part by its close tie to bodily as well as psychic experience.

To start with the first of these: the superimposition of organizing and disorganizing experiences. Bettelheim and Loewald have each addressed this aspect of the maternal role in essentially parallel ways. In a talk Bettelheim (1958) gave many years ago, he described the infant as being "like an orchestra tuning up," a raucous collection of unorganized stimuli coming as a barrage, with the mother having the role of orchestra conductor. By responding selectively and appropriately to the infant's behaviors and presumed experiences, she gives centrality to this or to that, potentially promoting relief and organization or, if her interventions are misplaced and mistimed, promoting further distress and disorganization. In this metaphor, one can recognize Loewald's (1960) well-known and much broader formulation that development is facilitated when higher level organizations place their order upon more diffuse organizations and help them take shape—a remarkably simple and powerful statement that captures a significant aspect of how development takes place.

These two linked formulations lead directly to an examination of organizing and disorganizing experiences in the infant. The overlay upon the infant of the mother's particular styles of organizing and disorganizing become what the later observer, when seeing the similarity of child to mother, will describe as the child's identification with her. Think of a random array of millions of metal filings; then think of casting a magnetic field over them. The filings immediately become organized along the pathways of the magnetic field. The infant, of course, is by no means as passive and receptive as inert metal filings, but nonetheless this feature is present in the mother-infant relationship.

So, imagine the infant, alone with its body, subject to the stimulation that that body puts forth from within or receives from without. Freud (1905) chose to focus on the psychosexual phases—oral, anal, and later genital/oedipal centers of stimulation. Empirically (that is, with the empiricism of the psychoanalytic process) we know these sites to be major foci clinically, and imagine them to be major foci during development. And there is no difficulty thinking of why this should be so, quite independent of the original (though now seriously critiqued) form of the libido theory. They are major sources of infant bodily stimulation; they are major foci of mother-child interaction in feeding, cleaning, and other caretaking activities, and they are susceptible to major pleasurable or acutely discomforting stimulus build-ups that can be resolved well or poorly, depending upon the mother's caregiving and specific aspects of the infant's state. As such they are sites of potential organizing or disorganizing experiences that will be developmentally forwarding or impairing.

But once we look to sources of organizing or disorganizing experiences, we can look beyond the erotogenic zones and psychosexual phases and find similar potential elsewhere as well. We see them in bodies that are too close or too removed and thus violate or fail to support boundaries, or in need-gratifying objects that are absent or are suffused with anxiety when present and thus violate attachment and support needs, or in too rough, intrusive, or affectively disconnected bodily handling that links fear, pain, and negative anticipation to the body-in-interaction altogether, or in overwhelming floods of stimuli from bodily pain (when present) or from the external surround. David Rapaport (1960) pointed to the cyclic and peremptory quality associated with bodily needs linked to oral, anal, and genital zones, qualities that give them particular motivational relevance. But, while not cyclic in the same sense of spontaneously arising from within, these other forms of interaction with the caretaker are certainly likely to be repetitive (given the formed character of the caretaker), with a high intensity and a high demand for resolution, qualities that are themselves parallel to the peremptory need for, for example, oral satisfaction.

Organizing or disorganizing experience in the infant can come in response to hunger, holding, or separation and attachment issues as well—and all of the issues in the normally expectable infant world. For the infant, the vast majority of these are bodily linked. When there is predictability and the stimulation is followed by relief or satisfaction, something calming and organizing must develop progressively. When the child's cry brings relief and when cycles of regularity can be anticipated, this itself *is* an organization of experience (in individualized ways of course); but when non-satiation occurs, or ineffectiveness of the child's call-for-help behavior, or when all that is predictable is a further increase in stimulation, then disorganization follows and the beginnings of anxiety/distress only "signal" the probable onset of more intense distress, and higher order defense mechanisms are unlikely to develop (Pine, 1986). Flooding and the rapid rise of traumatic anxiety are far more likely to be the result. Typically, the superimposition of the caregiver's organizing or disorganizing response significantly affects the outcome.

Such experiences, either pleasurable, comforting, and organizing or overwhelming and disorganizing, that flow from maternal handling in situations of high stimulation for the infant, become the basis not only for inner experience but for the ongoing object relation with that same mother and then others. We have come to recognize that trauma leads to repetition, starting from Freud's (1915) "spool" example. And even low level experiences, not traumatic in the single instance, but mounting to become chronic "strain trauma" (Kris, 1956) when repeated regularly within particular early object relations, also tend toward repetition. Pleasure and its particular forms and (especially) these forms of strain trauma are the engine of repetition of internalized object relations—in efforts to repeat the pleasure (which may be successful) or to master or undo the trauma (which is often not). And we also know that such early distress in relationships becomes the form of connection to the significant caretaker, automatically repeated because that is what the known relationship simply is—non-satisfaction, trauma and all. So, through many routes, organizing or disorganizing experiences get repeated and can become characteristic.

So much for the caretaker's role as orchestra conductor—a response to the infant (when that infant is experiencing intense stimulation) that quiets and fosters the organization of experience or a response that adds to the intensity and promotes disorganization. In those instances when these modes of organization/disorganization become part of the child, a later observer might say an identification has taken place. The caretaker's "shaping and molding" of the "clay" that is the infant and child may be a closer description.

There is a second way to understand components of the transfer from mother to child with regard to the bodily based and, increasingly, psychically represented stimulation the child is learning to regulate. It is what I have referred to in earlier writings (Pine, 1990) with the term: "magnification." When a normal, phase-appropriate, experience or state in the child intersects with a region of high conflict in the mother, it will stimulate those (dormant or active) conflicts in her. She will then be more likely to transmit those conflicts in some way, having them enter into her handling of the child, and she will thus promote conflict, anxiety, and developmental failure. In this way, the infant's developmentally normal state magnifies the mother's latent or active conflicts, and she in turn magnifies the import of the infant's otherwise normal movement through the particular phase-appropriate experience. In metaphor, the child's experience attracts the mother's pathological "rays" which she then sends into the child, distorting its experience. This is B. F. Skinner's (1971) "operant conditioning" in intense, personalized, affective form—not simply his description of positive or negative reinforcement or nonresponse that increases or decreases the likelihood of the subsequent appearance of particular behaviors, but a complex, entangling, insidious response that almost guarantees conflicted continuance. Many of these conflicts in the mother are those precisely attuned to bodily events in the child, be these of the sensual, psychosexual sort, like those connected with oral, anal, and genital zones, or of the whole body sort, like those connected with the child's independent motility, vigorous assertiveness, or physical expressions of aggression. That is, the mother's engagement with the child's bodily processes—the full range, from sensuality to aggression, from passive cuddling to active autonomous movement—activates old conflicts in her (specific of course to her own vulnerabilities and psychic make-up). She then brings these activated conflicts into her handling of the child, "magnifying" the affectivity of particular developmental events that match her internal issues. This magnification of affectively intense developmental events decreases the chances that the child can resolve those otherwise developmentally normal events smoothly. That the child later comes to carry the psychological conflicts of the mother, that he or she "identifies" with her, is no surprise given the mother's magnification of certain experiences. Here, then, is another microprocess of "identification": the child's phase appropriate behavior activates the mother's conflicts which she then brings into her handling of the child, magnifying the conflictual power of the phase appropriate experience for the child and guaranteeing continued conflict with its issues; the outcome is that the child carries conflicts like those of the caregiver. An "identification" has taken place. Naturally this only happens in certain areas for any particular mother-child pair.

Of course this magnification proceeds in two directions. There is "input" of conflict and anxiety into the child, or its absorption by a kind of osmosis, because of what has been activated in the mother via the infant's body. But the handling of the child's body also magnifies things for the mother in ways that she then has to cope with within herself—such things as the perceived fragility of the infant and the mother's own aggressive fantasies, the growing separateness of the two bodies, and the mother's experience of loss or efforts to hold on or to distance herself, and notably also the contact with the sucking, soiling, and miniature sexual being that the infant/child is. We cannot say that the result looks like an identification of the mother with her child, but the child's developmental presentations certainly leave their mark on her internal dynamics and their inner balance.

I now turn to one other concept that helps us understand how early, conflict/frustration/disorganization-filled, or, in reverse, organizing and satisfying experiences, tend to expand their place in the child during development—an expansion that will appear as an "identification," but that has taken place through a discernible (or inferable) process. In this instance the microprocess of identification originates in the child and pulls things inside. The concept has to do with how random or unpredictable environmental provisions, including but also beyond those provided by the mother, get taken in by the child, sometimes becoming central to his or her functioning. I have in mind what I referred to elsewhere (Pine, 1982) as the "appeal" phenomenon. This is not itself a bodily interactive phenomenon, but is readily seen to be based on bodily prototypes.

We use the phrase "it appeals to me." What does such a statement mean? In its depths, in its most psychoanalytically relevant meaning, it refers to states of unease or wish in the mind that respond to an environmental offering that "fits" with what the inner state requires. If I need bodily contact and it is uncertainly available as I need it, a soft cuddly toy may "appeal to me." A particular sight I see or story I hear may "appeal" to something unsettled and active inside me and provide a fantasy or give direction to a wish that becomes part of my psychic life. An apt example: a child I knew over time with serious neuropsychological problems involving organization of the visual field was, one day, given a gift of a camera. It "appealed to him"; that is, it fit with an inner unsettled need state. Years later, he became a photographer.

Like gravity—a force that operates at a distance, which can be used as a metaphoric parallel here—like gravity, the child's unsettled inner state "reaches out" across distance, so to speak, and pulls in environmental offerings, offerings that match what the inner state requires. These may be constructive, sublimatory, and organizing (as in my photographer example) or disturbing and painful, but familiar (as is characteristic of our repetitious relationship to internal objects).

And this tendency in the child is built in by evolution and probably has its prototype in early bodily relatedness—the first (evolution) because the receptor apparatuses attune the infant to the outside world from birth, an outside world that is thus always being taken in, and the second (bodily relatedness) because the hunger and feeding cycle from the start provides the anlage for all subsequent matches of an inner need and the "appeal" of something taken in from outside. Thus, in counterpoint to Loewald's formulation that development happens by the overlay, the superimposition, of the more-organized adult's functioning on the less-organized infant's and child's functioning, we can say that the child also "seeks" (teleologically speaking) or "needs" or is receptive to the adult overlay—and selectively assimilates environmental offerings when they fit with and satisfy some inner unsettled state.

As the concept of "magnification" helps us understand the transmission of significant and conflicted issues between mother and child, the concept of "appeal" helps us understand how the random offerings of the environment can be drawn upon when they fit with unsettled inner states. They provide an object or activity that momentarily at least resolves these states or permits them to be enacted, and thus is a major mode of expansion of the inner life to the world of character and of "choice" of defenses or symptoms or interests. While the mother's contribution is magnification, the child's contribution is magnetism, the inner "magnet" of unsettledness and receptivity drawing in from the outside what fits with the inner state, what "appeals" to the child—for good or ill. This, too, will appear as an "identification."

Three microprocesses of identification have now been inferred, processes that produce parent-child likenesses that will be descriptively viewed as the result of "identifications." There are others, no doubt, and other forms of internalization that will not appear as identifications. But these are three that can be formulated through a focus on bodily interrelatedness. They are: the mother's superimposition of modes of organizing and disorganizing at moments of intense stimulation in the child, the mother's "magnification" of her child's experiences when they intersect with her own areas of conflict, and the taking in process by the child when some maternal or other environmental offering has "appeal"—matches an inner need—for the child. And each of these three processes can be thought of as underlying specific instances of what would later be globally described as an "identification." Given the centrality that Piaget (1952) gave to accommodation and assimilation in the developmental process, it is of interest to note that the first two processes I have described (the maternal shaping and magnification) involve the child's "accommodation" to the mother's way of functioning, moving toward it, while the appeal process has the characteristic of assimilation, a taking in according to the child's needs.

The focus has been primarily on intense and potentially conflicted processes in the child until now. But magnification and appeal phenomena also come into the caretaker-child relationship with respect to the child's developing skills and interests, the expansion of the ego apparatuses into the region of preferences, interests, and talents, the area of the functional body, and the child's adaptive learning.

There is a parable about a king who wanted to see what the "natural" human language was, whether it was or was not the language of his own land. And to learn this he forbade anyone to utter a sound to his newborn child so as to see which language the child spoke when words eventually came. But, alas, the answer could never be found, for the child died. It is a tale of the need for stimulation, not only for the learning of language but for healthy developmental processes altogether. Is it so? Rene Spitz (1945), in his early studies of infants separated from their mothers and raised in institutions with astonishingly little stimulus input, reports not only stunted development but a much higher than normally expectable number of infant deaths.

A later study with more systematic observation, reported by Provence and Lipton (1962), makes one particular phenomenon more clear. Their institutionalized infants were raised with almost no human handling or face-to-face interaction (except for a minute or so of quick bathing and brief diaper changes each day); they were bottle

fed (with propped-up bottles so no holding of the infant was necessary), in cribs with sheets slung over the sides that increased visual
isolation (allowing a view only of a white ceiling and the white
sheets). They frequently lay in their cribs almost without movement,
as though in a state of suspended animation. When observed by the
researchers, they spontaneously produced none of the normal developmental markers (like hands meeting at the midline, eye-hand
coordination, the smiling response). And yet, when the researchers
worked consistently to elicit those behaviors when developmentally
expectable, the behaviors generally could be elicited. It seemed that
biologically programmed bodily developments grow as potential capabilities, but require responsive activation (a positive magnification) by a caretaker in order to be utilized by the infant. It is as
though ownership of the body, or the functional value of the behaviors for a nascent self, only develops when the mother's reactions
make the newly developing capacities matter. Built-in *capacities* (existing as potentials) become ego *functions* when they are functional *for*
something—and probably the main function early on is in the "dialogue" between mother and child. Who the child will become is
shaped everywhere and subtly through this dialogue.

Along similar lines, the mother's favorable, admiring responses to
the child's vigorous activity in Mahler's (1972) "practicing phase,"
the period of toddlerhood, may be one of the early powerful sup-
ports for, or inhibitors of, the whole development of an active sense
of agency—the "I want" and "I can do" of human experience. The
seeds of a sense of agency may already be planted even earlier in the
infant's capacity to "make things happen"—like reach*ing* out and
gett*ing* a toy, or squeez*ing* a rubber animal and mak*ing* it squeak (all
phrases including the "ing" of the active verb, of agency). But certainly the child's vigorous and sometimes risky or injurious activities
in the toddler period, and also the child's locomotor and autonomous movements away from the mother, are likely to incite sometimes problematic interaction between mother and child around the
achievements of the functional body's development. "Magnification"
processes, in the sense not just of encouragement or cautioning, but
of the conflict-ridden reactivity of certain predisposed mothers, will
come in here as at many other points regarding the child's increasingly capable and autonomous body. The child's development of particular areas of excellence and weakness in the use of its bodily capacities is determined at least by inborn levels of ability, the chance
dynamics of sublimation and the chance encounters that "appeal" to
the child, and, not least, by magnification processes, both positive

and negative, that stem from points of overlap with caretaker dynamics, the dynamics of emotional investment and of conflicted invasion. The overlay of the mother's style upon the child's developing modes of function, her magnification of certain experiences for good or ill, and the magnet in the child that draws in what appeals to him or her—which have been referred to here as the microprocesses of identification—are present in the region of the functional/learning body as well.

In summary of these remarks on the development of functional capacities in the child, two points have been emphasized: (1) the entry of the development of the child's capacities into the mother-child "dialogue," touched again by her organizing, disorganizing, or magnification processes, and the facilitation, inhibition, distortion, and direction of capacities through this entry; and (2) the appeal process in the child once again, the taking in of what fits with inner wishes, fantasies, and unsettled states.

CONCLUDING NOTE

In his influential book on the origins and structure of personality, Gardner Murphy (1947) used as a leitmotif the concept that development at all levels—biological, psychological, and social—moves from relatively global and undifferentiated forms, on into relative *differentiation*, and ultimately to relatively *integrated* forms. Recently, Chodorow (2003), examining Loewald's whole body of work, described how he worked centrally with this same dimension: global, differentiated, integrated—in his case, emphasizing a flow back and forth among them. Mahler's ideas are also an illustration and application of Murphy's more abstract and inclusive developmental line. For Mahler the form that the concept took was that the infant begins in a state of symbiosis (a global state, with an absence of clear differentiation) and moves to a greater awareness of separateness (differentiation). The further idea, sometimes explicit and always at least implicit, that object relationship brings a third stage—"integration" of the increasingly differentiated mother-infant pair—was taken for granted, though not fully theorized.

The discussion of microprocesses of identification can be set in the context of this developmental line. The infant begins with a primal attachment (Bowlby, 1969) and probably also with both merged and differentiated moments of experience vis-à-vis the mother (Pine, 2004). Increasing awareness of separateness (increasing differentiation) develops hand in hand with increasing experience-based ob-

ject relationship ("integration"). Simultaneously, identification processes also sew the child and the caretaker to one another. Thus, the
differentiated infant, with a sense of the separateness of self and
mother, is nonetheless tied to her through at least three psychological pathways: built-in attachment, experience-based object relationship, and identifications. Identifications, interestingly, by rejoining
subject and object, re-create a kind of undifferentiated state, but one
that is clearly at a more advanced developmental level, consisting, as
they do, of two separate selves with particular similarities. In describing some microprocesses of identification herein, I have thus tried to
contribute to the understanding of a process that contributes both to
the construction of a separate self and to the maintenance of a powerful (if often invisible to the subject) tie between caretaker and off-
spring.

Concluding with a last word on identification: We generally consider identification processes to be central in the evolution of particular personalities within the context of family dynamics. But what exactly does identification consist of? It is usually used in a descriptive
way, noting an end-result of child-parent likeness. But I would propose that some of the processes that I have described here can usefully be seen as microprocesses that specify how "identifications" actually come about. What I have tried to do in outlining the mother's
superimposition upon the child of her own organizing or disorganizing
style, and the mother's magnification of some of the child's experiences, and the appeal processes in the child that lead to its taking in
selectively from the parental (and larger environmental) offerings is
to imagine processes through which features of parental mind and
behavior get transferred to the child, incorporated by him or her, ultimately defining who he or she will be. I have done this through a focus on bodily interactions, but there is nothing in what I have said
that would not apply throughout development in later forms of affectively significant interaction as well.

BIBLIOGRAPHY

BETTELHEIM, B. (1958). Work with the severely disturbed child: A film pre-
    sentation and discussion. Austen Riggs Center, Stockbridge, Mass., August
    4, 1958.
BOWLBY, J. (1969). *Attachment and Loss. Volume 1: Attachment.* New York: Basic
    Books.
CHODOROW, N. J. (2003). The psychoanalytic vision of Hans Loewald. *Inter-
    national Journal of Psychoanalysis,* 84:897–913.

FREUD, A. (1936). The ego and the mechanisms of defense. *The Writings of Anna Freud: Volume 2.* New York: International Universities Press.

FREUD, S. (1905). Three essays on the theory of sexuality. *Standard Edition,* 7:135–243.

——— (1915). Mourning and melancholia. *Standard Edition,* 14:237–260.

——— (1920). Beyond the pleasure principle. *Standard Edition,* 18:7–64.

KRIS, E. (1956). The recovery of childhood memories in psychoanalysis. *The Psychoanalytic Study of the Child,* 11:54–88.

LOEWALD, H. W. (1960). On the therapeutic action of psychoanalysis. *International Journal of Psychoanalysis,* 41:16–33.

MAHLER, M. S. (1972). On the first three subphases of the separation-individuation process. *International Journal of Psychoanalysis,* 53:333–338.

MURPHY, G. (1947). *Personality: A Biosocial Approach to Origins and Structure.* New York: Harper and Bros.

PIAGET, J. (1952). *The Origins of Intelligence in Children.* New York: International Universities Press.

PINE, F. (1982). The experience of self: Aspects of its formation, expansion, and vulnerability. *Psychoanalytic Study of the Child,* 37:143–167.

——— (1986). On the development of the "borderline-child-to-be." *American Journal of Orthopsychiatry,* 56:450–457.

——— (1990). *Drive, Ego, Object and Self: A Synthesis for Clinical Work.* New York: Basic Books.

——— (2004). Mahler's concepts of "symbiosis" and "separation-individuation": Revisited, reevaluated, and refined. *Journal of the American Psychoanalytic Association,* 52:511–533.

PROVENCE, S., & LIPTON, R. (1962). *Infants in Institutions.* New York: International Universities Press.

RAPAPORT, D. (1960). On the psychoanalytic theory of motivation. *Nebraska Symposium on Motivation,* M. R. Jones, ed. Lincoln: University of Nebraska Press, 173–247.

SKINNER, B. F. (1971). Operant conditioning. *Encyclopedia of Education: Volume 1.* New York: Macmillan and Free Press, 29–33.

SPITZ, R. (1945). Hospitalism: An inquiry into the genesis of psychiatric conditions in early childhood. *Psychoanalytic Study of the Child,* 1:53–74.

RESEARCH STUDIES

Narrative in the Study of Resilience*

STUART T. HAUSER, M.D., PH.D., EVE GOLDEN, M.D., and JOSEPH P. ALLEN, PH.D.

*Winner of the Albert J. Solnit Award, 2006

The authors trace the contribution of narrative studies to the study of resilience. Narrative studies infiltrated the mental health field more slowly than they did the medical and social sciences, despite its long reliance on "talking therapies." With the development of the Adult Attachment Interview, however, narrative studies began to come into their own in developmental psychology, psychiatry, and psychoanalysis. Narrative studies are an especially apt tool in resilience studies. The authors discuss their use in this context, considering also some theoretical questions about the nature of narrative and its implications for psychotherapy.

Telling stories, about ourselves and about others to ourselves and to others, is the most natural and the

Stuart Hauser, Judge Baker Children's Center, Department of Psychiatry, Harvard Medical School, Boston, Norwegian Institute of Public Health, Division of Mental Health, Harvard Graduate School of Education, Psychoanalytic Institute of New England East (PINE); Eve Golden, independent scholar, Cambridge, Mass.; Joseph P. Allen, Department of Psychology, University of Virginia, Charlottesville.

We are indebted to Robbe Burnstine for her clear thinking and for her help in tracking down and working with many of the writings and ideas incorporated in this paper.

> earliest way in which we organize our experience
> and our knowledge.
> —Clifford Geertz (1997, p. 23)

DESPITE THE PRECEDENT OF THE PSYCHOANALYTIC PSYCHOTHERAPIES and their reputation as a "talking cure," it is only recently that personal narrative has gained recognition as a legitimate and important resource and tool in the world of developmental psychology. Similarly, while narrative has long been considered an invaluable source of information in the humanities and in sociology, only in the last twenty years or so have psychologists begun to establish reliable methods of analysis, looking systematically at narrative as a way of grasping how people create and maintain meaning over time.

But the process is gathering speed rapidly. Even in less "subjective" fields like clinical medicine, investigators are learning through the study of narrative something about how patients' stories influence the suffering that accompanies illness. Rita Charon describes this influence from a physician's point of view:

> As patient meets physician, a conversation ensues. A story—a state of affairs or a set of events—is recounted by the patient in his or her acts of narrating, resulting in a complicated narrative of illness told in words, gestures, physical findings, and silences, and burdened not only with the objective information about the illness but also with the fears, hopes and implications associated with it. As in psychoanalysis, in all of medical practice the narrating of the patient's story is a therapeutically central act, because to find words to contain the disorder and its attendant worries gives shape to and control over the chaos of illness (Charon, 2001, p. 1897).

Gay Becker, a medical anthropologist who studies groups of people in adversity, takes a similar view of the importance of stories. "Through stories, people organize, display and work through their experiences," she says; consequently, "narratives can be a potent force in diminishing disruption, whether the disruption is caused by illness or personal misfortune" (Becker, 1997). Becker uses the term *narrative* to mean the stories people tell about themselves—stories that reflect their experience as they see it and wish it to be seen by others. Not coincidentally, she sees a connection between the general use of stories in meaning-making and their use in the service of resilience.[1]

---

1. This view of narrative has been embraced in many medical studies (e.g., Charon, 2001; Cohler, 1991) and in other ethnographic studies of resilience (e.g., Cohler, 1991).

Resilience is the capacity of some individuals to prosper (often unexpectedly) in circumstances that defeat others, or to achieve adaptive outcomes following serious adversity. Clearly resilience is a matter of pressing concern, especially when children are at risk, and the "potent force" of narration has given us an important new window on it (Hauser, 1999, 2005; Hauser, Allen, and Golden, 2006).[2] Access to narrative greatly expands the purview of resilience studies, many of which have examined the personal and contextual forces that influence individual lives (e.g., Luthar, 2003). But until recently, there have been few explorations, other than in occasional crisis memoirs and biographical or autobiographical accounts (e.g., Brown, 1965; Bowlby, 1990; Chellis, 1992; Rubin, 1996; Higgins, 1994; Rhett, 1997; Walls, 2005) of how people's experiences of adversity *affect,* and are *influenced by,* their attitudes, thoughts, and feelings—not only at the time of trial, but also over the ensuing days, months, and years. Such explorations are important if we are to delineate more precisely the internal and relationship dimensions associated with risk (that is, the dimensions that can lead to dysfunctional outcomes) and protection (that is, the dimensions that can lead to optimal outcomes) in individuals exposed to adversity.

We do not yet know how risk and protective processes are actually *used* by individuals in ways that enable or undermine their adaptation, or why some people make effective use of protective factors while others do not. We also do not yet know how people deal with the internal consequences of disruption over time, or how their styles of coping influence the course of their plans, their relationships, and their overall adaptation. But there is reason to think that the study of narrative may shed some light on these unknowns (cf. Cohler, 1987, 1991; Cohler, Stott, and Musick, 1995).

NARRATIVE: CAUSE AND EFFECT

So far, two general positions on narrative and life course have received the lion's share of attention in the psychological literature. One holds that narrative *coherence*—the capacity to develop a "good story," in which circumstance and personal experience are meaningfully integrated—in some way *accounts for* successful adaptation

---

2. In addition to Hauser and colleagues' narrative approach, a highly accessible recent collection of non-narrative approaches to the study of resilience can be found in the recent book edited by Luthar (2003); and in an even more recent synthesis of these directions and findings (Luthar, 2006).

(Cohler, 1987, 1991; Becker, 1997). The second maintains that a person's narrative coherence *reflects* his capacity to handle adversity (Main et al., 1985).[3] Deeper exploration suggests, however, that this duality is probably false,[4] and a third possibility—that narrative *both* reflects *and* influences adaptation—is rapidly gaining credence. This possibility is poignantly evoked by Niobe Way in her study of five urban teenagers attending a "violent and dangerous" (Way, 1998, p. 30) minority school in a racist neighborhood. In her exploration of how some of these students managed—even thrived—under these oppressive conditions, Way shows how their narratives both reflected their conditions and led to immediate solutions at the moment and over the long term. Through their narratives, that is, "these students apprehend their complex experiences and invent ways to thrive in response to their realistic views of the world. . . . The hope and fear detected in their interviews are not contradictory at all. They are weaving together their life experiences and their future dreams and creating strategies for everyday living" (Way, 1998, p. 183). This is also the view we have elaborated at length in an extensive study of narrative and resilience in psychiatrically hospitalized adolescents (Hauser et al., 2006).

Our own lives show us that narrative has both causal and consequential aspects. We reflect on an experience, putting together events

---

3. The work of Mary Main and her colleagues Nancy Kaplan and Jude Cassidy on adult attachment representation clearly puts forth the idea that high narrative coherence in an interview about early separation and attachment figures reflects optimal attachment security (Main, Kaplan, and Cassidy, 1985). But some attachment theorists argue that narratives about secure attachment relationships may underlie successful coping in people faced with stressful situations. Inge Bretherton (1996), for example, conceptualizes "at least two ways [in which] inner resources are linked to secure attachment relationships. First, the confident knowledge that an attachment figure is available for emotional support when needed tends to increase an individual's ability to consider alternative solutions when faced with difficult and stressful situations. . . . Second, a secure relationship with one or more attachment figures affects coping more indirectly through the impact of such relationships on the organization and quality of an individual's representational system."

An inclusive collection of excellent theoretical and empirical discussions of adult attachment is Cassidy and Shaver, eds. (1999), *Handbook of Attachment: Theory, Research, and Clinical Applications.* For an even more direct connection among attachment, narrative coherence and resilience, see Roisman et al. (2002).

4. Social scientists writing about narrative and individual lives have appreciated the complex dynamics between an individual's stories, understandings, and actions. One of the earliest contributors to this literature was resilience pioneer Robert W. White, who in the early 1950s wrote about the need to study the complexities of unfolding lives as they were understood and lived by individual adolescents. See White (1950).

and responsibilities and hypotheses; the resulting reflections—our stories—alert us to new understandings and new possibilities; we act on these and acquire new experiences that further enlarge our capacity for story-telling. A two-year-old may kick the table on which he has just banged his head. He is responding to his story that the table hurt him—a story that an adult would see as limited in its explanatory power. Yet it will likely suffice to instill some respect for tables in the rambunctious toddler, slowing him down a bit and causing him to pay more attention to their whereabouts. This new behavior is adaptive in itself in that it protects him from further injury. But it also gives him the time, opportunity, and motivation to observe the table and learn something useful about it. In time a better story will emerge—that it is children who move and bang, not tables—and with it the probability that this child will take more responsibility for his own movements and for the consequences, both pleasurable and not, that result from them. From there his narrative about navigating physically in the world will continue to develop, in directions as individual as he is.

Narrative, therefore, is most profitably seen as both cause and effect. It reflects experience, but it also conditions new experience. Our stories are hubs in the wheel of our perpetual psychological work. From experiences we derive meaning; from meaning-making we imagine new actions; new actions lead us to new experiences; from new experiences we evolve new meanings—all in our own real-life contexts. The study of narrative across the life cycle illustrates *how* stories can trigger new perspectives about relationships, situations, goals, and all the other facts and forces that play decisive roles in individual's lives. In other words, it allows us to investigate a still-shadowy corner of resilience studies—how resilience *evolves,* how it is informed by a person's experience, and, especially, how the stories that we use to manage experience shape it and point to new courses of action and new and perhaps better stories.

NARRATIVE IN CONTEXT

With opportunity there is always risk. When the subject at hand is resilience, it is tempting—but dangerous—to overvalue individual stories, taking them out of context and mistaking them as the only significant engines of psychological change. That would discount the importance of the real surround of opportunities and constraints— environmental factors that can be very powerful and sometimes decisive. But close analysis of narrative displays in great detail (greater detail than most other techniques allow, in fact) not only a person, but also the influences of that person's context. Lives have many contexts, from the microcosmic (family) to the macrocosmic (current views of adolescence, availability of federal aid), and everything in between (a school system, a hospital ward, a set of community norms). These contexts are displayed with great clarity in personal narrative. The challenge and the promise of narrative research is its sensitivity *both to the individual and to his or her surround*, and it is gratifying to observe that the compelling possibilities of narrative[5] do not in fact compete with the need to consider individuals within the social and historical matrices that encompass them. Catherine Reissman, a sociologist who uses narrative to investigate divorce and other such complex events that clearly involve family and social issues as well as individual ones, captures the unique capacity of stories to portray individual lives in context. At its best, Reissman says, the study of narrative "illuminates the intersection of biography, history, and society" (Riessman, 2002, p. 697).[6]

Narratives and Resilience
NARRATIVE AND CHANGE: CLINICAL APPROACHES

Narrative bestows (apparent) order upon chaotic existence. That gives it great power, for good or for ill. Just as some new experiences foster resilience while others have potentially disastrous consequences, so do the narratives through which experience is explored. We all see destructive stories in action from time to time; if we are not clear-sighted enough to perceive our own, they are easy to spot in others. A teenager who doesn't try out for the cheerleading squad because she's "too fat" not only definitively destroys her chances of becoming a cheerleader, but also nurtures self-defeating convictions both about

---

5. There have been several masterful reviews of the narrative literature. A thoughtful overview of work in medical narrative can be found in a recent book edited by two medical anthropologists: Mattingly and Garro (2000). Arthur Kleinman, an anthropologically oriented psychiatrist, provided an early contribution (Kleinman 1988). Abraham Verghese, another physician and nonfiction writer, narrates finely textured accounts of his experiences with patients and of the significance of story-telling in medicine (Verghese 1994, 2001). Barbara Fiese focuses on family narratives in Fiese et al. (1999). More general reviews include Clifford Geertz, "Learning with Bruner" (1997). Other important contributions to this growing and multifaceted field of study include: Bruner (1990, 1996); Mishler (1995, 1999); Riessman (1993, 2002).

6. Riessman's approach shapes her 1990 book, *Divorce Talk: Women and Men Make Sense of Their Relationships*. Mishler's *Storylines* (1999) takes a narrative approach to a deft and intricate study of craft artists' lives and identities.

her body and about the uselessness of challenging other people's judgments—or her own. A person who blames all mishaps on someone else will never reap the growth in competence that comes with taking responsibility. Recognizing this ambivalent power of stories, recent psychoanalytic theorists have found it useful to contemplate the place of narrative in deep insight and psychological change.

In psychodynamic psychotherapy and psychoanalysis, story-making is a deliberate and active process between patient and therapist, a tool by which understanding of past, present, and the immediate moment are expanded. Developmental psychologist and theorist Jerome Bruner has pointed out that Freud's recognition of the salience of "psychic reality" was an early indication of interest in narrative construction and its influence on individuals' actions, relationships, and lives: "The malaise that led to the new interest in the narrative construction of reality long predates the rise of . . . perspectivally oriented post-modernism. Sigmund Freud probably had more to do with it than Derrida or Foucault, if only by proposing a psychic reality that seemed more driven by dramatic necessities than states of the objective world" (Bruner, 1996, p. 131). Donald Spence was one of the first psychoanalysts to consider at length the importance of narrative to the discovery of meaning in psychoanalysis. He distinguished between *historical truth* (a consensual account of public events) and *narrative truth* (an account whose form and content are shaped by an individual's past and current experience) (Spence, 1982).

Roy Schafer's *Retelling a Life* (1992) offered a psychoanalytic perspective different from Spence's—an eloquent and nuanced picture of how narratives of self and relationship change over time. Within the psychoanalytic dialogue, Schafer says:

> actions and happenings (for example, traumatic events) are continuously being told by the analysand and sooner or later re-told interpretively by both analyst and analysand. Closure is always provisional to allow for further retellings. . . . Insight . . . refers to those retellings that make a beneficial difference in a person's construction and reconstruction of experience and adaptively active conduct of life. Each retelling amounts to an account of the prior telling as something different, or more likely, something more than had been noted. In this dialogic way, each analysis amounts in the end to retelling a life in the past and present—and as it may be in the future. (1992, p. xv).

Schafer, like Spence, warns against too concrete a valuation of such retellings: "We have only versions of the true and the real. Narratively unmediated definitive access to truth and reality cannot be demonstrated. In this respect, therefore, there can be no absolute foundation on which an observer or thinker stands. Each must choose his or her narrative or version" (Schafer, 1992, p. xv).

Spence and Schafer contemplate narrative from the one-patient-at-a-time perspective of the clinical psychoanalyst, whose valuation of narrative truth is very high, and for whom historical truth is perhaps a less compelling concept than for other kinds of thinkers. At about the time they were writing, clinical psychologists were beginning to consider narrative in more general, and more generalizable, contexts. Bertram Cohler is a psychologist and psychoanalyst who has distinguished himself by his committed interest in people's life stories as a way of understanding their responses to adversity: "a central concern of the human sciences or social studies is to understand [the] personal narrative or life story in terms of an ordered sequence and in terms of the context, frame, or plot which the author employs in providing narrative integrity for a particular life story at a particular time" (1991, p. 177). Cohler has also drawn attention to a second way that the personal use of narrative may be relevant to resilience—it offers comfort as well as insight. A child's repeated request to "tell it again," as Cohler puts it, may try his parents, but it also reflects the solace inherent in story-telling. Older adults, he points out, "realize particular comfort" from the act of telling; it renews and reinforces the focus on one's own narrative and its potential for healing. Cohler concludes that "these observations point to the importance of additional study of storytelling for mental health" (p. 191).

Clinical psychologists Robert Neimeyer and Heidi Levitt (2001) have also underlined the meaning-making and organizing potential inherent in people's accounts of their experiences. It is important, they suggest, that people in difficult circumstances be able to allocate responsibility (or, equally, non-responsibility) accurately, both for specific events in their lives and for the effects of these events. Like Becker and Cohler, they emphasize how personal narrative influences a person's stance toward adversity. It may facilitate accountability when this is appropriate, and, just as important, identifying situations that cannot in fact be controlled. (Other narratives may foster a stance of victimhood or exploitation.) Neimeyer and Levitt offer the example of a young woman reflecting in narrative on her reaction when a stranger began stalking her:

> I was upset because I didn't do anything to this person and he went out of his way to make me feel uncomfortable when it was very obvious that I was trying to avoid contact with him. I felt like it was an-

other reminder of my being female, of my being less powerful than men, and . . . also my need to be defensive to be safe. And, of course, this is what I always seem to be struggling with—at home with my father, at work with my boss, and in my relationship with my husband. Always feeling somehow I have to work to prove myself equal and worthy of respect or otherwise I won't receive it. I always need to work to defend myself. I think this is especially affecting my relationship with my husband. I don't want to be defensive all the time (Neimeyer and Levitt, 2001, p. 53).

This woman's adaptive wish not to be "defensive all the time" is furthered in her narrative by a sensitive dissection of issues of responsibility with regard to the stalker. Past narratives, she tells us ("this is what I always seem to be struggling with") have taught her correctly that her defensiveness is her responsibility, and she is working to make her defensiveness meaningful by relating it to her past relationships and experiences. That process has enabled her to make a new and very important distinction between what is her responsibility and what is not; in this new experience she can resist the temptation to blame herself for the behavior of the stalker. This further accurate allocation of responsibility contributes a matter-of-fact rather than defensive view of a stressful situation as she constructs her current narrative about it.

All of these writers illustrate cascading loops of narration-action-narration, showing how personal narratives of disruptions may lead to organized accounts, and how the newly achieved level of integration can permit in turn new images and expectations, thus paving the way for change in the ways that relationships are sought and maintained, and experiences understood.

NARRATIVE AND CHANGE: THEORETICAL APPROACHES

Spence, Schafer, Cohler, and Neimeyer and Levitt are all clinical theorists. But narrative and its place in people's understanding of their lives has also attracted the attention of non-clinical social scientists of widely differing perspectives. Beginning in the 1980s, Jerome Bruner began urging his colleagues to address meaning-making (as revealed in narrative) and its role in individual actions. He was concerned that psychologists, in their pursuit of the "cognitive revolution" (a movement that he had promulgated and that was in fact very dear to his heart), were being distracted from investigation of mental activity into increasingly specialized and reductionistic studies of "information processing" and computation:

214   *Stuart T. Hauser, Eve Golden, & Joseph P. Allen*

To reduce meaning or culture to a material base, to say they "depend," say, on the left hemisphere, is to trivialize both in the service of misplaced concreteness. To insist upon explanations in terms of "causes" simply bars us from trying to understand how human beings interpret their worlds and how *we* interpret *their* acts of interpretation (Bruner, 1990, p. xiii).[7]

Bruner thought that autobiographical narratives would give access to the form and the substance of individuals' views of themselves and their place in the world. He was particularly interested in the perception of *agency* (or *agentivity*, as he calls it) and thought that this could be especially advantageously visualized through the study of autobiography. Most people, he says,

do not regard gravity as acting on their Selves (save perhaps in extreme situations). But if somebody grabs them or pushes them, or forcibly takes their purse, they will feel their Selves to have been violated, and invoke Self in their description of what happened. Agentivity is involved, their own and someone else's. . . . The range of what people will include under the influence of their own agentivity will vary from person to person . . . and with one's felt position within the culture (Bruner, 1990, p. 119).

Bruner's urging of his colleagues away from his own movement and back to the study of meaning did not go unheeded. A stream of narrative studies in several realms of psychology (cultural psychology, gender development, illness experience, and physician-patient interactions, to name only a few) appeared. As narrative gained greater acceptance as a legitimate topic (and tool) of scientific inquiry, psychologists began to test, and to contest, various approaches to its study and analysis.

Narrative perspective, both alone and in combination with more traditional quantitative approaches, has attracted the interest of several psychologists interested in adolescent development. Carol Gilligan and her colleagues, for instance, studied the fluctuations of the "voices" in which adolescents refer to self, other, and relationships (Gilligan, 1982; Gilligan et al., 1990). Camarena, Sarigiani, and Petersen (1997), building on Gilligan, investigated what psychological well-being meant for boys and for girls across the adolescent years.[8]

7. In addition to Bruner's 1990 *Acts of Meaning,* two other readable and important books by him are *Actual Minds, Possible Worlds* (1986); and *Making Stories: Law, Literature, Life* (2002).
8. In addition, in her narrative studies noted earlier Way (1998) focused on the experiences of working-class boys and girls.

In another recent study of narrative and resilience, James, Liem, and O'Toole (1997) explored how four resilient young women, survivors of serious childhood sexual abuse, now understood their mental health. They found in their interview narratives themes of mastery of adversity, overcoming challenges, and beating the odds. These women emphasized the importance of *agency:* the experience of personal causation and the awareness of having an effect upon their environment. In fact, James and colleagues offer yet another connection between narrative and resilience. Reflecting Bruner's observation (and anticipating a central theme of our own studies of the ongoing narratives of people hospitalized as adolescents with serious psychiatric disorders and subsequently identified as resilient young adults [Hauser, 1999; Hauser et al., 2006]), they argue that through their exercise of power in socially acceptable ways, these women "may be neutralizing the negative impact of sexual abuse by restoring power when power and status have been denied" (James et al., 1997, p. 227).

Elliot Mishler in an inclusive synthetic essay reviews much of the recent history of narrative scholarship and enumerates many of the fields where it is now being used—in anthropology, literary studies, and linguistics, for instance, as well as the clinical sciences and developmental and cognitive psychology (Mishler, 1995).

NARRATIVE RESEARCH AND THE ADULT ATTACHMENT INTERVIEW

However, it was the success of the Adult Attachment Interview (AAI) that opened the eyes of many developmental psychologists, psychiatrists, and allied workers to a whole new kind of potential in narrative studies. The AAI demonstrated that the way a person told a story could provide accurate, reliable, and useful information about very complex and subtle psychological constellations that had not been experimentally accessible before. The AAI was developed in the context of attachment theory—the study of the bonds that form between a young child and its caretakers, and the ramifications of these bonds in later life—and so it was in this broad area that intense excitement first arose about the ability of narrative studies to capture important aspects of development (Oppenheim and Waters, 1995).[9] Since the advent of the AAI, attention to narrative has accelerated rapidly among students of attachment, and develop-

9. Two accessible papers written for a clinical audience have also addressed this area: Main, 1993; and Lyons-Ruth, 1999.

ments within that field are now influencing the use of narrative in related areas. The AAI demonstrated that the narratives of children and adults can provide accurate information about such complex and not easily examined psychological phenomena as the security of attachment between infants and their caregivers, and internal representations that people develop of attachment figures and early experiences with them. That dramatic success in the field of attachment earned narrative studies a new respect. It released them from relegation to the "clinical" and "anecdotal" and allowed them to expand respectably into new empirical developmental and clinical psychology studies.

THE ADULT ATTACHMENT INTERVIEW AND ITS INFLUENCE

The turn to narrative in attachment studies owes much to the work of Mary Main and her colleagues, who demonstrated convincingly that mothers' attachment organizations (or, as Main and colleagues also call it, their *states of mind regarding attachment as determined by analysis of their narratives of their own early experiences*) show a high correspondence with the patterns of their infant children's independently studied attachments to them. The extraordinary success of the AAI is so rich in implications for narrative studies in general, and for narrative studies of resilience in particular, that a brief digression is in order here to make those implications clear. This is but a sketch; excellent studies of the history and development of the AAI are readily available. Main's colleague Erik Hesse has supplied a historical, theoretical, and clinical overview of this rich and rigorous assessment (Hesse, 1999), and the widening use of the AAI has been described in detail in summaries written for psychoanalytic clinicians by Main (2000) and by Main and Hesse (2000).

In brief, the AAI came out of a collaboration in the early 1980s between Main and Ruth Goldwyn, both developmental psychologists. Main had a background in attachment research and an interest in psycholinguistics. She and her colleagues administered to a group of parents a "semi-structured" interview[10] that required responses in some depth to a wide range of questions about early attachment: separations and reunions with caretakers, experiences of rejection and

10. A semi-structured interview addresses a prescribed topic in a flexible manner, allowing for spontaneous two-way conversation as well as previously determined questions and the answers to them.

abuse, experiences of loss, and so forth. This is a stressful experience. Hesse says that the central task of the interview is "producing and reflecting upon memories related to attachment while simultaneously remaining coherent [in] . . . discourse with the interviewer" (1999, pp. 396–397). Main and Goldwyn analyzed the resulting narratives by a carefully developed coding procedure that targeted both the structure of the narrative and its content. Their initial results showed that "[scores] appearing to reflect a parent's current state of mind [as reflected in the scoring] with respect to his or her own attachment experiences were substantially related to aspects of the infant's behavior toward that parent" (Hesse, 1999, pp. 395–396) as the infant's behavior had been observed five years earlier in an experimental protocol designed to elicit children's reactions to separation from and reunion with their caregivers (the so-called *strange situation*). Main and her colleagues supposed that the childhood experiences described in or inferred from the interview had contributed to the adult's "state of mind with regard to attachment," *but they classified the parents' "states of mind" not on the basis of those experiences, but on the basis of their own analysis of the parents' narratives.* That is, an infant's attachment behavior in the "strange situation" procedure was reliably correlated with the way that a mother or father *talked many years later about his or her own attachment experiences.* Years of subsequent replication and refinement have given empirical support to the theoretical conclusion that a parent's "state of mind with regard to attachment" could *predict* the attachment behavior of that parent's infant as measured experimentally later (Hesse, 1999, p. 407).

Since its first appearance in 1985, the AAI has shown excellent reliability and validity. That is, agreement between trained scorers is high, AAI findings have been extensively replicated, and classifications have been demonstrated to persist over time and across interviewers. Evidence continues to mount that the information derived from the interviews about the subject's "states of mind" with regard to attachment are valid; furthermore, this information relates *specifically* to attachment-related "states of mind," not to more general (and more commonly studied) factors such as social desirability, social adjustment, general personality style, intelligence, verbal fluency, or "memory" per se (Hesse, 1999; Cassidy and Shaver, 1999).

One of the "state of mind" scales used in the original AAI research was called *coherence.* It refers to the "maxims of conversation" of philosopher Herbert Paul Grice. According to Grice, adequacy of conversation can be judged by its quality, its quantity, its relevance, and its manner (1975). Coherence in the context of the AAI means not only that "the parts of the discourse are clearly related [and] form a logical whole," but also that they are "adapted to context" (Hesse, 1999; Main and Goldwyn, 1998).[11] AAI narratives are scored on contextual qualities of responsiveness, appropriateness, and cooperation as well as on internal consistency and organization. The coherence measure is not the only measure used in the AAI; others cover such phenomena as memory lapses, the tendency to allow narrative to trail off, and the devaluation or idealization of attachment. However, coherence is still viewed theoretically as the single best indicator of attachment security in the AAI.

Narrative coherence is considered a manifestation of security in *representations* of attachment—that is, in the internal models of attachment relationships that we are constantly constructing and revising out of our experiences with them. The AAI and its scoring procedures appear to capture accurately and consistently certain aspects of these representations, which have both content (ideas, thoughts, feelings) and structure (the degree to which they are accessible to consciousness, coherent, and integrated into action). Well-integrated attachment representations are consciously available to individuals for description and story-telling of an elaborated and reflective kind. Poorly integrated or traumatic ones are not; they are also stressful, which inhibits the narrative effort further. Inability to maintain coherence in the interview reflects the interference upon the narrative process of the stress of dealing with poorly integrated attachment experience, making structural disruptions in the narrative a tell-tale of attachment status.

The diagnostic and predictive success of the AAI, and its evidence of strong psychometric properties, gave narrative studies the bona fides to begin to integrate with traditional psychological research. In fact, the AAI made its own first appearance in concert with earlier observational studies of infants and mothers. For the first time, the narrative approach was demonstrated to be an enhancement to direct observation, rather than an alternative or an antagonist. Narrative measures are now being called "a new window" (Oppenheim and Waters, 1995, p. 203) on attachment relationships; we can extrapolate that they will also prove to be a window on the influence these relationships have on later development.

---

11. Hesse, The Adult Attachment Interview (1999, p. 404); the coherence description is quoted from Mary Main and Ruth Goldwyn's 1998 description of their scoring system.

BEYOND THE ADULT ATTACHMENT INTERVIEW —
IMPLICATIONS FOR RESILIENCE

Work inspired by the AAI suggests that similarly robust narrative instruments will be developed to study related facets of psychological
experience. In the meantime, the AAI itself has been refined, modified, and extended over the years, and is now available in forms ap-
plicable to children and adolescents. A new round of diagnostic and
predictive work is under way as investigators develop innovative
scales and investigate new situations (Allen and Land, 1999; Dozier,
Stovall, and Albus, 1999; Fonagy, 1999; Berlin, 1999; Main, 1999).

For instance, narrative is now being used to investigate aspects of
such varied subjects as cognitive development, how emotion is communicated, the development of narrative skills, and the representation of experience. Questions about how children experience the
world, and how a child infers "that others experience the world in a
manner similar to the way he or she experiences it" (Oppenheim
and Waters, 1995), have attracted particular interest. How people infer the internal experiences of others is a compelling preoccupation
in psychoanalytic practice and research (Schafer, 1992), and in the
study of medical illness from the patient's perspective (Mattingly and
Garro, 2001). It is easy to see that this question also has exciting implications for efforts to understand and help poorly socialized or im-
pulse-disordered children.

Psychoanalyst and attachment researcher Peter Fonagy and his colleagues have constructed a new scale that can be applied to AAI narratives to study how individual differences influence the ways people
grasp the internal mental states—wishes, feelings, unexpressed perceptions—of others (Fonagy et al., 1991). Fonagy's measure, called
reflective functioning, is a reliable scale that builds on one of Main's
original state-of-mind dimensions, *meta-cognitive monitoring*. This refers to a subject's active monitoring of thinking and recall (which is
evident in several places during the interview). Reflective functioning describes how individuals perceive and think about emotional
and intentional workings, their own and others'. Individuals with
high reflective functioning show intense "awareness of mental states
in the organization, development, and maintenance of attachment
relationships" (Fonagy et al., 1994). People who score high in reflective functioning are those "whose narratives [from the AAI] reflected a coherent mental representation of the psychological world
of their own caregivers, and of themselves as adults, and earlier as
children" (p. 242). Individuals who are adept at discerning the men-

tal states of others may infer them from observation or from interaction: "My parents didn't like each other very much, so it was important for them to make good friends with us" (p. 243). Fonagy and his colleagues found a significant relationship between a parent's reflective functioning and that parent's infant's security; they then went on to speculate about how reflective functioning might figure in the resilience of children of mothers with very adverse histories. They defined "resilient" children as those from adverse circumstances who nonetheless demonstrated high attachment security (Fonagy et al., 1994), and they asked: Could high reflective functioning in mothers with adverse histories be a protective factor, contributing to secure attachments in their infants? Their analyses revealed dramatic associations between high reflective functioning in mothers with adverse histories and the attachment security of their infants: Ten out of ten mothers in the adverse history group with high reflective functioning had children securely attached to them. In contrast, only one out of seventeen mothers with low reflective functioning had an infant with high levels of attachment security. Here again, narrative study has delineated delicate and subtle psychological capacities with important implications for resilience.

Fonagy's findings have attracted a great deal of attention among psychoanalysts as well as clinical and attachment researchers. Since impaired reflective functioning has been reported in the kind of psychopathology that indicates disturbed development, it is reasonable to ask whether high levels of reflective functioning may buffer the damaging effects of abuse and trauma (Fonagy et al., 1995). The work of Fonagy and his colleagues strongly suggests that narrative-based investigations can capture much more than attachment representations, and that the precursors of resilient development are likely to include such individual competences as reflective functioning. Some practitioners have noted that the capacity for reflection, which underlies empathy and other important aspects of clinical listening, may play a role in successful psychotherapy, permitting the identification of disruptions of empathy between therapist and patient (Slade, 1999), and more accurate description of moments of understanding within close pairs, be they therapist and patient, romantic partners, or parent and child.

More broadly still, this empirical direction allows for research focusing precisely on the places where general human potentials and the capacities of individual persons begin to diverge. For instance, research into the narratives of children shows that by five years of age they understand that they and other people have mental experiences out of which they construct their own representations of reality (Oppenheim and Waters, 1995). But children differ in how well they perceive boundaries between themselves and others, and in how clearly they understand the differences between other people's feelings, perceptions, and actions and their own. Questions about whether we could discern such variations, and if so what difference they might make, were powerful motivations underlying our extensive studies of resilient former psychiatrically hospitalized adolescents from High Valley Hospital (Hauser, 1999; Hauser et al., 2006). Similarly, with the development of new *clinical* studies based on attachment paradigms, interest has intensified in individual differences among groups of persons who share the same attachment pattern. Why, for example, and how does one person's attachment pattern change from a markedly compromised insecure one to a secure and open one, while another's does not (Roisman, Pardron, Sroufe, and Egeland, 2002; Badahur, 1998)? Questions like these, of course, are deeply relevant to the study of resilience.

Many investigators of attachment and development operate from the perspective of *co-construction*—that is, from the belief that children develop their narratives upon a scaffolding made available by their parents. One group of investigators looks to the links among narrative assessments of attachment, early observations of attachment behavior, and the core attachment phenomena that John Bowlby, the father of attachment theory, called *internal working models*—that is, the frameworks of beliefs and expectations that people develop, consciously and unconsciously, about how relationships "work" (Bretherton, 1999). Another group considers how a person's childhood and adolescent attachment experiences inform the adaptations and relationships that are later reflected in his or her narratives (Agrawal, Hauser, Miller, and Penn, 2002; Bretherton, 1999; Roisman et al., 2002).

In our study of resilient adolescents (Hauser et al., 2006), we took yet another direction. We asked three questions: How do the available features of a person's narratives—their content, their organization, their coherence—influence that person's adaptation *after* the experience of serious adversity? How are the individual's later narratives shaped by this adversity? And, how are the individual's subsequent narratives influenced by his or her new adaptation? These questions identify another point of contact among the various disciplines that share the growing interest in narrative. As noted above, recent clinical and ethnographic explorations posit the centrality of telling and retelling stories in handling disruptive life events, and more broadly in links between internal experience and interpersonal action (Becker, 1997; Cohler, 1991; Schafer, 1992). This view is beginning to converge with the developmental finding that supportive relationships later in life can help to "provide a benign perspective on early insecure attachments and dampen some of their negative effects" (Oppenheim and Waters, 1995, p. 213). Overall, though, most attachment theory and research still focuses on internal models and their narrative representations, together with the contributions that interpersonal relationships make to the narratives and the representations that underlie them. The contributions made *by narrative processes themselves* to continued development, and even to turning points in development, have so far received far less attention. One of our intentions in our own resilience work has been to test out an approach to that lack, and to demonstrate the importance of further study in this area.

Summary and Discussion

Narrative studies are relatively new in developmental research, but they are now securely integrated into the psychologist's repertoire of investigative techniques, and form the center of an exciting and fruitful body of work. Arising independently in a number of disciplines, and fertilized by work in attachment research and theory, research based on narrative is now actively pursued in many fields, some immediately relevant to psychoanalysis and, by extension, to questions about the nature of resilient development. The choice of which dimensions of narrative to study will, in the end, depend on the research questions being asked and the theoretical approach guiding the research, a point made by both Mishler (1993) and Riessman (1995). Cohler (1991) observes from his characteristic perspective that:

> Early, off-time, adverse life-changes, such as the death of a spouse or offspring, unexpected pregnancy, major health problem, or forced retirement represent misfortune requiring reorganization of the previously recounted personal narrative or life story. These unanticipated events are made "sensible," "followable," or coherent and internally consistent, within a life story that serves to manage meanings and to preserve a sense of self as coherent and integrated over time. Unanticipated adversity provides the dramatic quality . . . as the essential organizing principle of the life story, challenging a previously held sense of personal integration. Successful resolution of this tension reflects resilience to adversity and fosters enhanced personal vitality and increased sense of mastery.

There has been increased awareness regarding the importance of studying the means by which reconstructed experience of the past, particularly adversity, is interpreted as useful in turning present adversity into challenge or opportunity (pp. 184–185).

Cohler sees personal narratives as highlighting "both gains and costs arising from the effort to remain resilient through a continuing effort to manage the meaning of misfortune to preserve a coherent life story" (Cohler, 1991). Our view attributes to narrative a less causal influence on resilience; we see narrative as *reflecting* resilient processes strongly influenced by an interpersonal and environmental surround. Empirical studies like those of Fonagy and Roisman (Roisman et al., 2002) and their groups of colleagues (e.g., Stein, Fonagy, Ferguson, and Wisman, 2000) study the possible linkages between resilience and a person's narratives and attachment representations. Yet the role of narrative as an influence on behavior (or on change in behavior) has not been much explored so far in empirical studies of narration and action. Scholars of medical narrative such as Charon (2001) and Becker (1997) argue for the role of narratives in creating and sustaining personal coherence in the face of disruptions from illness and other calamities, but the interesting question implied in Cohler's (1987, 1991; Cohler et al., 1995) reflections on resilience and narrative has not yet been answered: *How does the form and content of a young person's thought shape his or her adaptation?* This is a question that tantalizes those of us who work with children at risk, and narrative studies are beginning to help us answer it.

BIBLIOGRAPHY

AGRAWAL, H. R., HAUSER, S. T., MILLER, M., & PENN, H. (2003). "My Father Did This to Me!" The Psychodynamic Treatment of an Angry, Sad, and Violent Young Man. *Harvard Review of Psychiatry,* 11:194–209.

ALLEN, J. P., & LAND, D. (1990). Attachment in Adolescence. In Jude Cassidy and Phillip R. Shaver, eds., *Handbook of Attachment: Theory, Research, and Clinical Application* (New York: Guilford Press), pp. 319–335.

BAHADUR, M. A. (1998). The Continuity and Discontinuity of Attachment: A Longitudinal Study from Infancy to Adulthood (Unpublished doctoral dissertation, New York University).

BECKER, G. (1997). *Disrupted Lives: How People Create Meaning in a Chaotic World* (Berkeley: University of California Press); quotation from p. 25.

BERLIN, L. J. (1999). Relations Among Relationships: Contributions from Attachment Theory and Research. In Cassidy and Shaver, eds. *Handbook of Attachment,* pp. 688–712.

BOWLBY, J. (1990). *Charles Darwin: A New Biography* (London: Hutchinson).

BRETHERTON, I. (1996). Internal Working Models of Attachment Relationships as Related to Resilient Coping. In Gil G. Noam and Kurt W. Fischer, eds., *Development and Vulnerability in Close Relationships* (Mahaw, N.J.: Erlbaum Associates), pp. 3–27; quotation from p. 3.

—— (1999). Internal Working Models in Attachment Relationships: A Construct Revisited. In Cassidy and Shaver, eds. *Handbook of Attachment*, pp. 89–111.

BROWN, C. (1965). *Manchild in the Promised Land* (New York: Macmillan).

BRUNER, J. (1986). *Actual Minds, Possible Worlds* (Cambridge, Mass.: Harvard University Press).

—— (1990). *Acts of Meaning* (Cambridge, Mass.: Harvard University Press).

—— (1996). *The Culture of Education* (Cambridge, Mass.: Harvard University Press).

—— (2002). *Making Stories: Law, Literature, Life* (New York: Farrar, Straus and Giroux).

CAMARENA, P. M., SARIGINI, P., & PETERSEN, A. C. (1997). Adolescence, Gender, and the Development of Mental Health, in Amia Lieblich and Ruthellen Josselson, eds., *The Narrative Study of Lives*, vol. 5 (Thousand Oaks, Calif: Sage), pp. 182–206.

CASSIDY, J., & SHAVER, P. R., EDS. (1999). *Handbook of Attachment: Theory, Research, and Clinical Applications* (New York: Guilford).

CHARON, R. (2001). Narrative Medicine: A Model for Empathy, Reflection, Profession, and Trust, *Journal of the American Medical Association* 286:1897–1902.

CHELLIS, M. (1992). *Ordinary Women: Extraordinary Lives* (New York: Penguin).

COHLER, B. J. (1987). Adversity, Resilience, and the Study of Lives. In E. James Anthony and Bertram J. Cohler, eds., *The Invulnerable Child* (New York: Guilford), pp. 363–424.

—— (1991). The Life Story and the Study of Resilience and Response to Adversity, *Journal of Narrative and Life History*, 1:169–200; quotation from p. 177.

COHLER, B. J., STOTT, F. M., & MUSICK, J. S. (1995). Adversity, Vulnerability, and Resilience: Cultural and Developmental Perspectives. In Dante Cicchetti and Donald J. Cohen, (eds.), *Developmental Psychopathology, vol. 2: Risk, Disorder, and Adaptation*, 753–800. New York: Wiley.

DOZIER, M. K., STOVALL, C., & ALBUS, K. E. (1999). Attachment and Psychopathology in Adulthood. In Cassidy and Shaver, eds. *Handbook of Attachment*, pp. 497–519.

FIESE, B. H., SAMEROFF, A. J., GROTEVANT, H. D., WAMBOLDT, F. S., DISKSTEIN, S., & FRAVEL, D. L. (1999). The Stories That Families Tell: Narrative Coherence, Narrative Interaction, and Relationship Beliefs, *Monographs of the Society for Research in Child Development* 257:1–162.

FONAGY, P. (1999). Psychoanalytic Theory from the Viewpoint of Attachment Theory and Research. In Cassidy and Shaver, eds., *Handbook of Attachment*, pp. 595–624.

FONAGY, P., STEELE, M., MORAN, G. S., STEELE, H., & HIGGITT, A. C. (1991). The Capacity for Understanding Mental States: The Reflective Self in Parent and Child and Its Significance for Security of Attachment, *Infant Mental Health Journal* 13:200–216.

FONAGY, P., STEELE, M., STEELE, H., HIGGIT, A. C., & TARGET, M. (1994). The Theory and Practice of Resilience, *Journal of Child Psychology and Psychiatry* 35:231–257; quotation from p. 242.

FONAGY, P., STEELE, M., STEELE, H., LEIGH, T., KENNEDY, R., MATTOON, G., TARGET, M. (1995). Attachment, the Reflective Self, and Borderline States: The Predictive Specificity of the Adult Attachment Interview and Pathological Emotional Development. In Susan Goldberg, Roy Muir, and John Kerr, eds., *Attachment Theory: Social, Developmental, and Clinical Perspectives* (Hillsdale, N.J.: Analytic Press), pp. 223–279.

GEERTZ, C. (1997). Learning with Bruner, *New York Review of Books*, April 10, pp. 22–24.

GILLIGAN, C. (1982). *In a Different Voice: Psychological Theory and Women's Development* (Cambridge, Mass.: Harvard University Press).

GILLIGAN, C., BROWN, L. M., & ROGERS, A. (1990). Joining the Resistance: Psychology, Politics, Girls, and Women, *Michigan Quarterly Review* 29:501–536.

GRICE, H. P. (1975). Logic and Conversation. In Peter Cole and Jerry L. Moran, eds., *Syntax and Semantics III: Speech Acts* (New York: Academic Press), pp. 41–58.

HAUSER, S. T. (1999). Understanding Resilient Outcomes: Adolescent Lives Across Time and Generations. *Journal of Research on Adolescence* 9:1–24.

——— (2005). Overcoming adversity in adolescence: Narratives of Resilience. In P. Giampieri-Deutsch, ed., *Psychoanalysis as an Empirical Interdisciplinary Science: Collected Papers on Contemporary Psychoanalytic Research* (Vienna: Verlag der Osterreischein Akademie der Wissenschaften), pp. 241–267.

HAUSER, S. T., ALLEN, J. P., & GOLDEN, E. (2006). *Out of the Woods: Tales of Resilient Teens* (Cambridge, Mass.: Harvard University Press.)

HESSE, E. (1999). The Adult Attachment Interview: Historical and Clinical Perspectives. In Cassidy and Shaver, eds., *Handbook of Attachment*, pp. 395–433; quotation from pp. 395–396.

HESSE, E., & MAIN, M. (2002). Disorganized Infant, Child, and Adult Attachment, *Journal of the American Psychoanalytic Association* 48:1055–1127.

HIGGINS, G. O. (1994). *Resilient Adults: Overcoming a Cruel Past* (San Francisco: Jossey-Bass).

JAMES, J. B., LIEM, J. H., & O'TOOLE, J. G. (1997). In Search of Resilience in Adult Survivors of Childhood Sexual Abuse: Linking Power Motivation to Psychological Health. In A. Lieblich and R. Josselson (eds.), *The Narrative Study of Lives*, vol. 5, p. 217.

KLEINMAN, A. (1998). *The Illness Narratives: Suffering, Healing, and the Human Condition* (New York: Basic Books).

LUTHAR, S. S., ED. (2003). *Resilience and vulnerability: Adaptation in the context of childhood adversities* (Cambridge (UK): Cambridge University Press).
———— (2006). "Resilience in Development: A Synthesis of Research across Five Decades." In Dante Cicchetti and Donald J. Cohen, eds., *Developmental Psychopathology: Risk, Disorder, and Adaptation, vol. 3,* 2nd ed. (New York: Wiley).

LYONS-RUTH, K. (1999). The Two-Person Unconscious: Intersubjective Dialogue, Enactive Relational Representation, and the Emergence of New Forms of Relational Organization, *Psychoanalytic Inquiry* 19:576–617.

MAIN, M. (1993). Discourse, Prediction, and Recent Studies in Attachment: Implications for Psychoanalysis, *Journal of the American Psychoanalytic Association* 41:209–244.

———— (1999). Epilogue. Attachment Theory: Eighteen Points with Suggestions for Future Studies, in Cassidy and Shaver, eds. *Handbook of Attachment,* pp. 845–888.

———— (2000). The Organized Categories of Infant, Child, and Adult Attachment, *Journal of the American Psychoanalytic Association* 48:1055–1127.

MAIN, M., & GOLDWYN, R. (1998). "Adult Attachment Scoring and Classification System," version 6.2, unpublished manuscript (Berkeley: University of California at Berkeley).

MAIN, M., KAPLAN, N., & CASSIDY, J. (1985). Security in Infancy, Childhood, and Adulthood: A Move to the Level of Representation, in Inge Bretherton and Everett Waters, eds., *Growing Points of Attachment Theory and Research, Monographs of the Society for Research in Child Development* 50, Serial No. 209:66–104.

MATTINGLY, C., & GARRO, L. (2000). *Narrative and the Clinical Construction of Illness and Healing* (Berkeley: University of California Press).

MISHLER, E. G. (1995). Models of Narrative Analysis: A Typology, *Journal of Narrative and Life History* 5:87–123.

———— (1999). *Storylines: Craftartists' Narratives of Identity* (Cambridge, Mass.: Harvard University Press).

NEIMEYER, R. A. & LEVITT, H. (2001). Coping and Coherence: A Narrative Perspective on Resilience. In C. R. Snyder, ed., *Coping with Stress: Effective People and Processes* (New York: Oxford University Press), pp. 47–67.

OPPENHEIM, D., & WATERS, H. (1995). Narrative Processes and Attachment Representations: Issues of Development and Assessment. In E. Waters, B. E. Vaughn, G. Posada, and K. Kondo-Ikemura, eds., *Caregiving, Cultural and Cognitive Perspectives on Secure-Base Behavior and Working Models: New Growing Points of Attachment Theory and Research, Monographs of the Society for Research in Child Development,* vol. 60, 2–3; pp. 197–215.

RHETT, K. (1997). *Survivor Stories: Memoirs of Crisis* (New York: Anchor Books).

RIESSMAN, C. (1990). *Divorce Talk: Women and Men Make Sense of Their Relationships* (New Bruswick, N.J.: Rutgers University Press).

———— (1993). *Narrative Analysis* (Newbury Park, Calif.: Sage).

———— (2002). Analysis of Interview Research. In Jaber F. Gubrium and

James A. Holstein, eds., *Handbook of Interview Research: Context and Method* (Thousand Oaks, Calif.: Sage), pp. 695–710.

ROISMAN, G. I., PARDRON, E., SROUFE, A., & EGELAND, B. (2002). Earned Secure Attachment Status in Retrospect and Prospect, *Child Development* 73:1204–1219.

RUBIN, L. B. (1996). *The Transcendent Child* (New York: Basic Books).

SCHAFER, R. (1992). *Retelling a Life: Narrative and Dialogue in Psychoanalysis* (New York: Basic Books).

SLADE, A. (1999). Attachment Theory and Research: Implications for the Theory and Practice of Individual Psychotherapy with Adults. In Cassidy and Shaver, eds., *Handbook of Attachment*, pp. 575–594.

SPENCE, D. P. (1982). *Narrative Truth and Historical Truth: Meaning and Interpretation in Psychoanalysis* (New York: W. W. Norton).

STEIN, H., FONAGY, P., FERGUSON, K. S., & WISMAN, M. (2000). Lives through Time: An Ideographic Approach to the Study of Resilience. *Bulletin of the Menninger Clinic* 64:281–305.

VERGHESE, A. (1994). *My Own Country: A Doctor's Story* (New York: Simon and Schuster).

——— (2001). "The Physician as Storyteller," *Annals of Internal Medicine* 135:1012–1017.

WALLS, J. (2005). *The Glass Castle* (New York: Scribner).

WAY, N. (1998). *Every-day Courage: The Lives and Stories of Urban Teenagers* (New York: NYU Press); quotation from p. 30.

WHITE, R. W. (1950). *Lives in Progress: A Study of the Natural Growth of Personality* (New York: Dryden Press).

Exploring the Role of Children's Dreams in Psychoanalytic Practice Today

A Pilot Study

OLIVIA LEMPEN, M.A., and
NICK MIDGLEY, Psych.D.

Aim: *The aim of this research study was to investigate the role of children's dreams in the practice of child psychoanalysis today, and to explore contemporary psychoanalytic understanding of children's dreams.* Methodology: *This pilot study consisted of two stages. The first involved a document analysis of published articles in* The Psychoanalytic Study of the Child, *making a comparison between those of the early 1950s and the 1990s, in order to see in what way the discourse around children's dreams within the psychoanalytic literature has changed over time. The second stage, based on questionnaires and in-depth interviews, attempted to understand in more detail the way contemporary child analysts, working in the Anna Freudian tradition, think about dreams and use them in their clinical practice.* Results: *Results suggest that there has been a decreased focus on dreams in a clinical context over time, and that this may partly be a consequence of changing theoretical models and changes in training. When work with dreams does take place, it appears that child analysts have*

Olivia Lempen, psychologist, Service Universitaire de Psychiatrie de l'Enfant et l'Adolescent, 1011 Lausanne, Switzerland; Nick Midgley, Clinical Tutor, Anna Freud Centre/University College London.

The Psychoanalytic Study of the Child 61, ed. Robert A. King, Peter B. Neubauer, Samuel Abrams, and A. Scott Dowling (Yale University Press, copyright © 2006 by Robert A. King, Peter B. Neubauer, Samuel Abrams, and A. Scott Dowling).

various different theoretical models of dreaming; and there is a variety of techniques for handling children's dreams in psychoanalytic practice today.

INTRODUCTION

IT WAS OVER ONE HUNDRED YEARS AGO THAT FREUD FIRST BEGAN TO make systematic use of dream interpretation, and since then, psychoanalytic theorists and clinicians have always acknowledged the major impact of "The Interpretation of Dreams" (1900) on the development of psychoanalysis. However, a number of authors (Brenner, 1969; Blum, 1976; Sachs, 1976; Lansky, 1992; Curtis & Flanders, 1993; Loden 2003) mention that the use of dreams in current psychoanalytic treatment is less than what it once was, and that they are now used in a whole range of different ways in clinical practice.

Surveying this post-Freudian literature on the role of dreams within psychoanalysis today, four main conclusions can be made:

(a) Dream analysis is no longer considered to be the primary way of investigating the unconscious;
(b) Psychoanalytic treatment today aims more at strengthening the adaptive function of the ego rather than seeking to reveal the impulses and desires contained in the unconscious, and this might be one reason why dreams are less of a feature of contemporary clinical practice;
(c) With the increasing emphasis on the ego, there has also been a greater interest in object relations, and, as a consequence, the phenomenon of transference is seen as more central to analytic treatment than dream interpretation;
(d) The interest in the analytic relationship has led therapists to give more importance to the manifest content of the dream, sometimes at the expense of an investigation of its latent content.

While these points are true for psychoanalysis generally, the situation within child analysis has always been a little different, because of questions about the place of dreams in early child development. Freud's "Interpretation of Dreams" (1900) offered what would now be considered an overly simplistic view of children's dreams. At this stage in his work, Freud thought there was little or no process of distortion in children's dreams and therefore no distinction needed to be made between manifest and latent content. However, he changed his mind later and acknowledged the more complex nature of children's dreams (Freud, 1909, 1916).

Developmental studies have also examined children's dream-life, although often from a purely descriptive perspective. Most such studies suggest that young children's dream content seems to be related quite directly to their everyday waking life. For example, Foulkes's (1982) longitudinal study of children's dreams shows that the capacity for dreaming is not acquired straightaway but appears and progresses with mental development in waking life. He reports that the telling of dreams gets longer with age and that in young children's dreams there are very few interactions. According to Foulkes, dreams are much more about body states like hunger or sleep and involve animals rather than humans, and the development of the capacity to dream—assessed according to the length and content of the dreams—only reaches an adult's level between nine and thirteen years old.

Such a view is echoed by more recent research, such as Murray's (1995) longitudinal and cross-sectional studies of REM awakenings in sleep laboratories, in which he found that children's dreams grow in complexity to near adult patterns by the early teen years, as cognitive ability increases. Likewise, in a longitudinal study of children's dreams in the transition from middle childhood to adolescence, Strauch (2005) reports that there was little change in the basic content categories of REM dreams, but that the frequency of unrealistic dream elements declined, whereas the ability to inventively put together separate contents of the memory system to produce meaningful scenes increased.

In a recent review of the psychological literature on children's dreams, Siegel (2005) summarized some of what has been established by developmental studies based in sleep laboratories and using other non-clinical approaches: that as children grow older, they are more able to recall dreams; that dream narratives increase in length; and that dreams are characterized by decreasing levels of passive victimization and have more elaborate character interactions.

Some studies, following the pioneering work of Despert (1949), have taken a more explicitly psychoanalytic perspective, looking at changes in both the manifest and latent meaning of dreams in the course of a child's development. Niederland (1957), in his longitudinal survey of early childhood dreams, showed how the landmarks in the child's psycho-sexual development appear in dreams—from the early nonverbal productions of the psyche to the sexual conflicts of the oedipal period. This view was largely supported by the work of Rambert (1969) in his study of the dreams of latency-age children. In a similar way, in a study of one analysand's dreams at age 5, 13, and

20, Mahon (1992) shows how the infantile oedipal wish found in a 5-year-old boy's dream goes through transformations as development proceeds.

The first child analysts were all interested to explore how the method of dream analysis could be translated into work with young children. Anna Freud was concerned throughout her career with the method of dream interpretation in child analysis. She first wrote, in 1926, that the method of analysis with adults in dream interpretation could be applied unchanged to children. Later, she changed her views and stressed how children were not able to free associate and that without free association, there was no reliable path from manifest to latent content (A. Freud, 1945, 1965). Melanie Klein (1937) introduced the idea of play as a substitute for free association in analytic sessions with children. In playing, she believed, the child makes use of the same language that adults use in dreams. Play would thus be the child's most important medium of expression.

Anna Freud and many other analysts did not subscribe to Klein's idea of children's play being equated with free association. According to Anna Freud (1980), play is one way to bring in material among others—verbal expression, painting, dramatizing, or acting out. Play can reveal a great deal of material but it can also serve the role of defense and resistance, for instance as a refusal of the child to verbalize. It does not supply free associations but could be a useful way of elaborating on dreams to gain insights and a greater understanding of the dreams of children.

In the more contemporary literature, frequent regrets are expressed that the analysis of dreams in the treatment of children has been a neglected area (Ablon and Mack, 1980; Gilman, 1987; Spiegel, 1994). There appears, indeed, to be little systematic research in this area, although a number of child analysts and psychotherapists have continued to write about the importance of dreams in the treatment of children (e.g., Jokipaltio, 1982; Catalano, 1990; Lewis and O'Brien, 1991) and some clinical papers continue to pay attention to the significance of dreams in the course of a particular analysis (e.g., Gillman, 1987; Karush, 1998). Thus, the present study is a contribution to exploring and understanding the place of dreams in contemporary child psychoanalysis. A qualitative approach was deemed appropriate for this study because, as a pilot study, the aim was not to test a particular hypothesis, but rather to discover something about the evolving place of dreams in child analysis and to understand something about the use of dreams clinically among child analysts working today.

THE RESEARCH STUDY

The study reported here was a pilot study for what we hope will be a broader investigation of the place of dreams in child analysis. This pilot study involved two stages, with different types of data and methodologies, thus enabling us to "triangulate" the data sources. The different stages of the study and the different types of data were necessary in order to get different perspectives on our topic—broad as well as deep, and historical as well as contemporary.

STAGE ONE: THE USE OF DREAMS IN CHILD ANALYSIS —
A HISTORICAL PERSPECTIVE

A systematic document analysis was undertaken of the context in which the word "dream(s)" appears in a major journal of child psychoanalysis, *The Psychoanalytic Study of the Child*. This journal was chosen because it is considered one of the foremost journals in the field of child psychoanalysis, and because it has been published continuously over a significant period of time, thus allowing a meaningful study of the changing conceptualization of children's dreams over a period of more than fifty years.

The purpose of this stage of the study was to see how dreams were represented in the professional literature of this leading journal of child psychoanalysis. Two time periods were studied—1945 to 1953 and 1992 to 1998—in order to assess in what ways the discourse has or has not changed over time. The first period was of nine years and the second of seven because the journal did not publish any issues in 1947 and 1948. The period of seven years was chosen because it was large enough to be able to make clear comparisons, as well as being limited enough to study the documents in some detail.

PROCEDURE

Drawing on a methodology described by Mosher (1998) for the study of the evolution of particular aspects of psychoanalytic thought, the analysis of the journal consisted in a search on the PEP CD-ROM version of the HYPERLINK "https://www.med.yale.edu/library/ journals/ pepweb.html", which includes the full text of thirteen premier psychoanalytic journals from 1920 to 2000. A specified year and the term "dream(s)" were entered as key search titles. All the papers of the journal published in the chosen year where the word "dream(s)" appears were selected.

On the basis of a preliminary study of the data, we established four broad, descriptive categories to classify the data according to the context in which the word "dream(s)" was used: (a) clinical context—child; (b) clinical context—adult; (c) theoretical context; (d) reference to the title of Freud's work only. We carried out a systematic review of selected papers in order to classify them in the appropriate category and to count the number of references that fell into each of them.

The search was conducted for the two periods at the same time in order to get an idea of comparative differences whilst undertaking the search. Inter-rater reliability for the categorization of the data was established with a colleague who was external to the research. The results were statistically analyzed with tests of proportions. The results of this document analysis are presented in Table One (below). The comparison of the proportions of papers in each time period with the word "dream(s)" shows a significant increase over time. When exploring this change in greater detail, it appeared that:

(1) the number of papers mentioning dreams in a clinical context with a child has significantly *decreased* over time;
(2) the number of papers referring theoretically to dreams has significantly *increased* over time.

This might suggest that there has been a greater increase of interest in *theoretical* aspects of dreams, but a decreased interest in the use of dreams in a *clinical* context, more specifically, in the context of child psychoanalysis.

This first stage of the study gave us the chance to make a survey of the topic of children's dreams in psychoanalysis from a broad and historical perspective. The next step was to try getting a sense, in a more focused way, of the contemporary attitude to dreams in child psychoanalysis.

STAGE TWO: THE USE OF DREAMS IN CONTEMPORARY CHILD ANALYSIS

In order to study the way in which child analysts use dreams in their clinical practice in a more in-depth way, we decided to move from our initial broad, historical perspective to a focused attention on modern clinical practice, by way of a series of in-depth, semi-structured interviews with child analysts. For the purpose of this pilot study, we decided to investigate analysts working in one particular setting, the Anna Freud Centre, London.[1] It was decided to limit the

---

1. Those trained at the Anna Freud Centre qualify as "child psychotherapists," although the approach is psychoanalytic. For this reason, the terms "child psychotherapist" and "child analyst" are used interchangeably in this study where those participants from the Anna Freud Centre are being discussed.

TABLE ONE

Comparison of the numbers of papers mentioning dreams

	1945–1953		1992–1998		TEST OF
	NUMBER	*PERCENTAGE*	*NUMBER*	*PERCENTAGE*	*PROPORTIONS*
Papers with word 'dream(s)' appearing in the text (a)	75	46	94	58	−2.17*
Papers with word 'dream(s)' appearing in the title (b)	2	3	3	3	−0.2
Papers referring to a clinical context-child (b)	33	44	26	28	2.21*
Papers referring to a clinical context-adult (b)	5	7	13	14	−1.5
Papers referring to a theoretical context (b)	30	40	50	53	−1.71**
Papers referring to Freud's work only (b)	5	7	2	2	1.5

(a) Calculated on the total number of papers in the PSC (162 in 1945–1953; 161 in 1992–1998)
(b) Calculated on the number of papers with the word 'dream(s)' appearing in the text (75 in 1945–1953; 94 in 1992–1998)
* Significant at 5% (|Statistic Test| > 1.96)
** Significant at 10% (|Statistic test| > 1.65)

participants to this one location in order to have a specific frame of reference, and because the theoretical model of the Anna Freud Centre has historically been close to the models of child analysis represented in the *Psychoanalytic Study of the Child.*

In order to select the participants for this interview study, we designed a short questionnaire about children's dreams in psychoanalytic practice. It was distributed to all twenty-eight child psychotherapists and analysts working at the Anna Freud Centre.[2]

The questionnaire consisted of six questions exploring the importance child analysts give or do not give to dreams in their practice (see Appendix One). The participants were asked about their level of experience which enabled us to compare the different attitudes toward dreams according to the experience of the analysts. At the end of the questionnaire, the analysts were also asked if they would agree to a further, more in-depth interview.

As well as helping us to select a group of participants who would represent as wide a range of attitudes as possible toward working with dreams, the questionnaire was the first step toward understanding how child analysts at the Anna Freud Centre consider children's dreams in their practice. This gave us an insight into the way dreams are used in psychoanalysis within one particular setting at the present time.

Seventeen questionnaires were returned and the full responses are presented in Appendix Two. Among the seventeen participants, there were ten trainees, five child analysts who qualified less than five years ago, and two who qualified more than five years ago. There were no obvious differences between those who did and did not return the questionnaire, except that the percentage of trainees who co-operated was higher than the percentage of qualified staff—perhaps suggesting a greater willingness to engage in research among the newer generation of child analysts and therapists.

The small number of participants did not allow any sophisticated statistical analysis but nevertheless certain trends emerged when we analyzed the data:

(a) A majority of the participants answered that working with dreams is important in "some of their cases," but not in all.
(b) Children were most often described as "sometimes" reporting

2. The training at the Anna Freud Centre leads to the qualification of "child psychotherapist," although the training itself is a purely analytic one. For the purposes of this paper, the terms "child psychotherapist" and "child analyst" will be used interchangeably.

dreams spontaneously. It appears that latency-age children and adolescents are more likely to speak about their dream-life than children
under five years of age.
(c) The majority of the psychotherapists would not suggest to the
child that they can talk about their dreams, either at the beginning of
the therapy or during its process.
(d) Dreams reported in therapy are more likely to be nightmares
than pleasant dreams.

Some differences between the more experienced and more recently qualified therapists were also found (see Figures 1–3). In summary, these were:

(a) Therapists who qualified more than five years ago attached more
importance to children's dreams in their practice than did trainees
or newly qualified child therapists.
(b) Trainees were less inclined than more experienced therapists to
suggest to the child, at the start of treatment, that he or she might
talk about dreams, or to ask a child about dreams during the course
of the therapy.

These were suggestive findings which we hoped to explore more
deeply through the in-depth interviews.

THE INTERVIEW STUDY

Of the seventeen child psychotherapists who returned the questionnaires, nine agreed to be interviewed. As this was a pilot study, we
chose four child analysts for the next stage of the study. Participants
were chosen following the principle of "purposive sampling," looking for the maximum variation within the sample, in order to represent as wide a variety of views as possible (Merriam, 2002). Within
such a small sample, the aim was not so much to be representative,
but rather to be inclusive of as many different views and positions as
possible. The criteria used for selecting the sample were the following:

(a) Varied levels of experience: one trainee, one newly qualified, and
two experienced child analysts;
(b) The greater or lesser importance they gave to children's dreams
in their practice as indicated in the initial questionnaire: two who answered dreams were important and two who answered they were not.

On the basis of the above, one of the authors (OL) then under-
took semi-structured interviews with these four child analysts linked
to the Anna Freud Centre. The informal context of a face-to-face interview had the advantages of giving an authentic insight into a ther-

Question 2: Is working with dreams important in:

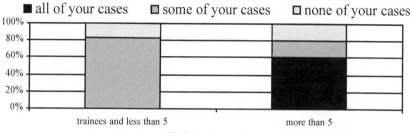

Figure One

Question 4: At the beginning of therapy, do you ever explain or suggest to the child that they can talk about their dreams?

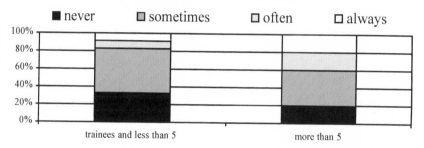

Figure Two

Question 5: During the process of therapy, do you ever ask the child if they have had a dream?

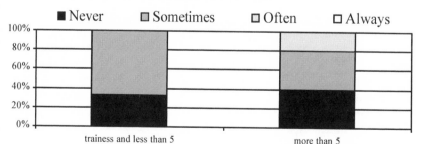

Figure Three

apist's working experience and the opportunity to create some new data which would not exist apart from this study. The interviews consisted of open-ended questions which encouraged the participants to offer their own understanding of the topic (see Appendix Two). A certain number of prompts were also prepared in order to enlarge and develop the participants' answers on important points of interest. However, the interviewer was always prepared to be open to any new ideas brought by the participants and was not restricted to any sequence of questions and prompts.

The interview was first tested on a young psychologist studying at the Anna Freud Centre which enabled us to see whether any changes were required in the structure and questions chosen. The outline of the interview was composed of questions concerning three main areas:

(a) General questions about the interviewee's analytic work with children;
(b) The participant's ideas about dreams and views on Freud's theory of dreams;
(c) The clinical experience of the participant in working with children's dreams.

The interviews lasted around one hour. They all took place at the work place of the participants. Each interview was taped and then transcribed.

PROCEDURE FOR THE ANALYSIS OF THE DATA

The four interviews were analyzed thematically, with the intention of exploring in detail the participants' views of the topic under investigation. The interviews were analyzed in a way that would stay close to the interviewees' subjective beliefs and experiences, while also looking for patterns across the different interviews (see Smith et al., 1999).

The analysis of the data was therefore idiographic, and we began by looking in detail at one of the transcripts before incorporating the others. A list of major and subordinate themes was established for each interview. The lists of themes could then be assessed together and clustered in order to construct a final master list of themes.

One of the authors (OL) carried out the initial analysis and then discussed the themes with the second author (NM) who had read the four interviews. Each interview was first analyzed in its own right, and we tried not to be overly influenced by the themes already found from the other analyses. Following the procedure known as the "constant comparative method" (Glaser and Strauss, 1967) the transcripts were also regularly checked back to make sure the themes were still connected with the primary material, and the whole analysis was then audited by a colleague external to the research. The table of themes of each of the interviews was also shown to the respective interviewees who gave us their feed-back on our choice of themes. These checks enabled us to have several external points of view on our analysis of the data, which helped us to avoid being overly committed to our own interpretations and to stay reflexive. In this way, it increased validity and reliability.

On the basis of this analysis, three major themes emerged. These will now be presented in narrative form, with data extracts from the interviews to help illustrate these themes.

THEME ONE. "WHERE IS THE ROYAL ROAD?"

A theme that emerged strongly from our analysis of the interview data was the interviewees' sense of a change in the use of dreams and the importance given to dreams in child analysis. Although one of the participants felt that "it is the same as it was many years ago," the others all felt that dream analysis was no longer central to their practice:

> I think it just changed. I think originally the emphasis in child therapy was upon interpretation, to make the unconscious conscious . . . But I think most child therapists will now put it down to the relationship.

As this quote indicates, there was the sense of a major shift in the methods and aims of child analysis, moving away from interpreting the unconscious; and so subsequently dream analysis had lessened in importance. Whether because of this lessening of significance, or as a result of it, all but one of those interviewed commented that children do not report many dreams during psychoanalysis. As one of the trainees we interviewed put it:

> None of the children [I have worked with] have brought many dreams, so I wouldn't be able to say that they had a particularly significant part to play within the whole therapy.

The one participant who saw things differently said that children do bring dreams during the course of therapy—although she was aware that many colleagues would say the opposite. This particular interviewee suggested that one reason for her different opinion to other child analysts might be because she always raises the subject of dreams at the beginning of every psychoanalysis. It seems, therefore, that the declared interest of the analyst in dreams may have a significant influence on the frequency with which the child patient will report a dream.

Opinion diverged on whether the therapist should mention to the child that they can bring dreams to the session. On the one hand, participants felt that it is for the child to decide what they want to say and how important it is to them. Telling the child that he or she can bring dreams is seen as encouraging certain types of material with the effect that the analyst may be "pushing something else away":

> It is a little bit like saying, "Come on, please dream!" You're trying to make them do something, so I wouldn't raise it as a routine part of the therapy.

On the other hand, the view was also expressed that children cannot be expected to know that dreams may have an important place in therapy, and that it is the responsibility of the analyst to mention and inquire about dreams. However, only one of those whom we interviewed made a point of saying to her patients during the course of analysis, if necessary, that they had not spoken to her about their dreams. Others preferred to encourage a child to elaborate only when the material was "a little bit dream-like."

Although dreams weren't seen as a central part of the analytic process overall, there was still a sense of what one interviewee described as "a significant dream at a particular time":

> In my practice dreams haven't been the most important part of any child's particular therapy, but there have been times where dreams have been particularly helpful in understanding something that's going on for the child at that particular point in time.

One participant gave the example of an adolescent girl suffering from anorexia who reported a dream about being spoon-fed by her mother, where the mother, when the girl was full, would regurgitate her own food into her daughter's mouth, while the father turned away. The analyst described how a step by step analysis of this dream led to the emergence of some important new understanding for this girl, although the dream's importance was more "in terms of the process at that point," rather than "the whole therapy."

Others spoke about the possible significance that a dream could have at a point in the analysis where resistance was especially great. Describing a particularly difficult period in one child's analysis, one interviewee described the significant moment when the child brought a dream to the session:

In a way I think that in bringing the dream, it felt very much like an attempt on her part to share something of herself that she would normally try to keep back and maybe she felt more able to do so because it was a dream, rather than allowing it to be enacted within the transference relationship, which she did take a very tight control of.

As this indicates, it was felt that a particular dream at a certain moment in the analysis could bring together, in a condensed way, various ideas that had been touched on elsewhere in the course of the therapy. And the participants agreed that children are more likely to bring dreams to the analyst when there is a strong therapeutic alliance. According to one interviewee, the child will feel like offering a dream to the analyst when the relationship is good and trustful. Yet this relationship also altered the understanding of the dream's role within the analysis. Another participant talked about how some children desperately want to be a good child, or good patient, and will bring dreams because "they want to bring something that they know you want to hear."

Theme Two. The Developmental Meaning of Dreams

Asked about their view of Freud's famous statement, "A dream is the fulfillment of a wish," the participants generally felt that these words expressed one possible aspect of the function of dreaming, but that there were other, equally important, aspects. "Defences, anxieties, anger, people you've just met," are all included in dreams, we were told, as are "complex layers of children's relationships, their thoughts and their feelings about themselves and about their parents." The participants also drew attention to Freud's later work on traumatic dreams in "Beyond the Pleasure Principle" (1920) and gave examples of dreams that children had described to them which appeared to be attempts at working over traumatic events that had really happened in their lives. As one interviewee put it, in describing one child's repeated dream: "It was his mind's way of trying to make sense of some very scary things."

One theme that emerged powerfully from the analysis of these interviews was the importance of seeing dreams from a developmental perspective. While agreeing with Freud's view that children's dreams are in some ways "simpler" than those of adults, the participants also felt that processes of distortion and disguise were significant. One analyst gave the example of a young child's dream about his sister, father, and mother being killed. She explained how the aggression in the dream appeared to relate to the child's anger against his mother;

although the dream was quite straightforward in some ways, the boy's murderous rage had nevertheless undergone a process of distortion, and was manifested in the dream by terrifying fires.

In relation to the relative lack of distortion in children's dreams, most of the participants talked about the difficulty for young children in distinguishing between reality and fantasy, and of knowing whether their dreams are real or not. One interviewee gave the example of a latency age child who had undergone traumatic experiences of invasive surgery, and had great difficulty in distinguishing between what he fantasized about these experiences and the actual reality. His dreams were often without distortion of any kind, but were simply a repetition of what had happened to him, or of his ideas of what had happened.

The analysts we interviewed suggested that those children who have difficulty in distinguishing fantasy from reality are more likely to report their dreams because the anxiety of believing the dreams might be real heightens their need to seek help. One of the interviewees suggested that younger children talked more about their nightmares when they had hopes that they might be helped with them: "they have the sort of feeling of the room being a container for difficult feelings and anxieties." On the other hand, the same analyst noticed how some children may not report their nightmares precisely because it can make them feel more anxious: "the telling of the dream can make it feel as if it was happening all over again."

THEME THREE. WORKING WITH DREAMS IN THE HERE AND NOW

Although all of the participants in this study were linked to a single clinic, with its own clear psychoanalytic traditions and models, there was a striking level of disagreement among those interviewed about the technique of working with dreams in child analysis.

One main disagreement among the interviewees was whether, or how far, to go in interpreting the manifest content of the dream. One interviewee expressed the idea that there is no essential difference between the dream and any other free association; she saw "the dream itself as a free association" and felt that it shouldn't be seen as "a special category." According to her, dreams do not need to be given further associations, and should be accepted for whatever they communicate in the analytic session. (The only exception she, like others, gave was in the case of adolescents.) She explained:

> Goodness knows there were other things behind it. But I felt it was useful to go with what it was, as he was bringing it to the session.

However, another interviewee argued that dealing only with the manifest content of the dream was an "oversimplification, an easy way out." She would always aim to access the latent content of a dream:

> It is much easier to say things, as many people do nowadays, in connection with the manifest content. Because it is easier and then they end up interpreting their own associations to the patient; but in fact, they should be interpreting the patient's associations, not their own.

One possible way in which these seemingly contradictory views were reconciled by the analysts we interviewed was in the emphasis that all of them gave to play. After a dream had been reported by a latency age child, one interviewee spoke about the importance of looking at the kind of play that followed:

> Obviously a child psychotherapist would not be using free association which was the method employed by Freud. What was particularly helpful in making sense of this little boy's dreams was the play that tended to follow after he talked about them.

What all the participants shared, however, was a belief in the importance of looking at the dream in terms of the child's relationship with the analyst at that point in time. One of the interviewees gave the following example:

> There was a lion in his room and he took a thorn out of the lion's foot and the lion became friendly. So there you have instantly pain instead of rage, the lion became friendly when the pain was taken away. But you also have something about the relationship, where somebody helps somebody. Now he was at the beginning of a relationship with me, he would not dare to say or even to feel, "I hope you will be able to help take away this pain."

This emphasis on the meaning of the dream in relationship to the transference did not necessarily lead to transference interpretations, however. As one participant put it, even if one does not interpret in the here and now, "I think it is always important to think in the here and now." Indeed, there was a concern about the way some analysts "compulsively" interpret dreams in the transference, but this was seen as potentially intrusive; the important thing was to "assess what the dream means to the child," and use this in deepening the analyst's own understanding.

The exception seemed to be in work with adolescents. After describing a piece of dream-work with an adolescent patient, one interviewee was asked to clarify whether her approach was interpretative.

She replied:

> Definitely, yes, that was mainly interpretation. [. . .] I think there
> were underlying wishes and these wishes were more concealed and
> needed to be analysed a little bit more in comparison with the four
> year old's dreams, where there was little distortion at all.

This issue of how to handle the child's material linked to the question of the technical difficulty of working with dream interpretation. The participants who were still in training or who had qualified as child analysts more recently spoke of their own uncertainty about how to work with dreams in a child's treatment. The issue of the relative lack of emphasis on working with dreams within training was raised, such that subsequent training and the impact of one's own training analysis became crucial. One participant spoke of the importance of gaining experience in this area:

> I learnt the technique of allowing the patient to bring their own asso-
> ciations, that's the vital thing. So after having kind of understood
> that, I was more confident to talk about dreams and to know what to
> do if somebody brings a dream.

DISCUSSION

The systematic analysis of the journal *The Psychoanalytic Study of the Child* during two time periods—1945–1953 and 1992–1998—suggested that in recent years, whilst the theoretical interest in dreams may have increased, the actual use of dreams as a clinical tool in a child treatment has declined. According to several authors (Rangell, 1956; Blum, 1976; Flanders, 1993) this change in the role of dreams in clinical practice is in relation to the general historical development of psychoanalytic methods, i.e. the focus on the ego at the expense of the unconscious. Because dreams were primarily thought of as the production of unconscious wishes, the focus on the ego might be one main reason why dreams are much less central in contemporary clinical practice. Brenner (1969) also points out that dream analysis is no longer the primary way of investigating unconscious processes and that association to symptoms and other production during the analytic session can be just as valuable and necessary.

Ablon and Mack (1980) consider that the dream provides a window onto various processes of development. According to them, children's dreams are of special interest because they express what matters most for the developing child. They think that anxiety dreams in particular provide a rich understanding of the contemporary struggles of children and of their link to earlier fears and conflicts. Such a developmental understanding of dreams emerged as a central theme in the current study.

Moreover, by looking at the interviews and the questionnaire results, there is a suggestion that children seem to report mainly bad dreams to the analyst. Several authors have pointed out the predominance of nightmares in the dreams reported by young children (Despert, 1949; Spiegel, 1994). We can thus wonder if one reason for children reporting mainly nightmares could be that they are struggling with normal developmental tasks, and that reporting nightmares is a way of dealing with the anxieties related to these struggles. Mack (1965) in a paper on children's nightmares focuses "upon the nightmare as a developmental phenomenon, occurring sporadically and, perhaps, inevitably even in healthy children" (p. 403).

One characteristic of children's dreams that emerged from this study concerns the difficulty young children have in distinguishing dreams from reality. Ablon and Mack (1980) write that recognizing the difference between dreams and actual events is a gradually learned process. Several references to cognitive developments have indicated that, before a certain age, children are not able to understand that a dream is a product of thought and does not belong to external reality (Piaget, 1929; Blom, 1960; Lewis and O'Brien, 1991).

The participants in this study suggest two possible consequences arising from this fact, especially in relation to nightmares. The first is that children report their nightmares because they seek help with the anxiety of believing they might be real. Alternatively, however, one participant commented that children who cannot differentiate dreams from real events may be reluctant to report them for fear of making the dream happen again.

The connection between dream interpretation and defenses has often been emphasized in the classical psychoanalytic literature (Furman, 1962; Harley, 1962; Root, 1962). This might be particularly strong with those children who cannot distinguish dreams from reality. In the case of anxiety dreams, the anxiety will increase the need for stronger defenses and stimulate the censoring forces. Children whose dreams are particularly terrifying may wish to avoid discussing their dreams.

The child analysts interviewed for this study all commented on the fact that children do not spontaneously report many dreams during analysis. Several authors have pointed out the infrequency of dreams reported in child treatment (Medici de Steiner, 1993; Spiegel, 1994). What is the reason for this? On the one hand, two of the participants pointed out that the relatively low importance they give to dreams is a consequence of children bringing so few dreams into therapy. On the other hand, one of the interviewees believed that this lack of dreams is due to the fact that analysts do not introduce the child to dreams at the beginning of, or during, the treatment. The declared interest of the therapist would therefore seem to influence the frequency with which children report dreams.

This may relate to the findings emerging from the questionnaires which showed that child analysts who qualified more than five years ago attach more importance to children's dreams in their practice, and are more inclined to suggest that the child might talk about dreams, than do trainees or newly qualified child analysts. Besides being linked with the historical change in the techniques of psychoanalysis mentioned above, this difference between newly and long qualified child analysts might also be related to a certain confidence which is acquired with experience.

Moreover, Greenson (1970) points out that because of the shift of emphasis toward ego psychology, many newly qualified therapists have not had their own dreams analyzed during their analysis. Without this experience it is unlikely they will later choose to work with dreams in practice.

This increasing emphasis on the ego has also been accompanied by a greater interest in object relations and, as a consequence, a greater interest in the phenomenon of transference and the *manifest* elements of a dream. The child analysts interviewed for this study mostly thought that they would not directly verbalize their interpretations of dreams to the child, although with adolescents the case might be different. Indeed Sugarman (2003) points out that the developmental immaturity of the child requires technical interventions beyond verbal interpretations of unconscious conflicts. It might be inappropriate to engage in introspection and in the verbalization of experience with children who are not developmentally ready for this.

The notion of a child's developing theory of mind (Mayes and Cohen, 1996) has to be taken into account to consider children's capacity for internalization and capacity for responding to therapeutic interventions. Joyce and Stoker (2000) show that young children are capable of a form of insight but that their mode of expression and communication is very different and requires other kinds of interventions—mainly through play.

The participants in this study seemed to consider the play which follows the reported dream to be a significant means of facilitating the emergence of unconscious material. Several authors have pointed out that play can be a useful way of elaborating on children's dreams (Lewis and O'Brien, 1991; Gensler, 1994). Mayes and Cohen (1993) and Cohen and Solnit (1993) discuss the therapeutic actions of play in child analysis. On the one hand, it can facilitate the therapeutic work, as a communicative medium and guide to interpretation and clarification. On the other hand, the act of playing in itself facilitates the return to developmentally appropriate and adaptive psychic functioning. Thus, it seems that, along with other aspects of psychoanalytic technique, including interpretation, play has a therapeutic meaning in child psychoanalysis, as the participants of this study point out in the case of dream interpretation.

However, whatever the interviewees' opinions on the techniques of interpretations were, the analysis of the interviews showed that they all gave importance to the role of the dream in the patient-analyst relationship. They introduced the notion of the dream as a present to the analyst, which they related to a good therapeutic alliance. Ablon and Mack (1980) discuss the desire of certain children to please, or displease, the analyst by bringing or withholding dreams. When the therapeutic alliance is good, children might bring dreams as a gift for which they expect the reciprocal gift of interpretation. The participants in this study did think that children might bring dreams to the analyst because they wanted to be appreciated, to be "good children" or "good patients."

However, one participant made the point that for this to happen, it is assumed that the analyst would be especially interested in dreams. This raises the question of the impact of the therapist's interest on the access to the dreams of the child. Gensler (1994) refers to the "interpersonal context of dream telling" and talks about the influence of the analyst's interest in the report of children's dreams in treatment. According to him, children are usually aware whether their dreams arouse interest in the analyst or not and they might use it as a tool, either to seduce the analyst or to withhold and maintain distance.

LIMITATIONS AND FURTHER DEVELOPMENTS TO THE STUDY

The current pilot study was limited in aim, and we are conscious of a number of limitations in the approach to the topic. While interviews with child analysts allowed us to get an "inside" perspective on the thinking process that informs their clinical work, an over-reliance on interview data from analysts may lead to a distorted picture of the clinical field. In order to ensure a more practical approach and outcome, less influenced by theoretical thinking, we would suggest a study of the therapist's case-notes or video-recordings of treatment of children. This would enable the researcher to have more direct contact with the actual substance of therapy, and would provide an op-

248   *Olivia Lempen & Nick Midgley*

portunity to analyze clinical material concerning dreams more thoroughly than by episodic accounts retold in interviews. It would also enable the researcher to study more systematically the developmental differences in the use of dreams with children of different age.

Although the use of a questionnaire to the whole staff group allowed us to check the results of our interview study against the general views of a wider group, there were also inevitable limitations to a study which relied on interviews with a relatively small number of people, all based in a single setting. Moreover, two of the people interviewed were also adult analysts and had considerable experience in adult psychoanalysis, which made it difficult for them to discuss only their work with children. This resulted in a wide range of attitudes and ideas being offered, which made it difficult to focus the information sharply on the main aim of the study—the use of dreams in child psychoanalysis practice today. Perhaps further study focusing on a more specific group—such as those undertaking a child analytic training—would be of value. It would also be helpful to make comparisons between child analysts working in different settings, in order to explore the possibility that approaches to dream-analysis in child treatment varies according to the particular setting.

Nevertheless, we believe that the current study offers some tentative findings that may be of some value. In recent years, while the theoretical interest in dreams may have increased, the actual use of dreams as a clinical tool in a child treatment appears to have declined. This might be in relation to a general historical shift in the focus of child analysis in relation to dreams, as suggested by our document analysis of papers in this journal in the 1950s and 1990s. As a possible consequence of this shift of emphasis, child analysts in this particular study notice that nowadays children do not report many dreams during their treatment, and they link this infrequency of reported dreams with their own relative lack of focus on dreams, and to a certain lack of confidence with the technique of dream interpretation. Nevertheless, although dreams were generally not seen as the most central part of the analytic process, it appeared in this study that a dream could be important in a child's treatment at a particular point in the treatment.

Besides suggesting the historical change in the techniques of child psychoanalysis, this study also showed the importance of seeing dreams from a developmental perspective. Children's dreams might be of special interest because they express what matters most for the developing child—as in traumatic and anxiety dreams. On the other hand, some developmental factors—such as the lack of cognitive skills to gain objective insight and the difficulty of young children in distinguishing reality from fantasy—make dream analysis with children difficult. Although the child analysts involved in this study disagreed on whether to interpret or how far to go in interpreting the manifest content of children's dreams, they all gave importance to the role of the dream in the patient-analyst relationship and shared a belief that play, especially with younger children, is a vital way to access and elaborate on unconscious material that may first emerge in the form of a dream.

APPENDIX ONE

Questionnaire given to child psychotherapists
Msc Research Project: Children's Dreams in Clinical Psychotherapy Practice
1. To which of these categories do you belong?

| A trainee | Qualified less than five years ago | Qualified more than five years ago |

2. Is working with dreams important in:

| All of your cases | Some of your cases | None of your cases |

3. Please state for each age category how often children spontaneously speak about their dreams in therapy session?

Under five:	Never	Rarely	Sometimes	Often
6 to 12 years:	Never	Rarely	Sometimes	Often
Adolescence:	Never	Rarely	Sometimes	Often

4. At the beginning of therapy, do you ever explain or suggest to the child that they can talk about their dreams?

| Never | Sometimes | Often | Always |

5. During the process of therapy, do you ever ask the child if they have had a dream?

| Never | Sometimes | Often | Always |

6. If children report dreams, how often are they:

| *Pleasant dreams:* | Never | Rarely | Sometimes | Often |
| *Nightmares:* | Never | Rarely | Sometimes | Often |

Within the context of my research, I would like to do a short interview about children's dreams in psychotherapy practice with a small number of child psychotherapists.
Would you agree to be contacted about the possibility of being interviewed?

| Yes | No |

If yes could you please write below your NAME and CONTACT DETAILS (with telephone number, if possible): THIS IS OPTIONAL.

APPENDIX TWO

#	Q1 trainees	Q1 less than 5	Q1 more than 5	Q2 all cases	Q2 some cases	Q2 no case	Q3 under 5 never	Q3 under 5 rarely	Q3 under 5 sometimes	Q3 under 5 often	Q3 6 to 12 never	Q3 6 to 12 rarely	Q3 6 to 12 sometimes	Q3 6 to 12 often	Q3 adolescents never	Q3 adolescents rarely	Q3 adolescents sometimes	Q3 adolescents often	Q4 never	Q4 sometimes	Q4 often	Q4 always	Q5 never	Q5 sometimes	Q5 often	Q5 always	Q6 pleasant dreams never	Q6 pleasant dreams rarely	Q6 pleasant dreams sometimes	Q6 pleasant dreams often	Q6 nightmares never	Q6 nightmares rarely	Q6 nightmares sometimes	Q6 nightmares often
1	✓				✓		✓					✓					✓				✓			✓				✓				✓		
2	✓				✓				✓								✓		✓				✓					✓					✓	
3	✓				✓			✓									✓			✓			✓					✓					✓	
4	✓				✓		✓						✓				✓		✓				✓					✓						✓
5	✓					✓	✓						✓			✓				✓			✓					✓					✓	
6	✓				✓								✓						✓					✓			✓						✓	
7	✓				✓		✓					✓						✓		✓				✓					✓					✓
8	✓				✓		✓						✓					✓		✓				✓				✓						✓
9	✓				✓								✓				✓			✓				✓					✓				✓	
10											✓					✓			✓					✓									✓	
11		✓			✓				✓				✓				✓					✓		✓					✓				✓	
12		✓			✓				✓				✓				✓			✓								✓						✓
13			✓			✓			✓				✓				✓		✓				✓						✓				✓	
14			✓			✓			✓				✓				✓			✓			✓					✓					✓	
15			✓	✓					✓				✓				✓				✓			✓										✓
16			✓	✓					✓				✓				✓			✓				✓				✓						✓
17			✓	✓						✓				✓		✓						✓			✓			✓						✓

BIBLIOGRAPHY

ABLON, S. L., & MACK, J. E. (1980). Children's Dreams Reconsidered. *Psychoanalytic Study of the Child, 35,* 179–217.

BLOM, G. E. (1960). Panel Reports—The Role of the Dream in Child Analysis. *Journal of the American Psychoanalytic Association, 8,* 517–525.

BLUM, H. P. (1976). The Changing Use of Dreams in Psychoanalytic Practice—Dreams and Free Association. *International Journal of Psychoanalysis, 57,* 315–324.

BRENNER, C. (1969). Dreams in Clinical Psychoanalytic Practice. In Flanders, S. (1993), *The Dream Discourse Today* (pp. 49–63). London: Routledge.

CATALANO, S. (1990). *Children's Dreams in Clinical Practice.* New York: Plenum Press.

CURTIS, H. C., & SACHS, D. M. (1976). Dialogue on "The Changing Use of Dreams in Psychoanalytic Practice." *International Journal of Psychoanalysis, 57,* 343.

DESPERT, J. (1949). Dreams in Children of Preschool Age. *Psychoanalytic Study of the Child, 3,* 141–180.

FLANDERS, S. (1993). *The Dream Discourse Today.* London: Routledge.

FOULKES, D. (1982). *Children's Dreams Longitudinal Studies.* New York: Wiley Interscience

FREUD, A. (1926). *The Psychoanalytic Treatment of Children.* London: Imago Publishing.

——— (1945). Indications for Child Analysis. *The Writings of Anna Freud, 4,* pp. 3–38.

——— (1965). *Normality and Pathology in Childhood.* New York: Hallmark Press.

FREUD, S. (1900). The Interpretation of Dreams. *S.E. 4.* London: Hogarth Press.

——— (1909). Analysis of a Phobia in a Five-Year-Old-Child. *S.E. 10.* London: Hogarth Press.

——— (1916). Introductory Lectures on Psycho-Analysis. *S.E. 22.* London: Hogarth Press.

——— (1920). Beyond the Pleasure Principle. *S.E. 18.* London: Hogarth Press.

FURMAN, E. (1962). Some Features of the Dream of a Severely Disturbed Young Child. *Journal of the American Psychoanalytic Association, 10,* 258–270.

GENSLER, D. (1994). Soliciting Dreams in Child Psychotherapy—The Influence of the Therapist's Interest. *Contemporary Psychoanalysis, 30,* 367–383.

GILMAN, R. (1987). A Child Analyzes a Dream. *Psychoanalytic Study of the Child, 42,* 263–273.

GREENSON, R. R. (1970). The Exceptional Position of the Dream in Psychoanalytic Practice. In Flanders, S. (1993). *The Dream Discourse Today* (pp. 64–88). London: Routledge.

HARLEY, M. (1962). The Role of the Dream in the Analysis of a Latency Child. *Journal of the American Psychoanalytic Association, 10,* 271–288.

HUG-HELLMUTH, H. (1919). *A Study of the Mental Life of the Child.* New York: Nervous and Mental Disease Publ. Co.

JOKIPALTIO, L. (1982). Dreams in Child Psychoanalysis. *Scand. Psychoanal. Rev.,* 5:31–47.

JOYCE, A., & STOKER, J. (2000). Insight and the Nature of Therapeutic Action in the Psychoanalysis of 4-and-5-Year-Old Children. *International Journal of Psychoanalysis,* 81, 1139–1154.

KARUSH, R. K. (1998). The Use of Dream Analysis in the Treatment of a Nine-year-old Obsessional Boy. *Psychoanalytic Study of the Child,* 53:199–211.

KLEIN, M. (1932). *The Psychoanalysis of Children.* London: Karnac Books, 1975.

LANSKY, M. R. (1992). The Legacy of *The Interpretation of Dreams.* In Lansky, M. R., *Essential Papers on Dreams* (pp. 3–31). New York: University Press.

LEWIS, O., & O'BRIEN, J. (1991). Clinical Use of Dreams with Latency-age Children. *American Journal of Psychotherapy, 65(4),* 527–543.

LODEN, S. (2003). The Fate of the Dream in Contemporary Psychoanalysis. *Journal of the American Psychoanalytic Association, 51(1),* 43–70.

MACK, J. E. (1965). Nightmares, Conflict, and Ego Development in Childhood. *International Journal of Psychoanalysis, 46,* 403–428.

MAHON, E. (1992). Dreams—A Developmental and Longitudinal Perspective. *Psychoanalytic Study of the Child, 47,* 49–65.

MAYES, L. C., & COHEN, D. J. (1993). Playing and Therapeutic Action in Child Analysis. *International Journal of Psychoanalysis, 74,* 1235–1244.

——— (1996). Children's Developing Theory of Mind. *Journal of the American Psychoanalytic Association, 44* (1), 117–142.

MEDICI DE STEINER, C. (1993). Children and Their Dreams. *International Journal of Psychoanalysis, 74,* 359–370.

MERRIAM, S. B. (2002). *Qualitative Research in Practice: Examples for Discussion and Analysis.* San Francisco: Jossey-Bass.

MOSHER, P. W. (1998). Frequency of Word Use as Indicator of Evolution of Psychoanalytic Thought. *Journal of the American Psychoanalytic Association,* 46, 577–581.

MURRAY, J. (1995). Children's Dreams. *Journal of Genetic Psychology,* 156 (3), 303–312.

NIEDERLAND, W. (1957). The Earliest Dreams of a Young Child. *Psychoanalytic Study of the Child, 12,* 190–208.

PIAGET, J. (1929). Dreams. In *The Child's Conception of the World* (pp. 88–122). New York: Harcourt Brace.

RANGELL, L. (1956). The Dream in the Practice of Psychoanalysis. *Journal of the American Psychoanalytic Association, 4,* 122–137.

ROOT, N. N. (1962). Some Remarks on Anxiety Dreams in Latency and Adolescence. *Journal of the American Psychoanalytic Association, 10,* 303–322.

SANDLER, J., KENNEDY, H., & TYSON, R. L. (1980). *The Technique of Child Psychoanalysis. Discussions with Anna Freud.* London: Karnac Books.

SIEGEL, A. (2005). Children's Dreams and Nightmares: Emerging Trends and Research. *Dreaming,* 15 (3), 147–154.

SMITH, J. A., JARMAN, M., & OSBORN, M. (1999). Doing Interpretative Phenomenological Analysis. In Murray, M. and Chamberlain, K., *Qualitative Health Psychology, Theories and Methods.* London: Sage.

SPIEGEL, S. (1994). An Alternative to Dream Interpretation with Children. *Contemporary Psychoanalysis, 30 (2),* 1994, 384–395.

STRAUCH, I. (2005). REM Dreaming in the Transition from Late Childhood to Adolescence: A Longitudinal Study. *Dreaming,* 15(3), 155–169.

SUGARMAN, A. (2003). A New Model for Conceptualizing Insightfulness in the Psychoanalysis of Young Children. *Psychoanal. Q.,* 72, 325–355.

Some Reflections on
Infancy-Onset Trichotillomania

MIRI KEREN, M.D., ADI RON-MIARA, M.A.,
RUTH FELDMAN, Ph.D.,
and SAMUEL TYANO, M.D.

Whether infancy-onset trichotillomania is best regarded as a habit, an early sign of obsessive compulsive disorder, a symptom of anxiety, or a sign of severe deprivation has been a topic of continuous debate. In this paper, we describe our clinical experience with nine consecutive cases of infancy-onset trichotillomania and detail the evaluation process and treatment course in one case. A distinct psychosocial stressor was identified in all cases, often accompanied by loss in the parents' histories. Most of the children had no transitional object. In six infants, the symptom resolved after treatment and did not recur, while in three others improvement was partial. Length of treatment varied from four to twenty-one sessions and outcome was unrelated to treatment duration. In all cases, mother-child interactions were characterized by a lack of maternal physical contact and warmth, sharp maternal transitions between under-involvement and intrusiveness, lack of mutual engagement, and no elaboration of symbolic play. The infant's behavior during play was marked by anxiety, irritability, and momentary withdrawal from the interaction. Our cases reveal an impaired affective interpersonal communication between mother and child, often masked by a fair overall family instrumental functioning. It is tenta-

Miri Keren, Adi Ron-Miara, and Samuel Tyano work in the Infant Mental Health Unit, Geha Mental Health Center, Petah Tiqva, Israel; Ruth Feldman works at Bar Ilan, Department of Psychology, and the Gonda Brain Science Center, Ramat-Gan, Israel.

The Psychoanalytic Study of the Child 61, ed. Robert A. King, Peter B. Neubauer, Samuel Abrams, and A. Scott Dowling (Yale University Press, copyright © 2006 by Robert A. King, Peter B. Neubauer, Samuel Abrams, and A. Scott Dowling).

tively suggested that infancy-onset trichotillomania represents an end-point symptom of several factors, such as a disturbed parent-infant relationship, a low pain threshold in the infant, and a parental hyper-sensitivity to overt expressions of aggressive impulses and negative affects. Issues related to treatment modalities are also addressed. Discussion focused on our experience that early-onset cases of trichotillomania are often not benign or homogenous in terms of etiology, course, or response to treatment and require much further study.

INTRODUCTION

FIRST DESCRIBED IN 1889 BY THE FRENCH DERMATOLOGIST HALLO-peau, trichotillomania, or the impulse to pull one's hair, usually begins in childhood, most often between 4 and 17 years of age. Trichotillomania is seven times as prevalent in children as in adults. Under the age of 6 years, boys seem to be more affected than girls (Hamdan-Allen, 1991). After that age, the pattern seems to reverse and during childhood, the symptom is 2.5 times more prevalent in females than in males (Muller et al., 1972). Recently, there has been an increased awareness of cases with very early onset that occur during the first year or two of life (Mansueto et al., 1997). The traditional view (Swedo et al., 1991) has been that the early onset form (2–6 years of age) is benign and self-limited. On the other hand, the later-onset condition, starting in adolescence and up to young adulthood, is considered to be more severe, long-lasting, and often related to psychopathology, such as depression (Weller et al., 1989), obsessive compulsive disorder (Greenberg, 1965; Swedo et al., 1992), drug or alcohol abuse, and panic disorder (Swedo et al., 1989), or impulse disorder (King et al., 1995). In this paper, we present our clinical experience with very early-onset trichotillomania (under the age of 2 years) and re-examine the view that it is a transient and benign phenomenon.

REVIEW OF THE SUGGESTED ETIOLOGIES

Little of the theorizing on the etiology of trichotillomania has distinguished between the infantile-onset and the later-onset forms of the disorder. To our best knowledge, no study has examined the longitudinal course of very early-onset cases of trichotillomania, and thus, the issue of continuity between the two forms remains unresolved.

Regardless of the age of onset, various models have been proposed to explain the condition of trichotillomania. Each of the explanatory frameworks reflects, regardless of age of onset, the dominant paradigm of its epoch (King et al., 1995). In general, three types of frameworks have been proposed for trichotillomania. *Psychodynamic models* have emphasized auto-erotic self-soothing drives as well as aggressive impulses that are turned against the self. *Learning theory models* point to the reinforcing nature of the tension reduction that is presumed to underlie hair pulling. Finally, *neurobiological models* have seen trichotillomania as a dysregulated fixed action-motor pattern (akin to disordered grooming behavior seen in various birds and mammals), perhaps related to basal ganglia dysfunction and other tic/obsessive spectrum disorders.

In addition to these general frameworks, several authors propose that severe disturbances in the early mother-child relationship underlie trichotillomania. Buxbaum (1960), for instance, emphasizes the use of hair as a transitional object and makes a link between hair pulling with unresolved conflict between auto-erotic and object-erotic satisfaction. It is important to note, however, that Winnicott (1971) viewed transitional phenomena as a normal and healthy process, and this hypothesis is incomplete without further elaboration.

Within the psychoanalytic perspective, authors have noted both pleasure and hostile aggressive components of hair pulling. Greenberg and Sarner (1965) studied adolescents and adopted the term "hair-pulling symbiosis" to describe the pathological mother-daughter relationship that is organized around the symptom and often includes the exclusion of the father. Mannino et al. (1969) investigated twelve cases of trichotillomania, among them one 2.5-year-old toddler and the others aged 6 years and more. Interestingly, in four of the children the symptom was an early-onset and began between 16 and 18 months of age. The most common family constellation was that of an aggressive, instrumental mother and a passive, adjunctive father. The mother-child relationship was characterized by an intermittent closeness and distance, a pattern that reflects both maternal ambivalence and self-centeredness. On the other hand, no distinct father-child relational pattern was evidenced in their sample. As a result, the authors viewed trichotillomania as a defensive, ego-syntonic process that functions to control anxiety through a narcissistic auto-erotic mechanism. In that sense, trichotillomania could be included in the list of what has been described as "self-soothing" or auto-erotic behaviors that are common in infancy, such as rumination, rocking, head-banging, or pica. Some children not only pull their hair but also mouth or swallow it (trichophagy), sometimes resulting in a tri-chobezoar (Frey et al., 2005).

The specific parent-child relationship disturbances that may lead to the development of trichotillomania, however, remain unclear. For instance, Aleksandrowitz et al. (1978) reported on a 2.5-year-old girl with trichotillomania and trichobezoar. They describe a desired and well-loved child who nonetheless started to pull out her hair at the age of 12 months. Good marital relationships and good overall functioning of the family were observed. Around the time of symp-tom onset, the mother became pregnant and the child had to face new frustrations that she, according to the authors, perceived as a narcissistic injury, for which she was totally unprepared. One may wonder whether the parent-child relationship was secure or over-gratifying and perhaps reinforced the 2-year-old child's omnipotent fantasies. "Too-good" mothering has been shown to impinge on the development of some aspects of the sense of self and hamper the de-velopment of interpersonal skills such as negotiation, concern for others, and the ability for reparation (Hopkins, 1996).

Another view of trichotillomania is as a habit that often develops in a climate of psychosocial stress in the family (Oranje et al., 1986). Hamdan-Allen (1991) also explained trichotillomania in young chil-dren as either a habit, like thumb sucking, or a symptom of anxiety, often provoked by actual or threatened separation from an attach-ment figure. One may argue that separation anxiety is in fact a symp-tom of a relational problem, which would bring us back to the par-ent-child relational etiology.

From a psychiatric perspective, trichotillomania has been viewed as a symptom of anxiety disorder. In a study by Reeve and colleagues (1992), overanxious disorder was the most common co-morbid DSM III R diagnosis of trichotillomania, at times with a concomitant mood disorder. Similarly, Wright and colleagues (2003) found anxiety (es-pecially separation anxiety) as the main symptom in a sample of ten hair-pulling toddlers (average age of 26 months). Swedo et al. (1992), in one of the larger studies on trichotillomania, examined ten early-onset cases (2 year olds) in addition to forty-three cases in older chil-dren, adolescents, and adults. They found that some of the young children exhibited anger or anxiety when prevented from pulling their hair, while others could be easily distracted from hair pulling by activity or positive attention. There was no manifest episode of anxi-ety preceding the hair pulling, although the children in this sample were too young to verbally report any possible anxious feelings. The clinical course was mostly episodic, with periods of complete remission. In contrast, the older children, adolescents, and adults often described an overwhelming urge to pull their hair, followed by a sense of temporary relief after pulling.

Walsh et al. (2001) differentiate between two clinical forms of hair pulling: The first type has been described as a "focused" type wherein time and attention is dedicated to the hair pulling. This type of hair pulling is associated with tension prior to the act and relief after pulling and is often accompanied by negative affect. The second, more common, type of trichotillomania is described as an "automatic" type. In this form of the disorder, hair pulling accompanies other activities, such as lying in bed, watching TV, or ruminating, and the individual is generally unaware of his or her hair pulling behavior (Du Toit et al., 2001). In our sample, seven of the cases presented the "automatic" type of hair pulling. The symptom in these cases often occurred when the child was in bed and seemed content and peaceful while playing with hair. Two of the cases were of the "focused" type; they pulled their hair at frustration times and often gazed angrily at the parents while pulling their hair.

TREATMENT MODALITIES

The different conceptualizations of trichotillomania are reflected in a wide variety of treatment modalities, such as response prevention (Massong et al., 1980; Byrd et al., 2002), elimination of thumb sucking ("thumb-post") (Watson et al., 1993), habit reversal, parent-child psychotherapy, pharmacotherapy with serotonin re-uptake inhibitors (Swedo et al., 1989), and cognitive-behavioral or habit-reversal treatment for older children and adolescents (Vitulano et al., 1992; Woods and Miltenberger, 2001).

According to Oranje et al. (1986) the following aspects should be taken into consideration when planning intervention in cases of young children with trichotillomania:

1. The family constellation where the symptom developed. Special attention should be paid to probable precipitating factors (e.g., birth of sibling, hospitalization of child or family member, disturbed mother-child relationship).
2. The context in which the symptom tends to occur, such as during watching TV, going to bed, or thumb sucking.
3. New maintenance factors (such as stressors in the child's family).
4. Whether the symptom initiated a cycle of deteriorating parent-child relationship, and what form these negative cycles tend to take.

In general, however, there is an agreement that the treatment course of trichotillomania is often difficult and requires "a broad, flexible approach" (O'Sullivan et al., 2000).

In our experience with nine cases of trichotillomania, we found that the early-onset cases seen were often not benign, necessitated professional intervention, and were not homogenous in terms of etiology, course, or response to treatment. This might be an artifact of our clinical setting—a community-based infant mental health clinic. It is likely that the "easy," habit cases may remit spontaneously or be treated successfully by pediatricians or dermatologists (Byrd et al., 2002) and only the more resistant cases are referred to the clinic. Still, none of our cases was referred by a dermatologist, and all were referred by well-baby clinics nurses or pediatricians, or they were self-referred. In the following, we present a detailed case description of one little girl, who in our opinion, provides a good example of the complexities of the etiology, treatment course, and mother-child relational pattern in cases of early-onset trichotillomania.

CASE PRESENTATION

Joy, a 1-year-and-11-month-old girl, was referred to our community-based Infant Mental Health Unit following symptoms of hair pulling that started a month and a half prior to referral. The referral was initiated by Joy's aunt who worked as a well-baby clinic nurse. No apparent trigger event could be recalled by the parents at first. In retrospect, however, it became apparent that Joy's hair pulling began at a time when her father was preoccupied with his own parents' second divorce. Joy's parents described her clinginess to the mother, but they did not make any connection between the hair-pulling symptom and mother-child relationship or the grandparents' divorce. Prior to symptom onset, Joy had not displayed a tendency to play with her own or others' hair. When she started to pull her hair, she would do so mostly while sucking her thumb and resting or falling asleep (the "automatic" type). She would also pull out her dolls' hair, and hair was found in Joy's feces, indicating that she also tended to swallow her hair.

Joy was the youngest daughter in a family of three children. The oldest child was an 8- year-old boy with developmental delays and motor difficulties, who was described as emotionally over-sensitive and was in therapy. Her sister, 4.5 years old, was described as well-developed and easy going.

Joy was born after a planned, full-term pregnancy, in a spontaneous, uncomplicated delivery. Joy's mother recalled being tense and overwhelmed after Joy's birth, as she was alone with the three children while the father was mostly on military duty. Mother planned to breastfeed Joy but stopped after 4 weeks because of lack of milk. Mother described Joy as a "too good baby" who would not even cry for food and had no feeding problems. Joy's psychomotor development was normal, and a mild delay in language was observed. The mother's main concern was Joy's sleeping pattern; she never slept through the night, often falling asleep on her own, waking up for a bottle, and spending the rest of the night in her parents' bed. It is of note that Joy *never had a transitional object. The mother deliberately did not allow her to acquire one indicating that she did not want Joy to become attached to an object that might be lost.* In place of a transitional object, mother would calm Joy with bottles of milk. During the first year, Joy stayed at home with her mother and was hardly ever cared for by someone other than the mother.

Asked by the therapist about the choice of Joy's first name, mother revealed some of the "ghosts in Joy's nursery." When Joy was a few months old, her mother had a nightmare in which Joy was suffocating and mother rescued her. Rushing to save her baby, the mother discovered her own grandmother lying in the crib dead with her face covered. The dream was interpreted by the mother as a sign that Joy had to be named after her deceased grandmother and a middle name was added to her first name. It turned out that the older siblings' names also stood for deceased family members. Joy was given a neutral first name, because the mother felt that both hers and her husband's families were plagued by illnesses, losses, and painful separations, and she unconsciously wished to break this "destiny" by giving her third child a different name. She interpreted the dream as a sign that no child can escape her family destiny.

Joy's father, a 34-year-old career army officer, was away from home most of the day. He grew up in an overprotective family atmosphere. He remembered being the favorite son of his parents, and he described how his parents had adopted a façade of "everything is great." His parents never openly addressed his difficulties at school and his sense of clumsiness and loneliness. The exacerbation of their longstanding marital problems destroyed this façade when he, himself, was already married. His parents divorced, and shortly after Joy's grandmother fell ill with a brain tumor and had surgery that left her with a facial paralysis and emotional distress. This turmoil led the grandparents to remarry but shortly afterward they divorced for a second time, right around the period of Joy's symptom onset. Joy's father took a mediating role in his parents' divorce and was overinvolved in his family of origin at the expense of attending to his own family's needs.

Joy's mother, a 31-year-old health professional, was working at home at the time of referral. The mother was an only child to her parents, each of whom had been previously married with children. Her father was divorced and had one son; her mother was a young widow with three children, and both of her parents died during the mother's early childhood. The mother's father died of a heart attack when she was 3.5 years old, and her mother died from cancer after a year of illness when she was 9.5 years old. After her parents' death, Joy's mother grew up in her aunt's home together with the aunt's three children. She remembers the aunt's family as loving, albeit not emotionally expressive, but experienced a deep sense of inferiority toward her cousins. Mother recalled how she would shut out her emotions (especially anger, sadness, and jealousy) and secretly mourned her parents' death each night. She still had episodes of intense crying, withdrawal, and isolation at the time of referral.

At the first evaluation session, Joy appeared to be a well-developed and chubby toddler. She stayed close to her parents, scanned the therapist and the room, and smiled from a distance. After a long warm-up time, she started exploring the toys and made an indecisive move toward the therapist. While her parents were busy telling the therapist about their own difficulties and families, Joy actively ignored her father (who similarly paid no attention to her) and approached her mother, trying unsuccessfully to gain her attention. She was strikingly attuned to her mother's emotions: when the mother started crying, Joy became distressed, handed her a tissue, and sat close to her. No less striking was the parents' lack of attention to Joy's behaviors. Joy enjoyed playing alone with a doll.

Joy's developmental status, assessed with the Bayley Scale of Infant Development (1993), was within normal range. Ten minutes of mother-child free play interaction was videotaped; mother was instructed to play with her child as she would at home. The quality of the interaction was coded, blind to the child's clinical status, by an independent coder in a university laboratory using the Coding Interactive Behavior coding system (Feldman, 1998).

The CIB is a global rating system for parent-infant interaction that includes 42 scales. Of these, 21 are parent scales that address parental behaviors such as gaze, observed positive and depressed affect, parental acknowledgment of the infant's communications, parental adaptation to infant signals, physical closeness, parental intrusion on the infant's play, teaching behavior, and so on. Sixteen of the CIB codes are infant codes, and assess infant alertness, negative emotionality, initiation, level of creative/symbolic output, competent use of the environment, child withdrawal, and so on. Finally, five codes address the dyadic atmosphere and index dyadic-systemic constructs such as the level of reciprocity between parent and child, rhythmic fluency of the interaction, or level of tension or constriction in the interacting dyad. CIB codes are aggregated into eight parent, child, and dyadic composites, including parental sensitivity and responsiveness, parent intrusiveness, parent limit-setting, child involvement, child withdrawal, and child compliance, dyadic reciprocity, and dyadic negative states.

The CIB system has been validated in studies of healthy and high-risk infants and has been found to differentiate interaction on the basis of child age, cultural background, interacting adult, biological and emotional risk-conditions, and improvement following intervention (Feldman, 2000; Feldman et al., 2001; Feldman et al., 2003; Feldman, 2004). In our clinic, we use CIB codes routinely to evaluate the interaction, assess the overall quality of the relationships as well as specific behavioral patterns of mother and child, target the interactive elements that require intervention, and often share with the mother our impression using the videotaped observations while pointing to specific moments in the interaction when the mother "missed" or misinterpreted the child's nonverbal communicative signals (Feldman et al., 2004).

The interactive behavior of the mother was coded as alternating between a depressed, under-involved stance and an over-directive, intrusive, and instrumental interactive style. No mutual enjoyment, dyadic reciprocity, or physical closeness was observed. Mother made no symbolic elaboration of Joy's play material, did not venture into imaginative play, and would only ask the child "What is it?" leaving play at a low functional level of symbolization. Numerous silent moments were noted. At one point, Joy threw her head backward, as if trying to exclude herself from this difficult, painful-to-watch exchange. In spite of the high level of dyadic tension, no overt signs of aggression were manifested in either mother or child. In general, mother scored low on the sensitivity/responsiveness construct and received a high score on the intrusiveness composite. The child scored high on the withdrawal cluster and medium-to-low on the involvement cluster. The level of dyadic reciprocity was low, and the level of negative dyadic states was medium-to-high.

Applying a psychiatric diagnosis from the Diagnostic Classification of Mental Health and Developmental Disorders of Infancy and Early Childhood (DC 0–3; 1994), Joy was diagnosed with a Disorder of Anxiety on the Axis I (Infant's Primary Diagnosis axis), and Mixed Over and Under-involved Mother-Infant Relationship disorder, and Under-involved Father-Infant Relationship disorder, on Axis II (Parent-Infant Relationship disorder). She had no diagnosis on the medical/developmental axis (Axis III). On the axis of psychosocial stressors (Axis IV), we put Maternal Dysthymic disorder with history of early loss of parents. The DC 0–3 is a widely used system for classifying disorders of infancy with established reliability and validity (see special sections in JAACAP, 2001, 40(1), and IMHJ, 2003, 24(4)). It includes five axes; I—primary diagnosis, II—parent-infant relational disorders, III—physical, neurological, and developmental disorders, IV—psychosocial stressors, and V—functional emotional developmental level.

Attempting to define the disorder in psychodynamic terms, we conceptualized Joy's trichotillomania symptom as a sign of significant emotional distress. We hypothesized that the distress has most likely been the result of Joy's feelings of anxiety and anger toward the distant father and the depressed mother. It appears that both parents had a very limited capacity for reflective functioning (Fonagy et al., 1991a) and neither thought of the possible link between Joy's clingy behavior and her hair pulling. Both parents were still deeply preoccupied with their own attachment figures and losses and had no positive internalized models of affective interpersonal communication. As a result, Joy was left to her own fears, anger, and sadness, just as each of her parents had felt alone in their own lives, from childhood to parenthood.

Still, we wondered why Joy, who was the third child in this family, became the identified patient. Joy was the youngest child in her family, as was the mother, and this may have triggered specific maternal projective identifications. Two main themes appeared to us as the "leading thread" in this case. The first was the mother's fear of loss of object, as reflected in her active avoidance of letting Joy have a transitional object (Mother said: "I cannot bear the thought of it getting lost"), and in her dream about Joy and her own deceased grandmother. The second was the trans-generational theme of "mothers being left alone with their young children." Because of her husband's psychological absence, Joy's mother found herself alone with three young children, in a similar state as her own widowed mother. The mother's basic insecure attachment was transmitted to Joy and within the therapy session, we could see a role reversal pattern as Joy attempted to comfort her mother. Mother's identification with Joy as the youngest child of the family led her to interfere with Joy's attempts at autonomy.

Above all, patterns of emotional communications and processes of mentalization were deficient in this family as a result of the extensive trans-generational use of repression and denial as defense mechanisms. There was no room for transitional space and therefore no opportunity to develop symbolization skills. The father's preoccupation with his own parents' divorce aggravated the mother's loneliness and depression, which in turn triggered the onset of their daughter's hair pulling. Joy was left with no effective coping mechanisms to deal with her own loneliness and anger. Although not assessed by means of the Strange Situation Paradigm, Joy's attachment to mother was clearly ambivalent, as manifested by her clingy behavior on the one hand and on the other hand withdrawal from mother observed momentarily during the interaction.

Based on this understanding of Joy's symptoms, we chose a triadic psychodynamically informed psychotherapy as the therapeutic modality. The treatment had three goals: To re-attach the father to his wife and infant in order to reduce the mother's loneliness; to engage parents and child in a secure, pleasurable playful interaction so as to promote the creation of a transitional space for the expression of feelings; and to increase the parent's reflectivity with regards to the child's mental state and their internal processes as parents.

As it turned out, the first sessions were indeed triadic, but the father's military profession did not allow him an ongoing participation, and the therapy became mainly mother-child dyadic psychotherapy. In the first triadic session, Joy's mother talked about her feelings of loneliness and of being "not heard." The father was unexpectedly receptive to his wife's new way of verbalizing her feelings rather than simply crying, and he was also able to become more involved with Joy by explaining to her that the mother was upset, would calm down soon, and that this distress was not the child's fault. This triadic session was special for all family members. It was the first time that Joy could experience her parents exchanging emotions and including her in the process. In Stern's terms (1995), a new "schema-of-being-with-Daddy-and-Mommy" had been constructed in Joy's representational world.

With the aim of reinforcing this new family "interpersonal communication trend" and noting the father's limited availability, we used the next session for a videotaped structured triadic play procedure termed the Lausanne Triadic Play (LTP; Fivaz-Depeursinge et al.,

1999; Harrison, 2005). This procedure is a standardized assessment of family interaction patterns used for research and clinical purposes and is routinely used in our clinic. Parents are instructed to "play as a family" in four successive episodes while both parents face the baby. During the first part, one of the parents starts playing with the infant and the other parent remains "just present." During the second part, parents reverse roles. In the third part, both parents play with the infant, and during the last part, the parents interact among themselves while the baby is "just present." During this procedure, it was the father's disengaged style that became most apparent during the third part, where he left the triadic play and let mother and Joy have a dyadic interaction. The therapist reviewed the tape with the parents and pointed to the nonverbal cues Joy made toward the father, and the role reversal attitude Joy had toward her mother. Father felt moved and the therapist suggested trying again the LTP. A change in the father's involvement was observed on both behavioral and affective levels, and a feeling of possible togetherness emerged. In the following session, the therapist attempted to maintain the "triadic space" in father's absence through "holding" the father's place in her own mind and repeatedly conveying it to mother and child. This stance facilitated the mother's verbalization of her fear of being overwhelmed by negative affects and feelings of loss. The therapist reflected upon the significance of interactional micro-events that occurred between Joy and her mother and enabled mother to become conscious of the link between her own fear of loss and Joy's ambivalent pattern of attachment. For instance, as Joy was playing somewhat far from her, mother called her back and at the same time said she wished Joy were more independent.

Joy's need for a transitional object was discussed in the light of this new understanding. Still, mother had a hard time giving Joy the freedom to choose a doll with "negative" characteristics—dirty with unkempt hair—and she suggested that Joy clean the doll and cut her hair (!). At that point, Joy needed the therapist's support to be able to express her own will. She obviously feared losing her mother while expressing overt resistance and anger. Mother's fear of loss of the loved object was the underlying motive of the resistance she expressed toward the therapist, whom she perceived as the one who encouraged Joy's autonomy. For instance, after a significant improvement in Joy's sleep habits, mother came and told about Joy's "regression" during the night. It turned out that mother herself took the child back to the parents' bed. With the therapist's help, she identified and verbalized her fear of losing Joy and her difficulty standing Joy's cry at night, which she interpreted as signs of loneliness and mourning similar to her own. As the therapist linked this insight to the mother's behavioral expression of resistance, there was a deepening of the therapeutic relationship and an enhancement of the mother's reflectivity.

Joy's language improved substantially with the emergence of aggressive themes in her play. At first, she felt safer sitting with her back to mother and only making eye contact with the therapist. With time, Joy's scribbling became more audacious, dolls were thrown away, and she would make "frightening" faces. Little by little, aggression and anxiety became externalized and three sessions later mother reported that hair pulling had completely stopped. A month later, mother reported further improvements: Joy, now 2 years and 2 months old, would wake up just once a night and return to sleep by herself in her bed. Toilet training was on its way and last, but not least, Joy's parents dared for the first time to go out and leave her with grandmother. At the end of sixteen sessions (over a period of 4 months), when Joy was 2 years and 3 months, mother decided to terminate the therapy. The link between Joy's past symptoms and her own conflict was now available to her, and she contemplated the possibility of having individual psychotherapy for herself. Unfortunately, the father did not attend the last session.

Three and one-half years later, on a follow-up phone call, we learned that trichotillomania had not recurred, though Joy would still touch her hair while relaxing and sucking her thumb. Joy was now a well-developed 5.5-year-old toddler, socially integrated in her kindergarten class, and was about to start elementary school. Mother, on her part, had just started individual psychotherapy a few weeks prior to our phone call.

DISCUSSION

Although the condition of trichotillomania has received clinical and empirical attention, very few early-onset cases have been described. In this paper, we described an early-onset case to illustrate the therapeutic process in cases of trichotillomania that are marked by a significant parent-child relational disturbance.

The diagnosis of relational disturbance underlies many, if not most, of the parent-infant dyads referred to our Unit. Such a diagnosis applies to infants presenting a variety of somatic symptoms, such as feeding problems, sleep problems, "self-soothing" behaviors, such as rumination, rocking, head banging, pica, and others (Keren et al.,

2001). Thus, trichotillomania is not unique in its link to a substantial disruption in the early attachment relationship.

However, hair pulling presents a puzzling, self-injurious behavior by young infants who are not autistic, mentally retarded, or are suffering from severe deprivation. We thus tried to assess the commonalities in our nine early-onset cases. This assessment was intended for hypothesis-generation and cannot be considered as a true prospective study since no adequate control group was included. The distribution of trichotillomania by gender was nearly half boys and half girls, with a slight preference for girls (five girls and four boys). We diagnosed all the cases with the DC: 0–3 Diagnostic Classification, and all of them met criteria for Parent-Infant Relationship disorders (Axis II). The main subtypes of parent-child relational disorder were that of "Overinvolved" (2), "Underinvolved" (4) or "Mixed" (3).

Our clinical diagnosis of relational disorder was supported by blind coders of the videotaped mother-infant interactions we had at our disposition using the CIB coding system (Feldman, 1998). In all cases, interactions were characterized by a lack of maternal physical contact and warmth, sharp maternal transitions between underinvolvement and intrusiveness, reduced mutual engagement, no parental elaboration of the child's symbolic play, and signs of anxiety and irritability in the infant, with momentary withdrawal from the dyadic interactions. During the structured "family play" triadic interaction (LTP), the least optimal family interaction was observed during the third section, which requires that both parents play together with the infant.

In addition to the detection of a parent-infant relationship disorder diagnosis, we noticed that seven out of the nine cases had no transitional object. Similarly, in all cases a distinct psychosocial stressor was identified, and in six cases there was substantial early loss in the parents' histories.

Although hair pulling is a painful activity, our infants did not seem to suffer while pulling their hair. Moreover, in seven of the cases, infants were pulling their hair while resting in bed or watching TV, as if unaware of any accompanying pain. Hence, one may ask whether these infants have a biological-rooted hyposensitivity to pain. Unfortunately, we did not make any standardized sensory assessment in these cases, but judging on the basis of our clinical observations, such as in instances when these toddlers bumped into objects or did not cry when falling, it is possible that these infants have a dispositional high threshold to pain.

The act of hair pulling may also represent an act of self-directed aggression. Based on our clinical experience, we suggest that parents of infants with trichotillomania may be "hypersensitive" to direct expressions of negative affect, especially aggression. In Joy's case, for instance, both parents learned not to express overtly their true feelings toward their caregivers in order to "keep peace." Joy was similarly very cautious not to aggravate her parents and only during treatment allowed herself to express direct aggression. In another 2-year-old girl, who was one of triplets, the symptomatic child was described as the quietest of the three children, the one who did not demand attention, and the child who was perceived as the easiest to take care of. The mother was preoccupied with the fear of losing control over her own aggressive impulses, whose origin was the harsh childhood she had experienced in her own parents' home. Having the mother try to remain engaged with the child in pleasurable interaction during the "vulnerable" bedtime (in terms of the hair pulling), as it has been suggested for treating self-soothing or auto-erotic behaviors in infancy, did not work. Instead, we gave the child one of the mother's hair kerchiefs (she was an orthodox Jew) to keep in her bed, and hair pulling resolved.

In light of these cases, we tentatively hypothesize that infant trichotillomania may be the somatic end-point of the combination of a physiological high pain threshold, aggressive impulses toward parents that are provoked by an underinvolved and/or an overinvolved parenting, and a parental vulnerability to the child's expression of aggression related to the parental attachment histories.

The choice of treatment modality for early-onset trichotillomania depends on the clinician's theoretical understanding of the disorder. Should treatment focus solely on the relationship disorder or is there a need to address the behavior as well? This is an important clinical question. If one accepts the multi-etiological approach to hair pulling, it is preferable to adopt a multi-faceted treatment that addresses the parent-infant relationship, the infant's habit of hair pulling as response specific situations, and the psychodynamic origins of the parents' reaction to negative affects.

Our clinical experience revealed that in six of the nine cases, the symptom resolved after treatment and no recurrence had been reported. In the three other cases, improvement was partial. Length of treatment was variable and lasted between 4 and 21 sessions, and treatment outcome was unrelated to therapy duration. In all cases but one we chose the parent-infant psychotherapy in combination with behavioral guidance as the treatment of choice.

CONCLUSIONS

In this paper, we presented the clinical course of nine infants with early-onset trichotillomania before the age of two years. The main limitations of this presentation are the small size of the sample and the lack of a comparison group of infants and parents referred to our clinic for symptoms other than trichotillomania. Therefore, we plan to use the tentative conclusions we have drawn from these cases as a basis for future research.

In our opinion, infancy-onset trichotillomania does not necessarily reflect a severe emotional deprivation. Nor does it seem to be the outcome of depression, as sometimes suggested in the literature. A more balanced view regards early-onset trichotillomania as the end-point of a complex interplay among several factors related to the quality of the parent-infant relationship, the infant's biological disposition, and the family history. Consequently, each of these parameters needs to be assessed independently prior to the initiation of treatment and evaluated again at termination. At present, it is unclear whether there is one specific treatment of choice that is clearly preferable in all cases of infancy-onset trichotillomania (e.g., behavioral, psychodynamic, or pharmacotherapy). A close monitoring of each case along the various lines described above would contribute to the further understanding of this disorder, its unique antecedents, clinical course, treatment, and developmental outcomes.

BIBLIOGRAPHY

ALEKSANDROWITZ, M. K., & MARES, A. J. (1978). Trichotillomania and Trichobezoar in an Infant. *J. Am. Acad. Child and Adolesc. Psychiatry, 17* (3): 533–539.
BAYLEY N. (1993). *Bayley Scale of Infant Development.* Second Edition, Psychological Cooperation.
BUXBAUM, E. (1960). Hair pulling and fetishism. *The Psychoanalytic Study of the Child,* 15:243–260.
BYRD, M. R., RICHARDS, D. F., HOVE, G., & FRIMAN, P. C. (2002). Treatment of Early Onset Hair Pulling as a Simple Habit. *Behavior Modification,* 26 (3):400–411.
Diagnostic Classification of Mental Health and Developmental Disorders of Infancy and Early Childhood. (1994). Washington DC: Zero to Three: National Center for Infants, Toddlers and Families.
DU TOIT, P. L., NIEHAUS, D. J. H., VAN KRADENBURG, J., & STEIN, D. J. (2001).

Characteristics and Phenomenology of Trichotillomania: An Exploration of Subtypes. *Comprehensive Psychiatry,* 42 (3):247–256.

FELDMAN, R. (1998). Coding Interactive Behavior (CIB) Manual. Unpublished manual, Bar-Ilan University (available from Prof. Feldman at: feldman @mail.biu.ac.il).

FELDMAN, R., EIDELMAN, A. I., & ROTENBERG, N. (2004). Parenting Stress, Infant Emotion Regulation, Maternal Sensitivity, and the Cognitive Development of Triplets: Model for Parent and Child Influences in a Unique Ecology. *Child Development,* 75 (December).

FELDMAN, R., GREENBAUM, C. W., MAYES, L. C., & ERLICH, H. S. (1997). Change in Mother-Infant Interactive Behavior: Relations to Change in the Mother, the Infant, and the Social Context. *Infant Behavior Development,* 20: 153–165.

FELDMAN R., & KEREN, M. (2004). Expanding the Scope of Infant Mental Health Assessment: A Community-based Approach. In *Handbook of Infant Mental Health Assessment.* Del-Carmen-Wiggins, R., Carter, A. S., eds. Cambridge: Oxford University Press, pp. 443–465.

FELDMAN, R., KEREN, M., GROSS-ROZVAL, O., & TYANO, S. (2004). Mother and Child's Touch Patterns in Infant Feeding Disorders: Relation to Maternal, Child, and Environmental Factors. *J. Am. Acad. Child and Adolesc. Psychiatry,* 43 (9):1089–1097.

FELDMAN, R., & KLEIN, P. S. (2003). Toddlers' Self-regulated Compliance with Mother, Caregiver, and Father: Implications for Theories of Socialization. *Developmental Psychology, 39:*680–692.

FELDMAN, R., MASALHA, S., & NADAM, R. (2001). Cultural Perspective on Work and Family: Dual-earner Jewish and Arab Families at the Transition to Parenthood. *Journal of Family Psychology,* 15:492–509.

FELDMAN, R., WELLER, A., EIDELMAN, A. I., & SIROTA, L. (2003). Testing a Family Intervention Hypothesis: The Contribution of Mother-Infant Skin-to-Skin Contact (Kangaroo Care) to Family Interaction and Touch. *Journal of Family Psychology,* 17:94–107.

FIVAZ-DEPEURSINGE, E., & CORBOZ-WARNERY, A. (1999). *The Primary Triangle. A Developmental Systems View of Fathers, Mothers and Infants.* New York: Basic Books.

FONAGY, P., STEELE, H., MORAN, G., STEELE, M., & HIGGITT, A. (1991a). The Capacity for Understanding Mental States: The Reflective Self in Parent and Child and Its Significance for Security of Attachment. *Infant Mental Health Journal,* 13:200–217.

FREY, A. S., MCKEE, M., KING, R. A., & MARTIN, A. (2005). Hair Apparent: Rapunzel Syndrome. *Amer. J. Psychiatry,* 162(2):242–248.

GREENBERG, H. R., & SARNER, C. A. (1965). Trichotillomania: Symptom and Syndrome. *Arch. Gen. Psychiat.* 12:482–489.

HALLOPEAU, M. (1889). Alopecie par grattage (trichomanie ou trichotillomania). *Ann. Derm. Syphiligraphie,* 10:440–441.

HAMDAN-ALLEN, G. (1991). Trichotillomania in Childhood. *Acta Psychiatr. Scand.,* 83:241–243.

HARRISON, A. M. (2005). Herding the Animals into the Barn: A Parent Consultation Model. *The Psychoanalytic Study of the Child*, 60:128–53.

HOPKINS, J. (1996). The Dangers and Deprivations of Too-Good Mothering. *J. of Child Therapy*, 22:407–422.

KEREN, M., FELDMAN, R., & TYANO, S. (2001). Emotional Disturbances in Infancy: Diagnostic Classification and Interactive Patterns of Infants Referred to a Community-based Infant Mental Health Clinic. *J. Am. Acad. Child and Adolesc. Psychiatry* 40:27–35.

KING, R. A., SCAHILL, L., VITULANO, L. A., SCHAWB-STONE, M., TERCYAK, K. P., & RIDDLE, M. A. (1995). Childhood Trichotillomania: Clinical Phenomenology, Comorbidity, and Family Genetics. *J. Am. Acad. Child and Adolesc. Psychiatry*, 34 (11):1451–1459.

MANNINO, F. V., & DELGADO, R. A. (1969). Trichotillomania in Children: A Review. *American J. Psychiat.* 126:4.

MANSUETO, C. S., STEMBERGER, R. M. T., THOMAS, A. M., & GOLOMB, R. G. (1997). Trichotillomania: A Comprehensive Behavioral Model. *Clin. Psychol. Rev.*, 17:567–577.

MASSONG, S. R., EDWARDS, R. P., RANGE SITTON, I., & HAILEY, B. J. (1980). A Case of Trichotillomania in a Three Year Old Treated by Response Prevention. *J. Behav. Ther. and Exper. Psychiat.*, 13:337–340.

MULLER, S. A., & WINKELMANN, R. K. (1972). Trichotillomania: A Clinicopathologic Study of 24 Cases. *Arch. Dermatol.* 105:535–540, 1972.

ORANJE, A. P., PEEREBOOM-WYNIA, J. D. R., & DE RAEYMAECKER, D. M. J. (1986). Trichotillomania in Childhood. *J. Am. Acad. Dermatol.* 15:614–619.

O'SULLIVAN, R. L., MANSUETO, C. S., LERNER, E. A., & MIGUEL, E. C. (2000). Characterization of Trichotillomania. A Phenomenological Model with Clinical Relevance to Obsessive-Compulsive Spectrum Disorders. *Psychiatrics Clinics of North America*, 23 (3):587–605.

REEVE, E. A., BERNSTEIN, G. A., & CHRISTENSON, G. A. (1992). Clinical Characteristics and Psychiatric Co-morbidity in Children with Trichotillomania. *J. Am. Acad. Child and Adolesc. Psychiatry*, 31 (1):132–138.

STERN, D. N. (1995). *The Motherhood Constellation: A Unified View of Parent-Infant Psychotherapy.* New York: Basic Books.

SWEDO, S. E., & LEONARD, H. L. (1992). Trichotillomania: An Obsessive Compulsive Spectrum Disorder? *Psychiatric Clinics of North America*, 15 (4): 777–790.

SWEDO, S. E., LEONARD, H. L., & RAPOPORT, J. L. (1991). Annotation: Trichotillomania. *J. Child Psychol. Psychiat.*, 32 (3):401–409.

SWEDO, S. E., LEONARD, H. L., RAPOPORT, J. L., LENANE, M. C., GOLDBERGER, E. L., & CHESLOW, D. L. (1989). A Double-blind Comparison of Clomipramine and Desipramine in the Treatment of Trichotillomania (Hair Pulling). *New England J. of Medicine*, 321:T497–501.

VITULANO, L. A., KING R. A., SCAHILL, L., & COHEN, D. J. (1992). Behavioral Treatment of Children and Adolescents with Trichotillomania. *J. Am Acad. Child and Adolesc. Psychiat.*, 31:139–146.

WALSH, K. H., & MCDOUGLE, C. T. T. (2001). Trichotillomania: Presentation, Etiology, Diagnosis and Therapy. *Am. J. Clin .Dermatology,* 2(5):323–333.

WATSON, T. S., & ALLEN, K. D. (1993). Elimination of Thumb Sucking as a Treatment for Severe Trichotillomania. *J. Am Acad. Child and Adolesc. Psychiat.,* 32:830–834.

WELLER, E. B., WELLER, R. A., & CARR, S. (1989). Imipramine Treatment of Trichotillomania and Co-existing Depression in a Seven-year-old. *J. Am. Acad. Child and Adolesc. Psychiatry,* 28:952–953.

WINNICOTT, D. W. (1971). *Playing and Reality.* Harmondsworth: Penguin Books.

WOODS, D. W., & MILTENBERGER, R. G. (EDS.). (2001). Tic Disorders, Trichotillomania, and Other Repetitive Behavior Disorders: Behavioral Approaches to Analysis and Treatment. Norwell, Mass.: Kluwer Academic Publishers.

WRIGHT, H. H., & HOLMES, G. R. (2003). Trichotillomania (Hair Pulling) in Toddlers. *Psychol. Rep.,* 92 (1):228–230.

APPLIED PSYCHOANALYSIS

Successful Mourning

Maternal Loss and Grieving by Proxy in *Fly Away Home*

FREDERICK C. MILLER, M.D.

Fly Away Home *is a captivating movie which beautifully portrays how profound losses can result in successful mourning. Movies can have lasting appeal when they convey universal themes such as loss and restitution in ways that not only illustrate underlying psychoanalytic processes but also confirm, clarify, or contradict them. A review of the literature on mourning reveals a preponderance of extrapolations from examples of unsuccessful grieving, resulting in an emphasis on a pathological perspective of an otherwise natural process. In* Fly Away Home *an adolescent girl whose own mother has recently died adopts orphaned goslings. They imprint on her as their mother, and she must learn to fly an airplane in order to lead them on their first migration. In doing so she eventually demonstrates a variety of displaced enactments of the consolidation of a healthy maternal identification, or grieving by proxy. The movie also illustrates the risks of loss manifested as injury or defectiveness, the father as a temporary maternal proxy, the reconstruction of a new family, and the resumption of adolescent development, which are discussed in this paper as important components of this natural process of loss and restitution resulting in successful grieving.*

Adult and Adolescent Psychoanalyst; Child, Adolescent, and Adult Psychiatrist, Wyndmoor and Philadelphia, Pennsylvania; Faculty of the Psychoanalytic Center of Philadelphia.

I appreciate the invaluable suggestions provided by Salman Akhtar, M.D. for this paper, and dedicate it to Susan, Lauren, and Jennifer, the home to whom I fly away.
The Psychoanalytic Study of the Child 61, ed. Robert A. King, Peter B. Neubauer, Samuel Abrams, and A. Scott Dowling (Yale University Press, copyright © 2006 by Robert A. King, Peter B. Neubauer, Samuel Abrams, and A. Scott Dowling).

INTRODUCTION

THERE IS SOMETHING CAPTIVATING AND POWERFULLY MOVING ABOUT the film *Fly Away Home* (1996). In the course of the movie, a young adolescent girl progresses from an almost fetal withdrawal after the sequential loss of her father (by parental divorce) and mother (by death in a later automobile accident) to a transcendent scene portrayed with luminescent beauty as she flies an airplane leading a flock of geese she has raised; a hauntingly beautiful song accompanies the scene and the suggestive first lines are:

> Fare thee well/my own true love/farewell for a while/I'm going away
> But I'll be back/though I go 10,000 miles
> —Carpenter, 1996

I wondered what could be the psychological reasons I found the telling of this story on film so haunting that it captivated me through numerous viewings. The following is an effort to identify and understand what had to be universal themes at the basis of such a profoundly affecting film, most importantly the themes of loss and restitution. I hoped that understanding the movie chronology would also shed light on what differentiates healthy from pathological mourning—i.e. loss and grieving that are resolved in a restitutive or adaptive way, in contrast to pathological grieving that leads to depression, other symptom neuroses, character disorders, developmental delays, or addictions.

Movies are an art form and popular entertainment that draw part of their appeal from depictions of universal psychological and developmental phenomena. Specifically, some films have more than metaphorical value when they provide evidence and confirmation outside of the hermetic realm of the analyst's office of important psychoanalytic clinical theories. More specifically, in *Fly Away Home* there appears striking confirmation of some of the clinical psychoanalytic theories of reaction to and restitution after a significant loss. Other examples, to mention a few of many, can be found in *My Girl* (the story of a girl whose severe hypochondriacism reflects her pathological grief due to guilt over her mother's death in childbirth); *Corina Corina* (presenting the elective mutism of a 9-year-old girl whose mother has died); *Drawn from Memory* (an animated autobiographical film reconstructing a childhood with abusive parents and many traumatic relocations); and *Frequency* (depicting the consequences of the death of a boy's father, albeit in a concretely science fiction manner).

The trauma of loss and attempts to master it dominate literature as well,[1] but that is a subject for another paper.

Fly Away Home

The movie begins with a happy, affectionate, and animated conversation between Amy, the young adolescent girl, and her mother, which is abruptly interrupted when the car in which they are riding is rammed by a large truck. The viewer experiences the trauma from the passenger's visual perspective as the car rolls over and over, shattering the windshield and smashing the car and its inhabitants. The scene closes as the girl loses consciousness, and the mother apparently dies.

The next scene takes place as Amy regains consciousness in a hospital room in New Zealand, to which her father had flown from his farm/studio outside Toronto, Canada. She awakens from her physical coma to find her sleeping father, who awakens and tears up when she asks, "Daddy, what are you doing here? . . . She died, didn't she?"

The third scene finds Amy arriving at her estranged father's farm, 6,000 miles from her home with her mother, although she had lived there as a young child while her artist parents were young and still married. Now the father's eccentric home, artist's studio, behavior, and life have little room or appropriateness for a young adolescent girl, especially one struggling with the loss of her mother and second home.

For example, on the first morning after her arrival Amy awakens to the noise in a nearby field of her father taking off on a hang glider, the flight ending with a harsh crash landing. The father looks to the girl for approval, seemingly without any awareness of how this risk to his life just witnessed could retraumatize his daughter, who quickly withdraws after expressing shock and disgust. Amy meets the father's sometimes live-in girlfriend, whom she initially rejects, along with classmates at the school to which she briefly returns.

Several days later Amy is awakened in the morning by the noise of construction near their farm, and the sight of her nearly naked father confronting the earthmoving company, whose work is interrupted while the father subsequently attends a town meeting to protest the risk to the local wildlife and flora by this construction. At

1. A recent best-selling nonfiction book *Tuesdays with Morrie* depicts a dying man's conversations with a sportswriter/surrogate son.

the same time Amy discovers eleven goose eggs whose mother had apparently been driven off or killed by the earthmovers. She retrieves one of her deceased mother's scarves[2] to carry these 11 eggs to the barn, where she sleeps with the unhatched eggs; upon return from the meeting, her father initially panics when she is not at home. When discovered asleep in the barn with the eggs, she pleads with her father to let her keep them, which he agrees to allow, but insists she resume her attendance at school.

The eggs had been placed by Amy in the top drawer of a bureau, which contained many of her mother's beautiful clothes and belongings, with an incandescent light to provide heat. Amy returns from school to discover the goslings hatching, and the gosling's eye view of the girl's face fills the screen, as they bond to her in the way they would ordinarily to their goose mother. Thus imprinted, they follow her everywhere.

The father then consults with the local wildlife constable, in an attempt to solve the dilemma that the geese when grown will need to be shown the migration path by the mother goose, who had been killed. Since the geese will instinctually (biologically) attempt to migrate, without the goose mother leading them they will become lost or be killed. During a visit to their home, the wildlife ranger abruptly attempts to pinion, or clip the wings of one of the goslings to prevent flight, prompting a terrified reaction by the girl, who retreats to the bathroom with her goslings and locks the door. The father, also shocked at the harsh action of the wildlife officer, throws him off his property to the officer's threats that the goslings would not be allowed to fly. Nonetheless, Amy blames her father for the ranger's threats.

Amy stays locked in the bathroom, nurturing her goslings who use the toilet as a pond. While taking a shower Amy accidentally squirts soap into her eyes and screams in pain. The father breaks down the door to "save" her, exposing her naked, early pubescent body to him and to his handsome young flying pal. After ejecting both, Amy is

---

2. Or consider the similar role of fabric in the following quotation from *Anil's Ghost* by Michael Ondaatje (author of *The English Patient*), spoken by Anil, an anthropologist who joined a forensic specialist in Sri Lanka to search for the missing people who were killed and hidden by the repressive government: "She used to believe that meaning allowed a door to escape grief and fear. But she saw that those who were slammed and stained by violence lost the power of language and logic. It was the way to abandon emotion, the last protection for the self. They held onto just the colored and patterned sarong a missing relative last slept in, which in normal times would have become a household rag but now was sacred."

consoled by father's girlfriend and accepts her offer of friendship: "I can never replace your mother, but we can be friends, which requires trust. . . . Your father did not know the wildlife constable would try to hurt the goslings, and we will never let that happen."

Amy then allies with her father and his girlfriend, pal, and father's brother, to prepare for the migration. They initially plan for the father to fly a small airplane to lead the flock south to their migration endpoint on the banks of South Carolina. Since the goslings will not shift their allegiance from the girl to her father and follow his airplane, they next plan to teach the girl to fly a small, simple, safe low-flying airplane, with the geese following her, as the father leads the girl with his airplane. After elaborate planning and practice, and numerous problems (e.g. one gosling has difficulty flying due to a deformity, and after flying, injures himself), the actual migratory flight in the movie is exciting and dramatic.

For the last and most poignant section of the journey, Amy and her father lose radio contact with their ground crew, and after a wire rudder strut on the father's plane snaps loose, his plane spirals to a rough landing in a field. Amy lands her plane nearby and finds her father grounded with a dislocated shoulder and a damaged plane. The father insists that Amy finish the remaining short flight on her own, despite her protests about needing to stay with him: "I want you to get into that plane and fly away home," to which she expresses her need for her mother's help. After he reminds her how much she is like her mother, both of them displaying independence and courage, and how her mother was with her "right next to you . . . she's in the geese, she's in the sky," she resumes the final leg of the flight. This is portrayed in stunningly beautiful visual terms, along with the elegiac words of the song *10,000 miles*[3] sung by Mary Chapin Carpenter on the background soundtrack.

Amy and her geese reach the migratory endpoint and are met by her father (who had hitched a car ride while she flew the geese down), his girlfriend, father's brother, and pal, but this is not the last scene, which next portrays the following early spring, when the geese

---

3.   Fare thee well/my own true love/farewell for a while/I'm going away
But I'll be back/though I go 10,000 miles/10,000 miles
My own true love/10,000 miles or more/the rocks may melt
And the seas may burn/if I should not return/Oh don't you see
That lonesome dove/sitting on an ivy tree/She's weeping for
Her own true love/as I shall weep for mine/Oh come ye back
My own true love/and stay a while with me/If I had a friend
All on this earth/you've been a friend to me

return to the Ontario farm, having traversed the 1,500 ("10,000") miles *on their own,* after having been shown the path just once by Amy, their mother by proxy.

RESTITUTIVE AND PATHOLOGICAL SOLUTIONS TO LOSS

The examples in *Fly Away Home* of the theme of loss are many and profound: Amy loses her father and native country due to the parental divorce, and then loses her mother to death, along with the losses of her second home and country, friends, school, and possessions. Even after she regains her father and original home, he crashes and almost dies in an airplane glider accident, and the house no longer seems nurturing. In fact, even the geese lose their breeding ground on their property, and their mother is driven away and killed. As the movie progresses, Amy is losing her childhood to her adolescence, which is developmentally replacing it.

Freud describes the required psychological process that occurs when an individual experiences "the loss by death of an emotionally important person" as the process of mourning, which is required before a person can adopt any new object of love, as follows: "Each single one of the memories and expectations in which the libido is bound to the object is brought up and hypercathected, and detachment of the libido is accomplished in respect of it . . . when the work of mourning is completed the ego becomes free and uninhibited again" (Freud, 1917).

There is much less written specifically about healthy rather than pathological grieving, especially when it occurs during adolescence. Siggins (1966) outlines and discusses the following clinical manifestations in adults which occur during "normal" mourning: anger, emancipation, relief, guilt, helplessness, anxiety, reactivation of old conflicts, somatic symptoms, and temporary denial, including absence of emotion. When any one or more of these reactions is exaggerated, the result is pathological mourning.

Wolfenstein (1969) describes two possible adaptive substitutes for mourning in earlier stages of development. One is the transfer of libido from the lost parent to a valued and trusted person in the child's life. The second is the incorporation of the lost parent into the child's ego ideal, which perpetuates the lost parent in his own person rather than finding an external substitute.

Schlesinger (2001) also highlights the healthy and natural aspects of loss and mourning: "Loss is the single universal and essential human experience. . . . Yet consider, this stark realization is not pessimistic, for without the ability to appreciate loss it is not possible to experience gain. Loss, or more precisely, the ability to recognize loss, to accept it and to let go, is the necessary condition for growth and maturation" (p. 118). He cautions against viewing and treating mourning per se as pathological: "Let us agree that mourning is a normal and adaptive reaction to loss. In the clinical situation it ought to be experienced for what it is and what it is about. We could say that it is one of the responsibilities of the analyst to protect the mourning process so that it may proceed toward its natural ending" (Schlesinger, p. 119).

In contrast to this emphasis on healthy grieving, the vast majority of the literature on mourning in childhood focuses on the pathological processes that can limit or interfere with the healthy mourning process, unlike the apparently successful grieving which Amy illustrates in the movie.[4] Pathological grieving has been described in a variety of ways, according to the following overlapping perspectives: quantitatively as an exaggeration of "normal" grieving, absence of grief, or abnormal intensity of grief; qualitatively as the result of different dynamic conflicts; temporally as grief that is either delayed, or prolonged; descriptively/symptomatically as the reactivation of the symptoms of preexisting emotional or somatic disorders; and developmentally as determined by interferences with ego and psychosexual development, and by variations in the separation individuation process.

Siggins (1966) describes pathological mourning in quantitative terms as mourning that is unusually intense as a result of exaggeration of one or more of the many clinical manifestations of "normal" mourning, or as evidence of the temporal extremes of either an absence or undue delay in the beginning of the mourning work, or prolongation of mourning.

From a qualitative perspective, Miller (1970) describes various dynamic formulations that contribute to pathological mourning, including guilt over unconscious hostile wishes toward the dead person; avoidance of the painful affects associated with the loss; idealization of the lost parent and displacement of hostile feelings for abandonment onto the surviving parent; and pathological identification with the deceased person, that is, with his/her symptoms.

Descriptive approaches to pathological mourning consider the

4. The duration of this process, previously thought to be a year, may last a lifetime, as lyrically described in *The Lovely Bones*, a novel by Alice Seabold depicting the resolution over 15 years of the losses due to the rape and murder of an 11-year-old girl and the mourning of parents, sister, and friends. The girl lives on in the novel in a spiritual realm called "my heaven," depicting a form of denial that is seemingly coexistent with healthy grieving, which gives the book some of its appeal (Akhtar, 2003).

complications that result when loss triggers a reactivation of symptoms of preexisting emotional disorders, ranging from anxiety disorders to psychoses, or the precipitation of latent somatic disorders, such as ulcerative colitis or asthma (Siggins, 1966, p. 21).

Developmental considerations address the impact of loss on the complicated process of ego maturation and psychosexual stages, and include the separation-individuation process, with special focus on the role of identifications and the ego ideal. Loewald (1962) describes how the nature of internalization that occurs in mourning is initially a means of defense against the intolerable pain of loss, as if to say "I need not suffer, since the person who died lives on within me." Siggins (1966) identifies the resulting danger "if this internal grasping of the object ceases to be a means to an end—namely the first step in relinquishing the object—and becomes instead an end in itself, so as to hold on to the object, deny its loss, and avoid a fresh confrontation with reality, then it dislocates the process of mourning" (p. 21). These identifications take many forms, from adaptively taking on the "vital and satisfying aspects of the relationship" (Siggins, 1960, p. 18), to pathologically adopting the symptoms of the last illness of the deceased, or of death itself in the form of a withdrawal of interest in activities in the world, as if to say "In order to deny death, I am identified with the deceased, which makes me dead." Another form of denial of death is the establishment of an ego-ideal based on over-idealizing the lost object so that unpleasant features of the relationship remain unprocessed. Relatedly, there are difficulties which occur when the contribution to the consolidation of identity formation by the early separation-individuation process (Mahler, 1975) is insufficient to withstand loss later in life, resulting in temporary identifications becoming permanent, or partial identifications becoming wholescale.

In addition, there has been a longstanding developmental view that children and early adolescents are constitutionally incapable of the grieving process, healthy or unhealthy, based on the idea that due to their incomplete ego development, loss is such a threat that they need to deny the loss, sometimes utilizing pathological identifications with the dead parent. Wolfenstein (1969) feels that adaptive identifications are extremely rare, due to "a fearful avoidance of identification with a lost parent, due to the terrifying image of the parent's illness and death," and that the adaptive reactions to loss that do occur follow a course different from mourning (1966, p. 97). In contrast, Bowlby (1960; 1961a; 1961b) considers the pattern of responses to loss by young children, including protest, despair, and detachment, as basically the same as adult mourning. This longstanding conceptual debate, with Anna Freud (1970), Humberto Nagera (1970), Wolfenstein, and many others doubting a child's capacity to grieve, while Bowlby (1960; 1961a; 1961b), Furman, Klein, and others argue that children are capable of grieving as adults do, remains controversial perhaps because it is usually discussed in "either-or" terms. Bowlby (1963) later offers a valuable alternative perspective which significantly bridges this apparent dichotomy. He notes the similarity of mourning in young children, a function of their incomplete psychological development, to *pathological* mourning in the adult. Both utilize a "complex series of defensive phenomena aimed at denying the reality of the event" (Miller, 1970) which is demonstrated more often by younger children as an early prototype that usually becomes replaced during latency and early adolescence with a more effective process for mourning that utilizes the gradual age-appropriate advancement in ego development and consolidation of object relations. It is to explore the elements that contribute to a healthy grieving process in adolescents, who are in developmental transition beyond childhood, and about whom little has been written regarding mourning, that this paper will now return.

At first Amy did not deny mother's death when she awoke from the car accident to find her father at her hospital bedside. But her next reaction to mother's death appeared pathological—she temporarily withdrew and retreated, to her bedroom, refused to attend school, and later retreated with the goslings to the bathroom, manifesting denial and apparent absence of grief (Deutsch, 1937). How can there be psychological restitution of such profound losses, and when are there traumatic consequences (Furman, 1984)? How were loss and pathological grieving transformed into a resumption of healthy adolescent psychological development? How can the pathological consequences of over-identification with a mother who has died be avoided? In an effort to respond to these important questions, the following six different but interrelated solutions to maternal loss are described and discussed. Although identified in the order they appear in the movie, no set sequence of stages of the restitutive process is suggested.

DISCUSSION

A dynamic discussion of a fictional movie character requires some caution. Although based on the true story of William Lishman's and Joseph Duff's experiments using airplanes to lead the migration of orphaned birds (Lishman, 1996), the screenwriter's intuitive insights and creativity, along with the director's structure and the actor's talent, all contribute to the detailed and complicated "clinical" picture of Amy in *Fly Away Home*. With this caveat in mind, I think there is more than metaphorical value in applying our dynamic and developmental knowledge to an understanding of Amy's efforts to resolve her loss and grief.

(1) *Initial Identifications in Response to Loss of a Parent*

The adoption of the goose eggs affords Amy her first major restitutive opportunity. When hatched, they imprint onto her as they would their mother, as described by Konrad Lorenz (1970). As they substitute Amy for their goose mother, Amy displays one of a number of examples of her identification with her own mother in the process of serving as the mother of the goslings. These reenactments of a maternal identification, which are later refined and consolidated, play a crucial part in Amy's progress in resolving her grief over the loss of her own mother and are clearly evident from early in the movie—for example, Amy uses her mother's scarf to gather the goose eggs, and places them in a bureau of mother's clothing, which provides the warmth in a womb-like environment needed to hatch. Later, her airplane is designed to look like a large version of the goose mother. Amy is allowed to keep and raise the goslings, with the requirement that she attend school, illustrating the resumption of normal development after the symbolic reunion between mother and child.

The juxtaposition of geese and Amy's mother's scarf suggests the role of the scarf and the geese that hatch in it as both variants of a transitional object for Amy, in this case serving the process of resolution of the loss of the mother to death, rather than the original meaning of a transitional object (Winnicott, 1953) as part of the developmental process instrumental in self and object differentiation (Mahler, 1975). That is, rather than a transition in differentiation of the self from object in order to qualitatively change the capacity for object relatedness, Amy's uses the scarf as a reminder of her mother to facilitate her recovery from the loss of an established relationship that has been interrupted by the mother's death. In this way the scarf might be an example of a "linking object" (Volkan, 1981), used to defensively protect from the separation anxiety and aggression stimulated by loss of an important figure. A parallel juxtaposition of the goose mother and the airplane designed to look like her (with Amy inside), suggests its role as another variant of a transitional object, in this case for the goslings, although it may be more accurate to view the airplane simply as a substitute for mother, allowing mothering by proxy. Amy is pivotal to both transitions, because her maternal disguise allows her to substitute for the goslings' mother at a crucial developmental period when they need guidance to migrate, which Amy simultaneously experiences as an enactment of the transitions in her identification with her mother, crucial for resolution of her mourning.

There is a further developmentally based complication for mourning during the adolescent process: "The painful, gradual decathexis of the parents that is the task of adolescence is an initiation into how to mourn" (Miller, 1970, p. 707). Wolfenstein (1969) proposes that "adolescence is a kind of trial mourning," and that there is a danger that "Where . . . the work of adolescence has remained uncompleted, the adult remains unable to accomplish the work of mourning in response to loss" (1966, p. 117). However, "Once this major transition has been achieved, it is as though a pattern has been established for decathecting a beloved object if the need arises, as when the individual is confronted with losses later in life. Having been initiated through the trial mourning of adolescence, he is then able to mourn" (1969, p. 458). Difficulties occur when the early separation-individuation experience has been insufficient to withstand a loss in later life, or when the identifications in response to loss become permanent rather than a temporary transition to traditional mourning (Masur, 2001), or are wholesale rather than partial (Meyer, 2001), a process which replaces rather than facilitates mourning, leading to a pathological absence or displacement of it.

Added to these universal developmental losses during early separation-individuation and later adolescence are the actual losses to Amy from parental divorce and death, and the likelihood for pathological grief seems increased, yet it did not occur. Perhaps Amy's loss of her father by parental divorce had allowed and accelerated the process of adolescent separation to begin, supported at first in a healthy direction by her mother and Amy's strong, supportive relationship with her, preparing and protecting her from the pathological consequences of mother's death.

Examples of a dramatic contrast to Amy's healthy identifications are the pathological identifications of the 11-year-old girl Veda with her mother's fatal illness and her boyfriend's terminal symptoms in the movie *My Girl* (1991). Veda feared she had caused her mother's death during childbirth, repeatedly presenting herself to the family doctor with symptoms of a variety of fatal illnesses, the most dramatic being her difficulty breathing after her friend dies of respiratory arrest. Veda's birth had not caused her mother's death, but her loss and guilt were expressed by identification with her mother's deadly symptoms, and those of her boyfriend's. She kept her mother and boyfriend alive via identifications with symptoms of their fatal illnesses, a pathological outcome that caused considerable suffering.

(2) *Grieving by Proxy: Displaced Enactments of Maternal Identification*

Scenes in which Amy assumes her mother's role alternate with memories of the mother pushing Amy on the swing in the barn/studio where the eggs hatch in a warm nest utilizing a (womblike) drawer of mother's scarves, heated by the father's (phallic) lamp. In this way, both parents symbolically participate in the gestation, birth, and subsequent nurturing and separation via migration of the goslings. After the trauma of being blinded by soap which provoked her being rescued by father and his girlfriend, Amy allies with father's girlfriend, who specifically says, "I can never replace your mother, but we can become friends," which Amy accepts, simultaneously becoming her father's symbolic Oedipal partner (in the geese migration project) while relinquishing that actual position to his girlfriend. Her adolescent development resumes, punctuated by her declaring independence by piercing her ears and nose, a reference also to the pinioning from which Amy protected her goslings. Clearly Amy's process of grieving by proxy was a more successful variant of displaced grief since there were no resulting developmental interferences.

(3) *Loss Manifesting as Injury and Defectiveness*

Episodes of mutilation, injury, and defectiveness, which illustrate the theme of castration that is commonly associated with loss, are prominent in Amy's development. The injury and death of the mother, and Amy's injuries, begin the movie, and the injury and death of the mother goose renew this trauma. The threat of pinioning the wings of the goslings prompts the elaborate project to lead them on their first migration. One of the ducks (Igor) is deformed from birth, and later is injured by the airplane.[5] As Amy resumes her adolescent development, she pierces her ears and nose; paradoxically the nose-ring of subjugation serves here as a declaration on independence.

In *Fly Away Home*, injury, both accidental and intentional, exemplifies a narcissistic injury, a form of loss, and a (pathological) way to prevent it. The constable's threat to pinion the goslings, literally "clipping their wings" to make flight impossible, would obviate loss

---

5. Igor, an injured bird that is carried in the airplane to migrate, shows that not all birds can fly, symbolizing how not all grief can be successful.

by preventing separation, at the expense of mutilation. Such symbolic castration by this "bad father," with its attendant defectiveness and arrest in development, is rejected by Amy and her family with horror. Amy retreats with her goslings to the bathroom, a temporary arrest or regression, only to emerge ready to resume development, symbolized by the successful migration. Thus Amy avoids one of the adverse reactions to the loss of a parent which results when the "compounding of narcissistic injury with object loss makes it more difficult to become reconciled to the loss" (Wolfenstein, 1969, p. 459).

In contrast, in the movie *My Girl*, Veda's recurring physical symptoms, which she fears signal her impending death, result from her pathological identification with her deceased mother, over whose death she feels guilty for having died while giving birth to Veda. These reach a crescendo when Veda panics at the bleeding from her first period, which she concludes is a mortal injury. Instead of heralding a variety of changes as part of adolescent physical and psychical development, Veda experiences her menarche as a severe narcissistic injury which serves as punishment for and remembrance of the death of her mother.

(4) *Reconstruction of a New Family and Resumption of Adolescent Development*

Another restitutive step is the reacquisition and reconstruction of a new family and home from the previous fragmented families and houses, which also symbolizes the partial or age appropriate resolution of the Oedipal conflicts. After his glider flying had earlier threatened himself with death and mutilation, Amy's father eventually provides immense support, stability, and creative solutions to Amy's struggles with loss. After the scene of the crisis in the bathroom, to which Amy had retreated with the goslings to protect them from mutilation ("pinioning") by the wildlife constable, Amy is able to accept the father's girlfriend as a friend, after the clear stipulation that in doing so Amy was not betraying her mother's memory.

This alliance with an auxiliary mother then allowed resumption of various relationships with men: her father (Oedipal), uncle (sublimated Oedipal), and the sexually charged adolescent (also Oedipal) relationship with the father's handsome younger male pal. Amy is thus able to avoid the twin dangers of stimulation of incestuous strivings toward father, who is no longer seen as alone and available, as well as the intensified negative feelings toward father, needed to protect the memory of her mother: "As the lost parent is idealized, the surviving parent is devalued" (Wolfenstein, 1966, p. 112). This new "family," resulting from the interplay of external as well as intrapsy-

chic changes, frees her to actively foster the achievement of independence by her goslings, which in turn allows Amy to further resolve
her mourning by proxy.

In contrast, in *My Girl*, Veda struggled in the absence of a mother
to hold onto her maternal role with the father, shown dramatically in
a scene at a carnival ride where she repeatedly rams her bumper car
into that of father's girlfriend, whose expression shifts from amuse-
ment to irritation to fear. Veda's rage rather than grief as her dominant emotion illustrates another pathological reaction to loss, resulting from the displacement of abandonment rage from the lost
parent, to protect it, onto the remaining figures in the environment
(Wolfenstein, 1969, p. 459). Father's new girlfriend serves as the inevitable focus of Veda's rage that is redirected in order to protect her
dead mother. Only later did the calm reassurance and sexual information provided by the father's girlfriend simultaneously herald
Veda's puberty, sexuality, and the beginning mother-daughter relationship, as part of Veda's beginning resolution of her Oedipal conflicts.

(5) *The Father as Temporary Maternal Proxy*

Amy had the advantage of having a second parent able to step in
and try to take over her parenting. Although he was at first detached,
eccentric, and irresponsible (e.g. risking his life to fly gliders that
crashed in front of his recently bereaved daughter), as an artist his
creativity allowed a flexibility and willingness to experiment with un-
conventional solutions[6] which allowed Amy to resume her adolescent development, albeit as the surrogate mother of a flock of
goslings. Also, the father's girlfriend was patient and unconditional
in her support of Amy, who herself never denied harsh truths, although they at first had overwhelmed her resulting in a temporary
arrest in development.

Wolfenstein (1969) describes one of two possible adaptive substitutes for mourning as "an available and acceptable parent substitute,
to whom the child can transfer piecemeal the libido he gradually at-
taches from the lost parent" (p. 458). The substitute must be a "valued and trusted person in the child's life," and although Amy's father was valued, he was not initially trusted, due to his unavailability

---

6. In contrast, in *Ponette*, a movie in which a girl similarly is in a car accident in
which her mother dies, the father not only provides little direct support for Ponette,
but leaves her for the initial weeks after mother's death, having confronted her with
the statement "mommy is dead . . . she was all broken."

after the divorce from Amy's mother. The other criteria for this process to occur is a "relatively low level of ambivalence toward the parent who has died," which Amy displayed.

The father attempted to substitute directly for the deceased goose mother in order to lead the goslings south, which the goslings rejected. Father then leads Amy, whom the goslings do follow as their substitute mother. But ultimately, father tells Amy to "fly away home," using the mother who is "right next to you . . . she's in the geese, she's in the sky, she's all around you, and she won't let you down."

Much less successfully, the father in *My Girl* immersed himself in his work as a mortician and remained distant from Veda because she reminded him of his deceased wife. Veda was experienced as an ongoing traumatic presence, contributing to the delay in successful grieving for both of them. Only later, when Veda and her father were both able to acknowledge her inappropriate guilt for mother's death, was Veda able to resume adolescent development.

(6) *Consolidation of a Healthy Identification with the Deceased Parent*

Amy relinquishes the father as a maternal substitute, as she consolidates a fuller identification with the mother, with whom Amy shares courage and independence, allowing her to assume the maternal position and lead her geese (i.e. "children") to safety. Amy's successful separation from, and consolidation of her identification with mother, provides the ultimate healthy solution to Amy's losses, allowing her to help her "children" to separate (i.e. migrate), and simultaneously allowing Amy's adolescent development to resume. This accomplishment may illustrate another adaptive reaction to parental loss described by Wolfenstein (1969) in which "the child incorporates the lost parent into his ego ideal and gains an increased impetus to striving for achievement" (p. 458). This is an example of a healthy narcissistic solution to loss when another object is not available, and requires a previous strong alliance between parent and child, focused on the child's achievements, which Amy and her mother certainly displayed.

Internalization in mourning initially serves as a means of defense from the intolerable pain of loss, but later can serve a new goal of achieving individuality and emancipation. Although a fictional character in the movie *Fly Away Home*, Amy illustrates how potentially pathological identifications with her mother, originally needed to make her profound loss tolerable, can be integrated and lead to the resumption of the healthy psychological development of a young woman.

There is a quip about successful parenting: "If you do it well, they leave home!" As impressive as the initial migration is in *Fly Away Home*, the ultimate migration is the actual return of the birds the next spring. The penultimate migration is symbolized in *Fly Away Home* by the artist father having created a full-scale model of Sputnik, the first satellite sent to "fly away" in space, only to circle the earth and relay information "home." Amy's father sells this satellite model to Japanese investors for a large amount of money, allowing him to finance the two small airplanes used to lead the migration of the geese, symbolically furthering Amy's grieving process and resumption of her adolescent development.

The title *Fly Away Home* symbolically recapitulates each of the six component restitutive solutions to loss offered in the movie and described in this paper as follows:

(1) *Initial identifications in response to loss of a parent*

Amy initially identifies with her dead mother to protect herself from the pain of profound loss, by adopting geese she mothers and leads on their flight south. To *fly* like a bird is to live in the air, not in the ground where the dead are buried. To *fly* is to magically transcend human limits, which include loss and death. The risk for this necessary but not sufficient response is a denial of death, via a manic defense (Winnicott, 1935; Klein, 1935) and the solidifying of a pathological identification, which Amy avoids.

(2) *Grieving by proxy: Displaced enactments of maternal identification*

Amy's mothering of the goslings, which starts as a symbolic identification with her mother, later includes the father's actual help in parenting the goslings, by showing them how to migrate, to go *away* from *home* and return. The father, geese, and eventually Amy all fly, but even though her airplane is designed to look like a large "mother" goose, and even though the geese can fly without an airplane, they still require maternal direction. Both parents, the father actually and the mother symbolically, are needed for Amy to parent the goslings, by showing them how to migrate, to leave *home* and return.

(3) *Loss manifesting as injury and defectiveness*

Amy protects the goslings from being pinioned, which is simultaneously a narcissistic injury, a form of loss, and a way to prevent losing them by preventing them from flying away (as if to say "if I am injured I can't fly south and will never lose my home"). They must *fly away* to avoid being pinioned, a pathological solution to loss.

(4) *Reconstruction of a new family and resumption of adolescent development*

Amy reconstructs a new family as part of the processes of resolution of her mourning, her further separation and individuation, and her adolescent Oedipal conflicts. Amy *flies away* as separation from her childhood family in order to return *home* as a developing adolescent.

(5) *The father as temporary maternal proxy*

Amy temporarily turns to her father as a substitute for mother, to teach the goslings to migrate *away* from *home* and back, but eventually father can provide only the vehicle and direction for Amy to do so.

(6) *Consolidation of a healthy identification with the deceased parent*

Amy's consolidation of her identification with her mother, in the context of the paradoxical forces of mourning for her mother while developmentally moving toward independence as part of her adolescence, is expressed in the oxymoron of having to *"fly away"* and *"home"*—two opposite directions at the same time, capturing the contradictions of internalizing enough *"home"* from the mother to be able to go *"away,"* and to return safely. The Fall migration and the return of the geese the following Spring, while both examples of instinctual processes, symbolize the importance of successful separation and individuation in order to leave home and return as a mature individual. The opposite of this is a pathological anniversary reaction (Siggins, 1966), a phenomenon which also addresses the identifications with a loved one who has died, but is manifested in the recurrent, often yearly appearance of symptoms the mourner had at the time or the date of the loss, or when the mourner attains the age at which the lost person died. In contrast to this pathological outcome of mourning, the migration symbolizes a healthy reenactment of the separation-individuation process.

CONCLUDING COMMENTS

"Uncomplicated grief is nature's exercise in loss and restitution" (Volkan, 1970), and "The healing may include creative restitution and adaptation that actually enriches the mourner" (Volkan, 1981). Loss leads to restitution throughout the movie *Fly Away Home,* as it also does in healthy grieving: loss of the mother leads Amy to a reconnection with her father, and his girlfriend becomes her friend and surrogate mother. Amy in turn substitutes for the missing mother of the goslings. The father loses his wife but regains his daughter, now a young adult, and his girlfriend joins in the developmental processes.

292   *Frederick C. Miller*

Amy loses her childhood but gains an adolescent maturity as a young woman, firmly identified with her mother as a healthy solution to both her grieving as well as to the resumption and further resolution of her adolescent development.

BIBLIOGRAPHY

AKHTAR, S. (2003). Personal communication.
BOWLBY, J. (1960). Grief and mourning in infancy and early childhood. *Psychoanalytic Study of the Child*, 15:9–52.
——— (1961a). Childhood mourning and its implications for psychiatry. *American Journal of Psychiatry*, 118:481–498.
——— (1961b). Processes of mourning. *International Journal of Psychoanalysis*, 42:317–340.
——— (1963). Pathological mourning and childhood mourning. *Journal of the American Psychoanalytic Association*, 11:500–541.
CARPENTER, MARY CHAPIN (1996). *10,000 miles*, traditional. Columbia Records.
DEUTSCH, H. (1937). Absence of Grief. *Psychoanalytic Quarterly* 6:12–22.
Drawn From Memory, The Animated Autobiography of Paul Fierlinger (1995). Commissioned for the PBS American Playhouse.
Fly Away Home (1996). Columbia Pictures.
FREUD, A. (1960). Discussion of Dr. John Bowlby's paper. *Psychoanalytic Study of the Child*, 41:191–208.
FREUD, S. (1917). Mourning and melancholia. *Standard Edition* 14:237–258. London: Hogarth Press, 1957.
FURMAN, E. (1984). When is the death of a parent traumatic? *Psychoanalytic Study of the Child*, 41:191–208.
KLEIN, M. (1935). A contribution to the psychogenesis of manic-depressive states. In *Love, Guilt and Reparation and Other Works 1921–1945*, pp. 262–289. New York: Free Press, 1992.
LISHMAN, B. (1996). *Father Goose: One Man, a Gaggle of Geese, and Their Real Life Incredible Journey South*. New York: Crown Publishers, Inc.
LOEWALD, H. W. (1962). Internalization, separation, mourning and the superego. *Psychoanalytic Quarterly*, 31:483–504.
LORENZ, K. (1970). *Studies in Animal and Human Behavior, Volume 1*. Cambridge: Harvard University Press.
MAHLER, M., PINE, F., & BERGMAN, A. (1975). The *Psychological Birth of the Human Infant-Symbiosis and Individuation*. New York: Basic Books, pp. 54–55, 65, 100.
MASUR, C. (2001). Can women mourn their mothers? Chapter 3, *Three Faces of Mourning: Melancholia, Manic Defense, and Moving on*, Margaret S. Mahler Symposium on Child Development. Salman Akhtar, editor. Northvale, N.J.: Jason Aronson, pp. 35–45.

MEYER, H. (2001). *Does mourning become Electra? Oedipal and separation-individuation issues in a woman's loss of her mother.* Chapter 2. *Three Faces of Mourning: Melancholia, Manic Defense, and Moving on,* Margaret S. Mahler Symposium on Child Development. Salman Akhtar, editor. Northvale, N.J.: Jason Aronson pp. 13–32.

MILLER, J., & MENES, B. (1970). Children's reactions to the death of a parent: A review of the psychoanalytic literature. *Journal the American Psychoanalytic Association,* 18:697–719.

My Girl (1991). Columbia Pictures.

SCHLESINGER, H. (2001). Technical problems in analyzing the mourning patient. Chapter 6, *Three Faces of Mourning: Melancholia, Manic Defense, and Moving on,* Margaret S. Mahler Symposium on Child Development. Salman Akhtar, editor. Northvale, N.J.: Jason Aronson, pp. 115–139.

SIGGINS, L. D. (1966). Mourning: A critical survey of the literature. *International Journal of Psychoanalysis,* 14:14–25.

VOLKAN, V. (1970). Typical findings in pathological grief. *Psychoanalytic Quarterly,* 45:255–273.

———— (1981). *Linking Objects and Linking Phenomena.* New York: International Universities Press, p. 49.

WINNICOTT, D. W. (1935). The manic defense. *Through Paediatrics to Psychoanalysis: Collected Papers.* New York: Brunner/Mazel, 129–144.

———— (1953). Transitional objects and transitional phenomena: A study of the first not-me possession. *International Journal of Psychoanalysis.* 34:89–97.

WOLFENSTEIN, M. (1966). How is mourning possible? *The Psychoanalytic Study of the Child,* 21:93–123. New York: International Universities Press.

———— (1969). Loss, rage, and repetition. *The Psychoanalytic Study of the Child,* 24:432–460. New York: International Universities Press.

For Better and For Worst

Romeo and Juliet

PAUL SCHWABER, Ph.D.

Shakespeare's famous young lovers, however "star-crossed," contribute crucially to their tragic fate. From a period between before "adolescence" was conceptualized or named, they offer vivid evidence of what we recognize as early adolescent passions, yearnings, and connections, their evocativeness and their dangers. Juliet especially is presented as eloquent in her remarkable awareness of powerful and unfamiliar feelings. The play exemplifies the useful bearings of imaginative literature and psychoanalysis on one another.

FROM THE MOMENT FREUD TURNED TO THE OEDIPUS STORY TO HELP him explain the pattern of his clinical observations, the interactions of psychoanalysis and imaginative literature have been fruitful. The two enterprises can be suspicious of one another, of course—the one not scientific enough, the other reductive, insufficient—but in the main they relate usefully. Sophocles' *Oedipus Rex* stood the test of time, and on that basis Freud could show the ancient truthfulness of devastating unconscious wishes in dreams, preparing the way—for his readers and himself—for his even more unsettling notions of infantile sexuality. The spread of psychoanalytic ideas for more than a century and multiple specific contributions of critics and psychoanalysts obviously have affected how we address imaginative works now. Conversely, the engaging, often startling power of imaginative works

Professor of Letters at Wesleyan University and a psychoanalyst in private practice. He and his wife, Dr. Rosemary Balsam, now edit the Book Review section of the *Journal of the American Psychoanalytic Association*.
The Psychoanalytic Study of the Child 61, ed. Robert A. King, Peter B. Neubauer, Samuel Abrams, and A. Scott Dowling (Yale University Press, copyright © 2006 by Robert A. King, Peter B. Neubauer, Samuel Abrams, and A. Scott Dowling).

continues to provoke applied and self-reflective commentary from psychoanalysts. At their best, both literary and psychoanalytic processes work against finality. No interpretation has the last word, however excellent it may be.

Which means, among other things, that the interpreter matters enormously, whether in a literary or a psychoanalytic encounter. Who the interpreter is, at what time and place, what he or she knows, how in touch with accumulated experiences of self and others, and at what point in the life cycle, all bear on the emerging meanings in the encounter. For example, one of the usually unacknowledged pleasures a teacher of literature has comes with the necessary task of rereading. Indeed, it is one of life's guarded secrets—the joys possible in rereading, realizations of what one missed at earlier times, of what amplitudes accrue as one's disciplinary and life experience accumulate. All psychoanalysts appreciate the enriched perceptiveness that comes with years of clinical practice; teachers of psychoanalysis know how much more one sees in Freud's writings each time through. To be sure, on occasion one finds previously marvelous works diminished. But I would call attention to rereading, because unlike more celebrated pleasures, it is not for the very young; it comes with ageing.

Literature, it is often said, imitates life: that in large part is what is so fascinating about it. The issue of imitation is vast, however, having to do with artifice: with form, style, genre, tradition, learning, and cultural idiom, with depicted circumstances, plot, and characters (Aristotle, 335–323? B.C.E.; Auerbach, 1953). Different historical moments, moreover, clearly affect judgment. I doubt that I can do anything like justice to imitation here. But as an ageing professor and not-so-old psychoanalyst, I'd like to reconsider Shakespeare's tragedy of young love, *Romeo and Juliet* (1596). As psychoanalysts or psychoanalytically informed critics, what can we understand about it that we may not have before? And what has the play to offer psychoanalysis?

Verona proves famously inhospitable to the young lovers, perhaps because no more ready for their feelings than they themselves are. Its prince and citizenry have run out of patience with Montagues and Capulets. Nonetheless, the young men of both feuding families itch for swordplay, when—with the heedlessness of youth—Romeo and his Montague mates crash a costume party of the Capulets. He catches sight of Juliet there and is transfixed—as, we soon learn, she is on seeing him—and the play's fusion of love and tragedy takes hold. Juliet's cousin Tybalt recognizes Romeo disguised, so from the first the lovers are specifically enmeshed in hate and intractability.

The bawdry and angry posturing of young men and the vicious narcissism of competing groups completes the picture. We are prepared early for young love thwarted by the folly and evil of others, for the "star-crossed" and "death-marked" pair, as the Prologue describes them, to play out their fate, and for the legend of Romeo and Juliet to flourish—begun by Capulet and Montague burying their feud as they bury their children. That is how persons of a certain age tend to recall the play, having read it in youth and remembered it nostalgically over time, like a first love.

The path to their deaths, though, cannot be merely "star-crossed"— that is, inevitable—or the play would hold little interest. What the youngsters experience, who they are, what they do, and how they contribute to their fate has to involve us. How, in other words, they love each other to death *and* engage our sympathy invites consideration. For Romeo and Juliet are partners in death and in art, but only briefly in life. That they engage our imaginations and identifications may therefore tell us something of ourselves—of the readinesses, impulses, and dire potentialities that we manage in time to channel into sustaining stabilities, when we do.

All is not without hope for the young couple at first. Capulet looks with favor on young Count Paris' suit for Juliet's hand, but only if his daughter—his only child—consents. Lady Capulet also favors the match, having herself married and borne Juliet by her daughter's present age, thirteen. She too explores rather than insists. Although clearly patriarchal in assumption, Juliet's parents seem to grant her the right of choice. She also has an ally, her garrulous, comical old wetnurse, now a family retainer, just as Romeo has his skeptical and witty friend, Mercutio. Soon the lovers will rely on the well-intentioned Friar to marry them and see them through.

There are customs and forms in place for the expression of young men's erotic aims that are not simply lustful, but none apparent for women other than passivity and prettiness. Count Paris approaches Juliet's father, for example, before trying hard to appeal to her. Although never a serious contender in her feelings, he is an honorable one. When we encounter Romeo initially, he is in agony over Rosaline—interestingly enough, also a Capulet—who has rejected him, indeed has apparently renounced sexuality. A young man's misery over an out-of-bounds woman invites oedipal tracing now, but it was recognizable then because it had been given ample representation in a genre of medieval poetry in which men painfully adored idealized and unavailable women. By Shakespeare's time, it was standard fare.

Romeo's instant rush of feeling upon seeing Juliet, unexplained

yet rendered unarguable by the strength of poetry, sweeps aside
precedents and forms and all sensible concern for safety. He exults:

> O, she doth teach the torches to burn bright!
> It seems she hangs upon the cheek of night
> As a rich jewel in an Ethiop's ear—
> Beauty too rich for use, for earth too dear! (I, v, 44–47)

One might puzzle over beauty too rich for use, too dear for earth—
hyperbole that could override unease, even fear. Yet his astonish-
ment is genuine, as is his summary: "Did my heart love till now? For-
swear it, sight!/ For I ne'er saw true beauty till this night!"(I, v, 52–53).
A moment's vision, a superb image, a closing couplet, and his love is
sealed. Though Tybalt rages, Capulet restrains him; and next we observe the lovers meet and kiss—charmingly. Romeo takes her hand
and presents himself as worshiping at a shrine:

> If I profane with my unworthiest hand
> This holy shrine, the gentle sin is this:
> My lips, two blushing pilgrims, ready stand
> To smooth that rough touch with a tender kiss.

She responds in kind, taking up the pilgrim image and amplifying it:

> Good pilgrim, you do wrong your hand too much,
> Which mannerly devotion shows in this;
> For saints have hands that pilgrims' hands do touch,
> And palm to palm is holy palmers' kiss.

They are flirting, dueting even, and in the process are also fashioning
a sonnet, in the Shakespearean rhyme scheme of three quatrains and
a couplet (abab cdcd efef gg):

> *Romeo:* Have not saints lips, and holy palmers too?
> *Juliet:* Ay, pilgrim, lips that they must use in prayer.
> *Romeo:* O, then, dear saint, let lips do what hands do! They pray; grant
> thou, lest faith turn to despair.
> *Juliet:* Saints do not move, though grant for prayers' sake.
> *Romeo:* Then move not while my prayer's effect I take (I, v, 93–107).
> [kiss]

Their fit is seamless; and when together they extend the metaphor of
pilgrim and saint gracefully to a second kiss, Juliet teases him: "You
kiss by the book." These are enchanting youngsters: attuned, intelligent, playful, and verbally felicitous. But they do not lack for trouble.
Learning each other's identity from the nurse, they recognize the
trap they are in.

Flush with overwhelming love, of course, they do not hesitate. The balcony scene ensues and the tragedy dependably unfolds. I want to pause here—put Romeo on hold for a while except as a foil—to ponder Juliet as she tries to catch up to and gauge all that she is feeling, because at this juncture her remarkable consciousness emerges to prominence. We've seen her josh with her nurse and promise her mother to consider Paris, but the text has registered Romeo's romantic epiphany, not hers. Now her monologues, interactions, and dialogues expose intense, rushing, and shifting emotions, her alacrity of mind and notable self-awareness. "My only love, sprung from my only hate!" she says on learning who he is. "Too early seen unknown, and known too late!/ Prodigious birth of love it is to me/ That I must love a loathed enemy" (I, v, 138–141). That "*must* love," loaded with insistence, deserves note. Juliet plunges into alliance with Romeo— or an idea of him—as if in part propelled to flee what she has been. Nor does she ask less of him. On the balcony, she famously reflects: "wherefore art thou Romeo?/ Deny thy father and refuse thy name;/ Or, if thou wilt not, be but sworn my love,/ And I'll no longer be a Capulet." Identity, family, and position are dismissible. She wants more, something at once sacrificial and unique to them: "Romeo, doff thy name;/ And for thy name, which is no part of thee,/ Take all myself" (II, ii, 33–48).

She is thinking aloud at this instant, unaware that he, risking his life to be there, overhears. They begin to talk and, embarrassed to have revealed her love, she offers to act coy. He tries to swear devotion, but she stops him. Words will not suffice, cannot equal the event. She urges him to leave: it isn't safe, they are rash, they are moving too fast. Yet in a blink she proclaims her love deep and infinite as the sea. Called in by her nurse, she bids him adieu, then asks that he stay, and in but a moment returns to say:

> Three words, dear Romeo, and good night indeed.
> If that thy bent of love be honorable,
> Thy purpose marriage, send me word to-morrow,
> By one that I'll procure to come to thee,
> Where and at what time thou wilt perform the rite;
> And all my fortunes at thy foot I'll lay
> And follow thee my lord throughout the world (II, ii, 142–148).

She wants, and proposes, marriage, tomorrow.

And Romeo is willing. "So thrive my soul," he begins, only to be silenced again. "A thousand times good night!," "Juliet affirms, and exits. He responds gallantly: "A thousand times the worse, to want thy light!,"—and proceeds to unintended illumination by remarking:

"Love goes toward love as schoolboys from their books,/ But love from love, toward school with heavy looks" (II, ii, 155–158). The sentiment is apt; he races to her and leaves unwillingly; but his schoolboy imagery reminds us of something crucial: that they are still children, and that their explosive, brave, immediate, and incomparable love is precocious.

In our terms, they are early adolescents. In their world, Juliet, at 13, is old enough to marry—recall that her mother had already married and borne Juliet by that age—although judging from a remark of Capulet's, her mother's experience may not have been happy. Recently, historians of early modernism have cast doubt on the long-standing assumption that women at that time married early to maximize childbirths, when many infants died—and many mothers did, giving birth (Wrigley and Schofield, 1981, pp. 254–256). The range, no doubt, was considerable. But the play is emphatic. Romeo and Juliet as presented are youngsters with rushing feelings and grownup bodies. They find one another suddenly, thrill to each other, and in fantasy merge. And there is frenzy in their love, a desperate demand for certainty and totality she in particular makes, which cannot be sufficiently explained by externalities—by the hostile families and daunting circumstances. It can be sighted in her "must love" as in her swirling contradictions and sudden proposal of marriage—and in an overt revelation she soon makes.

Reappearing on the balcony, Juliet asks when to send to him for word about the marriage ceremony. "By the hour of nine," he answers, and they linger, until she notes that dawn is near. "I would have thee gone," she says:

> And yet no farther than a wanton's bird,
> That lets it hop a little from her hand,
> Like a poor prisoner in his twisted gyves,
> And with a silken thread plucks it back again,
> So loving-jealous of his liberty.

Her enticement contains menace in this fantasy. She would imprison him, like a pet. Romeo's "I wish I were thy bird" follows her lead, to which she replies:

> Sweet, so would I.
> Yet I should kill thee with much cherishing.
> Good night, good night! Parting is such sweet sorrow
> That I shall say good night till it be morrow (II, ii, 159–186).

Few, I think, recall that prelude to the couplet that everyone remembers. She would kill him with much cherishing, take his very life. A tyrannical wish shows before it gets denied—or almost denied. "Parting is such sweet sorrow,/ That I shall say good night till it be morrow": considered closely, the lines are ambiguous. A continuous goodnight, after all, would keep him there and endanger him. So hostility that serves control complicates her love—and fuels it.

Varying characters, moods (there is much comedy), and social classes in rapid scenes, and presenting stark turns of loyalties and happenstance, the drama's structure and pace complement the tumult of the lovers. In quick order Romeo and Juliet are married by the Friar, Mercutio is killed by Tybalt as Romeo tries to part them, Romeo slays Tybalt and immediately is banished by the prince. Word of these horrors has not reached Juliet, however, when, in a remarkable soliloquy, she yearns for day's end and her wedding night.

"Gallop apace, you fiery-footed steeds," she urges the sun-god's horses, "And bring in cloudy night immediately." Impatiently, she awaits the bliss she would claim:

> Spread thy close curtain, love-performing night.
> That runaway's eyes may wink, and Romeo
> Leap to these arms untalked of and unseen.
> Lovers can see to do their amorous rites
> By their own beauties; or, if love be blind,
> It best agrees with night.

She acknowledges that love may be blind, but she wants darkness and secrecy, so even runaways (who presumably move by night) will not see the frankly sexual love she craves, her amorous rites that, however guilt-evoking, are legitimate.

> Come, civil night,
> Thou sober-suited matron, all in black,
> And learn me how to lose a winning match,
> Played for a pair of stainless maidenhoods.

Courteous and appropriate, "civil" night, personified as a mature woman, offers the cover and perhaps instruction that will enable Juliet's passion and paradox ("learn me how to lose a winning match")—and allow her, safely, to try out nascent, not yet graspable emotions:

> Hood my unmanned blood, bating in my cheeks,
> With thy black mantle till *strange* love grow bold,
> Think true love acted simple modesty [my italics].

This is fascinating. Her excitement is palpable, yet "hood my unmanned blood," a figure from falconry, suggests a wild creature tamed and trained by a man. In fact female hawks were and are used in falconry, being larger and more powerful than the males (*Encyclopedia Britannica,* 1960, 9:44–48). So her most exigent thought is gendered. Protective night will be female, both maternal and kind. But Juliet's coursing blood and rampant feelings, her "strange" love emerging from within, will need manning. It is not that Romeo will make her a woman. She can't wait for him to be present and passionately loving. But here she also adumbrates a wish for the power and skill with which to encounter her uncharted inner experience—and for her "strange" love—wild, not yet familiar—actively and boldly to meet his. For that, however—for such agency—she has no internalized female model. Neither the lower class nurse nor Juliet's mother apparently has qualified. In our terms, she aspires to an ego of her own, a female sense of self to manage and release her desire. But her thoughts reveal her dilemma. Such an imaginable ego would, for her, be male: it would "man" her the way a trainer would a hawk. Paradigmatic in Verona, male authority monopolizes her possibilities of active self-governance while affording no plausible access, by itself, to her pulsing, new, and wondrous feelings. External circumstances entrap her. But she is trapped psychologically too.

Turning tender and lyrical, she again enfolds Romeo in death:

> Come night; come, Romeo; come, thou day in night;
> For thou wilt lie upon the wings of night
> Whiter than new snow upon a raven's back.
> Come, gentle night; come, loving, black-browed night;
> Give me my Romeo; and, when he shall die,
> Take him and cut him out in little stars,
> And he will make the face of heaven so fine
> That all the world will be in love with night
> And pay no worship to the garish sun.

Juliet's sexual desire is undoubted, and the word "die," to Elizabethans, also signified orgasm. But her climactic fantasy here is of Romeo dismembered and commemorated. If it merges excitement with her continuing awareness of danger, it also suggests frantic displaced rage and a wish for finality. Internally she is apocalyptic. She cannot combine intimacy and life—cannot imagine it—and her fury feeds the very urgency of her love. Her thoughts wind back then to the wedding night and her impatience, but this time with an eye to childhood:

> O, I have bought the mansion of a love,
> But not possessed it; and though I am sold,
> Not yet enjoyed. So tedious is this day
> As is the night before some festival
> To an impatient child that hath new robes
> And may not wear them (III, ii, 1–31).

She can foresee no living future; but for her too, as for Romeo, things were easier once upon a time.

   This depiction of a young woman's consciousness is unprecedented in imaginative literature, to my knowledge. Her dynamic emergence, her excited, enchanting, still inchoate feelings, her pliancy and connectedness, her forcefulness, her sexual eagerness and destructive fantasies, her frenzy for immediacy, her longing, frustration, and fury, her actual social and internal barriers, her courage and intelligence, moreover, get augmented early in the play by the Nurse's reminiscences. She recalls weaning Juliet and much else from that time, especially how the little girl, walking unsteadily, once fell and bruised her forehead:

> And then my husband (God be with his soul!
> 'A was a merry man) took up the child.
> "Yea," quoth he, "dost thou fall upon thy face?
> Thou wilt fall backward when thou hast more wit;
> Wilt thou not, Jule?" and, by my holidam,
> The pretty wretch left crying and said "Ay."
> To see now how a jest shall come about!
> I warrant, an I should live a thousand years,
> I never should forget it. 'Wilt thou not, Jule?' quoth he,
> And, pretty fool, it stinted and said 'Ay' (I, iii, 39–48).

There is little doubt about this core gender assignment—but other matters emerge as well from the humorously perseverating account: that the Nurse's jolly husband died, as did Susan, their daughter, who was Juliet's age. These losses constellate in her mind with Juliet's weaning. Might Juliet have lost a sisterly playmate's presence and a fondly attentive man early on, and absorbed her wetnurse's sadnesses too, in addition to losing the breast? This is merely suggestive—based on the Nurse's memory, not Juliet's—but it comes from a key gendering source and it fits Juliet's characterization, providing credible childhood experience and cogent additional motivation for the vivid young woman who, loving instantly and surging within herself, demands everything of love and wants it now. Vulnerable about loss and appetitive for life—and for companionship—remarkably gifted, and constrained, she desperately, and with unconscious fury, wagers all.

She wanted to fuse with Romeo into something unnameable, to be neither Montague nor Capulet but bear no separateness. What he was to fulfill may be gauged from her agony when she learns of his banishment:

> Some word there was, worser than Tybalt's death,
> That murd'red me. I would forget it fain;
> But O, it presses to my memory
> Like damned guilty deeds to sinners' minds!
> 'Tybalt is dead, and Romeo—banished,'
> That 'banished,' that one word 'banished,'
> Hath slain ten thousand Tybalts. Tybalt's death
> Was woe enough, if it had ended there;
> Or if sour woe delights in fellowship
> And needly will be ranked with other griefs,
> Why followed not, when she said 'Tybalt's dead,'
> Thy father, or thy mother, nay, or both,
> Which modern lamentation might have moved?
> But with a rearward following Tybalt's death,
> 'Romeo is 'banished'—to speak that word
> Is father, mother, Tybalt, Romeo, Juliet,
> All slain, all dead. 'Romeo is banished'—
> There is no end, no limit, measure, bound,
> In that word's death; no words can that woe sound.
> Where is my father and my mother, nurse? (III, ii, 109–127).

He held all her representations (with the exception of the Nurse, who is there with her) in place, the felt foundations of her being. Without him she will expire of grief or stand empty of contents, a graveyard of consciousness. Touchingly, then, she asks like a child for her mother and father. This terrifying fantasy proves momentary, and she soon recovers her resourcefulness and will. But she has given expression to her dread that boldly loving Romeo and now suddenly being deprived of his presence, she might internally vanish.

Juliet is beguiling, frankly sexual, assertive, brave, and self-obser-vant, well-along in her self-making yet unfinished. Romeo, by con-trast, although passionate, vivid, devoted, and very eloquent, is less self-aware. Having fewer introspective moments, moreover, he does not reveal as much of what he brings from past and present to their urgent union.

After their initial exultation, his struggle proves two-fold: to adapt to his powerful desire and the lyrical tenderness he feels for her; and to manage to separate successfully not only from family but even more from his friends. For it is they—Mercutio and Benvolio most prominently—who constitute his companionable tie before Juliet. He frolics, boasts, and matches wits with them; he shares his unease with them; and when he rejoins them in that way, apparently cured of Rosaline, Mercutio revels: "Why is not this better now than groaning for love? Now art thou sociable, now art thou Romeo; now art thou what thou art" (II, iv, 83–87). Neither he nor they, however, are ready for a grown-up love. As Juliet's beloved, Romeo matches her feelings and expressiveness; and he acts resolutely. But as her husband, he makes an awful mess. Intervening to keep Mercutio and his new relative by marriage Tybalt from dueling, he enables Tybalt to kill Mercutio treacherously. "O sweet Juliet/ Thy beauty hath made me effeminate,/ And in my temper soft'ned valor's steel" (II, I, 111–113), he laments. His dear friend is dead, and his own sense of masculinity is undermined. So he kills Tybalt in turn and the predicted "star-crossed" process unfolds.

Shall we read unconscious as well as conscious intents in his actions? He *had* first yearned for a different out-of-bounds Capulet; and setting out with his mates for the Capulets' ball, he thought forebodingly:

> My mind misgives
> Some consequence, yet hanging in the stars,
> Shall bitterly begin his fearful date
> With this night's revels and expire the term
> Of a despised life, closed in my breast,
> By some vile forfeit of untimely death. (I, iv, 106–110)

Death figured as well in his plea to the Friar: "Do thou but close our hands with holy words,/ Then love-devouring death do what he dare—/ It is enough I may but call her mine"(II, vi, 6–8). Romeo begins, then, with a troubling agenda. And his crisis will involve overwhelming intimacy and responsibility, love and endangered masculinity, and bewildered loyalties and fear—all suddenly exigent. What results is devastation. By the end of the play Mercutio, Tybalt, Paris, Juliet, and he are dead—each death fully or mainly by his doing; his mother too has died of grief; and his father and Juliet's parents are bereft. The depth of Romeo's unleashed ferocity can be gauged by his words to his page when they reach Juliet's grave:

> Upon thy life I charge thee,
> Whate'er thou hearest or seest, stand all aloof
> And do not interrupt me in my course. . . .

> But if thou, jealous, dost return to pry
> In what I farther shall intend to do,
> By heaven, I will tear thee joint by joint
> And strew this hungry churchyard with thy limbs.
> The time and my intents are savage-wild,
> More fierce and more inexorable far
> Than empty tigers or the roaring sea. (V, iii, 25–39)

He taps a well of fury within himself, and only all those deaths can cap it. Hazlitt's remark of long ago is keen: "Romeo is Hamlet in love" (1817, p. 113).

Like Juliet, he is wracked by the banishment; and he resists the Friar's comfort that time would offer hope. "There is no world without Verona walls,/ But purgatory, torture, hell itself," he protests:

> 'Tis torture, and not mercy. Heaven is here
> Where Juliet lives; and every cat and dog
> And little mouse, every unworthy thing,
> Live here in heaven and may look on her;
> But Romeo may not. . . . .
>
> Hadst thou no poison mixed, no sharp-ground knife,
> No sudden mean of death, though ne'er so mean,
> But 'banished' to kill me—'banished'?
> O friar, the damned use that word in hell;
> Howling attends it! How has thou the heart,
> Being a divine, a ghostly confessor,
> A sin-absolver, and my friend professed,
> To mangle me with that word "banished"? (III, iii, 17–51)

Soon, raging, he moves to kill himself, only to be prevented and berated by the Friar and the Nurse for failing in manliness. "Hold thy desperate hand," the Friar cries:

> Art thou a man? Thy form cries out thou art;
> Thy tears are womanish, thy wild acts denote
> The unreasonable fury of a beast.
> Unseemly woman in a seeming man!
> And ill-beseeming beast in seeming both! (III, iii, 109–113)

This sequence uncovers a good deal. Romeo's hopeless despair releases his fury, potentially every which way, a fury fueled by pressure from without and within to be a man—which in Verona, with the exception of the Friar, means a bellicose and short-tempered one.

The play itself turns on that issue of manliness: the limits that define it, and the implicit demand—and challenge to it—by a bur-

geoning young woman for full sexual and social status and the room
to claim it. Her young husband unravels into swordplay and suicide.
Her father, frantic for authority after his nephew Tybalt's death and
flustered by her inordinate grief, imposes rigid patriarchal rule by insisting that she marry Paris—and does so angrily, not even knowing
she loves and has married Romeo. Her mother becomes equally firm
and stark. The Nurse too turns on her. The Friar's counsel of patience and his sleeping potion stratagem are foiled by plague. And
Romeo foolishly and impulsively kills Paris and, believing Juliet dead,
drinks poison. Awakening to find him dead, she chooses to die and
kills herself with his dagger, managing a Roman hero's death. To the
end she continues resourceful, intelligent, and steadfast. But the
irony is telling: even to die, her model of activity remains inescapably
patriarchal; and anxious or harried manliness, in this play, kills.

What, then, does my psychoanalytically informed rereading of
Romeo and Juliet accomplish? It bolsters any contention that the lovers
are more than star-crossed victims; they contribute to their fate and
participate in its resonances. My perspective offers quite a troubling
view of Romeo but, I think, a fair one. It also engages Juliet's erotic
awakening and genuineness, her complicating angers and rebellious-
ness, her distinct emotional intelligence befuddled by social limita-
tion and inner constrictions. No emerging young woman had ever
been so depicted in literature. Her existence is the more astonishing
when one recalls that the actors on the Elizabethan public stage were
all males. How could Shakespeare, with his troupe of male actors,
conceive of her? It no doubt matters that his daughters at that time
were 13 and 11, and his son Hamnet had just died (Honan, 1998,
pp. 235–236, 412). But there are mysteries to him that do not yield.

And what does his *Romeo and Juliet* offer to psychoanalysts some
four centuries after its composition—other than living poetry, vibrant characters, and a sad, monitory ending? It gives us—as *Oedipus
Rex* gave Freud—through the enduring evidence of art, a retrospect
that deepens, confirms, and enlivens. *Romeo and Juliet* captures the
rush and urgency of adolescent desires, even as it dramatizes the excitement, splendor, difficulties, and dangers of first loves. May we infer how important they are to go through, as practice? Surely it signals the hurdles to be gone over, sooner or later, for a more stable,
loving partnership—among which are sufficient separation from
one's family of birth and chosen peers, and sufficient consolidated
selfhood for merging that augments and enlivens but can also depend on trust of self and other without angry need of certainty.

Through a more encompassing developmental lens, *Romeo and Juliet* locates infantile grandiosities and transferences that feed and can poison loves which lack structure for sustained recognitions and mutualities, for the openness to learn, to accept, and to give. Most of all, if we give ourselves over to the words, world, and characters of the play, eventually to step back to go on with our lives, it vivifies and enlightens our awareness of what has been imitated. The passions that energize our most wonderful accomplishments of intimacy and of culture derive from primitive libidinal sources and, lest we forget, the death instinct.

BIBLIOGRAPHY

ARISTOTLE (335–323? B.C.E.). *Poetics.* Trans. S. H. Butcher. Intro., F. Fergusson. New York, Hill and Wang, 1961.
AUERBACH, E. (1953). *Mimesis: The Representation of Reality in Western Literature.* Trans., W. R. Trask. Princeton: Princeton U. Press.
Encyclopedia Britannica. (1960). Vol. 9, 44–48.
HAZLITT, W. (1817). *Characters of Shakespeare's Plays.* London: Dent & Sons, E. P. Dutton, 1906.
HONAN, P. (1998). *Shakespeare: A Life.* Oxford: Oxford U. Press.
SHAKESPEARE, W. (1596). *Romeo and Juliet.* Ed. J. E. Hankins. New York: Penguin Books, 1960.
WRIGLEY, E. A., & SCHOFIELD, R. S. (1981). *The Population History of England, 1541–1871: A Reconstruction.* Cambridge, Mass.: Harvard U. Press.

Psychopathic Characters on the Stage of Stephen Sondheim

MATTHEW ISAAC COHEN, Ph.D., and PHYLLIS M. COHEN, Ed.D.

Many of the characters in Stephen Sondheim's musical theater are burdened with a character pathology which results in their inability to establish intimate relationships. Drawing on Freud's "Psychopathic characters on the stage" and psychoanalytic theory, this article suggests that developmental, biological, and environmental factors from Sondheim's childhood contribute to his characters' social and interpersonal alienation. Sondheim's art is a partially successful attempt to re-assert connections and repair narcissistic injuries, introjecting the absent mother as part of the superego. The resistance to dramatizing character pathology through biography is both an expression of society's postmodern fragmentation and resistance to Oedipal drama.

FREUD'S ESSAY "PSYCHOPATHIC CHARACTERS ON THE STAGE," WRITTEN in 1905 or 1906, develops a thesis that audiences are able to identify with "abnormal characters" depicted in the theater, and thereby take masochistic pleasure in their suffering, by becoming "interested spectators" to the process by which pathology develops. "If we are faced by an unfamiliar and fully established neurosis, we shall be inclined to [. . .] pronounce the character inadmissible to the stage" (Freud, 1905–6, p. 310). Freud is of course thinking of the psycho-

Matthew Isaac Cohen is Senior Lecturer in the Department of Drama and Theatre, Royal Holloway, University of London. Phyllis M. Cohen is Edith B. Jackson Associate Professor, Yale University Child Study Center, is a child and adult psychoanalyst, and is on the faculty of the Western New England Institute of Psychoanalysis.

The Psychoanalytic Study of the Child 61, ed. Robert A. King, Peter B. Neubauer, Samuel Abrams, and A. Scott Dowling (Yale University Press, copyright © 2006 by Robert A. King, Peter B. Neubauer, Samuel Abrams, and A. Scott Dowling).

logically based Ibsenian theater of his own time and the theater of Goethe and Shakespeare that informed it.

Interested spectators today occupy a different position with respect to stage drama, both due to developments in the aesthetics of theater as well as the psychological makeup of the public en masse. Raymond Williams (1983) has described contemporary society as a "dramatized society." Drama is no longer enacted solely in the theater on special occasions, but is available on television constantly, reproduced in the heightened displays of celebrities, and reported in the mass media. As a public we have been conditioned to television commercial dramas lasting 30 seconds that collapse all the fine distinctions of character and narrative relations into stock images. "Real life" characters on talk shows and "reality" television shows are prepped to profess their deepest desires and fantasies in easily digestible sound bites.

This disjuncture between the horizons of expectation of what drama is and does between Freud's time and our own can be taken as one of the primary resistances to the Oedipal drama. Freud and his contemporary readers could empathize with Oedipus as dramatic character as their life rhythms coincided roughly with the agonistic classical dramas. "It appears as a necessary precondition of this form of art," Freud tells us of character dramas on the lines of *Hamlet,* "that the impulse that is struggling into consciousness, however clearly it is recognizable, is never given a definite name; so that in the spectator too the process is carried through with his attention averted, and he is in the grip of his emotions instead of taking stock of what is happening" (p. 309). Contemporary society does not give over to drama the inviolable time-space of leisure and meditation that is conducive to such identification; rather, drama is consigned to the time needed to finish a bowl of cereal or prepare for sleep. Attention needs to be grabbed through spectacle, not averted through misdirection. The complex triadic structuring, foreshadowing, illusion, and dramatic irony of Oedipus are antithetical to such a contemporary dramatic formation.

Psychopathic characters do appear on the stage, but contemporary audiences have a different set of resistances to their realization just as what Freud calls "the neurotic instability of the public" (p. 310) has been redefined in the dramatized society. The "interested spectators" of today's theater who can take on the role of privileged witness to the suffering of a dramatized character do not demand a narrative that represents the unfolding of a character's pathology on stage. What they do demand is that these characters can be slotted into dominant meta-narratives that inform shared conceptions of society.

In this age of soap opera sound bites, the American music-theater artist Stephen Sondheim returns the classical tradition of the dramatization of psychic abnormalities to the popular stage. However, unlike in the classical drama, where the audience witnesses the lifecycle of a pathology, the viewers of a Sondheim production witness characters with psyches that have been shattered long before the show has even begun. Sondheim's light-hearted characterization of pathological distress is suitable for a modern musical theater audience that accepts pathologies as preconditions for drama, not as reasons for drama. Sondheim's psychologically flawed characters and their impaired relations emerge from an obsessive wellspring of imagination and bear the marks of an ego defect which might be attributed to their creator.

Stephen Sondheim was born in New York in 1930 to a father who was a dress manufacturer and a mother who was his chief designer. He was an only child. His parents shared professional interests but were not close emotionally. His mother Janet (known by her nickname "Foxy") has been described as self-centered, narcissistic, aloof, with no feelings of warmth, and distant from her child from infancy (Secrest, 1998). Sondheim's parents divorced when he was age 10, but his father maintained a relation through weekly visitations, often taking his son to the Broadway theater. Sondheim was sent by his mother to a military academy immediately following the divorce. Possibly the psychologically abusive and distant relation with his mother contributed to an already compromised biological vulnerability. Sondheim appeared to show no separation anxiety and thoroughly adapted to the regime of military schooling, taking an enjoyment in the discipline and structure it provided. He appeared as a self-sufficient, adaptable boy but this outward tranquility might have been a defensive façade for separation trauma. We see distant echoes of the emotional chaos experienced upon the move from the comforts of a luxurious San Remo apartment on Central Park West to all the unknowns of military academy in the "cautionary note [that] is repeatedly sounded" by the fairy tale characters of *Into the Woods:* "Into the woods/It's time to go/I hate to leave/I have to, though" (Sondheim cited in Gordon, 1992, p. 303).

Sondheim began to spend summers with Oscar and Dorothy Hammerstein II, who were acquaintances of Sondheim's parents, when he was age 11. The Hammersteins became a second family for him. Oscar Hammerstein mentored the young Sondheim and became a role model for work in the theater. Dorothy became a surrogate mother of sorts and nurtured him emotionally and psychologically. The Hammersteins' son, Jimmy Hammerstein, described Sondheim's mother, "Foxy," as "too dangerous a mother to call even 'decent.' [. . .] She had to be the worst mother I've ever seen" (Gottfried, 1993, p. 13). Sondheim was later sent to a Friends Society school and attended Williams College, where he studied composition and piano. While both parents were Jewish, Sondheim did not have a bar mitzvah and has no memories of attending synagogue as a child or otherwise directly participating in a community of faith as a youth. His love of musicals (a genre identified with American Jews) and the Yiddish language are perhaps his only firm identity markers.

Sondheim began writing for musical theater, a populist genre by definition, from the age of 15. Sondheim has often reported that he "wrote for the theater [. . .] in order to be like Oscar. I have no doubt that if he'd been a geologist, I would have become a geologist" (Gottfried, 1993, p. 13). A more balanced view of Sondheim's professional development would also stress the significance of Sondheim's father in his choice of vocation; Herbert Sondheim played the piano, enacted musical sketches, and had numerous friends and professional colleagues in theater. What was pastime for father became profession for his son. One never knows what facets of a parent's personality, interests, and passions will be internalized by a child (Cohen, 2001). The musical theater, perhaps the most formulaic and emotionally bland form of artistic expression in the United States at the time, became a medium in Sondheim's hands for exploring his own psyche and the world around him. Sondheim's creative opus is considered by critics to be a radical departure from the musical tradition formalized by Rodgers and Hammerstein, painstakingly crafting "a new lyric, musical, and theatrical language for each work" (Gordon, 1992, p. 8). One of the functions of theater since ancient Athens is to expose social lies and free people from meaningless conventions. This is especially true in Sondheim's work.

Sondheim's fame as a songwriter and musical theater artist came early in his life, and he soon evolved into the most acclaimed musical creator of his generation. His single-minded commitment to his craft perhaps came at the expense of his personal social development. Sondheim was already branded by environmental insults and biological vulnerabilities; it can be hypothesized that his attachment to his work gave him yet another cause for alienation from comfortable peer relationships. Indeed, a recent biography has shown that he has had few sustained adult love relations (Secrest, 1998). Sondheim has largely avoided the public limelight, and beyond the broad details of his professional life, little is in fact known about him as a person. Sondheim's collaborator the director-playwright James Lapine has stated that he is fascinated by "the fact that you don't know a lot about" George Seurat (a character based on the French painter Georges Seurat, 1859–1891), the protagonist of the Sondheim-Lapine musical *Sunday in the Park with George.* "That told you a lot. The guy was clearly mysterious" (Lapine cited in Gottfried, 1993, p. 155). The same could be said about Sondheim himself.

Nonetheless it is possible to infer the ways Sondheim's personality intersects with his artistic efforts: beneath the multifarious artistry, the breadth of subjects he treats, and musical styles he deploys, there lie psychological issues that are constant motifs across Sondheim's opus. Behind the enormous variety of characters created by Sondheim, and the variations of relations he explores in his plays, is a fundamental ego defect burdening many of his characters. On the surface, characters appear obsessed over relations. But at their core they are unable to sustain meaningful human contacts. There is an emptiness in them. They appear to have resistances, be conflicted or obsessed. They appear to have a complexity of emotional experience. But in reality they are really void of the capacity to have genuine, internalized relations. Language is fragmented, musical tempos and keys switch without forewarning or signaling, foci and points of identification are elusive. Artifice and reality are not firmly distinguished as the musicals slip between caricature and the psychological. The struggle for spectators of these plays is to identify with misanthropic characters through this psychological matrix. Sondheim's work is in fact obsessed with the inability to understand what are the preconditions of establishing relations of intimacy. Much of his musical theater can be read as a struggle for the artist to understand his own self. Why am I so odd? Am I dumb? Am I unlovable? To the degree that these questions connect with interested spectators of Sondheim, such preoccupations and insecurities define the neurotic instability of the public.

Sondheim's psychologically abusive mother set up defenses in Sondheim's art and practice, and would seem to contribute to the way he portrays women and relations in his plays. The non-available primary object, absent and without the possibility of reciprocity, informs his dramatic re-creations which tend to have an "antiromantic, unsentimental depiction of marriage" (Gordon, 1992, p. 55).

Fredrik and Carl-Magnus, both in love with the glorious courtesan Desirée in *A Little Night Music,* sing the refrain:

Carl-Magnus: If only she'd been fearful . . .
Fredrik: Or married . . .
Carl-Magnus: Or tearful . . .
Fredrik: Or dead . . .
Both: It would have been wonderful.
 But the woman was perfection,
 And the prospects are grim
(Sondheim and Wheeler, 1991a, p. 150).

Both wish that Desirée were unavailable through death, emotional distance, or marital status so that they would not feel so passionate for this charming and beautiful woman.

This disconnection comes through musically in Sondheim's jaunty pointillism (particularly prevalent in *Sunday in the Park with George*), and the piano originals of the music, full of "coloristic devices such as repeated notes, arpeggios, broken chords, and the use of extreme registers" (Tunick in Sondheim and Wheeler, 1991a, p. 4).

The musical has provided the soundtrack for romantic love for the American public, but romantic relations in Sondheim's plays are consistently thwarted, and his songs and lyrics resist romantic appropriation. Characters yearn for cohesion, but struggle with instability and often end up alienated. The unstable love triangles and triple meters of *A Little Night Music* constantly struggle to resolve as stable couples and firm double meters. Some do: but there is a lingering sense of imbalance. Sondheim's characters display in general deep anxiety about the fixity of couples. "One's impossible, two is dreary,/Three is company, safe and cheery" (Sondheim and Furth, 1996, p. 81). A triad means not having to commit to a dyadic relation, while avoiding the desperate loneliness of the isolate. The first show that Sondheim wrote as a sophomore at Williams, *Finney's Rainbow,* has what Sondheim characterizes as a "parody" of the 1932 song, "How Deep Is the Ocean?" by Irving Berlin. Where Berlin gifts lyrics in "How Deep Is The Ocean?" that are ready-made for quotation in courting (How much do I love you/I'll tell you no lie/How deep is the ocean?/How high is the sky?), Sondheim shows discomfiture and an inability to make connections. "Why do I feel just the way I always feel,/When my feeling will never show?/You said good-bye when I said hello" (Sondheim cited in Gottfried, 1993, p. 17f). This is less parody than bewildered reaction to adult sexuality and intimacy. Berlin understands (and helps shape) the reciprocity of adult love while Sondheim articulates an inability to interpret others and struggles with the lack of attachment in his life. The best he can offer is that love depends on timing, and that love is a mysterious thing that is hard to express.

These ideas, which return in Sondheim's mature musicals (such as the celebrated Now/Later/Soon sequence of *A Little Night Music*), are defenses against the alienation of feeling. When Sondheim describes love he uses descriptors such as embarrassing, frightening, self-tormenting, full of quicksand and tricks. He also writes of love as enlightening, curious, and taking time, but the weight of the argument shows characters who are anxious and absent, devoid of feeling and lonely. Even with the reconciliation of lovers in the famous song "Send in the Clowns," the lovers remain spatially distant and distinct: "me here at last on the ground/you in mid-air" (Sondheim and Wheeler, 1991a, p. 169). Only by "sending in the clowns," a diversionary tactic used in circus to cover over accidents, can this fundamental discrepancy be overlooked. Intimate attachments are depicted repeatedly—this is a generic feature of the musical—but an emotional void shows underneath. As Madame Armfeldt, commenting on her many lovers and husbands of her youth to her grandchild, states at the beginning of Act 2 of *A Little Night Music*, "To lose a lover, or even a husband or two during one's lifetime can be vexing, but to lose one's teeth is a catastrophe. Bear that in mind, child, as you chomp so recklessly into that ginger snap" (Sondheim and Wheeler, 1991a, p. 135).

The same sentiment is seen in the detachment portrayed by Dot in *Sunday in the Park with George*, when she sings about her lover George Seurat. "Artists are bizarre. Fixed. Cold./That's you, George, you're bizarre. Fixed. Cold./I like that in a man. Fixed. Cold./God, it's hot out here" (Sondheim and Lapine, 1990, p. 6). Sondheim understands each character's neuroses. The characters are projections of aspects of Sondheim's psyche, but they are disclosed and fully analyzed. Dot, before leaving George, has the following exchange with him.

> *Dot:* Yes, George, run to your work. Hide behind your painting. I have come to tell you I am leaving because I thought you might *care* to know—foolish of me, because you care about nothing—
> *George:* I care about many things—
> *Dot:* Things—not people.
> *George:* People, too. I cannot divide my feelings up as neatly as you, and I am not hiding behind my canvas—I am living in it (Sondheim and Lapine, 1990, p. 52).

As George lives in his painting, Sondheim lives through his plays. Despite their protesting, there is no indication that his characters are capable of experiencing deep emotional attachments to others. "No one is you, George,/There we agree,/But others will do, George," Dot tells George (Sondheim and Lapine, 1990, p. 54).

The inability to make connections and the social awkwardness that we see in his depictions of heterosexual relationships is also demonstrated in the homosexual attachments in Sondheim's plays. For example, in *Company*, we see Robert's awkwardness and inability to connect with Peter's indirect sexual advances.

> *Peter:* I think that sometimes you can even know someone for, oh, a long, long time and then suddenly, out of nowhere, you just want to have them—I mean, even an old friend. You just, all of a sudden, desire that intimacy. That closeness.
> *Robert:* Probably. [. . .]
> *Peter:* Do you think that you and I could ever have anything like that?
> *Robert* (*Looks at him for a long and uncomfortable moment. Then a big smile*): Oh, I get it. You're putting me on. Man, you really had me going there, you son of a gun (Sondheim and Furth, 1996, pp. 102f).

Robert struggles to connect, and seems genuinely unable to read the nuances of person-to-person communication.

The characters and situations of the musicals examined so far are conventionally flawed. Not so for Sondheim's two most violent, and most controversial, works: *Sweeney Todd, the Demon Barber of Fleet Street* and *Assassins*. The two works demand special attention. Both focus on psychopathic characters that critics and spectators alike have pronounced "inadmissible to the stage," in Freud's words; both have also been Sondheim's most honest attempts to confront audiences with issues and themes of character pathology and obsession. The works push the envelope of what sorts of characters can be depicted on a musical stage, and simultaneously highlight the nuances of the lesser character pathologies articulated in *Company, A Little Night Music*, and *Sunday in the Park with George*. Sweeney Todd's campaign of death bizarrely is experienced as an attempt to reconstruct his family and his self after long exile to Australia. It begins, razor held aloft, with his exclamation: "My right arm is complete again!" (Sondheim and Wheeler, 1991b, p. 21). But at Todd's core, like for so many of Sondheim's characters, there is the inability to connect. He kills in "benign detachment" and when his partner in crime, the baker Mrs. Lovett, fantasizes about a life of "bourgeois gentility" with the barber, Todd appears completely oblivious to her desires (Gordon, 1992, pp. 241, 244). His relation to his significant others before his Australian exile was anything but complete, and no amount of killing or destruction can make him whole.

Critics have routinely tried to rehabilitate the murderous barber Sweeney Todd and the family of assassins from John Wilkes Booth to John Hinckley (the main characters of *Assassins*) as tragic heroes (see, e.g., Gordon, 1992). The characters themselves resist such easy typing. Sweeney Todd's murderous impulses initially are governed by the traditional logic of the revenge drama, but in the course of the play we observe Todd transform into "a superhuman creature determined upon a course of indiscriminate bloody purgation," a being who "lives to destroy" (Gordon, 1992, pp. 233f). The characters that attempt or succeed to assassinate presidents in *Assassins* are fully grounded in their social, political, and economic realities, but in the musical's penultimate scene Lee Harvey Oswald is persuaded to assassinate Kennedy by his adopted "family" of assassins, rather than being compelled by his own psychological makeup. "You think you can't connect. Connect to us," Sara Jane Moore tells Oswald (Sondheim and Weidman, 1991, p. 100).

CODA: CHILDREN AND ART

A normative psychoanalytic perspective of art understands artistic creation as a derivative of unfulfilled wishes and desires. Sondheim's work is a complex variant of this. His plays are his children which he dotes over, investing them with his current passions and enthusiasms, and then lets loose into the world after the gestation of writing and rehearsal. The relation of art to genealogy is most thoroughly explored in the second act of *Sunday in the Park with George*. Most critics were dissatisfied with this act, which leaves behind the painter George Seurat and his world for his artistic and biological descendents. But for Sondheim, the first act is only the "set up" for the payoff of the second act.

In the first act, the key image of *Sunday in the Park* is the family tree, and at the heart of the second act is a genealogical puzzle. In the second act, Seurat's great-grandson, himself a painter named George, is creating an "art piece commemorating George Seurat's painting A Sunday Afternoon on the Island of La Grande Jatte'" in 1983 (Sondheim and Lapine, 1990, p. 75). The George of the second act has no identifiable mother, which partly makes it so difficult for the audience to follow the genealogy (it can be argued that for Sondheim, this exclusion is no accident). George interacts with a surrogate, his grandmother Marie. Marie, played by the same actress who plays George Seurat's mistress and model Dot in Act One, is herself the daughter of Dot. She believes initially that her father was Louis, a baker who married Dot. But she discovers in this act that she is the daughter of George Seurat. The contemporary George sings repeatedly of "piece by piece [. . .]/putting it together—/that's what counts"; "link by link,/making the connections . . ."; "dot by dot,/ building up the image," "shot by shot," and "bit by bit,/ putting it together" (Sondheim and Lapine, 1990, pp. 86, 88, 89, 92). The sequence co-opts the language of pointillism, an art form that celebrates the atomic dot of color over linear connectedness. The magic of pointillism, of course, is that the dots add up to a complete image from afar. And yet, George stands too close—he cannot put the visual or social puzzle of dots together. George seems unable to grasp Marie's interjection "family—it's all you really have."

He relates to his social and artistic objects in such proximity that all becomes a blur. Like a person with autism, George is unable to determine the balance point for the optimal perspective. George understands the world in pieces; the gestalt for him is made up of many points that are connected only with lots of work. This is the tragedy and pain of the artist—he is unable to intuitively see the world around him as a whole. The contemporary George yearns for a sense of connection with family and the past, but is unable to achieve this. When George sings, "if you feel a sense of coalition,/then you never really stand alone./If you want your work to reach fruition,/What you need's a link with your tradition," he moves toward a holism and sense of identity and inter-relatedness. But this is immediately undermined by the next lines of the song: "And of course a prominent commission,/plus a little formal recognition" (Sondheim and Lapine, 1990, p. 92). Having zoomed in on the precise nature of his social dysfunction, George experiences vertigo and a dizzying lack of recognition.

It is important to recognize that the troubles that both Georges experience in relating to others does not make them social outcasts. They have social impacts on the lives of others, even if they are not able to derive the full benefits of intimacy themselves. Act Two shows Seurat afraid and alone; afraid of "leaving no mark" and "just passing through" (Sondheim and Lapine, 1990, pp. 104f). But Dot reassures him that she will never forget him and that he gave her a life.

George: What did I give you?
Dot: Oh, so many things. You taught me about concentration. At first I thought that meant just being still, but I was to understand it meant much more. You meant to tell me to be where I was—not some place in the past or future. I worried too much about tomorrow. I thought the world could be perfect. I was wrong (Sondheim and Lapine, 1990, p. 105).

The argument of Act One appears to be Seurat's inability to give to other people, but in Act Two we see that Seurat succeeds in stirring Dot's imagination, granting cultural literacy and gaining the fullness of his Being. The brief encounter of Seurat and Dot as lovers and artist-model leaves an eternal legacy of children and art behind them.

Sunday in the Park with George utilizes pointillist art as a metaphor for fractured relationships; *Company* provides a far less abstract model of personal and familial dysfunction. In this musical, Robert demonstrates an inability to form permanent relationships. One aspect of Robert's disconnection stems from his projection of maternal disapproval. Children typically interpret the absence of an unavailable mother as being their own fault. They fantasize that the mother is away because they are not good enough for the mother and speculate about the wrongs they have committed that might have displeased the mother. Sondheim views art as a mode for asserting connections and repairing these narcissistic injuries. The absent mother has been introjected as part of the superego. A lively dance in *Company* by Larry is accompanied by critical murmurings of his friends that might well be taken as meta-reflections on the frivolity of the musical as an artistic form, as seen through the eyes of a stern mother.

> *Robert:* I think they're going to hurt themselves.
> *Joanne:* What if their mothers came in and saw them up there doing that. Think of their poor mothers. He's embarrassing.
> *Robert:* Anyway, those people that laugh and carry on and dance like that—they're not happy.
> *Joanne (Yelling in Larry's direction):* Think of your poor mother!
> *Robert:* He's not what you'd call self-conscious.
> *Joanne:* [. . .] It really shocks me to see a grown man dance like that! (Sondheim and Furth, 1996, pp. 103f).

Indeed, Sondheim's musical theater, like much popular art, *is* embarrassing: it lays out deep emotions for the world to see. As Sondheim reports in an interview: "I get embarrassed hearing my own work. I assume that the cast is embarrassed to sing the stuff. I recognize this as a neurotic reaction, a foolish and unfounded reaction, but nevertheless it is my reaction" (Sondheim quoted in Savran 1994: xx).

Both Sondheim and his ideal "interested spectator" are fluent in the language of the unconscious, and capable of interpreting and expanding upon the intimations of character pathology that Sondheim so ably weaves into his plays. Freud's generation of playgoers demanded identification with a dramatic protagonist for sympathetic suffering in plays which gave "enjoyable shape even to forebodings of misfortune" (Freud, 1905–6, p. 306). Sondheim's theater speaks to a contemporary audience through non-narrative means, expressing the alienation of contemporary life through non-tragic psychopathological characters whose inner selves and psychic struggles are not told through unfolding biographies. Indeed, there is no need for such realist psychologism, for as Sondheim repeatedly asserts, the difficulties that his characters have in making deep connections with others is a shared problem for all who live in the "society of spectacle" (Debord, 1970), in which appearance of value is more precious than reality itself.

BIBLIOGRAPHY

COHEN, D. J. (2001). Life is with people. *Isr. J. Psychiatry Relat. Sci.,* 38 (3–4): 238–40.

DEBORD, G. (1970). *Society of the Spectacle.* Detroit: Black and Red.

FREUD, S. (1905–6). Psychopathic characters on the stage. *Standard Edition* 7:303–310.

GORDON, J. (1992). *Art Isn't Easy: The Theater of Stephen Sondheim.* New York: Da Cappo Press.

GOTTFRIED, M. (1993). *Sondheim.* New York: H. M. Abrams.

SAVRAN, D. (1994) [1988]. An interview with Stephen Sondheim. In *Sunday in the Park with George* by Stephen Sondheim and James Lapine. London: Nick Hern Books, ix–xxvi.

SECREST, M. (1998). *Stephen Sondheim: A Life.* London: Bloomsbury.

SONDHEIM, S., & FURTH, G. (1996) [1970]. *Company: A Musical Comedy.* New York: Theatre Communications Group.

SONDHEIM, S., & LAPINE, J. (1990) [1987]. *Sunday in the Park with George.* London: Nick Hern Books.

SONDHEIM, S., & WEIDMAN, J. (1991). *Assassins.* New York: Theatre Communications Group.

SONDHEIM, S., AND WHEELER, H. (1991a) [1973]. *A Little Night Music.* New York: Applause.

——— (1991b) [1979]. *Sweeney Todd, The Demon Barber of Fleet Street.* London: Nick Hern Books.

WILLIAMS, R. (1983). Drama in a dramatized society. In *Writing in Society.* New York: Verso, 11–21.1.

Blanche, Stella, Tennessee and Rose

The Sibling Relationship in
A Streetcar Named Desire

DANIEL JACOBS, M.D.

Tennessee Williams's guilty and loving relationship with his sister Rose haunted his life and influenced his writing. This paper explores that complex sibling relationship and Williams's attempt to both give voice to and resolve his conflicts over Rose through the writing of A Streetcar Named Desire.

TENNESSEE WILLIAMS'S RELATIONSHIP WITH HIS SISTER ROSE WAS both a close and troubled one. This intense sibling bond initially shored up but later threatened his precarious sense of self. Tennessee's struggle to come to terms with his intense attachment to Rose, as well as his need to separate from her, is expressed in many of his works. Nowhere is his conflict manifest in more searing and dramatic form than in *A Streetcar Named Desire*. This paper explores the ways in which Williams, through the creation of sisters Blanche and Stella (and Stanley Kowalski), expresses his ambivalent attachment to Rose. Through the act of writing, Williams expresses his desire to give his sister life and to sustain his attachment to her. At the same time, he gives voice to his desperate need to establish his own identity, to abandon a loved one to assure his own creative survival.

Training and Supervising Analyst, Boston Psychoanalytic Society and Institute.
The Psychoanalytic Study of the Child 61, ed. Robert A. King, Peter B. Neubauer, Samuel Abrams, and A. Scott Dowling (Yale University Press, copyright © 2006 by Robert A. King, Peter B. Neubauer, Samuel Abrams, and A. Scott Dowling).

INTRODUCTION

Tennessee Williams wrote: "If the writing is honest, it cannot be separated from the man who wrote it." For him the impulse to create arose from "the true expression of passionately personal problems and their purification through work" (*Selected Papers,* p. 120). If we take Williams at his word, and there is no reason not to, then it is fair to ask what was Williams trying to accomplish of a personal nature in writing *A Streetcar Named Desire?* What personal problems might he have been trying to resolve and how successful was he in doing so? In trying to answer these questions we are, of course, faced with the larger subject of creativity and its role in maintaining psychic equilibrium. Studying the way in which one artist, Tennessee Williams, dealt with an immense difficulty in his life by transforming private trauma into public drama may, in the end, help us to explore the role of creativity in our patients' and our own lives.

"Hell is yourself," Williams once said. But for him hell was also, as *Streetcar* amply illustrates, oneself in relation to another. For Williams one of the most painful and loving relationships of his life was that with his elder sister Rose, who was his muse, his alter ego, and his hell. Tennessee remained as faithful to Rose as Tom Wingfield does to his sister Laura in Williams's most autobiographical play, *The Glass Menagerie.* "I tried to leave you behind me, but I am much more faithful than I intended to be," Tom declares to a lost Laura at the end of the play (p. 115). The way in which Williams remained faithful to his sister Rose who was his icon and his albatross, how he transformed his private love and loss into public theater is the subject of this paper. At the center of much of Williams's creative efforts—and certainly in *A Streetcar Named Desire*—is the working through of his ambivalent feelings toward his sister and his anguish and guilt over her fate. For "just as Siamese twins may be joined at the hip or breastbone, Tennessee was joined to his sister, Rose, by the heart . . . In the history of love, there has seldom been such devotion as that which Tennessee showed his lobotomized sister" (Rasky, 1986, p. 51). Although Rasky (1986), Vidal (1985), and Williams himself emphasized his life-long love of Rose and his continuing care for her throughout her life, his relationship with his sister, I believe, was much more complex and troubled than Rasky's quote suggests.

For Tennessee Williams, his relationship with Rose provided him with a much-needed sense of protection and safety while, at the same time, his intense devotion to her and identification with her contributed to his precarious sense of self. Tennessee's relationship with his sister seems to be of the type that Bank and Kahn (1997) call "merging," characterized by the thought and feeling "I'm not sure who I am. Maybe I can be you" (p. 88). As Rasky suggested, Williams was so psychologically entwined with Rose that it was hard for him to know where he left off and she began. He could never fully separate his fate from hers, always feeling that only the most porous of membranes kept him from becoming mad as she was. There were times he referred to himself as Rose and would dress in woman's clothes. His greatest fear was that he would share the same fate as befell her. In his two early successes, *The Glass Menagerie* and *A Streetcar Named Desire*, we can witness Williams's conflict over his love for and identification with Rose and his guilt over the need to leave her to establish his own identity as an artist. *The Glass Menagerie* is, in good part, a justification for Tennessee's departure from his family. It is a plea for why he must leave the ineffective Laura (his castrated self) behind and pursue his own path as an artist. But Williams's own justifications and explanations that are expressed by Tom Wingfield in that play seem only a temporary stay against self-recrimination. For, in *Streetcar*, Williams returns in a much more searing and violent manner to the same theme of abandonment of a sibling in order to preserve oneself. Examining Williams's intense attachment to Rose and the effect of her illness upon him and his work is an interesting piece of biographical history, but it can also lead to a greater understanding of the role of creativity in maintaining psychic equilibrium and a sense of self.

CHILDHOOD

Rose Williams, the first child and only daughter of Cornelius and Edwina, was born on November 19, 1909. Two years after her birth, Thomas Lanier (called "Tom" by his family and later known as "Tennessee") was born. Eight years later another brother, William Dakin, arrived. Tom idolized his sister as a youngster. He spent hours playing with her and seemed to need her outgoing and imaginative spirit to counteract his own shyness. The intensity of his need for and identifications with Rose (and with his mother, Edwina) if not created by, were, no doubt, magnified by the conditions of family life.

Tom's early years were happy ones. This was, in main part, due to the fact that Edwina and her children were living with her parents whom Tom loved. His father, Cornelius, a traveling salesman at the time, was often on the road. At age five, however, Tom developed a serious case of diphtheria that was followed by sequelae of Bright's disease and an inability to walk that lasted two years. Whether this weakness of his legs was due to physical illness or was of an hysterical nature is unclear, but it did mean that Tom, instead of playing outdoors with other boys, was at home, thrown into the company of his doting mother, grandmother, and sister most of the time. Despite his difficulties, Tom remembered those times with great fondness. "My sister and I were gloriously happy. We sailed paper boats in washtubs of water, cut lovely paper dolls out of huge mail order catalogues, kept two white rabbits under the back porch, baked mud pies in the sun upon the front walk, climbed up and slid down the big wood pile, collected from neighboring alleys and trash piles bits of colored glass that were diamonds and rubies and sapphires and emeralds" (E. Williams, p. 19).

Things changed drastically when Cornelius got a desk job with the Shoe Company, and the family moved to St. Louis when Tom was nine. His beloved grandparents were left behind. The places where they lived in St. Louis were dreary, and the family moved nine times before settling into what was to be the family home. Cornelius's sedentary job meant he was home most nights where the animosity between himself and Edwina grew and was readily apparent to the children. While on the road, Cornelius's heavy drinking and womanizing was more easily overlooked, but now it could not be denied. "He had no sex from Mother," Dakin reported, "so he was not adverse to picking up a discreet female companion whenever opportunity beckoned. . . . Mother had a lot of faults—in that she overdid the puritan business—and she considered sex to be dirty" (Leverich, p. 133). The house was filled with bitter and violent quarrels. "He flew into a rage," Edwina recorded in her diary, "and threatened me. I locked my door and tried to reason with him through the closed door. 'Open that door or I'll bust it in!' Before I could obey the command he had suited the action to the word, the lock broke, the door flew open striking me on the nose and knocking me to the floor where I lay dazed" (p. 138). Such encounters no doubt terrified Tom. "Then the spell of perfect peace was broken. A loud voice was heard and heavy footsteps. Doors were slammed, furniture was kicked and banged. . . ." Williams recalled (E. Williams, p. 26). His own fears, along with his mother's disparagement of sexuality and male aggression, led Tom to have difficulties with his own assertiveness. He was called a sissy at school and was tormented by his peers. "I was scared to death of everyone on earth and particularly of public school boys," he reported later (E. Williams, p. 30). He found refuge from a frightening world in the relationship with his sister. "The poor children," Williams wrote, "used to run all over town, but my sister and I played in our own back yard . . . We were so close to each other, we had no need of others" (Nelson, p. 4). Tom reported that Rose had, like his character Laura Wingfield, a glass menagerie with which she and her brother played. "The glass figures," Williams wrote, "stood for all the small tender things that relieve the austere pattern of life and make it endurable to the sensitive" (Nelson, p. 8). In the fragile tenderness of a sibling only two years older than him, in the world they created out of shimmering glass, Williams found a safe haven. When they were older, Rose and Tom went to dances together and to the movies. Dakin, the youngest sibling, reported that while Rose was always affectionate toward him, it was Tom she truly loved (Leverich, 1995, p. 143).

ROSE'S ILLNESS

In her late adolescence, however, Rose began to show signs of disturbance. She suffered from complaints of indigestion and abdominal pain that compromised her studies and social functioning. By 1930, after several hospitalizations for these somatic complaints, accompanied, at times, by thoughts she'd been poisoned, her troubles were diagnosed as nervous. Her behavior over the next decade became more irrational. During those years when Rose's sexual preoccupations became prominent, her eagerness to have a gentleman caller grew more extreme, and her depressions more severe. Noting the disturbing changes in his sister, Tennessee began to mourn the loss of the Rose he had known. In his autobiographical story "The Resemblance Between a Violin Case and a Coffin," Tennessee wrote:

> They [grandmother and mother] never before bothered over the fact that I had depended so much on the companionship of my sister. But now they were continually asking me why I did not make friends with other children. I was ashamed to tell them that other children frightened me nor was I willing to admit that my sister's wild imagination and inexhaustible spirits made all other substitute companions seem like the shadows of shades, for now that she had abandoned me. . . . I too felt resentful even to acknowledge secretly how much had been lost through what she had taken away (*Collected Stories*, p. 272).

The continued task of separation and individuation and mourning that occurs in normal adolescence was compromised by real family grief and the severe loss of a loved one. Entering the "broken terrain and wilderness" of his own adolescence Tom grieved Rose's increasing separation from him, first into adolescent concerns of her own and then into madness. Tom "saw that it was all over . . . put away in a box like a doll no longer cared for, the magical intimacy of our childhood together, the soap bubble afternoons and the games with apple dolls cut out of catalogue dresses and the breathless races here and there on our wheels" (Leverich, pp. 62–63). He dealt with the increasing psychological separation from Rose through intense imitation and identification as his description in the short story mentioned illustrates. He wrote, "My sister's obsession with Richard may have been even more intense than mine. Since mine was copied from hers, hers was probably even more intense than mine. But while mine was of a shy and sorrowful kind, involved with my sense of abandonment, hers at first seemed joyous. She had fallen in love. As always I followed suit" (p. 275).

Rose grew increasingly moody and withdrawn, only to suddenly explode into bouts of weeping or rage. Never graduating from college, she worked sporadically, as her precarious mental health allowed. She argued at home with her mother, spoke aloud about her sexual fantasies, and became threatening toward her father. In 1935, she was dismissed from teaching Sunday school after supposedly spreading rumors that the rector of St. George and St. Michael's Episcopal Church had Jewish blood in him. Her dismissal precipitated one of her now frequent hospitalizations. By 1937, she had become frankly delusional and would be diagnosed as schizophrenic. Her language became increasingly vulgar—something her mother particularly could not abide—and her behavior more unpredictable and more violent. That year Tom wrote in his journal, "Tragedy. I write that word knowing the full meaning of it. We have had no deaths in our family, but slowly by degrees something was happening much uglier and more terrible than death. Now we are forced to see it, know it. The thought is an aching numbness—a horror" (E. Williams). In the use of "we" Tom indicates the way in which his sister's illness has thrown him once again back into the family and made separation from them even more difficult.

Rose entered Farmington State Hospital in 1937. Almost 60 years of institutional life lay ahead of her. The insulin shock treatments instituted at Farmington proved of little benefit. In 1939 Williams wrote of his visit to his psychotic sister: her talk "was so obscene—she laughed and spoke continual obscenities" (Leverich, p. 487). Her doctor appeared to Tennessee a cold, unsympathetic man who stated that her condition was hopeless, and her mental state was likely to deteriorate even more. It was a horrible ordeal for Tom, especially as he feared the same end for himself. In 1943, with the consent of her parents but without Tennessee's knowledge, Rose underwent a prefrontal lobe lobotomy. After the surgery, Edwina wrote to Tom of his sister's "head operation" that meant her permanent and irretrievable loss. Tom felt very guilty for having been away pursuing his studies, out of the loop of decision making, and inattentive to his sister's fate. For Williams the surgery was "a tragically mistaken procedure" that deprived her of any possibility of returning to normal life. "A cord breaking. 1000 miles away. Rose. Her head cut open. A knife thrust in her brain. Me. Here. Smoking" (Williams, 1972, p. 251).

INFLUENCE OF ROSE ON HER BROTHER'S EARLY PLAYS

The breaking of the magical childhood connection to Rose and the solace she represented, his inability to recall her to a full life together, and his guilt over his own tenuous mental survival were to haunt Tennessee and shape his plays. In his essay "The Catastrophe of Success" (1975), Williams wrote, "The monosyllable of the clock is Loss, loss, loss, unless you devote your heart to its opposition"(p.17). His heart's opposition took the form of writing and in his first two great plays, he finds and loses Rose who is transformed first into Laura in *The Glass Menagerie* and then into Blanche of *A Streetcar Named Desire*. Williams wrote, "When Wordsworth speaks of daffodils or Shelley of the skylark or Hart Crane of the delicate and aspiring structure of Brooklyn Bridge, the screen imagism is not so opaque that you cannot surmise at some distance behind it the ghostly and eluctable form of Ophelia" (Leverich, 1995, p. 536). And so, too, in creation of both Laura and Blanche, roses who never bloom, Tom's sister, lobotomized by a world that cannot understand or help her, hovers in the wings.

In his most clearly autobiographical play *The Glass Menagerie*, Laura, the protagonist's sister, is modeled on Rose in the earlier stages of her illness. Laura in the play is a shy, reclusive frightened girl unable to free herself from a domineering mother, and she is further destroyed by meeting her brother's friend Jim. Jim, who Amanda insists on treating as a gentleman caller for her daughter, is a representative of the world of progress. Literal, optimistic, forward-looking, he is a man who hopes to advance himself by "punching the clock" in an increasingly industrialized world. Jim is an average joe, the future stumblebum, that Tom Wingfield, the protagonist of the play, fears he will become if he does not leave the suffocating confines of family life. *The Glass Menagerie* was begun when Williams was thirty-two. Injured, broke, and unsuccessful, he had returned to his unhappy childhood home and visited for the first time since her surgery his now lobotomized sister in a state hospital nearby. The play worked on during this visit to St. Louis can be read, in part, as Williams's guilt ridden justification to himself and others for his departing again from his family. It is a plea as to why he must leave his forever-altered sister (his castrated self) behind and in order to find his own voice (Jacobs, 2003). But, while Tennessee does, after some months, leave St. Louis and family behind, he does not relinquish his attachment to his sister and his guilt over her institutionalized state and his own tenuous survival. In his second major play, *Streetcar,* Williams returns to a much more searing exploration of his need to leave a sibling he loves and to suppress the identifications with her in order to establish a clearer sense of himself.

A Streetcar Named Desire

In leaving St. Louis after the visit to his family in 1943 and in finishing *The Glass Menagerie* (first produced in 1945), Williams alters the course of his life. The play is a great success and propels him into fame and fortune beyond his imagining and beyond his capacity to tolerate (Williams, "The Catastrophe of Success"). By then another play is forming in his mind and he retreats from notoriety to Mexico where he begins for a short time to work on what was to become *A Streetcar Named Desire.*

   In that play Blanche Dubois, a sad and lonely southern belle of thirty, has suffered the loss of Belle Reve, her family's ancestral home. She arrives in New Orleans to visit her younger sister Stella, who has married the uncultured working class bloke Stanley Kowalski. Stanley enjoys bowling and poker and sex. He cannot stand Blanche's affectations and illusions of a grand life and is threatened by his sister-in-law's wish to separate Stella from him. Hurt and vengeful, Stanley exposes Blanche's tragic and sordid past, preventing Blanche's last chance for happiness and respectability with Stanley's friend Mitch. Stanley reveals to all that far from being a respectable school teacher who would only consider a chaste courtship with Mitch, Blanche has a reputation as a loose woman who has, among many men and boys, seduced one of her own high school students and has been dismissed. Having ruined the budding relationship of Mitch and Blanche and destroyed any chance of Blanche's starting a new life, in a last act of retributive cruelty Stanley rapes her. Blanche suffers a complete breakdown and is led away to an asylum where she will be, as she has been in her promiscuity, "dependent on the kindness of strangers." Her accusations that Stanley raped her are thought by Stella to be part of her delusions. Her sister in her own need to save herself and adequately nurture her newborn child can only think that her sister is mad. She goes along with her sister's institutionalization.

> *Stella:* I couldn't believe her story and go on living with Stanley.
> *Eunice* [her neighbor]: Don't ever believe it. Life has to go on. No matter what happens, you have to keep going.

Later in the scene, Stella filled with anguish cries: "Oh my God, Eunice help me! Don't let them do that to her, don't let them hurt her. Oh, God, please God, don't hurt her. What are they doing to her? What are they doing?" Eunice responds: "No, honey, no, no, honey. Stay here. Don't go back there. Stay with me and don't look"(p. 140).

The anguish of Stella reflects Tennessee's own anguish about his sister, her illness, and her lobotomy, with all its associations to primal scene and castration. Tennessee is also Eunice, encouraging himself to hold on to life, not to look back. It is the desperate wish to move forward into life, brutal as it can be, and the regressive pull toward disaster that comprises the dramatic tension in much of his work and in his life. Williams keeps asking what price must we pay for our own clinging to sanity, what part of us must be shut away in order to survive. For Stella to believe her sister's story of rape, to leave Stanley, means the end of her connection to hope and a life giving force of her husband's potency. At the play's very beginning he throws her a package of bloody, uncooked meat, the symbol of what he can provide. He is her nurturer, her connection to life and fecundity in however raw a form. Yet to keep him, she must not look on some truths. She must give up any dream of a return to Belle Reve (beautiful dream), just as Tennessee has to mourn the loss of his magical childhood with its intense closeness to his sister. Stella is left with a baby to sustain her. Tennessee without progeny is left with his own creativity to help him keep alive. Tennessee wrote, "the fear of the world, the fight to face it and not run away, is the realist things in all experience to me" (*Selected Letters*, pp. 401–402). Both Blanche and Stella try to fight and not run away. Blanche tries but like Rose cannot succeed. Stella is more successful, but the price of her survival is guilt and lingering doubt. Remorse and longing are evident as in her last words in the play, "Blanche! Blanche! Blanche!" echoing Stanley's earlier anguished cry of "Stella!" and what, I believe, is Tennessee's cry for his sister.

"I felt 'Streetcar' so intensely it terrified me," Williams wrote. "I couldn't work for several months I was so terrified" (Williams, *Conversations*, p. 215). What terrified Tennessee so? The reliving of his own family tragedy? Probably. His identification with Blanche and Rose and his fears for his own sanity? No doubt. But to my mind what threatened to overwhelm him was his intense conflict: the wish to be with Rose and his guilty wish to leave her—a departure that he felt had initially contributed to her destruction. (He was away from home pursuing his own studies when she, without his knowledge, was lobotomized.) And it is in Williams's creative impulse and the resulting plays that both wishes to re-find Rose and to leave her can be found. In *The Glass Menagerie* and then in *Streetcar* he resurrects a disabled sibling only to have her abandoned. And in each instance the justification is the same: One must go on no matter what happens as Eunice says near the end of *Streetcar.* So Stella chooses life—her husband and her child.

A play may be likened to a dream in which all of the characters speak for conflicting and wish fulfilling aspects of its author. There is little doubt that Blanche, trying to forget her past in promiscuity and alcohol, haunted by a love she betrayed, is a portrait of Williams. "We are both hysterics," he once said. "I don't want realism, I want magic." Blanche cries, "I don't tell the truth, I tell what ought to be the truth." Williams found his magic in the theater, in the artful dissembling of drama, in plays that are truth and fiction at the same time. He wrote: "It is only in his work that an artist can find reality and satisfaction, for the actual world is less intense than the world of his invention" (Williams, 1978, p. 19).

But if Williams resembles Blanche, he feels like Stanley. The lobotomy that Tennessee felt responsible for by his absence and lack of involvement with his sister is transformed into a rape. The knife cutting into Rose's brain becomes Stanley's invasion of Blanche's body that drives her into what one suspects is permanent madness and institutionalization. And Tennessee is capable, like Stanley, of buying for someone a one-way ticket out of his life. (During the time he was working on *Streetcar,* he bought such a ticket for his lover Poncho Rodriguez y Gonzales when Williams could no longer stand Poncho's jealous rages.) But Williams did not have Stanley's keen sense of who he is and what he wants from life. Stanley, unlike Tennessee, is a man unconflicted about his state of being. At the same time, Williams has made us feel, as he was, appalled by Stanley's aggression. In order to save his own life, he denies another life. Yet it was precisely that which Williams, I think, felt he had done to Rose.

Stella, in the end, must choose between loyalty to her sister and loyalty to Stanley. Cardullo (1997) suggests that hers is a spiritual death—that her future is to be tortured by self-recriminations and to live vicariously through her children. Certainly, that is a possibility, but the play's ending is ambiguous. In my view, Stella's dilemma is the plight of all of us who must live surrounded by both beauty and horror. But she also represents the artist who must create (procreate) in the midst of life's painful contradictions. Recalling his childhood Williams wrote, "The area way [the alley behind his family's flat in St. Louis where cats were torn to pieces by dogs] was one thing—my sister's white curtains and glass menagerie were another. Somewhere between them was the world we lived in" (Nelson, 191, p. 8). Faced with the contradictory nature of existence, the artist who creates beauty while still facing the horror is always in an untenable position, living like Stella between Blanche and Stanley, living like Tennessee between the memory of Rose and the reality of who she had become. Stella's giving birth represents William's own steely willingness to survive and to remain creative, to find comfort in that capacity, in the face of the world's brutality.

DISCUSSION

Melanie Klein described the creative impulse as arising within the depressive position. It is born, she believed, out of the need to repair the lost or damaged object that the individual in his mind has harmed. The creative act becomes one of the modes of achieving that reparation and reconciliation. Certainly, Tennessee's bringing back representations of his sister as Blanche in *Streetcar* and Laura in *The Glass Menagerie* keeps Rose alive and restores her, if only briefly, to some form of life outside of institutionalization and free of surgery. But if the aim of creativity is restoration of the lost object, we might ask why the representation of Rose is of a compromised woman and not the pre-psychotic exuberant girl of his childhood memory. Is it only an adherence to reality and the re-working of traumatic loss that keeps Williams from transforming Rose through the magic of theater into the healthy woman and dear companion he longed for? Or is his love for Rose more complicated than is often described?

Chasseguet-Smirgel begins to provide an answer to these questions. She suggests that the creative restoration of the other that Klein describes is based on the repression of sadistic drives toward the object and upon the use of reaction formations. She believes creation often brings about guilt feelings in the artist. The repressed aggression often returns in the form of intense self-reproach. Chasseguet-Smirgel posits that the main function of creative work is not the restoration of the other as Klein suggests, but rather the restoration of the artist's own integrity and sense of self, savaged by castration and loss. The artist, through the act of creating, fills in all the gaps in his maturation, at all levels of development, to attain a sense of narcissistic completeness. The creative work represents a higher degree of discharge of the sadistic drive in sublimated fashion rather than its repression as Klein suggested. Certainly one can see in the fate of crippled Laura and a violated Blanche the writer's sublimated sadism toward his sister. In neither *The Glass Menagerie* nor *Streetcar* does he restore a sister to health or write a fantasy of siblings who can help one another or live together in any kind of harmony. Rather through Tom Wingfield's and Stella Kowalski's wish and need to leave their sister and sister-in-law behind Williams portrays his own deep ambivalence toward Rose.

In the interchange between siblings in *Streetcar,* Williams in the voice of Stella, the one who survives, justifies the abandonment of a sibling:

> *Blanche:* You left. I stayed and struggled. You came to New Orleans and looked out for yourself.
> *Stella:* The best I could do was make my own living, Blanche. (p. 25)

Living here has a double meaning—to be alive as well as to earn an income. Living for Williams was writing—often writing about his sister from whom he must separate in order to write.

Chasseguet-Smirgel believes creativity is self creation and the creative act derives its deepest impulse from the desire to mitigate, by one's own means, the deficiencies left and caused by others. On a certain level, the creator expects nothing from anybody and attains total autonomy through his activity. "Creativity's deepest impulse, its living strength, as we know it, is essentially linked to freedom" (p. 404).

In *Streetcar* Williams tries to free himself from his identification with Rose and the threat of castration and loss of self she represents. Tennessee blamed his mother for making him into a sissy and for allowing Rose to undergo her fateful surgery. What comfort and repair the sibling relationship might give to the difficulties of the mother-son relationship were rent asunder by Rose's illness and lobotomy.

Edwardo Weiss in explaining trauma and its relations to castration
has written:

> Love objects become, as we know, libidinally bound to the ego, as if
> they were a part of it. If they are torn away from it, the ego acts as
> though it had sustained mutilation. The open wound thus produced
> in it is just what comes to expression as mental pain (1934, p. 12).

In the act of playwriting about this pain, his own and his sister's,
Williams, as Chasseguet-Smirgel suggests, repairs the severe injury to
himself. As Lawrence wrote, "one sheds one's sicknesses in books, re-
peats and presents again one's emotions to be master of them"
(Aberach, 1989, p. 274). Leichtman (1985) notes that older siblings
have a critical influence on the consolidation of identity and that sep-
arating and individuating from them constitutes an important developmental task (p.112). In *Streetcar*, Williams returns to this developmental task as he had in *The Glass Menagerie*. Through his writing, he
once again escapes the engulfment that Laura, Blanche, and Rose
represent. Despite, or perhaps because of, his success in making his
"own living," his aggression toward, guilt about, and longing for Rose
is apparent. They are demonstrated in the terrible way Blanche is
condemned to madness by the inability of others to understand or
help her. In the loss of Mitch, the rape by Stanley, and the abandonment by Stella, Blanche's psychic mutilation is complete. Her mental
anguish in finding herself alone and dependent only on the kindness
of strangers leads to her total collapse.

Tennessee's longing for Rose is manifest by the fact that he has in
the very act of writing the play linked himself to Blanche and thus to
Rose forever. Like figures on a Grecian urn, *Streetcar* forever both
unites him with and separates him from his sister who, I think, both
helped maintain his sanity when he was a child, only to pose a threat
to it in later life. If the creative act were entirely successful in its aims
at restoration of the artist's integrity and triumph over trauma, then
it would not have to be repeated. But as Robert Penn Warren noted,
poetry is only a temporary stay against confusion. The artist must
keep creating to maintain his sense of self. And so too, Williams over
and over would return in his work to his relationship with Rose, still
seeking to be with her while at the same time trying to free himself
from her.

Postscript: After his success made it possible, Tennessee took care
of Rose. Portions of the royalties he received were set aside for her
support. In 1951, he moved her to a sanitarium in Ossining, New
York, so she would be closer to him. He visited her frequently and of-

ten took her out with him to dinner or theater. For a while he moved her to Key West where he was living, but her behavior proved unmanageable. She died in a nursing home in Tarrytown, New York, on September 4, 1996, surviving Tennessee by thirteen years.

BIBLIOGRAPHY

ABERACH, D. (1989). Creativity and the survivor: The struggle for mastery. *Int. Rev. Psycho-anal.* 16:273–286.
ADLER, T. (1990). *The Moth and the Lantern.* Boston: Twayne Publishers.
BANK S., & KAHN, M. (1997). *The Sibling Bond.* New York: Basic Books.
CARDULLO, B. (1997). Drama of Intimacy and Tragedy of Incomprehension. In: Tharpe, J. Ed. *Tennessee Williams: A Tribute.* Jackson: University of Mississippi Press.
CHASSEGUET-SMIRGEL, J. (1984). Thoughts on the concept of reparation and the hierarchy of creative acts. *Int. R. Psycho-Anal.* 11:399–406.
JACOBS, D. (2003). Tennessee Williams: The uses of declarative memory in "The Glass Menagerie." *J. of Am. Psychoanal. Assoc.* 50:1259–1270.
LEICHTMAN, M. (1985). The influence of the older sibling on the separation-individuation process. *Psychoanal. S. Child* 40:111–161.
LEVERICH, L. (1995). *Tom.* New York: W. W. Norton.
NELSON, B. (1961). *Tennesseee Williams: The Man and His Work.* New York: Ivan Obolensky.
RASKY, H. (1986). *Tennessee Williams: A Portrait in Laughter and Lamentation.* Niagara Falls: Mosaic Press.
VIDAL, G. (1985). Introduction. In: *Tennessee Williams. Collected Stories.* New York: New Directions.
WEISS, E. (1934) Bodily pain and mental pain. *Int. J. Psychoanal.* 15:1–13
WILLIAMS, E., WITH L. FREEMAN (1963). *Remember Me to Tom.* New York: Putnam and Sons.
WILLIAMS, TENNESSEE (1945). *The Glass Menagerie.* New York: New Directions Paperback Edition, 1975.
——— (1947). A *Streetcar Named Desire.* New York: Signet Paperback (1951).
——— (1972). *Memoirs.* New York: Doubleday & Co.
——— (1975). "The catastrophe of success." In *The Glass Menagerie.* New York: New Directions paperback edition.
——— (1978). *Where I Live: Selected Essays.* Eds. C. Day and B. Woods. New York: New Directions.
——— (1986). *Conversations.* Ed. A. Devlin. Jackson: University of Mississippi Press.
——— (2000). *Selected Letters.* Eds. A. Devlin and N. Tischler. New York: New Directions.
——— "The Resemblance Between a Violin Case and a Coffin." In *Collected Stories* (1985). New York: New Directions.

The Invention of Purgatory

A Note on the Historical Pedigree of the Superego

EUGENE MAHON, M.D.

Stoppard (1998) in his great play "The Invention of Love" has suggested that the love poem "Like everything else, like clocks and trousers and algebra . . . had to be invented" *(emphasis added). In this essay I argue that the concept of Purgatory was not always with us either, but also had to be invented. If theology got the concept started, I suggest that eventually it may have found its way into psychology, even influencing psychoanalytic ideas about the origins of the Superego. If the concepts Heaven and Hell reflect primitive Superego absolutes, the concept of Purgatory seems like the primitive Superego modulating its own severity and becoming more mature in the process. This influence of a theological concept (Purgatory) on a psychoanalytic concept (Superego) is then outlined and explicated in some detail.*

THE CONCEPT OF AN AFTERLIFE MUST BE AS OLD AS HUMAN CONSCIOUS-ness of mortality, the mind's first attempt to disavow the unbearable realization of its own finiteness. Heaven, Hell, and eventually Purgatory were concepts that tried to imagine the scope and co-ordinates of this concept *afterlife*. For Purgatory, what began as a concept seems to have eventually become concrete fact, which includes specific geographic locations—with entrances into Purgatory being located in

Training and Supervising Analyst, Center for Psychoanalytic Training and Research, Columbia College of Physicians and Surgeons; private practice of Adult and Child Analysis, New York City.

The Psychoanalytic Study of the Child 61, ed. Robert A. King, Peter B. Neubauer, Samuel Abrams, and A. Scott Dowling (Yale University Press, copyright © 2006 by Robert A. King, Peter B. Neubauer, Samuel Abrams, and A. Scott Dowling).

Ireland and Sicily. If Heaven and Hell sound absolute in their depiction of total damnation or total eternal salvation, Purgatory seems to represent a yearning for continued communication with the afterlife in an attempt to modify the imagined sufferings of departed "souls." Is the psychology that led to the concept of Purgatory a possible forerunner of the later Freudian concept of the superego, which, at its most mature, rejects splitting and magical absolutism in favor of a more reasoned assessment of guilt and pleasure? This question is addressed in some detail in this paper. The irony of a theological concept being perhaps the necessary antecedent of a key concept in the godless subsequent psychology of psychoanalysis is presented and explored.

Since Dante's time Purgatory has always conjured up images of the aesthetic imagination of the great poet and how "real" he made the unsubstantial (Hell, Purgatory, Paradise) feel for all of us. While religion may have lost much of the power it once held as an artistic and intellectual phenomenon, Dante's brilliance seems to glow with supernatural, transcendent immutability. And Purgatory, once considered an actual place in Catholic imagination, but mere smoke and mirrors in the fierce Protestant assault on the concept, may have a kernel of humanistic yearning in it, that continues to inform modern consciousness whether it chooses to be aware of it or not. Or so I will argue in this essay, suggesting that Freud's conceptualization of the superego, startlingly original as its unconscious dimensions were, must have been influenced by the prior history of ideas in general, and the concept of Purgatory in particular. Freud's originality notwithstanding, I suggest that the "historical" consciousness that "invented" Purgatory is analogous and perhaps preparatory to the psychoanalytic intuition that spawned the concept of the superego.

Purgatory itself is obviously a product of "afterlife" psychology, which must be briefly described in general before the specific role of Purgatory and superego development can be addressed. The concept of the afterlife is as old as the consciousness of mortality itself: the mind's disbelief at the existential shock of mortality needed to conceptualize a space where life could begin again however transformed. The imagined space would soon become conceptually cluttered however. While one designated place, Sheol or Hades, seemed enough for Hebrew or Greek respectively, eventually the space got divided between Heaven and Hell, with Purgatory a late arrival historically speaking. Initially, Purgatory was "conceptual" but Le Goff (1981) traces how, by the twelfth century, it had become more concrete and even assumed a geographic identity. By the sixteenth century, a civil war practically developed between Protestants and Catholics when Luther denounced Rome for cashing in on the saving of souls in Purgatory through the marketing of "indulgences." The Protestant backlash led to the destruction of Catholic churches and purgatorial sites: this was an attempt to do away with the reification of these purgatorial souls and their exploitation by Rome in the interest of financial greed. Stephen Greenblatt, in his intriguing book on Hamlet, poses a fascinating question: Where did all the purgatorial ghosts go when banished by political, religious decree in the sixteenth century? They ended up on the Elizabethan stage, according to Greenblatt, exploited most dramatically by perhaps the greatest dramatist of all time, William Shakespeare. (That Shakespeare's father may have been a conflicted Catholic in precarious times and that his son's childhood may not have escaped such perilous influence is an irony that cannot be addressed at this time.)

If Greenblatt's Purgatorial ghosts ended up on the Elizabethan stage and then lost their dramatic allure when Shakespeare was no longer alive to exploit them, I would like to argue that after centuries of neglect they washed up again in Vienna, summoned by a very different type of conjurer, a neurologist, turned hypnotist, turned psychoanalyst, called Sigmund Freud. The spark of developmental, psychological decency that got the whole concept of Purgatory started couldn't be extinguished, it would seem. By decency I mean the human yearning for a way out of the theological impasse of the absolutes Heaven and Hell. These theological absolutes (Heaven and Hell) were the cultural, religious correlatives of splitting perhaps, before the psychology of such Manichean defense mechanisms was conceived or written about. Purgatory, it would seem, was an initial theological breakthrough of the religious mind, a way out of the choice between absolute terror and absolute redemption that Heaven and Hell posited. Purgatory suggested that splitting was not absolutely necessary. A psychoanalytic interpretation of this theological breakthrough would suggest that death wishes do not have to lead to absolute destruction of the object or absolute destruction of the self by imagined retaliations. Continuing dialogue might be possible if the landscape of the mind were not depicted so gothically, so grotesquely, so irrevocably. Le Goff argues that this "softening" of the sense of social justice was a result of the new optimism of the citizen of the twelfth century. In earlier centuries when life seemed a short-lived precarious thing balanced briefly on the doomed scales of birth and premature death, Heaven and Hell seemed absolutes that captured existential reality pretty accurately. But as a new sense of agency emerged in a less helpless citizenry, human psychology called for more than splitting. If Heaven could wait, Hell could too: maybe compromise could be entertained. Purgatory, a precursor of Freudian thought, was born.

Is it too fanciful to picture the Purgatorial ghosts ending up on Sigmund Freud's couch toward the end of the nineteenth century? Consider the climate of Freud's early research with Breuer into the psychosomatics that confronted them before there was a word for such symptomatology other than the pejorative *hysteria*. Sensing that memory was at the core of psychological illness, that hysterics were sick because of reminiscences, the two pioneers sought in their primitive chimney sweeping talking cure to *purge* the mind of its constipated memory blockages. If this is the language of intestinal enemas, it is also the language of *purgation*, the language of hope. Guilty memories causing a colic of the mind could be *purged* with hands on forehead, hypnotic suggestions, and verbal enemas that could free up the strangulated associations of the mind and release the soul from the *hell* of its internal misery. If the gates of Hell told a story of Dante's hopelessness ("Abandon hope all ye who enter here"), psychoanalysis suggested that "mind forged manacles" (William Blake's term) could be broken. The theological dialogue that Purgatory had suggested centuries earlier could now, without its primitive elements of fear and torture, be engaged psychoanalytically. The stage was set for the unconscious, the ego, the superego: a new language of mourning and psychic healing was nearing its gestation!

I am not suggesting that Freud had the slightest interest in Purgatory. I *am* suggesting that if one thinks of the history of ideas as one communal mind in the process of discovery and development, the psychological advance from splitting (Heaven and Hell) to a redemptive Purgatory, and from Purgatory to a psychoanalytic vision of a mature superego could be seen as a continuum: theological conscience became psychoanalytic and grew up as it learned more about the unconscious forces that not only determined its theories of original sin and damnation but could also inform its capacity to regulate guilt and pleasure in a non-neurotic fashion, using the power of insight.

Freud often wrote daringly and insightfully about religion (Demonological Neurosis, Totem and Taboo, etc.) but after he had "reduced" it to its oedipal roots, he seemed uninterested in it as an aesthetic or developmental window into the workings of the "historical" mind. Did Jung's less than rigorous brand of "mystical" psychoanalysis convince Freud to leave that kind of delving to his Swiss colleague whose character and "science" he was more and more eager to differentiate from, if not dismiss? I would like to argue that since religious ideas are products of the human mind like any other collective ideas, must they not reveal manifest and latent facets of the mind's contents and structures, not to mention the cultural aliment that nourished their origins? Take the concept of the soul for instance, and all its synonyms—ghost, spirit, etc. Since mortality first dawned on human consciousness surely this concept was hovering nearby, crying out for expression and explication. And if it has been abandoned by a more modern existential mind, its seductive regressive appeal is hardly extinct whenever human transience is hard to bear and the mind in extremis longs for an illusive permanence. I raise the issue of "soul" since obviously it is at the heart of the concept of Purgatory as well as the more ancient concepts, Heaven and Hell. Dante's Purgatory is clearly located on earth suggesting that the mind's prior inventions of Heaven and Hell were not "down to earth" enough for the great Italian poet or most of the citizens of the time. A mind that could concoct abstractions and imaginary locales of suffering and redemption needed, according to Le Goff, concrete "spatialization of thought" to really feel at home. According to Le Goff (1981), a concept that was an abstraction to Augustine, "Purgatory" being only *adjectival* in the fourth century, by the twelfth had assumed its verbal identity as a noun and began to be thought of as a place with portals of entry in Sicily and Ireland! The soul, born in abstraction perhaps, imagination reaching beyond the finiteness of flesh, had redefined itself as a concrete resident of an actual earthly location. If this seems preposterous to a modern skeptic, it is arresting to consider that as fine a mind as Thomas More's in the sixteenth century (in his "Supplication of Souls") writes as if he could transmit the actual communications of the souls in Purgatory as they cried out for memorial continuity, pleading with neglectful relatives not to be forgotten. Granted, More was defending the party line against the arch anti-Purgatorial lawyer and polemicist Simon Fish (Greenblatt, 2001, p. 10) and More's metaphors may have leaned on exaggeration for added emphasis: nonetheless it seems clear that to Thomas More souls were more than disembodied abstractions. They had voices and they could pull at heartstrings! What is an atheist psychoanalyst to make of all this five or fifteen centuries later?

If we assume that Purgatory as place, or soul as entity has no substantial reality, their *theological* reality and meaning for the human mind in the past and in the present cannot be dismissed, unless psychoanalysis adopts a prejudicial attitude toward human products and beliefs that run counter to its own. If nothing human is alien to man at least since the time of Protagoras, no human expression can fall beyond the inquiry of psychoanalysis without diminishing the scope and meaning of the whole enterprise, not to mention the loss of an opportunity to study yet another facet of that great adventure called mind.

I would like to suggest that the concept of souls in Purgatory raises interesting and challenging ideas for a psychoanalyst to grapple with. Are souls not concrete evocations of a dialogue between the living and the dead? The human dialogue, interrupted by death, can continue in absentia, furthering the process of mourning. "Death ends a life, but not a relationship," as Robert Anderson put it. Guilt, anger, sorrow can better be "actualized" in the purgatorial dialogue if the lost object is "pictured" as a soul. Affects can be better engaged perhaps in this imaginary theater that the souls in Purgatory invoke, and defense can also be fostered as the finality of death is denied and "harsh" reality is disavowed.

"Purgatory" and "soul," when considered as manifest content, surely suggest "latent" ideas that are not as immediately or visibly accessible. The concept of "souls" in "another world," clamoring for attention from a community that has turned its back on them, shut them out, is very evocative: it suggests the primal scene specifically or childhood generally. It suggests a metaphor of *child* as a curious communicative "soul," so much of which has to be repressed for either developmental or defensive or traumatic reasons. If the history of childhood is a nightmare the world is only beginning to awaken from (Freud can be hailed as the great awakener perhaps), I suggest that glimpses of the historic nightmare can still be caught in the *uncanny* shadows of Purgatory.

Purgatory could be seen as a pre-psychoanalytic precursor of superego development: If Heaven and Hell as abstractions represent splitting, Purgatory seems to represent the mind's revulsion at such Manichean absolutism. Purgatory seems to insist on resolution of conflict through less extreme measures. If "souls" represent projections of self and its conflicts into an afterworld, the communication with the souls that Purgatory offers allows these projections to be remetabolized in the process of dialogue. Defense reaches for insight in this precursor of analysis that Purgatory affords. One is tempted to suggest that before the momentous discovery of transference by Sigmund Freud, which allowed human imagination to project itself on a human screen in a consulting room the better to study itself, pre-Freudian mind needed the blank screen of the afterlife to project its worst fears on to, and its greatest hopes. The history of Art alone is a testimony to the extraordinary imaginings that were projected onto the screens of the afterlife from Bosch to Signorelli!

DISCUSSION

The "invention" of the concept of the superego is clearly attributable to the genius of Freud's *particular* way of thinking. It cannot have sprung ex nihilo however but owes some of its gestational identity to the antecedent history of ideas. As is well known, Freud had no trouble dipping his quill in the ink pots of history and literature and making off with insights that not only acknowledge the anxiety of influence but use it to further human knowledge. He invoked Oedipus, Hamlet, Leonardo, Eros, Thanatos, and others to act as armature for the erection of his psychological structures. Purgatory seems not to have engaged his thinking even though analogies between Heaven and Hell, the sublime and the repressed, "superos and acheronta" were often on his mind. In this essay I argue that the concept of Purgatory was a kind of preamble in the history of ideas to what Freud would later engage with more profoundly, more comprehensively, as the concept of the superego.

Freud's "superego" was many years in the making. What began as a reference to self-critical ideas in 1898, would eventually become conceptualized as a structure in 1920, his notion of *an ego ideal* being a pivotal insight along the way. As reality and development convince the infantile mind that separateness, not symbiosis, is the existential lot of each human, the startled mind reaches for illusion as a soothing stopgap. An ego ideal is born that comforts the mind saying in essence to the ego: "The way you were once loved by mother in the primary narcissism of instant unconditional gratification, I, a conceptual abstract substitute, will now love you." The ego ideal has a more ambiguous voice when it adds, "Of course I will love you most *if...*" The unconditional becomes conditional, the itemized conditions of love very much the new province of an overseer called the superego. Much has been written about all of this and I summarize only to set the stage for the introduction of a concept such as Purgatory into this discussion. If the ego ideal and the superego can at their most absolute sound like the Heaven one yearns for and the Hell one may be condemned to, a concept such as Purgatory allows some "play" between the clash of absolutes that would give the historical mind, and perhaps even the current more "psychoanalyzed" mind, more room to move.

I have tried to imagine the human mind removed from its historical, religious perspective, Catholic and Protestant bigotries set aside momentarily, trying to come to grips with ambition, sexuality, guilt, memory, mortality, conscience, reparation, forgiveness, the usual ferment of issues called the "human condition" in other words. The mind I am "imagining" stretches from Augustine to Dante to Luther, but perhaps it is better conceptualized as stretching from Homer to Freud. It is a mind that seems to believe in an immortal soul with less skepticism perhaps than the current atheistic mind of the twenty-first century. It is, however, the "developmental" mind out of which "current" mind emerged, and it is this "pedigree" which makes it pertinent to this discussion. This mind's conception of and attitude toward the soul has a "psychology" to it that has a bearing on modern concepts of the superego. If Heaven and Hell seem to offer perfection or damnation, Purgatory as a mental concept seems less absolute. Dante's Purgatory was clearly part of terra firma and the medieval traveler, as already mentioned, could find the entrance to Purgatory itself in Ireland or Sicily! The geographic location does suggest that the concept was more "down to earth" than the snootier abstractions Heaven and Hell. It is this down to earthness I would like to examine, since I mean to compare it to another down-to-earth phenomenon of the human mind, the child at play.

I believe it is possible to conceptualize play as a semiotic activity of the child that is one part symbolism and one part action (Mahon 1993). This mixture of the conceptual and the practical allows the child to bring the highfalutin communications of adults, which he is awash in and often overwhelmed by, down to earth literally and figuratively on the surface of his playroom where he can experiment and conduct trials and errors with his beloved playthings. In this theater, absolutes like extreme perfection and extreme punishment can be "modified" as towers get built and rebuilt, playthings get banished and returned, animals are executed and reprieved, death itself is undone in playful enactments of resurrection. Piaget (1965) has argued that the moral judgment of the child gets less harsh as the years go by, which is a tribute to the dynamics of development: as one decenters oneself from total infantile omnipotence, a less magical, less concrete, less absolute, less perceptually bound mind advances toward a conceptual world where even forgiveness can be tolerated and guilt does not have to mean immediate consignment to Hell's fire. Purgatory would seem to be an offshoot of this kind of playful working out of aggression, crime, punishment, retribution, and forgiveness in *down to earth* compromises rather than the absolutes Heaven and

Hell seem wedded to. The souls in Purgatory, pictured as the disembodied voices of the once living, now dead, who nevertheless speak
to the living from beyond the grave, surely is a reflection of *living*
guilt and loss and mourning trying to work out its affects, not in silence, but in an imagined dialogue with the dead. I would like to suggest another, more provocative interpretation of soul, not as death
personified for the defensive reasons of the living, a kind of mourning
that uses an imagined afterlife to resume its interrupted dialogue,
but soul as a living entity, the unfulfilled or stifled or compromised or
even "murdered" developmental spirit of a child, that cries out from
its internal purgatory for "a hearing" that will help it to complete its
development. Could all neurosis be characterized perhaps as an infantile soul, trapped in a Purgatory of its own making, but appealing
nonetheless with parent or analyst for the dialogue that would set it
free? Can neurosis, in other words, be depicted as an interrupted dialogue, a conflict that couldn't be resolved, and whose "voice" was
therefore silenced? Is psychoanalysis an attempt to resume the dialogue, and was Purgatory a historical precursor of this healing dialogue?

The soul as the silenced voice of child development yearning to
fulfill itself is an aspect of the purgatorial concept which has been in-
sufficiently emphasized in my opinion. The psychological drive to
complete one's development would probably fall into the category of
Freud's concept of ego instincts. That Purgatory may have been a
concept that sought to address this need is an irony that Sigmund
Freud seems to have ignored, even though as I have argued, its derivatives may have ended up on his couch!

If it is not too fanciful to imagine the stifled voices of unfulfilled
child developmental wishes as the return of the repressed yearnings
of infantile souls, these souls have not died, nor do they speak from
the afterlife. They speak when they are able to overcome the effects
of repression, inhibition, neglect, abuse, and trauma and thereby
resume their developmental tasks and fulfill the potential legacy
of their birthright. The image of these undead but unheard souls
eventually finding their voice and pleading their case on Freudian
couches is analogous perhaps to Greenblatt's hypothesis that the
purgatorial ghosts of Shakespeare's England, when banished from
the religious scene, ended up on another, the Elizabethan stage! The
point here is not to be analogous and fanciful but to draw a comparison between the work of child development and play and the work of
psychoanalysis (Mahon 2004). In childhood play, morality in a kind
of purgatorial process of aggression and guilt modulation can wean

itself from initial primitive harshness in which "crime" leads to dire punishment and can embrace instead a less dire, more reasoned and reasonable attitude toward psychological reality. This "purgatorial" play could be seen as a preamble to a childhood and adolescent superego that in ideal developmental outcomes is a structure that modulates guilt and pleasure in a non-neurotic manner. Similarly in the adult psychoanalytic situation an analysand initially "tortured" by superego pathology will invest the transference neurosis with the "transferred" ghosts of childhood imaginary crimes and imagined punishments until in a kind of "purgatorial" process he sheds these distortions through unrelenting interpretations of transferred primitive convictions. Heaven and Hell are rejected in this purgatorial psychoanalytic process which insists that aggression and guilt are human affects and that the fair assessment of the affects is the function of a decent, mature humanistic conscience. Purgatory itself, as a primitive historical invention of the guilty mind, is rejected also obviously even though the kernel of humanistic decency that got the idea started can be nostalgically retained. At the end of Dante's extraordinary Purgatorio, memory has been stripped of all the bad stuff ("the perilous stuff that weighs upon the heart," as Macbeth called it), and a new vision of memory has been invoked, the river Lethe no longer necessary as the new river Eunoe (a new imaginative creation of Dante's) flows with newly purged memorial integrity. Psychoanalysis is not quite as religious or as ambitious as Dante, but memory-work (Mahon and Battin-Mahon 1983) is surely one of its abiding principles.

If Purgatory was the historic mind's attempt to break free from the split psychology of Heaven and Hell, psychoanalysis is surely a continuation of that "healing" process. But whereas Dante would replace one kind of repression (Lethe) with another perhaps more adaptive one (Eunoe), Freud insists that, in the theory of conservation of psychological mass known as psychoanalysis, no mental product is ever "forgotten" totally. If it is possible to imagine the history of ideas as one historic mind in search of psychological truth, Freud, peering over Dante's shoulder, would describe Paradise not as a heavenly place of forgetfulness, but as a place where flesh, spit, teeth, shit, sex, love, hate, aging, and death can see themselves in a mirror that reflects all the fear and courage of a conflicted mind. This psychoanalytic mirror resides not in the afterlife, but in the finite span of each human life. Psychoanalysis rescued the finite from the abstractions of infinity, a dubious achievement for some, the distinctive mark of its intellectual courage for others. Earth was redeemed at the expense of Heaven, Hell, and Purgatory, but, as Robert Frost maintained, "Earth is the only place for Love, I don't know where it's likely to go better." Surely it diminishes psychoanalysis not a whit to acknowledge that the framers of a constitution called Purgatory cleared the way a little for the more enlightened psychological democracy of psychoanalysis.

BIBLIOGRAPHY

ANDERSON, ROBERT (1968). *I Never Sang for My Father.* New York: Random House.
DANTE ALIGHIERI (2000). *Purgatorio.* Tr. W. S. Merwin. New York: Random House.
FROST, R. (1965). *The Poetry of Robert Frost.* New York: Holt, Rinehart & Winston.
GREENBLATT, S. (2001). *Hamlet in Purgatory.* Princeton: Princeton University Press.
LE GOFF, J. (1981). The Birth of Purgatory. Chicago: University of Chicago Press.
MAHON, E. J. (1993). Play: Its Role in Child Analysis, Its Fate in Adult Analysis. In *The Many Meanings of Play.* Ed. A. J. Solnit, D. Cohen, and P. B. Neubauer. New Haven: Yale University Press.
MAHON, E. J. (2004). Playing and Working Through: A Neglected Analogy. *Psychoanalytic Quarterly,* 73.
MAHON, E. J., & BATTIN-MAHON, D. (1983). The Fate of Screen Memories in Psychoanalysis. *The Psychoanalytic Study of the Child,* 38:459–479.
PIAGET, J. (1965). *The Moral Judgment of the Child.* New York: Free Press.
STOPPARD, TOM (1998). *The Invention of Love.* New York: Grove Press.

Index

Freud, S. (*continued*)
  phases, 175, 192; on puberty, 102n7; on religion, 337–38; on "spool" example, 193; on trauma, 48. *See also* specific works
Frey, A. S., 257
Friedman, R. J., 21
Friedman, S., 45
Frost, R., 344
Furman, E., 245, 283
Furst, S., 17
Furth, G., 313, 318

Gaddini, E., 45
Garro, L., 210n5, 219
Geertz, C., 205–6, 210n5
Gensler, D., 246, 247
George, C., 182
Ghent, E., 160
Gill, M., 105n13
Gilligan, C., 142, 214
Gilman, R., 231
Gladwell, M., 76
Glaser, 239
Glass Menagerie, The (Williams), 321, 322, 326–27, 329–32
Goethe, J., 309
Golden, E., 205–23, 207
Goldwyn, R., 216–17, 218
Gordon, J., 310, 311, 312, 315
Gottfried, M., 311, 313
Grandparent Syndrome, 82–97
Green, A., 21
Greenacre, P., 5, 30n5, 45, 46, 49, 50
Greenberg, H. R., 255, 256
Greenberg, J. R., 161
Greenblatt, S., 336, 338, 342
Greenson, R. R., 246
Grice, H. P., 217–18
Grieving. *See* Mourning
Grusky, Z., 24

Hair pulling. *See* Trichotillomania
Hallopeau, M., 255
Hamdan-Allen, G., 255, 257
Hamlet (Shakespeare), 309, 336, 340
Hammerstein family, 310–11
Harley, M., 245
Harpaz-Rotem, I., 170–86
Harris, A., 177, 185
Harrison, A. M., 265
Harrison, S., 58
Hartke, R., 48
Hauser, S. T., 142, 205–23
Heaven and hell, 321, 334–35, 337–44
Hegel, G. W. F., 159, 160

Hell. *See* Heaven and hell
Herbert, J. C., 20–22, 42
Hesse, E., 216, 217, 218
Higgins, G. O., 207
Hitchcock, J., 15
Hofer, M., 171–72
Hoffman, I. Z., 161
Homer, 341
Homosexuality, 59–61, 89, 92
Honan, P., 306
Hopkins, J., 257
Horner, 181
Hurry, A., 102n8
Hysteria, 337

Ibsen, Henrik, 309
Id, 15, 160
Idealization, 136–37
Identification: with aggressor, 190; and "appeal" phenomenon in child, 191, 195–200; definition of, 190; description of, 146–47; and Grandparent Syndrome, 82–97; microprocesses of, 190–200; and mother's "magnification" of behavior, 191, 194–95, 197–200; and mourning, 282, 284–86, 289–90, 291; projective identification, 23, 156–58; and superimposition of mother's forms of organizing and disorganizing, 191–94, 197, 200
Identity: and adolescents, 66–67, 156; ego identity, 127–28; self-definition, 155–67; sexual identity, 129–31
Incest. *See* Sexual abuse
Infancy-onset trichotillomania. *See* Trichotillomania
"Inhibitions, Symptoms and Anxiety" (S. Freud), 111n20
Instinctual anxiety, 14–15
Institutionalized infants, 197–98
Internalization, 17, 147–50
"Interpretation of Dreams, The" (S. Freud), 229
Intersubjective delineation, 161–63, 166–67
Intersubjectivity: and intersubjective delineation, 161–63, 166–67; and mother-child relationship, 175; and musician/performer (Sallie) case, 20–52; mutual intersubjective delineation, 161–63; and psychoanalysis, 21; and self-definition, 155–67
Into the Woods (Sondheim), 310
Introjection, 84–86
Invention of Love, The (Stoppard), 334
Isay, R., 111n23

Mother-child relationship (*continued*)
parent Syndrome, 86–97; and identification, 190–200; and intersubjectivity, 175;
and magnification processes, 191, 194–
95, 197–200; mother's role as interlocutor and interpreter during, 178–79; in
musician/performer (Sallie) case, 26,
38–40, 38–39n9, 41, 46, 48–50; and objective reality, 177; and rapprochement,
170–86; and RIGS, 173; and self-reflexivity of child, 173–74; and separation
anxiety, 15, 178–84, 186; and subjective
omnipotence, 177; superimposition of
mother's forms of organizing and disorganizing, 191–94, 197, 200; and trichotillomania, 256–57, 259–69
Mourning: by children and adolescents,
282–83; and component restitutive solutions to loss, 284–91; and consolidation
of healthy identification with deceased
parent, 289–90, 291; and father as temporary maternal proxy, 288–89, 291; in
Fly Away Home, 275–80, 283–92; healthy
and natural aspects of, 280–81; and
identification, 282, 284–86, 289–90,
291; and initial identifications in response to loss of parent, 284–86, 290;
and loss manifesting as injury and defectiveness, 286–87, 290; in *My Girl,* 276,
285–86, 287, 288; pathological mourning, 281–83, 285–86, 287, 288; and reconstruction of new family and resumption of adolescent development, 287–88,
291; and restitutive and pathological solutions to loss, 280–83
"Mourning and Melancholia" (S. Freud),
191
Muller, S. A., 255
Murphy, G., 199
Murray, J., 230
Musician/performer (Sallie) case: acting
out in, 24, 32–38, 43–47; analyst's emotional reactions in, 34–35, 37, 38; artistic
talents in, 30–31, 49, 50–51; beginning
of psychoanalysis in, 30–32; change of
strategy in, 35–41; childhood in, 39–41;
clinical beginnings in psychoanalysis in,
24–30; countertransference in, 22, 24,
28, 29, 35, 39, 42, 46, 48, 50; dramatic
performances in, 43–47; dreams in,
29–30, 31, 35–37, 37n8; early psychic
trauma in, 44–45, 48–52; gift giving
in, 26, 32, 35; language in, 25–26, 31,
41n10, 44, 49–52; and latency, 45–46;
and marriage, 26–27; mental structure
of client in, 25–29, 36–38, 47, 48–49;

and mother, 26, 38–40, 38–39n9, 41, 46,
48–50; and performance of madrigal
singers, 33–34; power struggles in, 32–
35; practical jokes in, 34–38; psychoanalysis in, 20–52; self-disclosure by analyst in, 21–24, 27–28, 34, 41–42; superego in, 45–46; tattoos in, 34–35, 37;
transference in, 24, 29, 35, 46–47, 49, 50
Musick, J. S., 207
Mutual intersubjective delineation, 161–
63, 166–67
My Girl, 276, 285–86, 287, 288

Nagera, H., 283
Narrative studies: and Adult Attachment
Interview (AAI), 215–19; and cause and
effect, 207–9; and change, 210–15; in
context, 209–10; definition of narrative,
206; and meta-cognitive monitoring,
219; and reflective functioning, 219–20;
and resilience, 210–23
Nass, M., 50
Neimeyer, R., 212–13
Nelson, B., 324, 330
Niederland, W., 230
Novick, J., 127, 142
Novick, K. K., 127, 142

Object Relation Inventory (ORI), 173, 182
Object relations, 156–58, 160, 166
O'Brien, J., 231, 245, 246
Oedipal transference, 120, 131
Oedipus, 294, 309, 340
Oedipus complex, 61–62, 83, 85, 88, 90,
92–93, 103, 105, 136
Oedipus Rex (Sophocles), 294, 306
Offer, D., 143
Ogden, T. H., 23, 156–57, 160–61, 175
Omer, H., 72
Ondaatje, M., 278n2
Only children, 93–94, 96
Operant conditioning, 194
Oppenheim, D., 215, 218, 219, 221, 222
Orange, D. M., 162
Oranje, A. P., 257, 258
Organization/disorganization of mother,
191–94, 197, 200
ORI (Object Relation Inventory), 173, 182
O'Shaughnessy, E., 38
O'Sullivan, R. L., 259
O'Toole, J. G., 215

Pardron, E., 221
Parents. *See* Father-child relationship;
Mother-child relationship
Parker, G., 85